The Mahabharata
Vana, Parva
Part II

by

Krishna-Dwaipayana Vyasa

The Mahabharata Vana, Parva
Part II
by Krishna-Dwaipayana Vyasa

ISBN: 978-93-59329-52-9

Published by

DOUBLE 9 BOOKS

2/13-B, Ansari Road
Daryaganj, New Delhi – 110002
info@double9books.com
www.double9books.com
Tel. 011-40042856

ABOUT THE AUTHOR

Krishna Dvaipayana is a respected sage who is depicted in almost all Hindu traditions. He is widely recognized as the author of the epic Mahabharata. Many Hindus consider Vyasa to be a partial incarnation of the god Vishnu and the compiler of the Vedic mantras into four Vedas, as well as the author of the eighteen Puranas and the Brahma Sutras. He is one of Chiranjeevis' eight immortals, meaning that he is still alive in the current Kali yuga. Vyasa's birth name is Krishna Dvaipayana, which may refer to his dark skin and birthplace, but he is better known as "Veda Vyasa" (Veda Vysa) because he divided the single, everlasting Veda into four independent books: Rigveda, Samaveda, Yajurveda, and Atharvaveda. The term "Vyasa" (Vysa) indicates "compiler" or "arranger" and also "separation" or "division." Other definitions include "split", "differentiate", and "describe." It is additionally a term bestowed upon "a holy sage or a pious educated man," in addition to "persons distinguished for their writings." Swami Vivekananda believes that Vyasa was a lineage of sages who were satisfied to simply develop ideas without claiming credit since they were free of desire for the consequences of their work, and hence assigned authorship to Vyasa.

CONTENTS

SECTION CXLV

And the ruddy geese, and the gallinules and the ducks and the *karandavas* and the *plavas* and the parrots and the male *kokilas* and the herons in confusion flew in all directions, while some proud elephants urged by their mates, as also some lions and elephants in rage, flew at Bhimasena. And as they were distracted at heart through fear, these fierce animals discharging urine and dung, set up loud yells with gapping mouths. Thereupon the illustrious and graceful son of the wind-god, the mighty Pandava, depending upon the strength of his arms, began to slay one elephant with another elephant and one lion with another lion while he despatched the others with slaps. And on being struck by Bhima the lions and the tigers and the leopards, in fright gave loud cries and discharged urine and dung. And after having destroyed these the handsome son of Pandu, possessed of mighty strength, entered into the forest, making all sides resound with his shouts. And then the long-armed one saw on the slopes of the Gandhamadana a beautiful plantain tree spreading over many a *yojana*. And like unto a mad lion, that one of great strength proceeded amain towards that tree breaking down various plants. And that foremost of strong persons—Bhima—uprooting innumerable plaintain trunks equal in height to many palm-trees (placed one above another), cast them on all sides with force. And that highly powerful one, haughty like a male lion, sent up shouts. And then he encountered countless beasts of gigantic size, and stags, and monkeys, and lions, and buffaloes, and aquatic animals. And what with the cries of these, and what with the shouts of Bhima, even the beasts and birds that were at distant parts of the wood, became all frightened. And hearing those cries of beasts and birds, myriads of aquatic fowls suddenly rose up on wetted wings. And seeing these fowls of water, that bull among the Bharatas proceeded in that direction; and saw a vast and romantic lake. And that fathomless lake was, as it were, being fanned by the golden plantain trees on the coast, shaken by the soft breezes. And immediately descending into the lake abounding in lilies and lotuses, he began to sport lustily like unto a mighty maddened elephant. Having thus sported there for a long while, he of immeasurable effulgence ascended, in order to penetrate with speed into that forest filled with trees. Then the Pandava winded with all his might his loud-blowing shell. And striking his arms with his hands, the mighty Bhima made all the points of heaven resound. And filled with the sounds of the shell, and with the shouts of Bhimasena, and also with the reports produced by the striking of his arms, the caves of the mountain seemed as if they were roaring. And hearing those loud arm-strokes, like unto the crashing of thunder, the lions that were slumbering in the caves, uttered mighty howls. And being terrified by the yelling of the lions, the elephants, O Bharata, sent forth tremendous roars, which filled the mountain. And hearing those sounds emitted, and knowing also Bhimasena to be his brother, the ape Hanuman, the chief of monkeys, with the view of doing good to Bhima, obstructed the path leading to heaven. And thinking that he (Bhima) should not pass that way, (Hanuman) lay across the narrow path, beautified by plantain trees, obstructing it for the sake of the safety of Bhima. With the object that Bhima might not come by curse or defeat, by entering into the plantain wood, the ape Hanuman of huge body lay down amidst the plantain trees, being overcome with drowsiness. And he began to yawn, lashing his long tail, raised like unto the pole consecrated to Indra, and sounding like thunder. And on all sides round, the mountains by the mouths of caves emitted those sounds in echo, like a cow lowing. And as it was being shaken by the reports produced by the lashing of the tail, the mountain with its summits tottering, began to crumble all around. And overcoming that roaring of mad elephants, the sounds of his tail spread over the varied slopes of the mountain.

"On those sounds being heard the down of Bhima's body stood on end; and he began to range that plantain wood, in search of those sounds. And that one of mighty arms saw the monkey-chief in the plantain wood, on an elevated rocky base. And he was hard to be looked at even as the lightning-flash; and of coppery hue like that of the lightning-flash; and endued with the voice of the lightning-flash; and quick moving as the lightning-flash; and having his short flesh neck supported on his shoulders; and with his waist slender in consequence of the fullness of his shoulders. And his tail covered with long hair, and a little bent at the end, was raised like unto a banner. And (Bhima) saw Hanuman's head furnished with small lips, and coppery face and tongue, and red ears, and brisk eyes, and bare white incisors sharpened at the edge. And his head was like unto the shining moon; adorned with white teeth within the mouth; and with mane scattered over, resembling a heap of *asoka* flowers. And amidst the golden plantain trees, that one of exceeding effulgence was lying like unto a blazing fire, with his radiant body. And that slayer of foes was casting glances with his eyes reddened with intoxication. And the intelligent Bhima saw that mighty chief of monkeys, of huge body, lying like unto the Himalaya, obstructing the path of heaven. And seeing him alone in that mighty forest, the undaunted athletic Bhima, of long arms, approached him with rapid strides, and uttered a loud shout like unto the thunder. And at that shout of Bhima, beasts and birds became all alarmed. The powerful Hanuman, however, opening his eyes partially looked at him (Bhima) with disregard, with eyes reddened with intoxication. And then smilingly addressing him, Hanuman said the following words, 'Ill as I am, I was sleeping sweetly. Why hast thou awakened me? Thou shouldst show kindness to all creatures, as thou hast reason. Belonging to the animal species, we are ignorant of virtue. But being endued with reason, men show kindness towards creatures. Why do then reasonable persons like thee commit themselves to acts contaminating alike body, speech, and heart, and destructive of virtue? Thou knowest not what virtue is, neither hast thou taken council of the wise. And therefore it is that from ignorance, and childishness thou destroyest the lower animals. Say, who art thou, and what for hast thou come to the forest devoid of humanity and human beings? And, O foremost of men, tell thou also, whither thou wilt go to-day. Further it is impossible to proceed. Yonder hills are inaccessible. O hero, save the passage obtained by the practice of asceticism, there is no passage to that place. This is the path of the celestials; it is ever impassable by mortals. Out of kindness, O hero, do I dissuade thee. Do thou hearken unto my words. Thou canst not proceed further from this place. Therefore, O lord, do thou desist. O chief of men, to-day in every way thou art welcome to this place. If thou think it proper to accept my words, do thou then, O best of men, rest here, partaking of fruits and roots, sweet as ambrosia, and do not have thyself destroyed for naught.'"

SECTION CXLVI

Vaisampayana said, "O represser of foes, hearing these words of the intelligent monkey-chief, the heroic Bhima answered, 'Who art thou? And why also hast thou assumed the shape of a monkey? It is a Kshatriya—one of a race next to the Brahmanas—that asketh thee. And he belongeth to the Kuru race and the lunar stock, and was borne by Kunti in her womb, and is one of the sons of Pandu, and is the off spring of the windgod, and is known by the name of Bhimasena.' Hearing these words of the Kuru hero, Hanuman smiled, and that son of the wind-god (Hanuman) spake unto that offspring of the windgod (Bhimasena), saying, 'I am a monkey, I will not allow thee the passage thou desirest. Better desist and go back. Do thou not meet with destruction.' At this Bhimasena replied, 'Destruction at anything else do I not ask thee about, O monkey. Do thou give me passage. Arise! Do not come by grief at my hands.' Hanuman said, 'I have no strength to rise; I am suffering from illness. If go thou must, do thou go by overleaping me.' Bhima said, 'The Supreme Soul void of the properties pervadeth a body all over. Him knowable alone by knowledge, I cannot disregard. And therefore, will I not overleap thee. If I had not known Him from Whom become manifest all creatures, I would have leapt over thee and also the mountain, even as Hanuman had bounded over the ocean.' Thereupon Hanuman said, 'Who is that Hanuman, who had bounded over the ocean? I ask thee, O best of men. Relate if thou canst.' Bhima replied, 'He is even my brother, excellent with every perfection, and endued with intelligence and strength both of mind and body. And he is the illustrious chief of monkeys, renowned in the Ramayana. And for Rama's queen, that king of the monkeys even with one leap crossed the ocean extending over a hundred *yojanas*. That mighty one is my brother. I am equal unto him in energy, strength and prowess and also in fight. And able am I to punish thee. So arise. Either give me passage or witness my prowess to-day. If thou do not listen to my bidding, I shall send thee to the abode of Yama.'"

Vaisampayana continued. "Then knowing him (Bhima) to be intoxicated with strength, and proud of the might of his arms, Hanuman, slighting him at heart, said the following words, 'Relent thou, O sinless one.

In consequence of age, I have no strength to get up. From pity for me, do thou go, moving aside my tail.' Being thus addressed by Hanuman, Bhima proud of the strength of his arms, took him for one wanting in energy and prowess, and thought within himself, 'Taking fast hold of the tail, will I send this monkey destitute of energy and prowess, to the region of Yama.' Thereat, with a smile he slightingly took hold of the tail with his left hand; but could not move that tail of the mighty monkey. Then with both arms he pulled it, resembling the pole reared in honour of Indra. Still the mighty Bhima could not raise the tail with both his arms. And his eye-brows were contracted up, and his eyes rolled, and his face was contracted into wrinkles and his body was covered with sweat; and yet he could not raise it. And when after having striven, the illustrious Bhima failed in raising the tail, he approached the side of the monkey, and stood with a bashful countenance. And bowing down, Kunti's son, with joined hands, spake these words, 'Relent thou, O foremost of monkeys; and forgive me for my harsh words. Art thou a Siddha, or a god, or a Gandharva, or a Guhyaka? I ask thee out of curiosity. Tell me who thou art that hast assumed the shape of monkey, if it be not a secret, O long-armed one, and if I can well hear it. I ask thee as a disciple, and I, O sinless one, seek thy refuge.' Thereupon Hanuman said, 'O represser of foes, even to the extent of thy curiosity to know me, shall I relate all at length. Listen, O son of Pandu! O lotus-eyed one, I was begotten by the windgod that life of the world—upon the wife of Kesari. I am a monkey, by name Hanuman. All the mighty monkey-kings, and monkey-chiefs used to wait upon that son of the sun, Sugriva, and that son of Sakra, Vali. And, O represser of foes, a friendship subsisted between me and Sugriva, even as between the wind and fire. And for some cause, Sugriva, driven out by his brother, for a long time dwelt with me at the Hri-syamukh. And it came to pass that the mighty son of Dasaratha the heroic Rama, who is Vishnu's self in the shape of a human being, took his birth in this world. And in company with his queen and brother, taking his bow, that foremost of bowmen with the view of compassing his father's welfare, began to reside in the Dandaka forest. And from Janasthana, that mighty Rakshasa monarch, the wicked Ravana, carried away his (Rama's) queen by stratagem and force, deceiving, O sinless one, that foremost of men, through the agency of a Rakshasa, Maricha, who assumed the form of a deer marked with gem-like and golden spots.'"

SECTION CXLVII

"Hanuman said, 'And after his wife was carried away, that descendant of Raghu, while searching with his brother for his queen, met, on the summit of that mountain, with Sugriva, chief of the monkeys. Then a friendship was contracted between him and the high-souled Raghava. And the latter, having slain Vali installed Sugriva in the kingdom. And having obtained the kingdom, Sugriva sent forth monkeys by hundreds and by thousands in search of Sita. And, O best of men, I too with innumerable monkeys set out towards the south in quest of Sita, O mighty-armed one. Then a mighty vulture Sampati by name, communicated the tidings that Sita was in the abode of Ravana. Thereupon with the object of securing success unto Rama, I all of a sudden bounded over the main, extending for a hundred *yojanas*. And, O chief of the Bharatas, having by my own prowess crossed the ocean, that abode of sharks and crocodiles, I saw in Ravana's residence, the daughter of king Janaka, Sita, like unto the daughter of a celestial. And having interviewed that lady, Vaidehi, Rama's beloved, and burnt the whole of Lanka with its towers and ramparts and gates, and proclaimed my name there, I returned. Hearing everything from me the lotus-eyed Rama at once ascertained his course of action, and having for the passage of his army constructed a bridge across the deep, crossed it followed by myriads of monkeys. Then by prowess Rama slew those Rakshasas in battle, and also Ravana, the oppressor of the worlds together with his Rakshasa followers. And having slain the king of the Rakshasas, with his brother, and sons and kindred, he installed in the kingdom in Lanka the Rakshasa chief, Vibhishana, pious, and reverent, and kind to devoted dependants. Then Rama recovered his wife even like the lost Vaidic revelation. Then Raghu's son, Rama, with his devoted wife, returned to his own city, Ayodhya, inaccessible to enemies; and that lord of men began to dwell there. Then that foremost of kings, Rama was established in the kingdom. Thereafter, I asked a boon of the lotus-eyed Rama, saying, "O slayer of foes, Rama, may I live as long as the history of thy deeds remaineth extant on earth!" Thereupon he said, "So be it." O represser of foes, O Bhima, through the grace of Sita also, here all excellent objects of entertainment are supplied to me, whoever abide at this place. Rama reigned for the thousand and ten hundred years. Then he ascended to his own abode. Ever since, here Apsaras and Gandharvas delight me, singing for aye the deeds of that hero, O sinless one. O son of the Kurus, this path is impassable to mortals. For this, O Bharata, as also with the view that none might defeat or curse thee, have I obstructed thy passage to this path trod by the immortals. This is one of the paths to heaven, for the celestials; mortals cannot pass this way. But the lake in search of which thou hast come, lieth even in that direction.'"

SECTION CXLVIII

Vaisampayana continued, "Thus addressed, the powerful Bhimasena of mighty arms, affectionately, and with a cheerful heart, bowed unto his brother, Hanuman, the monkey-chief, and said in mild words, 'None is more fortunate than I am; now have I seen my elder brother. It is a great favour shown unto me; and I have been well pleased with thee. Now I wish that thou mayst fulfil this desire of mine. I desire to behold, O hero, that incomparable form of thine, which thou at that time hadst had, in bounding over the main, that abode of sharks and crocodiles. Thereby I shall be satisfied, and also believe in thy words.' Thus addressed, that mighty monkey said with a smile, 'That form of mine neither thou, not any one else can behold. At that age, the state of things was different, and doth not exist at present. In the Krita age, the state of things was one; and in the Treta, another; and in the Dwapara, still another. Diminution is going on this age; and I have not that form now. The ground, rivers, plants, and rocks, and *siddhas*, gods, and celestial sages conform to Time, in harmony with the state of things in the different yugas. Therefore, do not desire to see my former shape, O perpetuator of the Kuru race. I am conforming to the tendency of the age. Verily, Time is irresistible.' Bhimasena said, 'Tell me of the duration of the different yugas, and of the different manners and customs and of virtue, pleasure and profit, and of acts, and energy, and of life and death in the different yugas.' Thereupon Hanuman said, 'O child, that yuga is called Krita when the one eternal religion was extant. And in that best of yugas, every one had religious perfection, and, therefore, there was no need of religious acts. And then virtue knew no deterioration; nor did people decrease. It is for this that this age is called Krita (perfect). But in time the yuga had come to be considered as an inferior one. And, O child, in the Krita age, there were neither gods, nor demons, nor Gandharvas, nor Yakshas, nor Rakshasas, nor Nagas. And there was no buying and selling. And the Sama, the Rich, and the Yajus did not exist. And there was no manual labour. And then the necessaries of life were obtained only by being thought of. And the only merit was in renouncing the world. And during that yuga, there was neither disease, nor decay of the senses. And there was neither malice, nor pride, nor hypocrisy, nor discord, nor ill-will, nor cunning, nor fear, nor misery, nor envy, nor covetousness. And for this, that prime refuge of Yogis, even the Supreme Brahma, was attainable to all. And Narayana wearing a white hue was the soul of all creatures. And in the Krita Yuga, the distinctive characteristics of Brahmanas, Kshatriyas, Vaisyas, and Sudras were natural and these ever stuck to their respective duties. And then Brahma was the sole refuge, and their manners and customs were naturally adapted to the attainment of Brahma and the objects of their knowledge was the sole Brahma, and all their acts also had reference to Brahma. In this way all the orders attained merit. And one uniform Soul was the object of their meditation; and there was only one *mantra* (the *Om*), and there was one ordinance. And although of different characteristics, all of them followed a single Veda; and they had one religion. And according to the divisions of time, they led the four modes of life, without aiming at any object, and so they attained emancipation. The religion consisting in the identification of self with Brahma indicates the Krita Yuga. And in the Krita Yuga, the virtue of the four orders is throughout entire in four-fold measure. Such is the Krita Yuga devoid of the three qualities. Do thou also hear from me of the character of the Treta Yuga. In this age, sacrifices are introduced, and virtue decreaseth by a quarter. And Narayana (who is the Soul of all creatures) assumeth a red colour. And men practise truth, and devote themselves to religion and religious rites. And thence sacrifices and various religious observances come into existence. And in the Treta Yuga people begin to devise means for the attainment of an object; and they attain it through acts and gifts. And they never deviate from virtue. And they are devoted to asceticism and to the bestowal of gifts. And the four orders adhere to their respective duties; and perform rites. Such are the men of the Treta Yuga. In the Dwapara Yuga, religion decreaseth by one half. And Narayana weareth a yellow hue. And the Veda becometh divided into four parts. And then some men retain (the knowledge of) the four Vedas, and some of three Vedas, and some of one Veda, while others do not know even the Richs. And on the Shastras becoming thus divided, acts become multiplied. And largely influenced by passion, people engage in asceticism and gifts. And from their incapacity to study the entire Veda, it becomes divided into several parts. And in consequence of intellect having decreased, few are established in truth. And when people fall off from truth, they become subject to various diseases; and then lust, and natural calamities ensue. And afflicted with these, people betake themselves to penances. And some celebrate sacrifices, desiring to enjoy the good things of life, or attain heaven. On the coming of the Dwapara Yuga, men become degenerate, in consequence of impiety. O son of Kunti, in the Kali Yuga a quarter only of virtue abideth. And in the beginning of this iron age, Narayana weareth a black hue. And the Vedas and the institutes, and virtue, and sacrifices, and religious observances, fall into disuse. And (then) reign *iti* 1 , and disease, and lassitude, and anger and other deformities, and natural calamities, and anguish, and fear of scarcity. And as the yugas wane, virtue dwindles. And as virtue dwindles away, creatures degenerate. And as creatures degenerate, their natures undergo deterioration. And the religious acts performed at the waning of the yugas, produce contrary effects. And even those that live for several yugas, conform to these changes. O represser of foes, as regards thy curiosity to know me, I say this,—Why should a wise person be eager to know a superfluous matter? (Thus), O long-armed one, have I narrated in full what thou hadst asked me regarding the characteristics of the different yugas. Good happen to thee! Do thou return.'"

SECTION CXLIX

"Bhimasena said, 'Without beholding thy former shape, I will never go away. If I have found favour with thee, do thou then show me thine own shape.'"

Vaisampayana continued, "Being thus addressed by Bhima, the monkey with a smile showed him that form of his in which he had bounded over the main. And wishing to gratify his brother, Hanuman assumed a gigantic body which (both) in length and breadth increased exceedingly. And that monkey of immeasurable effulgence stood there, covering the plantain grove furnished with trees, and elevating himself to the height reached by the Vindhya. And the monkey, having attained his lofty and gigantic body like unto a mountain, furnished with coppery eyes, and sharp teeth, and a face marked by frown, lay covering all sides and lashing his long tail. And that son of the Kurus, Bhima, beholding that gigantic form of his brother, wondered, and the hairs of his body repeatedly stood on end. And beholding him like unto the sun in splendour, and unto a golden mountain, and also unto the blazing firmament, Bhima closed his eyes. Thereupon Hanuman addressed Bhima with a smile, saying, 'O sinless one, thou art capable of beholding my size up to this extent. I can, however, go on swelling my size as long as I wish. And, O Bhima, amidst foes, my size increaseth exceedingly by its own energy.'"

Vaisampayana said, "Witnessing that dreadful and wonderful body of Hanuman, like unto the Vindhya mountain, the son of the wind-god became bewildered. Then with his down standing erect, the noble-minded Bhima, joining his hands, replied unto Hanuman saying (there), 'O lord, by me have been beheld the vast dimensions of thy body. Do thou (now), O highly powerful one, decrease thyself by thy own power. Surely I cannot look at thee, like unto the sun risen, and of immeasurable (power), and irrepressible, and resembling the mountain Mainaka. O hero, to-day this wonder of my heart is very great, that thou remaining by his side, Rama should have encountered Ravana personally. Depending on the strength of thy arms, thou wert capable of instantly destroying Lanka, with its warriors, and horses, elephants and chariots. Surely, O son of the wind-god, there is nothing that is incapable of being achieved by thee; and in fight, Ravana together with his followers was no match for thee single-handed.'"

Vaisampayana continued, "Thus addressed by Bhima, Hanuman, the chief of monkeys, answered in affectionate words uttered in solemn accents. 'O mighty-armed one, O Bharata, it is even as thou sayest. O Bhimasena, that worst of Rakshasas was no match for me. But if I had slain Ravana—that thorn of the worlds—the glory of Raghu's son would have been obscured;— and for this it is that I left him alone. By slaying that lord of the Rakshasas together with his followers, and bringing back Sita unto his own city, that hero hath established his fame among men. Now, O highly wise one, being intent on the welfare of thy brothers, and protected by the wind-god, do thou go along a fortunate and auspicious way. O foremost of the Kurus, this way will lead thee to the Saugandhika wood. (Proceeding in this direction), thou wilt behold the gardens of Kuvera, guarded by Yakshas and Rakshasas. Do thou not pluck the flowers (there) personally by thy own force; for the gods deserve regard specially from mortals. O best of the Bharata race, the gods confer their favour (upon men), (being propitiated) by offerings, and *homas*, and reverential salutations, and recitation of *mantras*, and veneration, O Bharata. Do thou not, therefore, act with rashness, O child; and do thou not deviate from the duties of thy order. Sticking to the duties of thy order, do thou understand and follow the highest morality. Without knowing duties and serving the old, even persons like unto Vrihaspati cannot understand profit and religion. One should ascertain with discrimination those cases in which vice goeth under the name of virtue, and virtue goeth under the name of vice,—(cases) in which people destitute of intelligence become perplexed. From religious observances proceedeth merit; and in merit are established the Vedas; and from the Vedas sacrifices come into existence; and by sacrifices are established the gods. The gods are maintained by the (celebration of) sacrifices prescribed by the Vedas and the religious ordinances; while men maintain themselves by (following) the ordinances of Vrihaspati and Usanas and also by these avocations, by which the world is maintained,—serving for wages, (receiving) taxes, merchandise, agriculture and tending kine and sheep. The world subsisteth by profession. The (study of the) three Vedas and agriculture and trade and government constitutes, it is ordained by the wise, the professions of the twice born ones; and each order maintaineth itself by following the profession prescribed for it. And when these callings are properly pursued, the world is maintained with ease. If, however, people do not righteously lead their lives, the world becometh lawless, in consequence of the want of Vedic merit and government. And if people do not resort to (their) prescribed vocations, they perish, but by regularly following the three professions, they bring about religion. The religion of the Brahmanas consisteth in the knowledge of the soul and the hue of that order alone is universally the same. The celebration of sacrifices, and study and bestowal of gifts are well-known to be the three duties common (to all these orders). Officiating at sacrifices, teaching and the acceptance of gifts are the duties of a Brahmana. To rule (the subjects) is the duty of the Kshatriya; and to tend (cattle), that of the Vaisya, while to serve the twice-born orders is said to be the duty of the Sudra. The Sudras cannot beg alms, or perform *homas*, or observe vows; and they must dwell in the habitation of their masters. Thy vocation, O son of Kunti, is that of the Kshatriya, which is to protect (the subjects). Do thou carry out thy own duties, in an humble spirit, restraining thy senses. That king alone can govern, who taketh counsel of experienced men, and is helped by honest, intelligent and learned ministers; but a king who is addicted to vices, meeteth with defeat. Then only is the order of the world secured, when the king duly punisheth and conferreth favours. Therefore, it is necessary to ascertain through spies the nature of the hostile country, its fortified places and the allied force of the enemy and their prosperity and decay and the way in which they retain the adhesion of the powers they have drawn to their side. Spies are among the important auxiliaries of the king; and tact, diplomacy, prowess, chastisement, favour and cleverness lead to success. And success is to be attained through these, either in separation, or combined—namely, conciliation, gift, sowing dissensions, chastisement, and sight. And, O chief of the Bharatas, polity hath for its root diplomacy; and diplomacy also is the main qualification of spies. And polity, if well judged conferreth success. Therefore, in matters of polity the counsels of Brahmanas should be resorted to. And in secret affairs, these should not be consulted,—namely, a woman, a sot, a boy, a covetous person, a mean-minded individual, and he that betrayeth signs of insanity. Wise men only should be consulted, and affairs are to be despatched through officers that are able. And polity must be executed through persons that are friendly; but dunces should in all affairs be excluded. In matters religious, pious men; and in matters of gain, wise men; and in guarding families, eunuchs; and in all crooked affairs, crooked men, must be employed. And the propriety or impropriety of the resolution of the enemy, as also their strength or weakness, must be ascertained through one's own as well as hostile spies. Favour should be shown to honest persons that have prudently sought protection;

but lawless and disobedient individuals should be punished. And when the king justly punisheth and showeth favour, the dignity of the law is well maintained. O son of Pritha, thus have I expounded, unto thee the hard duties of kings difficult to comprehend. Do thou with equanimity observe these as prescribed for thy order. The Brahmanas attain heaven through merit, mortification of the senses, and sacrifice. The Vaisyas attain excellent state through gifts, hospitality, and religious acts. The Kshatriyas attain the celestial regions by protecting and chastising the subjects, uninfluenced by lust, malice, avarice and anger. If kings justly punish (their subjects), they go to the place whither repair meritorious persons.'"

SECTION CL

Vaisampayana said, "Then contracting that huge body of his, which he had assumed at will, the monkey with his arms again embraced Bhimasena. And O Bharata, on Bhima being embraced by his brother, his fatigue went off, and all (the powers of body) as also his strength were restored. And having gained great accession of strength, he thought that there was none equal to him in physical power. And with tears in his eyes, the monkey from affection again addressed Bhima in choked utterance, saying, 'O hero, repair to thy own abode. May I be incidentally remembered by thee in thy talk! O best of Kurus, do not tell any one that I abide here. O thou of great strength, the most excellent of the wives of the gods and Gandharvas resort to this place, and the time of their arrival is nigh. My eyes have been blessed (by seeing thee). And, O Bhima, having felt a human being by coming in contact with thee, I have been put in mind of that son of Raghu, who was Vishnu himself under the name of Rama, and who delighted the heart of the world; and who was as the sun in regard to the lotus face of Sita, and also to that darkness—Ravana. Therefore, O heroic son of Kunti, let not thy meeting with me be fruitless. Do thou with fraternal feeling ask of me a boon, O Bharata. If this be thy wish, that going to Varanavata, I may destroy the insignificant sons of Dhritarashtra—even this will I immediately do. Or if this be thy wish that, that city may be ground by me with rocks, or that I may bind Duryodhana and bring him before thee, even this will I do to-day, O thou of mighty strength.'"

Vaisampayana said, "Hearing those words of that high-souled one, Bhimasena with a cheerful heart answered Hanuman, saying, 'O foremost of monkeys, I take all this as already performed by thee. Good happen to thee. O mighty-armed one! I ask of thee this,—be thou well pleased with me. O powerful one, on thy having become our protector, the Pandavas have found help. Even by thy prowess shall we conquer all foes.' Thus addressed, Hanuman said unto Bhimasena, 'From fraternal feeling and affection, I will do good unto thee, by diving into the army of thy foes copiously furnished with arrows and javelins. And, O highly powerful one, O hero, when thou shall give leonine roars, then shall I with my own, add force to shouts. Remaining on the flagstaff of Arjuna's car will I emit fierce shouts that will damp the energy of thy foes. Thereby ye will slay them easily.' Having said this unto Pandu's son, and also pointed him out the way. Hanuman vanished at that spot."

SECTION CLI

Vaisampayana said, "When that foremost of monkeys had gone away, Bhima, the best of strong men, began to range the huge Gandhamadana along that path. And he went on, thinking of Hanuman's body and splendour unrivalled on earth, and also of the greatness and dignity of Dasaratha's son. And proceeding in search of the place filled with lotuses of that kind, Bhima beheld romantic woods, and groves, and rivers, and lakes graced with trees bearing blossoms, and flowery woodlands variegated with various flowers. And, O Bharata, he beheld herds of mad elephants besmeared with mud, resembling masses of pouring clouds. And that graceful one went on with speed, beholding by the wayside woods wherein there stood with their mates deer of quick glances, holding the grass in their mouths. And fearless from prowess, Bhimasena, as if invited by the breeze-shaken trees of the forest ever fragrant with flowers, bearing delicate coppery twigs, plunged into the mountainous regions inhabited by buffaloes, bears and leopards. And on the way, he passed by lotus-lakes haunted by maddened black-bees, having romantic descents and woods, and on account of the presence of lotus-buds, appearing as if they had joined their hands (before Bhima). And having for his provisions on the journey the words of Draupadi, Bhima went on with speed, his mind and sight fixed on the blooming slopes of the mountain. And when the sun passed the meridian, he saw in the forest scattered over with deer, a mighty river filled with fresh golden lotuses. And being crowded with swans and Karandavas, and graced with Chakravakas, the river looked like a garland of fresh lotuses put on by the mountain. And in that river that one of great strength found the extensive assemblage of Saugandhika lotuses, effulgent as the rising sun, and delightful to behold. And beholding it, Pandu's son thought within himself that his object had been gained, and also mentally presented himself before his beloved worn out by exile."

SECTION CLII

Vaisampayana said, "Having reached that spot, Bhimasena saw in the vicinity of the Kailasa cliff, that beautiful lotus lake surrounded by lovely woods, and guarded by the Rakshasas. And it sprang from the cascades contiguous to the abode of Kuvera. And it was beautiful to behold, and was furnished with a wide-spreading shade and abounded in various trees and creepers and was covered with green lilies. And this unearthly lake was filled with golden lotuses, and swarmed with diverse species of birds. And its banks were beautiful and devoid of mud. And situated on the rocky elevation this expanse of excellent water was exceedingly fair. And it was the wonder of the world and healthful and of romantic sight. In that lake the son of Kunti saw, the water of ambrosial taste and cool and light and clear and fresh; and the Pandava drank of it profusely. And that unearthly receptacle of waters was covered with celestial Saugandhika lotuses, and was also spread over with beautiful variegated golden lotuses of excellent fragrance having graceful stalks of *lapis lazulis*. And swayed by swans and Karandavas, these lotuses were scattering fresh farina. And this lake was the sporting region of the high-souled Kuvera, the king of the Yakshas. And it was held in high regard by the Gandharvas, the Apsaras and the celestials. And it was frequented by the celestial sages and the Yakshas and the Kimpurushas and the Rakshasas and the Kinnaras; and it was well-protected by Kuvera. And as soon as he beheld that river and that unearthly lake, Kunti's son, Bhimasena of mighty strength became exceedingly delighted. And agreeably to the mandate of their king, hundreds and thousands of Rakshasas, named Krodhavasas, were guarding that lake, wearing uniforms and armed with various weapons. And as that repressor of foes, Kunti's son, the heroic Bhima of dreadful prowess, clad in deer-skins and wearing golden armlets and equipped with weapons and girding his sword on, was fearlessly proceeding, with the view of gathering the lotus, those (Rakshasas) saw him and immediately began to address each other, shouting forth, 'It behoveth you to enquire for the errand on which this foremost of men, clad in deer skins, and equipped with arms, hath come.' Then they all approached the effulgent Vrikodara of mighty arms and asked, 'Who art thou? Thou shouldst answer our questions. We see thee in the guise of an ascetic and yet armed with weapons. O thou of mighty intelligence, do thou unfold unto us the object with which thou hast come (hither).'"

SECTION CLIII

"Bhima said, 'I am the son of Pandu, and next by birth to Yudhishthira the just, and my name is Bhimasena. O Rakshasas, I have come with my brothers to the jujube named Visala. At that place, Panchali saw an excellent Saugandhika lotus, which, of a certainty, was carried thither by the wind from this region. She wisheth to have those flowers in abundance. Know ye, ye Rakshasas, that I am engaged in fulfilling the desire of my wedded wife of faultless features, and have come hither to procure the flowers.' Thereat the Rakshasas said, 'O foremost of men, this spot is dear unto Kuvera, and it is his sporting region. Men subject to death cannot sport here. O Vrikodara, the celestial sages, and the gods taking the permission of the chief of the Yakshas, drink of this lake, and sport herein. And, O Pandava, the Gandharvas and the Apsaras also divert themselves in this lake. That wicked person who, disregarding the lord of treasures, unlawfully attempteth to sport here, without doubt, meeteth with destruction. Disregarding him, thou seekest to take away the lotuses from this place by main force. Why then dost thou say that thou art the brother of Yudhishthira the just? First, taking the permission of the lord of Yakshas, do thou drink of this lake and take away the flowers. If thou dost not do this, thou shall not be able even to glance at a single lotus.' Bhimasena said, 'Ye Rakshasas, I do not see the lord of wealth here. And even if I did see that mighty king, I would not beseech him: Kshatriyas never beseech (any body). This is the eternal morality; and I by no means wish to forsake the Kshatriya morality. And, further this lotus-lake hath sprung from the cascades of the mountain; it hath not been excavated in the mansion of Kuvera. Therefore it belongeth equally to all creatures with Vaisravana. In regard to a thing of such a nature, who goeth to beseech another?'"

Vaisampayana said, "Having said this unto the Rakshasas, the mighty-armed and exceedingly unforbearing Bhimasena of great strength plunged into the lotus-lake. Thereat that powerful one was forbidden by the Rakshasas, saying, 'Do not do this;' and they from all sides began to abuse him in anger. But slighting these Rakshasas, that mighty one of dreadful prowess plunged (farther and farther). Now they all prepared for opposing him. And with eyes rolling, they upraised their arms, and rushed in wrath at Bhimasena, exclaiming, 'Seize him! Bind him! Hew him! We shall cook Bhimasena, and eat him up!' Thereupon that one of great force, taking his ponderous and mighty mace inlaid with golden plates, like unto the mace of Yama himself, turned towards those, and then said, 'Stay!' At this, they darted at him with vehemence, brandishing lances, and axes, and other weapons. And wishing to destroy Bhima, the dreadful and fierce Krodhavasas surrounded Bhima on all sides. But that one, being endued with strength, had been begotten by Vayu in the womb of Kunti; and he was heroic and energetic, and the slayer of foes, and ever devoted to virtue and truth, and incapable of being vanquished by enemies through prowess. Accordingly this high-souled Bhima defeating all the manoeuvres of the foes, and breaking their arms, killed on the banks of the lake more than a hundred, commencing with the foremost. And then witnessing his prowess and strength, and the force of his skill, and also the might of his arms, and unable to bear (the onset), those prime heroes all of a sudden fled on all sides in bands.

"Beaten and pierced by Bhimasena, those Krodhavasas quitted the field of battle, and in confusion quickly fled towards the Kailasa cliff, supporting themselves in the sky. Having thus by the exercise of his prowess defeated those hosts, even as Sakra had defeated the armies of Daityas and Danavas, he (Bhima), now that he had conquered the enemy, plunged into the lake and began to gather the lotuses, with the object of gaining his purpose. And as he drank of the waters, like unto nectar, his energy and strength were again fully restored; and he fell to plucking and gathering Saugandhika lotuses of excellent fragrance. On the other hand, the Krodhavasas, being driven by the might of Bhima and exceedingly terrified, presented themselves before the lord of wealth, and gave an exact account of Bhima's prowess and strength in fight. Hearing their words, the god (Kuvera) smiled and then said, 'Let Bhima take for Krishna as many lotuses as he likes. This is already known to me.' Thereupon taking the permission of the lord of wealth, those (Rakshasas) renouncing anger, went to that foremost of the Kurus, and in that lotus-lake beheld Bhima alone, disporting in delight."

SECTION CLIV

Vaisampayana said, "Then, O best of the Bharatas, Bhima began to collect those rare unearthly, variegated and fresh flowers in abundance.

"And it came to pass that a high and violent wind, piercing to the touch, and blowing about gravels, arose, portending battle. And frightful meteors began to shoot, with thundering sounds. And being enveloped by darkness, the sun became pale, his rays being obscured. And on Bhima displaying his prowess, dreadful sounds of explosion rang through the sky. And the earth began to tremble, and dust fell in showers. And the points of the heavens became reddened. And beasts and birds began to cry in shrill tones. And every thing became enveloped in darkness; and nothing could be distinguished. And other evil omens besides these appeared there. Witnessing these strange phenomena, Dharma's son Yudhishthira, the foremost of speakers, said, 'Who is it that will overcome us? Ye Pandavas who take delight in battle, good betide you! Do ye equip yourselves. From what I see, I infer that the time for the display of our prowess hath drawn nigh.' Having said this, the king looked around. Then not finding Bhima, that represser of foes, Dharma's son, Yudhishthira, enquired of Krishna and the twins standing near regarding his brother, Bhima, the doer of dreadful deeds in battle, saying, 'O Panchali, is Bhima intent upon performing some great feat, or hath that one delighting in daring deeds already achieved some brave deed? Portending some great danger, these omens have appeared all around, indicating a fearful battle.' When Yudhishthira said this, his beloved queen, the high-minded Krishna of sweet smiles, answered him, in order to remove his anxiety. 'O king, that Saugandhika lotus which to-day had been brought by the wind, I had out of love duly shown unto Bhimasena; and I had also said unto that hero, If thou canst find many of this species, procuring even all of them, do thou return speedily,—O Pandava, that mighty armed one, with the view of gratifying my desire, may have gone towards the north-east to bring them.' Having heard these words of hers, the king said unto the twins, 'Let us together follow the path taken by Vrikodara. Let the Rakshasas carry those Brahmanas that are fatigued and weak. O Ghatotkacha, O thou like unto a celestial, do thou carry Krishna. I am convinced and it is plain that Bhima hath dived into the forest; for it is long since he hath gone, and in speed he resembleth the wind, and in clearing over the ground, he is swift like unto Vinata's son, and he will ever leap into the sky, and alight at his will. O Rakshasas, we shall follow him through your prowess. He will not at first do any wrong to the Siddhas versed in the Vedas.' O best of the Bharatas, saying, 'So be it,' Hidimva's son and the other Rakshasas who knew the quarter where the lotus lake of Kuvera was situated, started cheerfully with Lomasa, bearing the Pandavas, and many of the Brahmanas. Having shortly reached that spot, they saw that romantic lake covered with Saugandhika and other lotuses and surrounded by beautiful woods. And on its shores they beheld the high-souled and vehement Bhima, as also the slaughtered Yakshas of large eyes, with their bodies, eyes, arms and thighs smashed, and their heads crushed. And on seeing the high-souled Bhima, standing on the shore of that lake in an angry mood, and with steadfast eyes, and biting his lip, and stationed on the shore of the lake with his mace upraised by his two hands, like unto Yama with his mace in his hand at the time of the universal dissolution, Yudhishthira the just, embraced him again and again, and said in sweet words, 'O Kaunteya, what hast thou done? Good betide thee! If thou wishest to do good unto me, thou shouldst never again commit such a rash act, nor offend the gods.' Having thus instructed the son of Kunti, and taken the flowers those god-like ones began to sport in that very lake. At this instant, the huge-bodied warders of the gardens, equipped with rocks for weapons, presented themselves at the spot. And seeing Yudhishthira the just and the great sage Lomasa and Nakula and Sahadeva and also the other foremost of Brahmanas, they all bowed themselves down in humility. And being pacified by Yudhishthira the just, the Rakshasas became satisfied. And with the knowledge of Kuvera, those foremost of Kurus for a short time dwelt pleasantly at that spot on the slopes of the Gandhamadana, expecting Arjuna."

SECTION CLV

Vaisampayana said, "Once upon a time Yudhishthira, while living at that place, addressed Krishna, his brother, and the Brahmanas, saying, 'By us have been attentively seen one after another sacred and auspicious *tirthas*, and woods, delightful to beheld, which had ere this been visited by the celestials and the high-souled sages, and which had been worshipped by the Brahmanas. And in various sacred asylums we have performed ablutions with Brahmanas, and have heard from them the lives and acts of many sages, and also of many royal sages of yore, and other pleasant stories. And with flowers and water have the gods been worshipped by us. And with offerings of fruits and roots as available at each place we have gratified the *pitris*. And with the high-souled ones have we performed ablutions in all sacred and beautiful mountains and lakes, and also in the highly sacred ocean. And with the Brahmanas we have bathed in the Ila, and in the Saraswati, and in the Sindhu, and in the Yamuna, and in the Narmada, and in various other romantic *tirthas*. And having passed the source of the Ganga, we have seen many a lovely hill and the Himalaya mountains, inhabited by various species of birds, and also the jujube named Visala, where there is the hermitage of Nara and Narayana. And (finally) we have beheld this unearthly lake, held in veneration by the Siddhas, the gods and the sages. In fact, O foremost of Brahmanas, we have one by one carefully seen all celebrated and sacred spots in company with the high-souled Lomasa. Now, O Bhima, how shall we repair to the sacred abode of Vaisravana, inhabited by the Siddhas? Do thou think of the means of entering (the same).'"

Vaisampayana said, "When that king had said this, an aerial voice spake, saying. 'Thou will not be able to go to that inaccessible spot. By this very way, do thou repair from this region of Kuvera to the place whence thou hadst come even to the hermitage of Nara and Narayana, known by the name of Vadari. Thence, O Kaunteya, thou wilt repair to the hermitage of Vrishaparva, abounding in flowers and fruit, and inhabited by the Siddhas and the Charanas. Having passed that, O Partha, thou wilt proceed to the hermitage of Arshtishena, and from thence thou wilt behold the abode of

Kuvera.' Just at that moment the breeze became fresh, and gladsome and cool and redolent of unearthly fragrance; and it showered blossoms, And on hearing the celestial voice from the sky, they all were amazed,—more specially those earthly *rishis* and the Brahmanas. On hearing this mighty marvel, the Brahmana Dhaumya, said, 'This should not be gainsaid. O Bharata, let this be so.' Thereupon, king Yudhishthira obeyed him. And having returned to the hermitage of Nara and Narayana, he began to dwell pleasantly, surrounded by Bhimasena and his other brothers, Panchali, and the Brahmanas."

SECTION CLVI

Vaisampayana continued, "Thus dwelling with the Brahmanas in that best of mountains, in expectation of Arjuna's return, when the Pandavas had grown confident and when all those Rakshasas together with Bhima's son had departed, one day while Bhimasena was away, a Rakshasa all of a sudden carried off Yudhishthira the just and the twins and Krishna. That Rakshasa (in the guise of a Brahmana) had constantly remained in the company of the Pandavas, alleging that he was a high-class Brahmana, skilled in counsel, and versed in all the *Sastras*. His object was to possess himself of the bows, the quivers and the other material implements belonging to the Pandavas; and he had been watching for an opportunity of ravishing Draupadi. And that wicked and sinful one was named Jatasura. And, O king of kings, Pandu's son (Yudhishthira) had been supporting him, but knew not that wretch like unto a fire covered with ashes.

"And once on a day while that represser of foes, Bhimasena, was out hunting, he (the Rakshasa), seeing Ghatotkacha and his followers scatter in different directions and seeing those vow-observing great *rishis*, of ascetic wealth, viz., Lomasa and the rest, away for bathing and collecting flowers, assumed a different form, gigantic and monstrous and frightful; and having secured all the arms (of the Pandavas) as also Draupadi, that wicked one fled away taking the three Pandavas. Thereupon that son of Pandu, Sahadeva, extricated himself with exertion, and by force snatched the sword named Kausika from the grasp of the enemy and began to call Bhimasena, taking the direction in which that mighty one had gone. And on being carried off Yudhishthira the just, addressed him (that Rakshasa), saying, 'O stupid one, thy merit decreaseth (even by this act of thine). Dost thou not pay heed unto the established order of nature? Whether belonging to the human race, or to the lower orders, all pay regard to virtue,—more specially the Rakshasas. In the first instance, they knew virtue better than others. Having considered all these, thou ought to adhere to virtue. O Rakshasa, the gods, the *pitris*, the Siddhas, the *rishis*, the Gandharvas, the brutes and even the worms and ants depend for their lives on men; and thou too liveth through that agency. If prosperity attendeth the human race, thy race also prospereth; and if calamities befall the former, even the celestials suffer grief. Being gratified by offerings, do the gods thrive. O Rakshasa, we are the guardians, governors and preceptors of kingdoms. If kingdoms become unprotected, whence can proceed prosperity and happiness? Unless there be offence, a Rakshasa should not violate a king. O man-eating one, we have committed no wrong, ever so little. Living on *vighasa*, we serve the gods and others to the best of our power. And we are ever intent upon bowing down to our superiors and Brahmanas. A friend, and one confiding, and he whose food hath been partaken of, and he that hath afforded shelter, should never be injured. Thou hast lived in our place happily, being duly honoured. And, O evil-minded one, having partaken of our food, how canst thou carry us off? And as thy acts are so improper and as thou hast grown in age without deriving any benefit and as thy propensities are evil, so thou deservest to die for nothing, and for nothing wilt thou die to-day. And if thou beest really evil-disposed and devoid of all virtue, do thou render us back our weapons and ravish Draupadi after fight. But if through stupidity thou must do this deed, then in the world thou wilt only reap demerit and infamy. O Rakshasa, by doing violence to this female of the human race, thou hast drunk poison, after having shaken the vessel.' Thereupon, Yudhishthira made himself ponderous to the Rakshasa. And being oppressed with the weight, he could not proceed rapidly as before. Then addressing Draupadi, Nakula and Sahadeva, Yudhishthira said, 'Do ye not entertain any fear of this wretched Rakshasa, I have checked his speed. The mighty-armed son of the Wind-god may not be far away; and on Bhima coming up at the next moment, the Rakshasa will not live.' O king, staring at the Rakshasa bereft of sense, Sahadeva addressed Yudhishthira, the son of Kunti, saying, 'What can be more meritorious for a Kshatriya than to fall in fight, or defeat a foe? O repressor of foes, we will fight and either this one will slay us, or we shall slay him, O mighty-armed one. Verily this is the place and time, O king. And, O thou of unfailing prowess, the time hath come for the display of our Kshatriya virtue. It behoveth us to attain heaven either by gaining victory or being slain. If the sun sets to-day, the Rakshasa living yet, O Bharata, I will not any more say that I am a Kshatriya. Ho! Ho! Rakshasa, say! I am Pandu's son, Sahadeva. Either, after having killed me, carry off this lady, or being slain, lie senseless here.'

"Madri's son, Sahadeva, was speaking thus, when Bhimasena made his appearance, with a mace in his hand, like unto Vasava himself wielding the thunder-bolt. And here he saw his two brothers and the noble-minded Draupadi (on the shoulders of the demon), and Sahadeva on the ground rebuking the Rakshasa and also that stupid Rakshasa himself deprived of sense by Fate, going round in different directions through bewilderment caused by Destiny. And finding his brothers and Draupadi being carried off, Bhima of mighty strength was fired with wrath, and addressed the Rakshasa, saying, 'I had ere this found thee out for a wicked wight from thy scrutiny of our weapons; but as I had no apprehension of thee, so I had not slain thee at that time. Thou wert in the disguise of a Brahmana—nor didst thou say anything harsh unto us. And thou didst take delight in pleasing us. And thou also didst not do us wrong. And, furthermore, thou wert our guest. How could I, therefore, slay thee, who wert thus innocent of offence, and who wert in the disguise of a Brahmana? He that knowing such a one to be even a Rakshasa, slayeth him, goes to hell. Further, thou canst not be killed before the time cometh. Surely to-day thou hast reached the fullness of thy time in as much as thy mind hath been thus turned by the wonder-performing Fate towards carrying off Krishna. By committing thyself to this deed, thou hast swallowed up the hook fastened to the line of Fate. So like unto a fish in water, whose mouth hath been hooked, how canst thou live to-day? Thou shall not have to go whither thou intendest to, or whither thou hadst already gone mentally; but thou shall go whither have repaired Vaka and Hidimva.'

"Thus addressed by Bhima, the Rakshasa in alarm put them down; and being forced by Fate, approached for fight. And with his lips trembling in anger he spake unto Bhima, saying, 'Wretch! I have not been bewildered; I had been delaying for thee. Today will I offer oblations of thy blood to those Rakshasas who, I had heard, have been slain by thee in fight.' Thus addressed, Bhima, as if bursting with wrath, like unto Yama himself at the time of the universal dissolution, rushed towards the Rakshasa, licking the corners of his mouth and staring at him as he struck his own arms with the hands. And seeing Bhima waiting in expectation of fight, the Rakshasa also darted towards him in anger, like unto Vali towards the wielder of the thunderbolt, repeatedly gaping and licking the corners of his mouth. And when a dreadful wrestling ensued between those two, both the sons of Madri, waxing exceeding wroth rushed forward; but Kunti's son, Vrikodara, forbade them with a smile and said, 'Witness ye! I am more than a match for this Rakshasa. By my own self and by my brothers, and by my merit, and by my good deeds, and by my sacrifices, do I swear that I shall slay this Rakshasa.' And after this was said, those two heroes, the Rakshasa and Vrikodara challenging each other, caught each other by the arms. And they not forgiving each other, then there ensued a conflict between the infuriated Bhima and the Rakshasa, like unto that between a god and a demon. And repeatedly uprooting trees, those two of mighty strength struck each other, shouting and roaring like two masses of clouds. And those foremost of athletes, each wishing to kill the other, and rushing at the other with vehemence, broke down many a gigantic tree by their thighs. Thus that encounter with trees, destructive of plants, went on like unto that between the two brothers Vali and Sugriva—desirous of the possession of a single woman. Brandishing trees for a moment, they struck each other with them, shouting incessantly. And when all the trees of the spot had been pulled down and crushed into fibres by them endeavouring to kill each other, then, O Bharata, those two of mighty strength, taking up rocks, began to fight for a while, like unto a mountain and a mighty mass of clouds. And not suffering each other, they fell to striking each other with hard and large crags, resembling vehement thunder-bolts. Then from strength defying each other, they again darted at each other, and grasping each other by their arms, began to wrestle like unto two elephants. And next they dealt each other fierce blows. And then those two mighty ones began to make chattering sounds by gnashing their teeth. And at length, having clenched his fist like a five-headed snake, Bhima with force dealt a blow on the neck of the Rakshasa. And when struck by that fist of Bhima, the Rakshasa became faint, Bhimasena stood, catching hold of that exhausted one. And then the god-like mighty-armed Bhima lifted him with his two arms, and dashing him with force on the ground, the son of Pandu smashed all his limbs. And striking him with his elbow, he severed from his body the head with bitten lips and rolling eyes, like unto a fruit from its stem. And Jatasura's head being severed by Bhimasena's might, he fell besmeared with gore, and having bitten lips. Having slain Jatasura, Bhima presented himself before Yudhishthira, and the foremost Brahmanas began to eulogise him (Bhima) even as the Marutas (eulogise) Vasava."

SECTION CLVII

Vaisampayana continued, "On that Rakshasa having been slain, that lord, the royal son of Kunti, returned to the hermitage of Narayana and began to dwell there. And once on a time, remembering his brother Jaya (Arjuna), Yudhishthira summoned all his brothers, together with Draupadi and said these words, 'We have passed these four years peacefully ranging the woods. It hath been appointed by Vibhatsu that about the fifth year he will come to that monarch of mountains, the excellent cliff Sweta, ever graced with festivities held by blooming plants and maddened Kokilas and black bees, and peacocks, and chatakas and inhabited by tigers, and boars and buffaloes, and gavayas, and deer, and ferocious beasts; and sacred; and lovely with blown lotuses of a hundred and a thousand petals, and blooming lilies and blue lilies and frequented by the celestials and the Asuras. And we also, eagerly anxious of meeting him on his arrival have made up our minds to repair thither. Partha of unrivalled prowess hath appointed with me, saying, "I shall remain abroad for five years, with the object of learning military science." In the place like unto the region of the gods, shall we behold the wielder of Gandiva arrive after having obtained the weapons.' Having said this, the Pandava summoned the Brahmanas, and the sons of Pritha having gone round the ascetics of rigid austerities and thereby pleased them, informed them of the matter mentioned above. Thereupon the Brahmanas gave their assent, saying, 'This shall be attended by prosperity and welfare. O foremost of the Bharatas, these troubles shall result in happiness. O pious one, gaining the earth by the Kshatriya virtue, thou shall govern it.' Then in obedience to these words of the ascetics, that represser of foes, Yudhishthira, set out with his brothers and those Brahmanas, followed by the Rakshasa and protected by Lomasa. And that one of mighty energy, and of staunch vows, with his brothers, at places went on foot and at others were carried by the Rakshasas. Then king Yudhishthira, apprehending many troubles, proceeded towards the north abounding in lions and tigers and elephants. And beholding on the way the mountain Mainaka and the base of the Gandhamadana and that rocky mass Sweta and many a crystal rivulet higher and higher up the mountain, he reached on the seventeenth day the sacred slopes of the Himalayas. And,

O king, not far from the Gandhamadana, Pandu's son beheld on the sacred slopes of the Himavan covered with various trees and creepers the holy hermitage of Vrishaparva surrounded by blossoming trees growing near the cascades. And when those repressers of foes, the sons of Pandu, had recovered from fatigue, they went to the royal sage, the pious Vrishaparva and greeted him. And that royal sage received with affection those foremost of Bharatas, even as his own sons. And those repressers of foes passed there seven nights, duly regarded. And when the eighth day came, taking the permission of that sage celebrated over the worlds, they prepared to start on their journey. And having one by one introduced unto Vrishapava those Brahmanas, who, duly honoured, remained in his charge as friends; and having also entrusted the highsouled Vrishaparva with their remaining robes, the sons of Pandu, O king, left in the hermitage of Vrishaparva their sacrificial vessels together with their ornaments and jewels. And wise and pious and versed in every duty and having a knowledge of the past as well as the future, that one gave instructions unto those best of the Bharatas, as unto his own sons. Then taking his permission those high-souled ones set out towards the north. And as they set out the magnanimous Vrishaparva followed them to a certain distance. Then having entrusted the Pandavas unto the care of the Brahmanas and instructed and blessed them and given directions concerning their course, Vrishaparva of mighty energy retraced his steps.

"Then Kunti's son, Yudhishthira of unfailing prowess, together with his brothers, began to proceed on foot along the mountain path, inhabited by various kinds of beasts. And having dwelt at the mountain slopes, densely overgrown with trees, Pandu's son on the fourth day reached the Sweta mountain, like unto a mighty mass of clouds, abounding in streams and consisting of a mass of gold and gems. And taking the way directed by Vrishaparva, they reached one by one the intended places, beholding various mountains. And over and over they passed with ease many inaccessible rocks and exceedingly impassable caves of the mountain. And Dhaumya and Krishna and the Parthas and the mighty sage Lomasa went on in a body and none grew tired. And those highly fortunate ones arrived at the sacred and mighty mountain resounding with the cries of birds and beasts and covered with various trees and creepers and inhabited by monkeys, and romantic and furnished with many lotus-lakes and having marshes and extensive forests. And then with their down standing erect, they saw the mountain Gandhamadana, the abode of Kimpurushas, frequented by Siddhas and Charanas and ranged by Vidyadharis and Kinnaris and inhabited by herds of elephants and thronged with lions and tigers and resounding with the roars of Sarabhas and attended by various beasts. And the war-like sons of Pandu gradually entered into the forest of the Gandhamadana, like unto the Nandana gardens, delightful to the mind and heart and worthy of being inhabited and having beautiful groves. And as those heroes entered with Draupadi and the high-souled Brahmanas, they heard notes uttered by the mouths of birds, exceedingly sweet and graceful to the ear and causing delight and dulcet and broken by reason of excess of animal spirits. And they saw various trees bending under the weight of fruits in all seasons, and ever bright with flowers—such as mangoes and hog-plums and bhavyas and pomegranates, citrons and jacks and lakuchas and plantains and aquatic reeds and parvatas and champakas and lovely kadamvas and vilwas, wood-apples and rose-apples and kasmaris and jujubes and figs and glomerous figs and banians and aswatthas and khirikas and bhall atakas and amalkas and bibhitakas and ingudas and karamardas and tindukas of large fruits—these and many others on the slopes of the Gandhamadana, clustered with sweet and nectarine fruits. And besides these, they beheld champakas and asokas and ketakas and vakulas and punnagas and saptaparnas and karnikaras, and patals, and beautiful kutajas and mandaras, and lotuses, and parijatas, and kovidaras and devadarus, and salas, and palmyra palms, and tamalas, and pippalas, and salmalis and kinsukas, and singsapas, and saralas and these were inhabited by Chakoras, and wood-peckers and chatakas, and various other birds, singing in sweet tones pleasing to the ear. And they saw lakes beautiful on all sides with aquatic birds, and covered all around with kumudas, and pundarikas, and kokanadas, and utpalas, and kalharas, and kamalas and thronged on all sides with drakes and ruddy geese, and ospreys, and gulls and karandavas, and plavas, and swans, and cranes, and shags, and other aquatic birds. And those foremost of men saw those lotus-lakes beautified with assemblages of lotuses, and ringing with the sweet hum of bees, glad, and drowsy on account of having drunk the intoxicating honey of lotuses, and reddened with the farina falling from the lotus cups. And in the groves they beheld with their hens peacocks maddened with desire caused by the notes of cloud-trumpets; and those woods-loving glad peacocks drowsy with desire, were dancing, spreading in dalliance their gorgeous tails, and were crying in melodious notes. And some of the peacocks were sporting with their mates on kutaja trees covered with creepers. And some sat on the boughs of the kutajas, spreading their gorgeous tails, and looking like crowns worn by the trees. And in the glades they beheld the graceful sindhuvaras like unto the darts of Cupid. And on the summits of the mountain, they saw blooming karnikaras bearing blossoms of a golden hue, appearing like ear-rings of excellent make. And in the forest they saw blossoming kuruvakas, like unto the shafts of Cupid, which smiteth one with desire and maketh him uneasy. And they saw tilakas appearing like unto beauty-spots painted on the forehead of the forest. And they saw mango trees graced with blossoms hummed over by black bees, and serving the purpose of Cupid's shafts. And on the slopes of the mountain there were diverse blossoming trees, looking lovely, some bearing flowers of a golden hue, and some, of the hue of the forest-conflagration, and some, red and some sable, and some green like unto lapises. And besides these, there were ranges of salas and tamalas and patalas and vakula trees, like unto garlands put on by the summits of the mountain. Thus gradually beholding on the slopes of the mountain many lakes, looking transparent like crystal, and having swans of white plumage and resounding with cries of cranes, and filled with lotuses and lilies, and furnished with waters of delicious feel; and also beholding fragrant flowers, and luscious fruits, and romantic lakes, and captivating trees, the Pandavas penetrated into the forest with eyes expanded with wonder. And (as they proceeded) they were fanned by the breeze of balmy feel, and perfumed by kamalas and utpalas and kalharas and pundarikas. Then Yudhishthira pleasantly spake unto Bhima saying, 'Ah! O Bhima, beautiful is this forest of the Gandhamadana. In this romantic forest there are various heavenly blossoming wild trees and creepers, bedecked with foliage and fruit, nor are there any trees that do not flower. On these slopes of the Gandhamadana, all the trees are of sleek foliage and fruit. And behold how these lotus-lakes with fullblown lotuses, and ringing with the hum of black bees, are being agitated by elephants with their mates. Behold another lotus-lake girt with lines of lotuses, like unto a second Sree in an embodied form wearing garlands. And in this excellent forest there are beautiful ranges of woods, rich with the aroma of various blossoms, and hummed over by the black bees. And, O Bhima, behold on all sides the excellent sporting ground of the celestials. By coming here, we have attained extra-human state, and been blessed. O Partha, on these slopes of the Gandhamadana, yon beautiful blossoming trees, being embraced by creepers with blossoms at their tops, look lovely. And, O Bhima, hark unto the notes of the peacocks crying with their hens on the mountain slopes. And birds such as chakoras, and satapatras, and maddened kokilas, and parrots, are alighting on these excellent flowering trees. And sitting on the twigs, myriads of jivajivakas of scarlet, yellow and red hues, are looking at one another. And the cranes are seen near the spots covered with green and reddish grass, and also by the side of the cascades. And those birds, bhringarajas, and upachakras, and herons are pouring forth their notes charming to all creatures. And, lo! with their mates, these elephants furnished with four tusks, and white as lotuses, are agitating that large lake of the hue of lapises. And from many cascades, torrents high as several palmyra palms (placed one upon another) are rushing down from the cliffs. And many argent minerals splendid, and of the effulgence of the sun, and like unto autumnal clouds, are beautifying this mighty mountain. And in some places there are minerals of the hue of the collyrium, and in some those like unto gold, in some, yellow orpiment and in some, vermilion, and in some, caves of red arsenic like unto the evening clouds and in some, red chalk of the hue of the rabbit, and in some, minerals like unto white and sable clouds; and in some, those effulgent as the rising sun, these minerals of great lustre beautify the mountain. O Partha, as was said by Vrishaparva, the Gandharvas and the Kimpurushas, in company with their loves, are visible on the summits of the mountain. And, O Bhima, there are heard various songs of appropriate measures, and also Vedic hymns, charming to all creatures. Do thou behold the sacred and graceful celestial river Mahaganga, with swans, resorted to by sages and Kinnaras. And, O represser of foes, see this mountain having minerals, rivulets, and beautiful woods and beasts, and snakes of diverse shapes and a hundred heads and Kinnaras, Gandharvas and Apsaras.'"

Vaisampayana said, "Having attained excellent state, those valiant and warlike repressers of foes with Draupadi and the high-souled Brahmanas were exceedingly delighted at heart, and they were not satiated by beholding that monarch of mountains. Thereafter they saw the hermitage of the royal sage Arshtishena, furnished with flowers and trees bearing fruits. Then they went to Arshtishena versed in all duties of rigid austerities, skeleton-like, and having muscles bare."

SECTION CLVIII

Vaisampayana continued, "Having approached that one, whose sins had been consumed by asceticism, Yudhishthira announced his name, and gladly greeted him, bending his head. And then Krishna, and Bhima, and the devout twins, having bowed down their heads unto the royal sage, stood (there) surrounding him. And that priest of the Pandavas, the virtuous Dhaumya, also duly approached that vow-observing sage. And by his prophetic eye that virtuous Muni had already known (the identity of) those foremost of the Kurus, the sons of Pandu. And he said unto them. 'Be ye seated.' And that one of rigid austerities, after having duly received that chief of the Kurus, when the latter with his brothers had seated himself enquired after his welfare saying, 'Dost thou not turn thy inclination upon untruth? And art thou intent upon virtue? And, O Partha, hath not thy attention to thy father and thy mother diminished? Are all thy superiors, and the aged, and those versed in the Vedas, honoured by thee? And O Pritha's son, dost thou not turn thy inclination unto sinful acts? And dost thou, O best of the Kurus, properly know how to perform meritorious acts, and to eschew wicked deeds? Dost thou not exalt thyself? And are pious men gratified, being honoured by thee? And even dwelling in the woods, dost thou follow virtue alone? And, O Partha, doth not Dhaumya grieve at thy conduct? Dost thou follow the customs of thy ancestors, by charity, and religious observances, and asceticism, and purity, and candour, and forgiveness? And dost thou go along the way taken by the royal sages? On the birth of a son in their (respective) lines, the *Pitris* in their regions, both laugh and grieve, thinking—Will the sinful acts of this son of ours harm us, or will meritorious deeds conduce to our welfare? He conquereth both the worlds that payeth homage unto his father, and mother, and preceptor, and Agni, and fifthly, the soul.' Yudhishthira said, 'O worshipful one, those duties have been mentioned by thee as excellent. To the best of my power I duly and properly discharge them.'

"Arshtishena said, 'During the Parvas sages subsisting on air and water come unto this best of the mountains ranging through the air. And on the summits of the mountain are seen amorous Kimpurushas with their paramours, mutually attached unto each other; as also, O Partha, many

Gandharvas and Apsaras clad in white silk vestments; and lovely-looking Vidyadharas, wearing garlands; and mighty Nagas, and Suparnas, and Uragas, and others. And on the summits of the mountain are heard, during the Parvas, sounds of kettle-drums, and tabors, shells and mridangas. O foremost of the Bharatas, even by staying here, ye shall hear those sounds; do ye by no means feel inclined to repair thither. Further, O best of the Bharata race, it is impossible, to proceed beyond this. That place is the sporting-region of the celestials. There is no access thither for mortals. O Bharata, at this place all creatures bear ill-will to, and the Rakshasas chastise, that man who committeth aggression, be it ever so little. Beyond the summit of this Kailasa cliff, is seen the path of the celestial sages. If any one through impudence goeth beyond this, the Rakshasas slay him with iron darts and other weapons. There, O child, during the Parvas, he that goeth about on the shoulders of men, even Vaisravana is seen in pomp and grandeur surrounded by the Apsaras. And when that lord of all the Rakshasas is seated on the summit, all creatures behold him like unto the sun arisen. O best of Bharatas, that summit is the sporting-garden of the celestials, and the Danavas, and the Siddhas, and Vaisravana. And during the Parvas, as Tumburu entertaineth the Lord of treasures, the sweet notes of his song are heard all over the Gandhamadana. O child, O Yudhishthira, here during the Parvas, all creatures see and hear marvels like this. O Pandavas, till ye meet with Arjuna, do ye stay here, partaking of luscious fruits, and the food of the Munis. O child as thou hast come hither, do thou not betray any impertinence. And, O child, after living here at thy will and diverting thyself as thou listest, thou wilt at length rule the earth, having conquered it by the force of thy arms.'"

SECTION CLIX

Janamejaya said, "How long did my great grandsires, the highsouled sons of Pandu of matchless prowess, dwell in the Gandhamadana mountain? And what did those exceedingly powerful ones, gifted with manliness, do? And what was the food of those high-souled ones, when those heroes of the worlds dwelt (there)? O excellent one, do thou relate all about this. Do thou describe the prowess of Bhimasena, and what that mighty-armed one did in the mountain Himalayan. Surely, O best of Brahmanas, he did not fight again with the Yakshas. And did they meet with Vaisravana? Surely, as Arshtishena said, the lord of wealth cometh thither. All this, O thou of ascetic wealth, I desire to hear in detail. Surely, I have not yet been fully satisfied by hearing about their acts."

Vaisampayana continued, "Having heard from that one of incomparable energy, (Arshtishena), that advice conducive to their welfare, those foremost of the Bharatas, began to behave always accordingly. Those best of men, the Pandavas, dwelt upon the Himavan, partaking of the food eaten by the Munis, and luscious fruit, and the flesh of deer killed with unpoisoned shafts and various kinds of pure honey. Living thus, they passed the fifth year, hearing various stories told by Lomasa. O lord, saying, 'I shall be present when occasion ariseth,' Ghatotkacha, together with all the Rakshasas, had ere this already gone away. Those magnanimous ones passed many months in the hermitage of Arshtishena, witnessing many marvels. And as the Pandavas were sporting there pleasantly, there came to see them some complacent vow-observing Munis and Charanas of high fortune, and pure souls. And those foremost of the Bharata race conversed with them on earthly topics. And it came to pass that when several days has passed, Suparna all of a sudden carried off an exceedingly powerful and mighty Naga, living in the large lake. And thereupon that mighty mountain began to tremble, and the gigantic trees, break. And all the creatures and the Pandavas witnessed the wonder. Then from the brow of that excellent mountain, the wind brought before the Pandavas various fragrant and fair blossoms. And the Pandavas, and the illustrious Krishna, together with their friends, saw those unearthly blossoms of five hues. And as the mighty-armed Bhimasena was seated at ease upon the mountain, Krishna addressed him, saying, 'O best of the Bharata race, in the presence of all the creatures, these flowers of five hues, carried by the force of the wind raised by Suparna, are falling in amain on the river Aswaratha. In Khandava thy high-souled brother, firm in promise, had baffled Gandharvas and Nagas and Vasava himself, and slain fierce Rakshasas, and also obtained the bow Gandiva. Thou also art of exceeding prowess and the might of thy arms is great, and irrepressible, and unbearable like unto the might of Sakra. O Bhimasena, terrified with the force of thy arms, let all the Rakshasas betake themselves to the ten cardinal points, leaving the mountain. Then will thy friends be freed from fear and affliction, and behold the auspicious summit of this excellent mountain furnished with variegated flowers. O Bhima, I have for long cherished this thought in my mind,—that protected by the might of thy arms, I shall see that summit.'

"Thereupon, like a high-mettled bull that hath been struck, Bhimasena, considering himself as censured by Draupadi, could not bear (that). And that Pandava of the gait of a lion or a bull, and graceful, and generous, and having the splendour of gold, and intelligent, and strong, and proud, and sensitive, and heroic, and having red eyes, and broad shoulders, and gifted with the strength of mad elephants, and having leonine teeth and a broad neck, and tall like a young sala tree, and highsouled, and graceful in every limb, and of neck having the whorls of a shell and mighty-armed, took up his bow plaited at the back with gold, and also his sword. And haughty like unto a lion, and resembling a maddened elephant, that strong one rushed towards that cliff, free from fear or affliction. And all the creatures saw him equipped with bows and arrows, approaching like a lion or a maddened elephant. And free from fear or affliction, the Pandava taking his mace, proceeded to that monarch of mountains causing the delight of Draupadi. And neither exhaustion, nor fatigue, nor lassitude, nor the malice (of others), affected that son of Pritha and the Wind-god. And having arrived at a rugged path affording passage to one individual only, that one of great strength ascended that terrible summit high as several palmyra palms (placed one upon another). And having ascended that summit, and thereby gladdened Kinnaras, and great Nagas, and Munis, and Gandharvas, and Rakshasas, that foremost of the Bharata line, gifted with exceeding strength described the abode of Vaisravana, adorned with golden crystal palaces surrounded on all sides by golden walls having the splendour of all gems, furnished with gardens all around, higher than a mountain peak, beautiful with ramparts and towers, and adorned with door-ways and gates and rows of pennons. And the abode was graced with dallying damsels dancing around, and also with pennons waved by the breeze. And with bent arms, supporting himself on the end of his bow, he stood beholding with eagerness the city of the lord of treasures. And gladdening all creatures, there was blowing a breeze, carrying all perfumes, and of a balmy feel. And there were various beautiful and wonderful trees of diverse hues resounding with diverse dulcet notes. And at that place the foremost of the Bharatas surveyed the palace of the Lord of the Rakshasas scattered with heaps of gems, and adorned with variegated garlands. And renouncing all care of life the mighty-armed Bhimasena stood motionless like a rock, with his mace and sword and bow in his hands. Then he blew his shell making the down of his adversaries stand erect; and twanging his bow-string, and striking his arms with the hands he unnerved all the creatures. Thereat with their hairs standing erect, the Yakshas and Rakshasas began to rush towards the Pandavas, in the direction of those sounds. And taken by the arms of the Yakshas and Rakshasas the flamed maces and clubs and swords and spears and javelins and axes, and when, O Bharata, the fight ensued between the Rakshasas and Bhima, the latter by arrows cut off the darts, javelins and axes of those possessing great powers of illusion, and he of exceeding strength with arrows pierced the bodies of the roaring Rakshasas, both of those that were in the sky, and of those that remained on the earth. And Bhima of exceeding strength was deluged with the mighty sanguine rain sprung from the bodies of the Rakshasas with maces and clubs in their hands and flowing on all sides from their persons. And the bodies and hands of the Yakshas and Rakshasas were seen to be struck off by the weapon discharged by the might of Bhima's arms. And then all the creatures saw the graceful Pandava densely surrounded by the Rakshasas, like unto the Sun enveloped by clouds. And even as the Sun surrounds everything with his rays, that mighty-armed and strong one of unfailing prowess, covered all with arrows destroying foes. And although menacing and uttering yells, the Rakshasas did not see Bhima embarrassed. Thereupon, with their bodies mangled, the Yakshas afflicted by fear of Bhimasena began to utter frightful sounds of distress, throwing their mighty weapons. And terrified at the wielder of a strong bow, they fled towards the southern quarter, forsaking their maces and spears and swords and clubs and axes. And then there stood, holding in his hands darts and maces, the broad-chested and mighty-armed friend of Vaisravana, the Rakshasa named Maniman. And that one of great strength began to display his mastery and manliness. And seeing them forsake the fight, he addressed them with a smile, 'Going to Vaisravana's abode, how will ye say unto that lord of wealth, that numbers have been defeated by a single mortal in battle?' Having said this unto them that Rakshasa, taking in his hands clubs and javelins and maces, set out and rushed towards the Pandava. And he rushed in amain like a maddened elephant. Bhimasena pierced his sides with three choice arrows. And the mighty Maniman, on his part, in wrath taking and flourishing a tremendous mace hurled it at Bhimasena. Thereupon Bhimasena beset with innumerable shafts sharpened on stones, hurled that mighty mace in the sky, dreadful, and like unto the lightning flash. But on reaching the mace those shafts were baffled; and although discharged with force by that adept at hurling the mace, still they could not stay its career. Then the mighty Bhima of dreadful prowess, baffled his (the Rakshasa's) discharge by resorting to his skill in mace-fighting. In the meanwhile, the intelligent Rakshasa had discharged a terrible iron club, furnished with a golden shaft. And that club, belching forth flames and emitting tremendous roars, all of a sudden pierced Bhima's right arm and then fell to the ground. On being severely wounded by that club, that bowman, Kunti's son, of immeasurable prowess, with eyes rolling in ire, took up his mace. And having taken that iron mace, inlaid with golden plates, which caused the fear of foes and brought on their defeat, he darted it with speed towards the mighty Maniman, menacing (him) and uttering shouts. Then Maniman on his part, taking his huge and blazing dart, with great force discharged it at Bhima, uttering loud shouts. Thereat breaking the dart with the end of his mace, that mighty-armed one skilled in mace-fighting, speedily rushed to slay him, as Garuda (rushed) to slay a serpent. Then all of a sudden, advancing ahead in the field, that mighty-armed one sprang into the sky and brandishing his mace hurled it with shouts. And like unto the thunder-bolt hurled by Indra, that mace like a pest, with the speed of the wind destroyed the Rakshasa and then fell to the ground. Then all the creatures saw that Rakshasa of terrible strength slaughtered by Bhima, even like a bull slain by a lion. And the surviving Rakshasas seeing him slain on the ground went towards the east, uttering frightful sounds of distress."

SECTION CLX

Vaisampayana said, "Hearing various sounds resounding in the caves of the mountain and not seeing Bhimasena, Kunti's son, Ajatasatru and the twin sons of Madri and Dhaumya and Krishna and all the Brahmanas and the friends (of the Pandavas), were filled with anxiety. Thereupon, entrusting Draupadi to the charge of Arshtishena and equipped in their arms, those valiant and mighty charioteers together began to ascend the summit of the mountain. And having reached the summit, as those repressors of foes and mighty bowmen and powerful charioteers they were looking about, saw Bhima and those huge Rakshasas of mighty strength and courage weltering in a state of unconsciousness having been struck down by Bhima. And holding his mace and sword and bow, that mighty-armed one looked like Maghavan, after he had slain the Danava hosts. Then on seeing their brother, the Pandavas, who had attained excellent state, embraced him and sat down there. And with those mighty bowmen, that summit looked grand like heaven graced by those foremost of celestials, the highly fortunate Lokapalas. And seeing the abode of Kuvera and the Rakshasas, lying slain on the ground, the king addressed his brother who was seated, saying, 'Either it be through rashness, or through ignorance, thou hast, O Bhima, committed a sinful act. O hero, as thou art leading the life of an anchorite, this slaughter without cause is unlike thee. Acts, it is asserted by those versed in duties, as are calculated to displease a monarch, ought not to be committed. But thou hast, O Bhimasena, committed a deed which will offend even the gods. He that disregarding profit and duty, turneth his thoughts to sin must, O Partha, reap the fruit of his sinful actions. However, if thou seekest my good, never again commit such a deed.'"

Vaisampayana continued, "Having said this to his brother, Vrikodara the virtuous, the highly energetic and firm-minded son of Kunti, Yudhishthira versed in the particulars of (the science of) profit, ceased, and began to reflect on that matter.

"On the other hand, the Rakshasas that had survived those slain by Bhima fled in a body towards the abode of Kuvera. And they of exceeding fleetness having speedily reached Vaisravana's abode, began to utter loud cries of distress, being afflicted with the fear of Bhima. And, O king bereft of their weapons and exhausted and with their mail besmeared with gore and with dishevelled hair they spake unto Kuvera, saying. 'O lord, all thy foremost Rakshasas fighting with maces and clubs and swords and lances and barbed darts, have been slain. O lord of treasures, a mortal, trespassing into the mountain, hath, singlehanded, slaughtered all thy Krodhavasa Rakshasas assembled together. And, O lord of wealth, there lie the foremost of the Yakshas and Rakshasas senseless and dead, having been struck down; and we have been let off through his favour. And thy friend, Maniman also hath been slain. All this hath been done by a mortal. Do thou what is proper, after this.' Having heard this, that lord of all the Yaksha hosts waxing wroth, with eyes reddened in anger, exclaimed, 'What!' And hearing of Bhima's second (act of) aggression, that lord of treasures, the king of the Yakshas, was filled with wrath, and said, 'Yoke' (the horses). Thereat unto a car of the hue of dark clouds, and high as a mountain summit, they yoked steeds having golden garments. And on being yoked unto the car, those excellent horses of his, graced with every noble quality and furnished with the ten auspicious curls of hair and having energy and strength, and adorned with various gems and looking splendid, as if desirous of speeding like the wind, began to neigh at each other the neighing emitted at (the hour of) victory. And that divine and effulgent king of the Yakshas set out, being eulogised by the celestials and Gandharvas. And a thousand foremost Yakshas of reddened eyes and golden lustre and having huge bodies, and gifted with great strength, equipped with weapons and girding on their swords, followed that high-souled lord of treasures. And coursing through the firmament they (the steeds) arrived at the Gandhamadana, as if drawing forward the sky with their fleetness. And with their down standing erect, the Pandavas saw that large assemblage of horses maintained by the lord of wealth and also the highsouled and graceful Kuvera himself surrounded by the Yaksha hosts. And seeing those mighty charioteers the son of Pandu, possessed of great strength, equipped with bows and swords, Kuvera also was delighted; and he was pleased at heart, keeping in view the task of the celestials. And like unto birds, they, (the Yakshas) gifted with extreme celerity, alighted on the summit of the mountain and stood before them (the Pandavas), with the lord of treasures at their head. Then, O Bharata, seeing him pleased with the Pandavas, the Yakshas and the Gandharvas stood there, free from agitation. Then thinking themselves as having transgressed, those high-souled and mighty charioteers, the Pandavas, having bowed down unto that lord, the giver of wealth stood surrounding the lord of treasures with joined hands. And the lord of treasures sat on that excellent seat, the elegant Pushpaka, constructed by Viswakarma, painted with diverse colours. And thousands of Yakshas and Rakshasas, some having huge frames and some ears resembling pegs, and hundreds of Gandharvas and hosts of Apsaras sat in the presence of that one seated, even as the celestials sit surrounding him of a hundred sacrifices and wearing a beautiful golden garland on his head and holding in his hands his noose and sword and bow, Bhima stood, gazing at the lord of wealth. And Bhimasena did not feel depressed either on having been wounded by the Rakshasas, or even in that plight seeing Kuvera arrive.

"And that one going about on the shoulders of men, on seeing Bhima stand desirous of fighting with sharpened shafts, said unto Dharma's son, 'O Partha, all the creatures know thee as engaged in their good. Do thou, therefore, with thy brothers fearlessly dwell on this summit of the mountain. And, O Pandava, be thou not angry with Bhima. These Yakshas and Rakshasas had already been slain by Destiny: thy brother hath been the instrument merely. And it is not necessary to feel shame for the act of impudence that hath been committed. This destruction of the Rakshasas had been foreseen by the gods. I entertain no anger towards Bhimasena. Rather, O foremost of the Bharata race, I am pleased with him; nay,—even before coming here, I had been gratified with this deed of Bhima.'"

Vaisampayana said, "Having spoken thus unto the king, (Kuvera) said unto Bhimasena, 'O child, O best of the Kurus, I do not mind this, O Bhima, as in order to please Krishna, thou hast, disregarding the gods and me also, committed this rash act, namely, the destruction of the Yakshas and the Rakshasas, depending on the strength of thy arms, I am well-pleased with thee. O Vrikodara, to-day I have been freed from a terrible curse. For some offence, that great Rishi, Agastya, had cursed me in anger. Thou hast delivered me by this act (of thine). O Pandu's son, my disgrace had ere this been fated. No offence, therefore, in any way, attaches unto thee, O Pandava.'

"Yudhishthira said, 'O divine one, why wast thou cursed by the high-souled Agastya? O god, I am curious to hear about the occasion of that imprecation. I wonder that at that very moment, thou together with thy forces and attendants wast not consumed by the ire of that intelligent one.'

"Thereupon the lord of treasures said, 'At Kusasthali, O king, once there was held a conclave of the gods. And surrounded by grimvisaged Yakshas, numbering three hundred maha-padmas, carrying various weapons, I was going to that place. And on the way, I saw that foremost of sages, Agastya, engaged in the practice of severe austerities on the bank of the Yamuna, abounding in various birds and graced with blossoming trees. And, O king, immediately on seeing that mass of energy, flaming and brilliant as fire, seated with upraised arms, facing the sun, my friend, the graceful lord of the Rakshasas, Maniman, from stupidity, foolishness, hauteur and ignorance discharged his excrement on the crown of that Maharshi. Thereupon, as if burning all the cardinal points by his wrath, he said unto me, "Since, O lord of treasures, in thy very presence, disregarding me, this thy friend hath thus affronted me, he, together with thy forces, shall meet with destruction at the hands of a mortal. And, O wicked-minded one, thou also, being distressed on account of thy fallen soldiers, shalt be freed from thy sin, on beholding that mortal. But if they follow thy behests, their (the soldier's) powerful sons shall not incur by this dreadful curse." This curse I received formerly from that foremost of Rishis. Now, O mighty king, have I been delivered by thy brother Bhima.'"

SECTION CLXI

"The lord of treasures said, 'O Yudhishthira, patience, ability, (appropriate) time and place and prowess—these five lead to success in human affairs. O Bharata, in the Krita Yuga, men were patient and able in their respective occupations and they knew how to display prowess. And, O foremost of the Kshatriyas, a Kshatriya that is endued with patience and understandeth the propriety regarding place and time and is versed in all mortal regulations, can alone govern the world for a long time,—nay, in all transactions. He that behaveth thus, acquireth, O hero, fame in this world and excellent state in the next. And by having displayed his prowess at the proper place and time, Sakra with the Vasus hath obtained the dominion of heaven. He that from anger cannot see his fall and he that being naturally wicked and evilminded followeth evil and he that knoweth not the propriety relative to acts, meet with destruction both in this world and the next. The exertions of that stupid person become fruitless, who is not conversant with the expediency regarding time and acts, and he meeteth with destruction both in this world and the next. And the object of that wicked and deceitful persons is vicious, who, aiming at mastery of every kind, committeth some rash act. O best of men, Bhimasena is fearless, and ignorant of duties, and haughty, and of the sense of a child, and unforbearing. Do thou, therefore, check him. Repairing again to the hermitage of the pious sage Arshtishena, do thou reside there during the dark fortnight, without fear or anxiety. O lord of men, deputed by me, all the Gandharvas residing at Alaka, as also those dwelling in this mountain, will, O mighty-armed one, protect thee, and these best of the Brahmanas. And, O king, O chief among virtuous men, knowing that Vrikodara hath come hither out of rashness, do thou check him. Henceforth, O monarch, beings living in the forest will meet you, wait upon you and always protect you all. And, ye foremost of men, my servants will always procure for you various meats and drinks of delicious flavour. And, O son, Yudhishthira, even as by reason of your being the progeny of spiritual intercourse, Jishnu is entitled to the protection of Mahendra, and Vrikodara, of the Wind-god, and thou, of Dharma, and the twins possessed of strength, of the Aswins,—so ye all are entitled to my protection. That one next by birth to Bhimasena, Phalguna, versed in the science of profit and all mortal regulations, is well in heaven. And, O child, those perfections that are recognised in the world as leading to heaven, are established in Dhananjaya even from his very birth. And self-restraint, and charity, and strength, and intelligence, and modesty, and fortitude, and excellent energy—even all these are established in that majestic one of magnificent soul. And, O Pandava, Jishnu never committed any shameful act through poverty of spirit. And in the world, none ever say that Partha hath uttered an untruth. And, O Bharata, honoured by the gods, *pitris*, and the Gandharvas, that enhancer of the glory of the Kurus is learning the science of weapons in Sakra's abode. And, O Partha, in heaven he that with justice had brought under his subjection all the rulers of the earth, even that exceedingly powerful and highly energetic monarch, the grandsire of thy father, Santanu himself, is well-pleased with the behaviour of that wielder of the Gandiva—the foremost of his race. And, O king, abiding in Indra's regions, he who on the banks of the Yamuna had worshipped the gods, the *pitris*, and the Brahmanas, by celebrating seven grand horse sacrifices, that great grandsire of thine, the emperor Santanu of severe austerities, who hath attained heaven, hath enquired of thy welfare.'"

Vaisampayana said, "Having heard these words of the dispenser of wealth, the Pandavas were well-pleased with them. Then lowering his club and mace and sword and bow, that foremost of the Bharatas bowed down unto *Kuvera*. And that giver of protection, the lord of treasures, seeing him prostrate, said, 'Be thou the destroyer of the pride of foes, and the enhancer of the delight of friends. And ye oppressors of enemies, do ye live in our romantic region. The *Yakshas* will not cross your desires. Gudakesa, after having acquired mastery over weapons, will come back soon. Bidden adieu by Maghavat himself, Dhananjaya will join you.'

"Having thus instructed Yudhishthira of excellent deeds, the lord of the *Guhyakas*, vanished from that best of mountains. And thousands upon thousands of *Yakshas*, and *Rakshasas* followed him in vehicles spread over with checkered cushions, and decorated with various jewels. And as the horses proceeded towards the abode of Kuvera, a noise arose as of birds flying in the air. And the chargers of the lord of treasures speedily coursed through the sky as if drawing forward the firmament, and devouring the air.

"Then at the command of the lord of wealth, the dead bodies of the *Raksha*sas were removed from the summit of the mountain. As the intelligent Agastya had fixed this period as the limit of (the duration of) his curse, so being slain in conflict, the Rakshasas were freed from the imprecation. And being honoured by the Rakshasas, the Pandavas for several nights dwelt pleasantly in those habitations."

SECTION CLXII

Vaisampayana continued, "Then, O represser of foes, at sunrise, having finished his daily devotions, *Dhaumya* came unto the Pandavas, with *Arshtishena*. And having bowed down unto the feet of Arshtishena and Dhaumya, they with joined hands paid homage unto all the Brahmanas. Then Dhaumya taking Yudhishthira's right hand, said these words, looking at the east, 'O mighty monarch, this king of mountains, Mandara lieth vast, covering the earth up to the ocean. O Pandava, Indra and Vaisravana preside over this point graced with woods and forests and mountains. And, O child, the intelligent sages versed in every duty, say, that this (region) is the abode of Indra and king Vaisravana. And the twice-born ones, and the sages versed in the duties, and the *Sidhas*, and the *Sadhyas*, and the celestials pay their adorations unto the Sun as he riseth from this point. And that lord of all living beings, king *Yama*, conversant with duty, presideth over yonder southern region whither come the spirits of the departed. And this is *Sanyamana*, the abode of the lord of departed spirits, sacred, and wonderful to behold, and crowned with prime prosperity. And the intelligent ones call that monarch of mountains (by the name of) Asta. Having, O king, arrived at this, the Sun ever abideth by the truth. And king *Varuna* protects all creatures, abiding in this king of mountains, and also in the vast deep. And, O highly fortunate one, there illumining the northern regions, lieth the puissant Mahameru, auspicious and the refuge of those knowing *Brahma*, where is the court of *Brahma*, and remaining where that soul of all creatures, *Prajapati*, hath created all that is mobile and immobile. And the *Mahameru* is the auspicious and healthy abode even of the seven mind-born sons of *Brahma*, of whom *Daksha* was the seventh. And, O child, here it is that the seven celestial *rishis* with Vasishtha at their head rise and set. Behold that excellent and bright summit of the Meru, where sitteth the great sire (*Brahma*) with the celestials happy in self-knowledge. And next to the abode of *Brahma* is visible the region of him who is said to be the really primal Cause or the origin of all creatures, even that prime lord, god Narayana, having neither beginning nor end. And, O king, that auspicious place composed of all energies even the celestials, cannot behold. And the region of the high-souled *Vishnu*, by its native splendour, exceeding in effulgence the sun or fire, cannot be beheld by the gods, or the Danavas. And the region of Narayana lieth resplendent to the east of the *Meru*, where, O child, that lord of all creatures, the self-create primal Cause of the universe, having manifested all beings, looketh splendid of his excellent grace. O child, not to speak of the *Maharshis*-even *Brahmarshis* have no access to that place. And, O best of the Kurus, it is the *Yatis* only who have access to it. And, O Pandu's son, (at that place) luminaries cannot shine by him; there that lord of inconceivable soul alone shineth transcendental. There by reverence, and severe austerities, Yatis inspired by virtue of pious practices, attain Narayana Hari. And, O Bharata, repairing thither, and attaining that universal Soul— the self-create and eternal God of gods, high-souled ones, of *Yoga* success, and free from ignorance and pride have not to return to this world. O highly fortunate Yudhishthira, this region is without beginning, or deterioration, or end for it is the very essence of that God. And, O son of the Kurus, the Sun and the Moon every day go round this Meru, coursing in an opposite direction. And, O sinless one, O mighty monarch, the other luminaries also go round this king of mountains in the self-same way. Thus the worshipful Sun who dispelleth darkness, goeth round this (mountain) obscuring other luminaries. Then having set, and passed the evening, that Maker of day, the Sun, taketh a northerly course. Then again nearing the *Meru*, the divine Sun (ever) intent on the good of all beings, again courseth, facing the east. And in this way, the divine Moon also together with the stars goeth round this mountain, dividing the month unto several sections, by his arrival at the Parvas. Having thus unerringly coursed round the mighty *Meru*, and, nourished all creatures, the Moon again repaireth unto the *Mandar*. In the same way, that destroyer of darkness—the divine Sun—also moveth on this unobstructed path, animating the universe. When, desirous of causing dew, he repaireth to the south, then there ensueth winter to all creatures. Then the Sun, turning back from the south, by his rays draweth up the energy from all creatures both mobile and immobile. Thereupon, men become subject to perspiration, fatigue, drowsiness and lassitude; and living beings always feel disposed to slumber. Thence, returning through unknown regions, that divine effulgent one causeth shower, and thereby reviveth beings. And having, by the comfort caused by the shower, wind, and warmth, cherished the mobile and the immobile, the powerful Sun resumeth his former course. O Partha, ranging thus, the Sun unerringly turneth on the wheel of Time, influencing created things. His course is unceasing; he never resteth, O Pandava. Withdrawing the energy of all beings, he again rendereth it back. O Bharata, dividing time into day and night, and Kala, and Kashiba, that lord, the Sun, dealeth life and motion to all created things.'"

SECTION CLXIII

Vaisampayana continued, "Dwelling in that best of mountains those high-souled ones observing excellent vows, felt themselves attracted (to that place), and diverted themselves, eager to behold Arjuna. And multitudes of *Gandharvas* and *Maharshis* gladly visited those energetic ones, possessing prowess, of chaste desires and being the foremost of those endued with truth and fortitude. And having arrived at that excellent mountain furnished with trees bearing blossoms, those mighty charioteers were exceedingly delighted, even as the *Marutas*, on arriving at the celestial regions. And experiencing great exhilaration, they lived (there), seeing the slopes and summits of that mighty mountain, filled with flowers, and resonant with the cries of peacocks and cranes. And on that beautiful mountain they beheld lakes filled with lotuses, and having their shores covered with trees, and frequented by darkness, and *karandavas* and swans. And the flourishing sporting-regions, graceful on account of the various flowers, and abounding in gems, was capable of captivating that king, the dispenser of wealth (*Kuvera*). And always ranging (there), those foremost of ascetics (the Pandavas) were incapable of conceiving (the significance of) that Summit, furnished with mighty trees, and masses of wide-spreading clouds. And, O great hero, owing to its native splendour, and also on account of the brilliance of the annual plants, there was no difference there between night and day. And staying in the mountain, remaining in which the Sun of unrivalled energy cherisheth the mobile and immobile things, those heroes and foremost of men beheld the rising and the setting of the Sun. And having seen the rising and the setting points of the Sun and the rising and the setting mountain, and all the cardinal points, as well as the intervening spaces ever blazing with the rays of the Dispeller of darkness, those heroes, in expectation of the arrival of that mighty charioteer firm in truth, became engaged in reciting the *Vedas*, practising the daily rituals, chiefly discharging the religious duties, exercising sacred vows, and abiding by the truth. And saying, 'Let us even here experience delight by joining without delay Arjuna accomplished in arms,' those highly blessed Parthas became engaged in the practice of *Yoga*. And beholding romantic woods on that mountain, as they always thought of *Kiriti*, every day and night appeared unto them even as a year. From that very moment joy had taken leave of them when, with Dhaumya's permission, the high-souled *Jishnu*, matting his hair, departed (for the woods). So, how could they, absorbed in his contemplation, experience happiness there? They had become overwhelmed with grief ever since the moment when at the command of his brother, Yudhishthira, *Jishnu* of the tread of a mad elephant had departed from the *Kamyaka* forest. O Bharata, in this way, on that mountain those descendants of Bharata passed a month with difficulty, thinking of him of the white steeds, who had gone to *Vasava's* abode for learning arms. And Arjuna, having dwelt for five years in the abode of him of a thousand eyes, and having from that lord of celestials obtained all the celestial weapons,—such as those of *Agni*, of *Varuna*, of *Soma*, of *Vayu*, of *Vishnu*, of *Indra*, of *Pasupati*, of *Brahma*, of *Parameshthi*, of *Prajapati*, of *Yama*, of *Dhata*, of *Savita*, of *Tvashta*, and of *Vaisravana*; and having bowed down to and gone round him of a hundred sacrifices, and taken his (Indra's) permission, cheerfully came to the Gandhamadana."

SECTION CLXIV

Vaisampayana continued, "And it came to pass that one day as those mighty charioteers were thinking of Arjuna, seeing Mahendra's car, yoked with horses of the effulgence of lightning, arrive all on a sudden, they were delighted. And driven by Matali, that blazing car, suddenly illuminating the sky, looked like smokeless flaming tongues of fire, or a mighty meteor embosomed in clouds. And seated in that car appeared *Kiriti* wearing garlands and new-made ornaments. Then Dhananjaya possessing the prowess of the wielder of the thunder-bolt, alighted on that mountain, blazing in beauty. And that intelligent one decked in a diadem and garlands, having alighted on the mountain, first bowed down at the feet of *Dhaumya*, and then at those of *Ajatasatru*. And he also paid homage unto Vrikodara's feet; and the twins also bowed down unto him. Then going to Krishna, and having cheered her, he stood before his (elder) brother in humble guise. And on meeting with that matchless one, they were exceedingly delighted. And he also meeting with them rejoiced exceedingly, and began to eulogise the king. And seeing before them that car driving in which the slayer of Namuchi had annihilated seven phalanxes of *Diti's* offspring, the magnanimous Parthas went round it. And being highly pleased, they offered excellent worship unto Matali, as unto the lord of the celestials himself. And then the son of the Kuru king duly enquired of him after the health of all the gods. And Matali also greeted them. And having instructed the Parthas even as a father doth his sons, he ascended that incomparable car, and returned to the lord of the celestials.

"And when Matali had gone away, that foremost of the royal race, Sakra's son, the high-souled destroyer of all foes made over unto his love, the mother of *Sutasoma*, beautiful precious gems and ornaments having the splendour of the sun, which had been presented to him by Sakra. Then, sitting in the midst of those foremost of the Kurus, and those best of the *Brahmanas*, effulgent like unto fire or the sun, he began to relate all as it had happened, saying, 'In this way, I have learnt weapons from *Sakra*, *Vayu*, and the manifest *Siva*; and all the celestials with Indra also have been pleased with me, on account of my good behaviour, and concentration.'

"After having briefly narrated unto them his sojourn in heaven, *Kiriti* of spotless deeds agreeably slept that night with the two sons of Madri."

SECTION CLXV

Vaisampayana said, "Then when the night had been spent, Dhananjaya, together with his brothers, paid homage unto Yudhishthira the just. And, O Bharata, at this moment, proceeding from the celestials there arose mighty and tremendous sounds of a musical instrument, and the rattling of car-wheels, and the tolling of bells. And there at all the beasts and beasts of prey and birds emitted separate cries. And from all sides in cars resplendent as the sun, hosts of *Gandharvas* and *Apsaras* began to follow that represser of foes, the lord of the celestials. And ascending a car yoked with steeds, decorated with burnished gold, and roaring like clouds, that king of the celestials, *Purandara* blazing in beauty came unto the Parthas. And having arrived (at that place), he of a thousand eyes descended from his car. And as soon as Yudhishthira the just saw that high-souled one, he together with his brothers, approached that graceful king of the immortals. And in accordance with the ordinance that generous one duly worshipped him of immeasurable soul, in consequence with his dignity. And then Dhananjaya possessed of prowess, having bowed down unto *Purandara*, stood before the lord of the celestials in humble guise, like unto a servant. And seeing the sinless Dhananjaya having ascetic merit, bearing clotted hair, stand in humility before the lord of celestials, Yudhishthira, the son of Kunti, of great energy, smelt (the crown) of his head. And beholding *Phalguna* (in that attitude), he was exceedingly glad; and by worshipping the king of the celestials, he experienced the highest bliss. Then unto that strongminded monarch, swimming in felicity, the intelligent lord of the celestials, Purandara, spake, saying, 'Thou shalt rule the earth, O Pandava. Blessed be thou! Do thou, O Kunti's son, again repair unto Kamyaka.'

"That learned man who for a year leading the *Brahmacharya* mode of life, subduing his senses and observing vows, peruseth with rapt attention this meeting of *Sakra* with the Pandavas, liveth a hundred years free from disturbances, and enjoying happiness."

SECTION CLXVI

Vaisampayana continued, "When *Sakra* had gone to his proper place, *Vibhatsu* together with his brothers and Krishna, paid homage unto the son of Dharma. Then smelling the crown of the head of that Pandava, who was thus paying homage, (Yudhishthira) in accents faltering on account of joy, addressed Arjuna, saying, 'O Arjuna, how didst thou pass this period in heaven? And how has thou obtained the weapons, and how also hast thou gratified the lord of the celestials? And, O Pandava, has thou adequately secured the weapons? Have the lord of the celestials and *Rudra* gladly granted thee the weapons? And how hast thou beheld the divine *Sakra*, and the wielder of *Pinaka*? And how has thou obtained the weapons? And in what manner didst thou worship (them)? And what service hadst thou done unto that repressor of foes, the worshipful one of a hundred sacrifices, that he said unto thee, "By thee have I been gratified?" All this, O highly effulgent one, I wish to hear in detail. And, O sinless one, the manner in which thou didst please Mahadeva and the king of the celestials and, O repressor of foes, the service thou hadst done to the wielder of the thunderbolt, — do thou, O Dhananjaya, relate all this in detail.'

"Arjuna said, 'O mighty monarch, listen how I duly beheld him of a hundred sacrifice and the divine *Sankara* also. O grinder of foes, O king, having acquired that science which thou hadst directed me (to learn), I at thy command went to the forest, for practising penances. From *Kamyaka* repairing to the *Bhrigutunga*, I spent there one night, being engaged in austerities. And it came to pass that on the next I saw a certain *Brahmana*. And he asked me, saying, "O son of Kunti, whither wilt thou go?" Thereupon, O descendant of the Kurus, I truly related unto him everything. And, O best of kings, having heard the true account, the *Brahmana* became well-pleased with me, and, O king, praised me. Then the *Brahmana*, pleased with me, said, "O Bharata, be thou engaged in austerities. By performing penances, thou wilt in a short time behold the lord of the celestials." And according to his advice I ascended the *Himavan*, and, O mighty king, began to practise penances, (the first) month subsisting on fruit and roots. I spent the second month, subsisting on water. And, O Pandava, in the third month I totally abstained from food. And in the fourth month I remained with upraised arms. And a wonder it is that I did not lose any strength. And it came to pass that when the first day of the fifth month had been spent, there appeared before me a being wearing the form of a boar, turning up the earth with his mouth, stamping the ground with his feet, rubbing the earth with his breast, and momentarily going about in a frightful manner. And him followed a great being in the guise of a hunter furnished with the bow, arrows, and the sword, and surrounded by females. Thereupon, taking my bow and the two inexhaustible quivers, I pierced with shafts that terrible and frightful creature. And simultaneously (with me) that hunter also drawing a strong bow, more severely struck at (the animal), as if shaking my mind. And, O king, he also said unto me, "Why hast thou, transgressing the rules of hunting, hit the animal first hit at by me? With these sharpened shafts will I destroy thy pride. Stay!" Then that mighty-bodied one holding the bow rushed at me. And with volleys of mighty shafts, he covered me entirely, even as a cloud covereth a mountain with showers. Then, on my part, I covered him with a mighty discharge of arrows. Thereupon, with steady arrows having their points aflame, and inspired with *mantras*, I pierced him even as (Indra) riveth a mountain with a thunderbolt. Then his person began to be multiplied a hundredfold and a thousandfold. At this, I pierced all his bodies with shafts. Then again all those forms became one, O Bharata. Thereat I struck at it. Next, he now assumed a small body with a huge head, and now a huge body with a small head. And, O king, he then assumed his former person and approached me for fight. And, O foremost of the Bharata race, when in the encounter I failed to overwhelm him with arrows, I fixed the mighty weapon of the Wind-god. But I failed to discharge it at him, and this was a wonder. And when that weapon thus failed of effect, I was struck with amazement. However, O king, exerting myself more vigorously, I again covered that being with a mighty multitude of shafts. Then taking *Sthuna-karna*, and *Varuna* and *Salava*, and *Asmavarsha* weapons, I assailed him, profusely showering shafts. But, O king, he instantly swallowed up even all these weapons of mine. And when all those (weapons) had been swallowed up, I discharged the weapon presided over by Brahma. And when the blazing arrows issuing from that weapon were heaped upon him all around, and being thus heaped over by that mighty weapon discharged by me, he increased (in bulk). Then all the world became oppressed with the energy begotten of the weapon hurled by me, and the firmament and all the points of the sky became illumined. But that one of mighty energy instantly baffled even that weapon. And, O monarch, when that weapon presided over by *Brahma* had been baffled I was possessed with terrible fear. Thereupon immediately holding even my bow and the two inexhaustible quivers, I shot at that being, but he swallowed up all those weapons. And when all the weapons had been baffled and swallowed up, there ensued a wrestling between him and myself. And we encountered each other first with blows and then with slaps. But incapable of overcoming that being, I fell down stupefied on the ground. Thereupon, O mighty king, with a laugh, that wonderful being at my sight vanished at that spot together with the women. Having accomplished this, O illustrious monarch, that divine one assumed another and unearthly form (clad in) wonderful raiment. And renouncing the form of a hunter, that divine lord of the gods, resumed his own unearthly appearance and that mighty god stood (there). Then appeared before me with *Uma* that manifest divine one, having the bull for his mark, wielding the *Pinaka*, bearing serpents and capable of assuming many forms. And, O repressor of foes, advancing towards me, standing even then in the field ready for conflict, that wielder of the trident addressed me saying, "I am well-pleased with thee." Then that divine one held up my bows and the couple of quivers furnished with inexhaustible shafts and returned them unto me saying, "Do thou ask some boon, O Kunti's son. I am well-pleased with thee. Tell me, what I shall do for thee. And, O hero, express the desire that dwelleth in thy heart. I will grant it. Except immortality alone, tell me as to the desire that is in thy heart." Thereat with my mind intent on the acquisition of arms, I only bowed down unto Siva and said, "O divine one, if thou beest favourably disposed towards me, then I wish to have this boon,—I wish to learn all the weapons that are with thy god-head." Then the god *Tryamvaka* said unto me, "I will give. O Pandava, my own weapon *Raudra* shall attend upon thee." Thereupon *Mahadeva*, well-pleased, granted to me the mighty weapon, *Pasupata*. And, having granted that eternal weapon, he also said unto me, "This must never be hurled at mortals. If discharged at any person of small energy, it would consume the universe. Shouldst thou (at any time) be hard pressed, thou mayst discharge it. And when all thy weapons have been completely baffled, thou mayst hurl it." Then when he having the bull for his mark, had been thus gratified, there stood manifest by my side that celestial weapon, of resistless force capable of baffling all weapons and destructive of foes and the hewer of hostile forces and unrivalled and difficult to be borne even by the celestials, the demons and the *Rakshasas*. Then at the command of that god, I sat me down there. And in my very sight the god vanished from the spot.'"

SECTION CLXVII

"Arjuna said, 'O Bharata, by the grace of that god of gods the Supreme Soul, *Tryamvaka*, I passed the night at that place. And having passed the night, when I had finished the morning rituals, I saw that foremost of the *Brahmanas* whom I had seen before. And unto him I told all as it had happened, O Bharata, namely, that I had met the divine *Mahadeva*. Thereupon, O king of kings, well-pleased, he said unto me, "Since thou hast beheld the great god, incapable of being beheld by any one else, soon wilt thou mix with *Vaivaswata* and the other *Lokapalas* and the lord of the celestials; and Indra too will grant thee weapons." O king, having said this unto me and having embraced me again and again, that *Brahmana* resembling the Sun, went away whither he listed. And, O slayer of foes, it came to pass that on the evening of that day refreshing the whole world, there began to blow a pure breeze. And in my vicinity on the base of the *Himalaya* mountain fresh, fragrant and fair flowers began to bloom. And on all sides there were heard charming symphony and captivating hymns relating to Indra. And before the lord of the celestial hosts of *Apsaras* and *Gandharvas* chanted various songs. And ascending celestial cars, there approached the *Marutas* and the followers of *Mahendra* and the dwellers of heaven. And afterwards, Marutvan together with *Sachi* and all the celestials appeared on the scene in cars yoked with horses elegantly adorned. And at this very moment, O king, he that goeth about on the shoulders of men manifested himself unto me in excellent grace. And I saw *Yama* seated on the south and *Varuna* and the lord of the celestials at their respective regions. And, O foremost of men, O mighty monarch, they after having cheered me said, "O Savyasachin, behold us— the Lokapalas—seated. For the performance of the task of the gods thou hast obtained the sight of *Sankara*. Do thou now receive weapons from us seated around." Thereupon, O lord, having bowed down unto those foremost of the celestials with regard, I duly accepted those mighty weapons. And then they recognised me as one of their own. Afterwards the gods repaired to the quarter from whence they had come. And that lord of the celestials, the divine Maghavan too having ascended his glorious chariot, said, "O *Phalguna*, thou shalt have to repair unto the celestial region. O Dhananjaya, even before this thy arrival I knew that thou wouldst come hither. Then I have, O best of the Bharatas, manifested myself unto thee. As formerly thou hadst performed thy ablution in the various *tirthas* and now hast performed severe austerities, so thou wilt be able to repair unto the celestial regions, O Pandava. Thou wilt, however, again have to practise extreme penance, for thou shouldst at any rate journey to heaven. And at my command, Matali shall take thee to the celestial regions. Thou hast already been recognised by the celestials and the celestial sages of high soul." Thereupon I said unto Sakra, "O divine one, be thou favourable unto me. With the view of learning arms do I beseech thee that thou mayst be my preceptor." At this Indra said, "O child, having learnt weapons thou wouldst perform terrible deeds and with this object thou desirest to obtain the weapons. However, obtain thou the arms, as thou desirest." Then I said, "O slayer of foes, I never would discharge these celestial weapons at mortals except when all my other arms should have been baffled. Do thou, O lord of the celestials, grant me the celestial weapons (so that) I may hereafter obtain the regions attainable by warriors." Indra said, "O Dhananjaya it is to try thee that I have said such words unto thee. Having been begotten of me this speech of thine well becometh thee. Do thou, O Bharata, repairing unto my abode learn all the weapons of *Vayu*, of *Agni*, of the *Vasus*, of *Varuna*, of the *Marutas*, of the *Siddhas*, of Brahma, of the Gandharvas, of the Uragas, of the Rakshasas, of Vishnu and of the *Nairitas*; and also all the weapons that are with me, O perpetuator of the Kuru race." Having said this unto me *Sakra* vanished at the very spot. Then, O king, I saw the wonderful and sacred celestial car yoked with steeds arrive conducted by Matali. And when the Lokapalas went away Matali said unto me, "O thou of mighty splendour, the lord of the celestials is desirous of seeing thee. And O mighty-armed one, do thou acquire competence and then perform thy task. Come and behold the regions, attainable by merit and come unto heaven even in this frame. O Bharata, the thousand-eyed lord of the celestials wisheth to see thee." Thus addressed by Matali, I, taking leave of the mountain Himalaya and having gone round it ascended that excellent car. And then the exceedingly generous Matali, versed in equine lore, drove the steeds, gifted with the speed of thought or the wind. And when the chariot began to move that charioteer looking at my face as I was seated steadily, wondered and said these words, "Today this appeareth unto me strange and unprecedented that being seated in this celestial car, thou hast not been jerked ever so little. O foremost of Bharata race, I have ever remarked that at the first pull by the steeds even the lord of the celestials himself getteth jerked. But all the while that the car had moved, thou hast been sitting unshaken. This appeareth unto me as transcending even the power of *Sakra*."

"'Having said this, O Bharata, Matali soared in the sky and showed me the abodes of the celestials and their palaces. Then the chariot yoked with steeds coursed upwards. And the celestials and the sages began to worship (that car), O prince of men. And I saw the regions, moving anywhere at will, and the splendour also of the highly energetic *Gandharvas, Apsaras,* and the celestial sages. And *Sakra's* charioteer, Matali, at once showed me *Nandana* and other gardens and groves belonging to the celestials. Next I beheld Indra's abode, *Amaravati,* adorned with jewels and trees yielding any sort of fruit that is desired. There the Sun doth not shed heat; nor doth heat or cold or fatigue there affect (one), O king. And, O great monarch, the celestials feel neither sorrow nor poverty of spirit, nor weakness, nor lassitude, O grinder of foes. And, O ruler of men, the celestials and the others have neither anger nor covetousness. And, O king, in the abodes of the celestials, the beings are ever contented. And there the trees ever bear verdant foliage, and fruits, and flowers; and the various lakes are embalmed with the fragrance of lotuses. And there the breeze is cool, and delicious, and fragrant, and pure, and inspiring. And the ground is variegated with all kinds of gems, and adorned with blossoms. And there were seen innumerable beautiful beasts and in the air innumerable rangers of the sky. Then I saw the *Vasus,* and the *Rudras,* and the *Sadhyas* with the *Marutas,* and the *Adityas,* and the two *Aswins* and worshipped them. And they conferred their benison on me, granting me strength and prowess, and energy, and celebrity, and (skill in) arms, and victory in battle. Then, entering that romantic city adored by the *Gandharvas* and the celestials, with joined hands, I stood before the thousand-eyed lord of the celestials. Thereupon, that best of bestowers gladly offered unto me half of his seat; and *Vasava* also with regard touched my person. And, O Bharata, with the view of acquiring arms and learning weapons, I began to dwell in heaven, together with the gods and the *Gandharvas* of generous souls. And *Viswavana's* son, *Chitrasena* became my friend. And he, O king, imparted unto me the entire *Gandharva* (science). And, O monarch, I happily lived in *Sakra's* abode, well cared for having all my desires gratified, learning weapons, listening to the notes of songs, and the clear sounds of musical instruments, and beholding the foremost of *Apsaras* dance. And without neglecting to study the arts, which I learnt properly, my attention was specially fixed on the acquisition of arms. And that lord of a thousand eyes was pleased with that purpose of mine. Living thus in heaven, O king, I passed this period.

"'And when I had acquired proficiency in weapons, and gained his confidence that one having for his vehicle the horse (*Uchchaisrava*), (Indra), patting me on the head with his hand, said these words, "Now even the celestials themselves cannot conquer thee,—what shall I say of imperfect mortals residing on earth? Thou hast become invulnerable in strength, irrepressible, and incomparable in fight." Then with the hair of his body standing on end, he again accosted me saying, "O hero, in fighting with weapons none is equal unto thee. And, O perpetuator of the Kuru race, thou art even watchful, and dexterous, and truthful, and of subdued senses, and the protector of the *Brahmanas* and adept in weapons, and warlike. And, O Partha, together with (a knowledge of) the five modes, using (them), thou hast obtained five and ten weapons and, therefore, there existeth none, who is thy peer. And thou hast perfectly learnt the discharge (of those weapons) and (their) withdrawal, and (their) re-discharge and re-withdrawal, and the *Prayaschitta* connected (with them), and also their revival, in case of their being baffled. Now, O represser of foes, the time hath arrived for thy paying the preceptor's fee. Do thou promise to pay the fee; then I shall unfold unto thee what thou wilt have to perform." Thereat, O king, I said unto the ruler of the celestials, "If it be in my power to do the work, do thou consider it as already accomplished by me." O king, when I had said these words, Indra with a smile said unto me "Nothing is there in the three worlds that is not in thy power (to achieve). My enemies, those *Danavas*, named *Nivata-Kavachas*, dwell in the womb of the ocean. And they number thirty million and are notorious, and all of equal forms and strength and splendour. Do thou slay them there, O Kunti's son; and that will be thy preceptor's fee."

"'Saying this he gave unto me the highly resplendent celestial car, conducted by Matali, furnished with hair resembling the down of peacocks. And on my head he set this excellent diadem. And he gave me ornaments for my body, like unto his own. And he granted unto me the impenetrable mail—the best of its kind, and easy to the touch; and fastened unto the *Gandiva* this durable string. Then I set out, ascending that splendid chariot riding on which in days of yore, the lord of the celestials and vanquished *Vali*—that son of *Virochana*. And, O ruler of men, startled by the rattling of the car, all the celestials, approached (there), taking me to be the king of the celestials. And seeing me, they asked, "O Phalguna, what art thou going to do?" And I told them as it had fallen out,—and said, "I shall even do this in battle. Ye that are highly fortunate, know that I have set out desirous of slaying the *Nivata-Kavachas*. O sinless ones, do ye bless me." Thereupon, they began to eulogise me even as they (eulogise) the god, *Purandara*. And they said, "Riding on this car, *Maghavan* conquered in battle *Samvara*, and *Namuchi*, and *Vala*, and *Vritra*, and *Prahrada*, and *Naraka*. And mounted on this car also Maghavan, had conquered in battle many thousands and millions and hundreds of millions of *Daityas*. And, O *Kaunteya*, thou also, riding on this car, by thy prowess shalt conquer the *Nivata-Kavachas* in conflict, even as did the self-possessed Maghavan in days of yore. And here is the best of shells; by this also thou shalt defeat the *Danavas*. And by this it is that the high souled *Sakra* conquered the words." Saying this, the gods offered (unto me) this shell, *Devadatta*, sprung in the deep; and I accepted it for the sake of victory. And at this moment, the gods fell extolling me. And in order to be engaged in action, I proceeded to the dreadful abode of the *Danavas*, furnished with the shell, the mail, and arrows, and taking my bow.'"

SECTION CLXVIII

"Arjuna continued, 'Then at places eulogised by the *Maharshis*, I (proceeded, and at length) beheld the ocean—that inexhaustible lord of waters. And like unto flowing cliffs were seen on it heaving billows, now meeting together and now rolling away. And there (were seen) all around barks by thousands filled with gems. And there were seen *timingilas* and tortoises and *makaras* like unto rock submerged in water. And on all sides round thousands of shells sunk in water appeared like stars in the night covered by light clouds. And thousands upon thousands of gems were floating in heaps and a violent wind was blowing about in whirls—and this was wonderful to behold. And having beheld that excellent lord of all waters with powerful tides, I saw at a short distance the city of the demons filled with the *Danavas*. And even there, entering underneath the earth, Matali skilled in guiding the car, sitting fast on the chariot drove it with force; and he dashed on, frightening that city with the rattling of his chariot. And hearing that rattling of the chariot like unto the rumbling of the clouds in the sky, the *Danavas*, thinking me to be the lord of the celestials, became agitated. And thereupon they all, frightened at heart, stood holding in their hands bows and arrows and swords and javelins and axes and maces and clubs. Then having made arrangements for the defence of the city, the *Danavas*, with minds alarmed, shut the gates, so that nothing could be discovered. Thereupon taking my shell, *Devadatta*, of tremendous roars, I again and again winded it with exceeding cheerfulness. And filling all the firmament, those sounds produced echoes. Thereat mighty beings were terrified and they hid (themselves). And then, O Bharata, all of them adorned with ornaments, those offsprings of *Diti*—the *Nivata-Kavachas*—made their appearance by thousands, donning diverse mail and taking in their hands various weapons and equipped with mighty iron javelins and maces and clubs and hatchets and sabres and discs and *sataghnis* and *bhusundis* and variegated and ornamented swords. Then, after deliberating much as to the course of the car, Matali began to guide the steeds on a (piece of) level ground, O foremost of the Bharatas. And owing to the swiftness of those fleet coursers conducted by him, I could see nothing—and this was strange. Then the *Danavas* there began to sound thousands of musical instruments, dissonant and of odd shapes. And at those sounds, fishes by hundreds and by thousands, like unto hills, having their senses bewildered by that noise, fled suddenly. And mighty force flew at me, the demons discharging sharpened shafts by hundreds and by thousands. And then, O Bharata, there ensued a dreadful conflict between me and the demons, calculated to extinguish the *Nivata Kavachas*. And there came to the mighty battle the *Devarshis* and the *Danavarshis* and the *Brahmarshis* and the *Siddhas*. And desirous of victory, the *Munis eulogised* me with the same sweet-speeches that (they had eulogised) Indra with, at the war, (which took place) for the sake of *Tara*.'"

SECTION CLXIX .

"Arjuna continued, 'Then, O Bharata, vehemently rushed at me in battle in a body the *Nivata-Kavachas*, equipped with arms. And obstructing the course of the car, and shouting loudly, those mighty charioteers, hemming me in on all sides, covered me with showers of shafts. Then other demons of mighty prowess, with darts and hatchets in their hands, began to throw at me spears and axes. And that mighty discharge of darts, with numerous maces and clubs incessantly hurled fell upon my car. And other dreadful and grim-visaged smiters among the *Nivata-Kavachas*, furnished with bows and sharpened weapons, ran at me in fight. And in the conflict, shooting from the *Gandiva* sundry swift arrows coursing straight, I pierced each of them with ten. And they were driven back by those stone-whetted shafts of mine. Then on my steeds being swiftly driven by Matali, they began to display various movements with the speed of the wind. And being skilfully guided by Matali, they began to trample upon the sons of *Diti*. And although the steeds yoked unto that mighty chariot numbered hundreds upon hundreds, yet being deftly conducted by Matali, they began to move, as if they were only a few. And by their tread, and by the rattling of the chariot wheels and by the volleys of my shafts, the *Danavas* began to fall by hundreds. And others accoutred in bows, being deprived of life, and having their charioteers slain, were carried about by the horses. Then, covering all sides and directions, all (the *Danavas*) skilled in striking entered into the contest with various weapons, and thereat my mind became afflicted. And I witnessed (this instance of) the marvellous prowess of Matali, viz., that he guided those fiery steeds with ease. Then, O king, in the conflict, with diverse fleet weapons I pierced by hundreds and by thousands (demons) bearing arms. And, O slayer of foes, seeing me thus range the field putting forth every exertion, the heroic charioteer of *Sakra* was well-pleased. And oppressed by those steeds and that car, some (of them) met with annihilation; and others desisted from fight; while (other) *Nivata-Kavachas*, challenged by us in battle and being harassed with shafts offered opposition unto me, by (discharging) mighty showers of arrows. Thereupon, with hundreds and thousands of sundry fleet weapons inspired with the *mantras* relating to *Brahma's* weapons, I swiftly began to burn them. And being sore pressed by me, those mighty *asuras* waxing wroth afflicted me together, by pouring torrents of clubs and darts and swords. Then, O Bharata, I took up that favourite weapon of the lord of the celestials, Maghavan by name, prime and of fiery energy and by the energy of that weapon I cut into a thousand pieces the *Tomaras*, together with the swords and the tridents hurled by them. And having cut off their arms I in ire pierced them each with ten shafts. And in the field arrows were shot from the *Gandiva* like unto rows of black-bees; and this Matali admired. And their shafts also showered upon me; but those powerful (arrows) I cut off with my shafts. Then on being struck the *Nivata-Kavachas* again covered me on all sides with a mighty shower of arrows. And having neutralised the force of the arrows by excellent swift and flaming weapons capable of baffling arms, I pierced them by thousands. And blood began to flow from their torn frames, even as in the rainy season waters run down from the summits of mountains. And on being wounded by my fleet and straight-coursing shafts of the touch of Indra's thunder-bolt, they became greatly agitated. And their bodies were pierced at hundreds of places; and the force of their arms diminished. Then the *Nivata-Kavachas* fought me by (the help of) illusion.'"

SECTION CLXX

"Arjuna said, 'Then with rocks of the proportions of trees, there commenced a mighty shower of crags; and this exercised me exceedingly. And in that high encounter, I crushed (those crags) by swift-speeding showers of arrows, issuing from Mahendra's weapon, like unto the thunderbolt itself. And when the rocks had been reduced to powder, there was generated fire; and the rocky dust fell like unto masses of flames. And when the showers of crags had been repelled, there happened near me a mightier shower of water, having currents of the proportions of an axle. And falling from the welkin, those thousands of powerful torrents covered the entire firmament and the directions and the cardinal points. And on account of the pouring of the shower, and of the blowing of the wind, and of roaring of the *Daityas*, nothing could be perceived. And touching heaven and the entire earth, and incessantly falling on the ground, the showers bewildered me. Thereupon, I discharged that celestial weapon which I had learnt from Indra—even the dreadful and flaming *Visoshana*: and by that the water was dried up. And, O Bharata, when the rocky shower had been destroyed, and the watery shower had been dried up, the *Danavas* began to spread illusions of fire and wind. Then by aqueous appliances I extinguished the flames; and by a mighty rock-issuing arm, resisted the fury of the winds. And when these had been repelled, the *Danavas*, irrepressible in battle, O Bharata, simultaneously created various illusions. And there happened a tremendous horrifying shower of rocks and dreadful weapons of fire and wind. And that illusory downpour afflicted me in fight. And then on all sides there appeared a dense and thick darkness. And when the world had been enveloped in deep and dense darkness, the steeds turned away, Matali fell off, and from his hand the golden lash fell to the earth. And, O foremost of the Bharatas, being frightened, he again and again cried, "Where art thou?" And when he had been stupefied, a terrible fear possessed me. And then in a hurry, he spake unto me, saying, "O Partha, for the sake of nectar, there had taken place a mighty conflict between the gods and the demons. I had seen that (encounter), O sinless one. And on the occasion of the destruction of Samvara, there had occurred a dreadful and mighty contest. Nevertheless I had acted as charioteer to the lord of the celestials. In the same way, on the occasion of the slaying of *Vritra*, the steeds had been conducted by me. And I had also beheld the high and terrific encounter with *Virochana's* son, and, O Pandava, with *Vala*, and with *Prahrada* and with others also. In these exceedingly dreadful battles, I was present; but, O Pandu's son, never (before) had I lost my senses. Surely the Greatfather hath ordained the destruction of all creatures; for this battle cannot be for any other purpose than destruction of the universe." Having heard these words of his, "pacifying my perturbation by my own effort, I will destroy the mighty energy of the illusion spread by the *Danavas*" quoth I unto the terrified Matali. "Behold the might of my arms, and the power of my weapons and of the bow, *Gandiva*. To-day even by (the help of) illusion-creating arms, will I dispel this deep gloom and also this horrible illusion of theirs. Do not fear, O charioteer. Pacify thyself." Having said this, O lord of men, I created for the good of the celestials, an illusion of arms capable of bewildering all beings. And when (their) illusion had been dispelled, some of the foremost amongst the *Asuras*, of unrivalled prowess, again spread diverse kinds of illusion. Thereupon, now (the world) displayed itself, and now it was devoured by darkness; and now the world disappeared from view and now it was submerged under water. And when it had brightened up, Matali, sitting in front of the car, with the wellconducted steeds, began to range that hair-erecting field. Then the fierce *Nivata-Kavachas* assailed me. And finding my opportunity, I began to send them to the mansion of Yama. Thereupon, in that conflict then raging, calculated to annihilate the *Nivata-Kavachas* on a sudden, I could not see the *Danavas* concealed by illusion.'"

SECTION CLXXI

"Arjuna continued, 'Remaining invisible the *Daityas* began to fight with the help of illusion. And I too fought with them, resorting to the energy of visible weapons. And the shafts duly discharged from the *Gandiva*, began to sever their heads at those different places where they were respectively stationed. And thus assailed by me in the conflict, the *Nivata-Kavachas*, all on a sudden withdrawing the illusion, entered into their own city. And when the *Daityas* had fled, and when all had become visible, I there discovered hundreds and thousands of the slain. And there I saw by hundreds their shivered weapons, ornaments, limbs, and mail. And the horses could not find room for moving from one place to another; and on a sudden with a bound, they fell to coursing in the sky. Then remaining invisible, the *Nivata-Kavachas* covered the entire welkin with masses of crags. And, O Bharata, other dreadful *Danavas*, entering into the entrails of the earth, took up horses' legs and chariot-wheels. And as I was fighting, they, hard besetting my horses with rocks, attacked me together with (my) car. And with the crags that had fallen and with others that were falling, the place where I was, seemed to be a mountain cavern. And on myself being covered with crags and on the horses being hard pressed, I became sore distressed and this was marked by Matali. And on seeing me afraid, he said unto me, "O Arjuna, Arjuna! be thou not afraid; send that weapon, the thunder-bolt, O lord of men." Hearing those words of his, I then discharged the favourite weapon of the king of the celestials—the dreadful thunderbolt. And inspiring the Gandiva with *mantras*, I, aiming at the locality of the crags, shot sharpened iron shafts of the touch of the thunder-bolt. And sent by the thunder, those adamantine arrows entered into all those illusions and into the midst of those *Nivata-Kavachas*. And slaughtered by the vehemence of the thunder, those *Danavas* resembling cliffs, fell to the earth together in masses. And entering amongst those *Danavas* that had carried away the steeds of the car into the interior of the earth, the shafts sent them into the mansion of Yama. And that quarter was completely covered with the *Nivata-Kavachas* that had been killed or baffled, comparable unto cliffs and lying scattered like crags. And then no injury appeared to have been sustained either by the horses, or by the car, or by Matali, or by me, and this seemed strange. Then,

O king, Matali addressed me smiling, "Not in the celestials themselves, O Arjuna, is seen the prowess that is seen in thee." And when the *Danava* hosts had been destroyed, all their females began to bewail in that city, like unto cranes in autumn. Then with Matali I entered that city, terrifying with the rattling of my car the wives of the *Nivata-Kavachas*. Thereupon, seeing those ten thousand horses like unto peacocks (in hue), and also that chariot resembling the sun, the women fled in swarms. And like unto (the sounds of) rocks falling on a mountain, sounds arose of the (falling) ornaments of the terrified dames. (At length), the panic-stricken wives of the *Daityas* entered into their respective golden places variegated with innumerable jewels. Beholding that excellent city, superior to the city of the celestials themselves, I asked Matali, saying, "Why do not the celestials reside in such (a place)? Surely, this appeareth superior to the city of Purandara." Thereat, Matali said, "In days of yore, O Partha, even this was the city of our lord of the celestials. Afterwards the celestials were driven from hence by the *Nivata-Kavachas*. Having performed the most rigid austerities, they had gratified the Grand-father and had asked (and obtained) the boons— namely, that they might reside here, and that they might be free from danger in wars with the gods." Then *Sakra* addressed the self-create lord saying, "Do thou, O lord, desirous of our own welfare do what is proper." Thereupon, O Bharata, in this matter the Lord commanded (Indra), saying, "O slayer of foes, in another body, even thou shalt be (the destroyer of the *Danavas*)." Then, in order to slaughter them, *Sakra* rendered unto thee those weapons. The gods had been unable to slay these, who have been slain by thee. O Bharata, in the fullness of time, hadst thou come hither, in order to destroy them and thou hast done so. O foremost of men, with the object that the demons might be killed, Mahendra had conferred on thee the excellent prime energy of these weapons.'

"Arjuna continued, 'After having destroyed the *Danavas*, and also subdued that city, with Matali I again went to that abode of the celestials.'"

SECTION CLXXII

"Arjuna continued, 'Then while returning, I happened to descry a mighty unearthly city, moving at will, and having the effulgence of fire or the sun. And that city contained various trees composed of gems, and sweet-voiced feathered ones. And furnished with four gates, and gateways, and towers, that impregnable (city) was inhabited by the *Paulamas* and *Kalakanjas*. And it was made of all sorts of jewels and was unearthly, and of wonderful appearance. And it was covered with trees of all kinds of gems, bearing fruits and flowers. And it contained exceedingly beautiful unearthly birds. And it always swarmed throughout with cheerful *Asuras*, wearing garlands, and bearing in their hands darts, two edged swords, maces, bows, and clubs. And, O king, on seeing this wonderful city of the Daityas, I asked Matali saying, "What is this that looketh so wonderful?" Thereat, Matali replied, "Once on a time a *Daitya's* daughter, named *Pulama* and a mighty female of the *Asura* order, *Kalaka* by name, practised severe austerities for a thousand celestial years. And at the end of their austerities, the self-create conferred on them boons. And, O king of kings, they received these boons,—that their offspring might never suffer misfortune; that they might be incapable of being destroyed even by the gods, the *Rakshasas* and the *Pannagas*; and that they might obtain a highly effulgent and surpassingly fair aerial city, furnished with all manner of gems and invincible even by the celestials, the *Maharshis*, the *Yakshas*, the *Gandharvas*, the *Pannagas*, the *Asuras* and the *Rakshasas*. O best of the Bharatas, this is that unearthly aerial city devoid of the celestials, which is moving about, having been created for the *Kalakeyas*, by *Brahma* himself. And this city is furnished with all desirable objects, and is unknown of grief or disease. And, O hero, celebrated under the name of *Hiranyapura*, this mighty city is inhabited by the *Paulamas* and the *Kalakanjas*; and it is also guarded by those mighty *Asuras*. And, O king, unslayed by any of the gods, there they dwell cheerfully, free from anxiety and having all their desires gratified, O foremost of kings. Formerly, *Brahma* had destined destruction at the hands of mortals. Do thou, O Partha, in fight, compass with that weapon—the thunder-bolt—the destruction of the mighty and irrepressible *Kalakanjas*.'"

"Arjuna continued, 'O lord of men, learning that they were incapable of being destroyed by the celestials and the *Asuras*, I cheerfully said unto Matali, "Do thou speedily repair into yonder city. With weapons will I compass the annihilation of the haters of the lord of the celestials. Surely, there exist no wicked haters of the gods who ought not to be slain by me." Thereupon Matali took me to the vicinity of *Hiranyapura* on the celestial chariot yoked with steeds. And seeing me, those sons of Diti, wearing various kinds of attire and ornament and accoutred in mail, flew at me with a mighty rush. And those foremost of the *Danavas*, of exceeding prowess, in wrath attacked me with arrows and *bhallas* and clubs and two-edged swords, and *tomaras*. Thereat, O king, resorting to my strength of lore, I resisted that great volley of weapons by a mighty shower of shafts; and also confounded them in conflict by ranging around in my car. And being bewildered, the *Danavas* began to push each other down. And having been confounded, they rushed at one another. And with flaming arrows, I severed their heads by hundreds. And hard pressed by me, the offspring of Diti, taking shelter within (their) city, soared with it to the firmament, resorting to the illusion proper to the *Danavas*. Thereupon, O son of the Kurus, covering the way of the *Daityas*, with a mighty discharge of shafts I obstructed their course. Then by virtue of the bestowal of the boon, the *Daityas* supported themselves easily on that sky-ranging unearthly aerial city, going anywhere at will and like unto the sun. And now (the city) entered unto the earth and now it rose upwards; and at one time it went in a crooked way and at another time it submerged into water. At this, O represser of foes, I assailed that mighty city, going anywhere at will, and resembling *Amaravati*. And, O best of the Bharatas, I attacked the city containing those sons of Diti, with multitudes of shafts, displaying celestial weapons. And battered and broken by the straight-coursing iron shafts, shot by me, the city of the *Asuras*, O king, fell to the earth. And they also, wounded by my iron arrows having the speed of the thunder, began, O monarch, to go about, being urged by destiny. Then ascending to the sky, Matali, as if falling in front, swiftly descended to the earth, on that chariot of solar resplendence. Then, O Bharata, environed me sixty thousand cars belonging to those wrathful ones eager to battle with me. And with sharpened shafts graced with feathers of the vulture, I destroyed those (cars). At this, thinking, "These our hosts are incapable of being vanquished by mortals," they became engaged in the conflict, like unto the surges of the sea. Thereupon I gradually began to fix (on the string) unearthly weapons. At this, thousands of weapons (shot) by those wonderfully warring charioteers, by degrees opposed my unearthly arms and in the field I saw hundreds and thousands of mighty (demons) ranging on their cars, in various manoeuvres. And being furnished with variegated mail and standards and diverse ornaments, they delighted my mind. And in the conflict I could not afflict them by showers of shafts, but they did not afflict me. And being afflicted by those innumerable ones, equipped in weapons and skilled in fight, I was pained in that mighty encounter and a terrible fear seized me. Thereupon collecting (my energies) in fight, I (bowed down) unto that god of gods, *Raudra*, and saying, "May welfare attend on all beings!" I fixed that mighty weapon which, celebrated under the name of *Raudra*, is the destroyer of all foes. Then I beheld a male person having three heads, nine eyes, three faces, and six arms. And his hair was flaming like fire or the sun. And, O slayer of foes, for his dress, he had mighty serpents, putting out their tongues. And saying, O best of the Bharatas, the dreadful and eternal *Raudra*, I being free from fear, set it on the *Gandiva*; and, bowing unto the three-eyed *Sarva* of immeasurable energy, let go (the weapon), with the object of vanquishing those foremost of the *Danavas*, O Bharata. And, O lord of men, as soon as it had been hurled, there appeared on the scene by thousands, forms of deer, and of lions, and of tigers, and of bears and of buffaloes, and of serpents, and of kine, and of sarabhas, and of elephants, and of apes in multitudes, and of bulls, and of boars, and of cats, and of dogs, and of spectres, and of all the *Bhurundas*, and of vultures, and of Garudas, of *chumaras*, and of all the leopards, and of mountains, and of seas, and of celestials, and of sages, and of all the *Gandharvas*, and of ghosts with the *Yakshas*, and of the haters of the gods, (*Asuras*), and of the *Guhyakas* in the field, and of the *Nairitas* and of elephant-mouthed sharks, and of owls, and of beings having the forms of fishes and horses, and of beings bearing swords and various other weapons, and of *Rakshasas* wielding maces and clubs. And on that weapon being hurled all the universe became filled with these as well as many others wearing various shapes. And again and again wounded by beings of various sights with (pieces of) flesh, fat, bones, and marrow on their persons,—some having three heads, and some four tusks, and some four mouths, and some four arms,—the *Danavas* met with destruction. And, then, O Bharata, in a moment I slew all those *Danavas*, with other swarms of arrows composed of the quintessence of stone, flaming like fire or the sun, and possessed of the force of the thunder-bolt. And, seeing them hewn by the *Gandiva*, and deprived of life, and thrown from the sky, I again bowed unto that god—the Destroyer of *Tripura*. And, seeing those adorned with unearthly ornaments, crushed by the weapon, the *Raudra*, the charioteer of the celestials, experienced the greatest delight. And having witnessed the accomplishment of that unbearable feat incapable of being achieved even by the celestials themselves, Matali, the charioteer of Sakra, paid homage unto me; and well-pleased, with joint hands said these words. "The feat that hath been achieved by thee, is incapable of being borne even by the gods, nay,—in battle, the lord of the celestials himself cannot perform this deed. The sky-coursing mighty city incapable of being destroyed by the gods and the Asuras hast thou, O hero, crushed by thy own prowess and by the energy of asceticism." And when that aerial city had been destroyed, and when the *Danavas* also had been slain, their wives, uttering cries of distress, like unto Kurari birds, with hair dishevelled came out of the city. And bewailing for their sons and brothers and fathers, they fell on the ground and cried with distressful accents. And on being deprived for their lords, they beat their breasts, their garlands and ornaments fallen off. And that city of *Danavas*, in appearance like unto the city of the *Gandharvas* filled with lamentations and stricken with dole and distress, and bereft of grace even like unto a lake deprived of (its) elephants, or like unto a forest deprived of trees and (deprived of its) masters, looked no longer beautiful—but it vanished, like a cloud-constructed city. And when I had accomplished the task, from the field Matali took me of delighted spirits, unto the abode of the lord of the celestials. And having slain those mighty Asuras, and destroyed *Hiranyapura*, and having also killed the *Nivata-Kavachas*, I came unto Indra. And, O exceedingly resplendent one, as it had fallen out, Matali related in detail unto Devendra that entire achievement of mine. And with the Marutas, hearing of the destruction of *Hiranyapura*, of the neutralisation of the illusion, and of the slaughter of the highly powerful Nivatakavachas in fight, the prosperous thousand-eyed divine *Purandara* was well pleased, and exclaimed, "Well done; Well done!" And the king of the celestials together with the celestials, cheering me again and again, said these sweet words, "By thee hath been achieved a feat incapable of being achieved by the gods and the Asuras. And, O Partha, by slaying my mighty enemies, thou hast paid the preceptor's fee. And, O Dhananjaya, thus in battle shalt thou always remain calm, and discharge the weapons unerringly, and there shall not stand thee in fight celestials, and *Danavas*, and *Rakshasas*, and *Yakshas*, and *Asuras*, and *Gandharvas* and birds and serpents. And, O Kaunteya, by conquering it even by the might of thy arms, Kunti's son Yudhishthira, will rule the earth."'"

SECTION CLXXIII

"Arjuna continued, 'Then firmly confident, the sovereign of the celestials considering as his own, pertinently said these words unto me wounded by cleaving shafts, "All the celestial weapons, O Bharata, are with thee, so no man on earth will by any means be able to over-power thee. And, O son, when thou art in the field, Bhishma and Drona and Kripa and Karna and Sakuni together with other Kshatriyas shall not amount unto one-sixteenth part of thee." And the lord Maghavan granted me this golden garland and this shell, Devadatta, of mighty roars, and also his celestial mail impenetrable and capable of protecting the body. And Indra himself set on my (head) this diadem. And *Sakra* presented me with these unearthly apparels and unearthly ornaments, elegant and rare. In this manner, O king, (duly) honoured, I delightfully dwelt in Indra's sacred abode with the children of the *Gandharvas*. Then, well-pleased, *Sakra*, together with the celestials, addressed me, saying, "O Arjuna, the time hath come for thy departure; thy brothers have thought of thee." Thus, O Bharata, remembering the dissensions arising from that gambling, did I, O king, pass those five years in the abode of Indra. Then have I come and seen thee surrounded by our brothers on the summit of this lower range of the *Gandhamadana*.'

"Yudhishthira said, 'O Dhananjaya, by fortune it is that the weapons have been obtained by thee; by fortune it is that the master of the immortals hath been adored by thee. O repressor of foes, by fortune it is that the divine *Sthanu* together with the goddess had become manifest unto thee and been gratified by thee in battle, O sinless one; by fortune it is that thou hadst met with the Lokapalas, O best of the Bharatas. O Partha, by fortune it is that we have prospered; and by fortune it is that thou hast come back. To-day I consider as if the entire earth engarlanded with cities hath already been conquered, and as if the sons of Dhritarashtra have already been subdued. Now, O Bharata, I am curious to behold those celestial weapons wherewith thou hadst slain the powerful *Nivata-Kavachas*.'

"Thereat Arjuna said, 'Tomorrow in the morning thou wilt see all the celestial weapons with which I slew the fierce *Nivata-Kavachas*.'"

Vaisampayana said, "Thus having related (the facts touching) the arrival, Dhananjaya passed that night there, together with all his brothers."

SECTION CLXXIV

Vaisampayana continued, "And when the night had passed, Yudhishthira the just, arose and together with his brothers, performed the necessary duties. He then spake unto Arjuna, that delight of his mother, saying, 'O Kaunteya, do thou show (me) those weapons with which thou vanquished the *Danavas*.' Thereat, O king, the exceedingly powerful Dhananjaya, the son of Pandu, duly practising extreme purity, showed those weapons, O Bharata, which had been given unto him by the celestials. Dhananjaya seated on the earth, as his chariot, which had the mountain for its pole, the base of the axle and the cluster of beautiful-looking bamboo trees for its socket-pole, looked resplendent with that celestial armour of great lustre, took his bow *Gandiva* and the conch-shell given to him by the gods, commenced to exhibit those celestial weapons in order. And as those celestial weapons had been set, the Earth being oppressed with the feet (of Arjuna), began to tremble with (its) trees; and the rivers and the mighty main became vexed; and the rocks were riven; and the air was hushed. And the sun did not shine; and fire did not flame; and by no means did the Vedas of the twice-born once shine. And, O Janamejaya, the creatures peopling the interior of the earth, on being afflicted, rose and surrounded the Pandava, trembling with joined hands and contorted countenances. And being burnt by those weapons, they besought Dhananjaya (for their lives). Then the *Brahmarshis*, and the *Siddhas*, and the *Maharshis* and the mobile beings—all these appeared (on the scene). And the foremost *Devarshis*, and the celestials and the *Yakshas* and the *Rakshasas* and the *Gandharvas* and the feathered tribes and the (other) sky-ranging beings—all these appeared (on the scene). And the Great-sire and all the Lokapalas and the divine Mahadeva, came thither, together with their followers. Then, O great king, bearing unearthly variegated blossoms *Vayu* (the Wind-god) fell to strewing them around the Pandava. And sent by the celestials, the *Gandharvas* chanted various ballads; and, O monarch, hosts of the *Apsaras* danced (there). At such a moment, O king, sent by the celestials, Narada arrived (there) and addressed Partha in these sweet words, 'O Arjuna, Arjuna, do thou not discharge the celestial weapons. These should never be discharged when there is no object (fit). And when there is an object (present), they should also by no means be hurled, unless one is sore pressed; for, O son of the Kurus, to discharge the weapons (without occasion), is fraught with great evil. And, O Dhananjaya, being duly kept as thou hast been instructed to these powerful weapons will doubtless conduce to thy strength and happiness. But if they are not properly kept, they, O Pandava, will become the instrument for the destruction of the three worlds. So thou shouldst not act in this way again. O Ajatasatru, thou too wilt behold even these weapons, when Partha will use them for grinding (thy) enemies in battle.'"

Vaisampayana continued, "Having prevented Partha the immortals with others that had come there, went to each his place, O foremost of men. And, O Kaurava, after they had all gone, the Pandavas began to dwell pleasantly in the same forest, together with Krishna."

SECTION CLXXV

Janamejaya said, "When that prince among heroes, having been accomplished in arms, had returned from the abode of the slayer of Vritra, what did Pritha's sons do in company with the warlike Dhananjaya?"

Vaisampayana said, "In company with that hero equal unto Indra, Arjuna—that foremost of men, sported in the pleasure-gardens of the lord of treasures (situated) in those woods on that romantic and excellent mountain. And surveying those peerless and various pleasure-grounds filled with diverse trees, that chief of men, *Kiriti*, ever intent upon arms, ranged at large, bow in hand. And having through the grace of king Vaisravana obtained a residence, those sons of a sovereign cared not for the prosperity of men. And, O king, that period of their (lives) passed peacefully. And having Partha in their company, they spent four years there even like a single night. And as the Pandavas lived in the wood, (these four years) and the former six, numbering ten, passed smoothly with them.

"Then having seated themselves before the king, the vehement son of the Wind-god, with *Jishnu* and the heroic twins, like unto the lord of the celestials, earnestly addressed the king in these beneficial and pleasant words. 'It is only to render thy promise effectual and to advance thy interests, that, O king of the Kurus, forsaking the forest, we do not go to slay Suyodhana together with all his followers. Although deserving of happiness, yet have we been deprived of happiness. And this is the eleventh year that (in this state) we have been living (in the forest). And hereafter, deluding that one of evil mind and character, shall we easily live out the period of non-discovery. And at thy mandate, O monarch, free from apprehension, we have been ranging the woods, having relinquished our honour. Having been tempted by our residence in the vicinity, they (our enemies) will not believe that we have removed to a distant realm. And after having lived there undiscovered for a year, and having wreaked our revenge on that wicked wight, Suyodhana, with his followers, we shall easily root out that meanest of men, slaying him and regaining our kingdom. Therefore, O Dharmaraja, do thou descend unto the earth. For, O king, if we dwell in this region like unto heaven itself, we shall forget our sorrows. In that case, O Bharata, thy fame like unto a fragrant flower shall vanish from the mobile and the immobile worlds. By gaining that kingdom of the Kuru chiefs, thou wilt be able to attain (great glory), and to perform various sacrifices. This that thou art receiving from *Kuvera*, thou wilt, O foremost of men, be able to attain any time. Now, O Bharata, turn thy mind towards the punishment and destruction of foes that committed wrongs. O king, the wielder of the thunderbolt himself is incapable of standing thy prowess. And intent upon thy welfare, he, having *Suparna* for his mark (Krishna), and also the grandson of Sini (Satyaki) never experience pain, even when engaged in encounter with the gods, O Dharmaraja. And Arjuna is peerless in strength, and so am I too, O best of kings. And as Krishna together with the Yadavas is intent upon thy welfare, so am I also, O foremost of monarchs, and the heroic twins accomplished in war. And encountering the enemy, we, having for our main object the attainment by thee of wealth and prosperity, will destroy them.'"

Vaisampayana continued, "Then having learnt that intention of theirs, the magnanimous and excellent son of Dharma, versed in religion and profit, and of immeasurable prowess, went round Vaisravana's abode. And Yudhishthira the just, after bidding adieu unto the palaces, the rivers, the lakes, and all the *Rakshasas*, looked towards the way by which (he) had come (there). And then looking at the mountain also, the high-souled and pure-minded one besought that best of mountains, saying, 'O foremost of mountains, may I together with my friends, after having finished my task, and slain my foes, and regained my kingdom, see thee again, carrying on austerities with subdued soul.' And this also he determined on. And in company with his younger brothers and the *Brahmanas*, the lord of the Kurus proceeded even along that very road. And Ghatotkacha with his followers began to carry them over the mountain cascades. And as they started, the great sage *Lomasa*, advising them even as a father doth his son, with a cheerful heart, went unto the sacred abode of the dwellers of heaven. Then advised also by Arshtishena, those first of men, the Parthas, went alone beholding romantic *tirthas* and hermitages, and other mighty lakes."

SECTION CLXXVI

Vaisampayana said, "When they had left their happy home in the beautiful mountain abounding in cascades, and having birds, and the elephants of the eight quarters, and the supernatural attendants of *Kuvera* (as dwellers thereof), all happiness forsook those foremost of men of Bharata's race. But afterwards on beholding *Kuvera's* favourite mountain, *Kailasa*, appearing like clouds, the delight of those pre-eminent heroes of the race of Bharata, became very great. And those foremost of heroic men, equipped with scimitars and bows, proceeded contentedly, beholding elevations and defiles, and dens of lions and craggy causeways and innumerable water-falls and lowlands, in different places, as also other great forests inhabited by countless deer and birds and elephants. And they came upon beautiful woodlands and rivers and lakes and caves and mountain caverns; and these frequently by day and night became the dwelling place of those great men. And having dwelt in all sorts of inaccessible places and crossing *Kailasa* of inconceivable grandeur, they reached the excellent and surpassingly beautiful hermitage of *Vrishaparba*. And meeting king Vrishaparba and received by him, they became free from depression and then they accurately narrated in detail to Vrishaparba the story of their sojourn in the mountains. And having pleasantly passed one night in his sacred abode frequented by gods and *Maharshis*, those great warriors proceeded smoothly towards the jujube tree called Visala and took up their quarters there. Then all those magnanimous men having reached the place of Narayana, continued to live there, bereft of all sorrow, at beholding *Kuvera's* favourite lake, frequented by gods and *Siddhas*. And viewing that lake, those foremost of men, the sons of Pandu traversed that place, renouncing all grief even as immaculate *Brahmana rishis* (do) on attaining a habitation in the *Nandana* gardens. Then all those warriors having in due course happily lived at Badari for one month, proceeded towards the realm of Suvahu, king of the *Kiratas*, by following the same track by which they had come. And crossing the difficult Himalayan regions, and the countries of China, Tukhara, Darada and all the climes of Kulinda, rich in heaps of jewels, those warlike men reached the capital of Suvahu. And hearing that those sons and grandsons of kings had all reached his kingdom, Suvahu, elated with joy, advanced (to meet them). Then the best of the Kurus welcomed him also. And meeting king Suvahu, and being joined by all their charioteers with Visoka at their head and by their attendants, Indrasena and others, and also by the superintendents and servants of the kitchen, they stayed there comfortably for one night. Then taking all the chariots and chariot-men and dismissing Ghatotkacha together with his followers, they next repaired to the monarch of mountains in the vicinity of the *Yamuna*. In the midst of the mountain abounding in waterfalls and having grey and orange-coloured slopes and summits covered with a sheet of snow, those warlike men having then found the great forest of Visakhayupa like unto the forest of Chitraratha and inhabited by wild boars and various kinds of deer and birds, made it their home. Addicted to hunting as their chief occupation, the sons of Pritha peacefully dwelt in that forest for one year. There in a cavern of the mountain, Vrikodara, with a heart afflicted with distraction and grief, came across a snake of huge strength distressed with hunger and looking fierce like death itself. At this crisis Yudhishthira, the best of pious men, became the protector of Vrikodara and he, of infinite puissance, extricated Bhima whose whole body had been fast gripped by the snake with its folds. And the twelfth year of their sojourn in forests having arrived, those scions of the race of Kuru, blazing in effulgence, and engaged in asceticism, always devoted principally to the practice of archery, repaired cheerfully from that Chitraratha-like forest to the borders of the desert, and desirous of dwelling by the *Saraswati* they went there, and from the banks of that river they reached the lake of *Dwaitabana*. Then seeing them enter *Dwaitabana*, the dwellers of that place engaged in asceticism, religious ordinances, and self-restraining exercises and in deep and devout meditation and subsisting on things ground with stone (for want of teeth) having procured grass-mats and water-vessels, advanced to meet them. The holy fig, the rudaraksha, the rohitaka, the cane and the jujube, the catechu, the sirisha, the bel and the inguda and the karira and pilu and sami trees grew on the banks of the *Saraswati*. Wandering about with contentment in (the vicinity of) the *Saraswati* which was, as it were, the home of the celestials, and the favourite (resort) of *Yakshas* and *Gandharvas* and *Maharshis*, those sons of kings lived there in happiness."

SECTION CLXXVII

Janamejaya said, "How was it, O sage! that Bhima, of mighty prowess and possessing the strength of ten thousand elephants, was stricken with panic at (the sight of) that snake? Thou hast described him, that slayer of his enemies, as dismayed and appalled with fear, even him, who by fighting at the lotus lake (of Kuvera) became the destroyer of *Yakshas* and *Rakshasas* and who, in proud defiance, invited to a single combat, Pulastya's son, the dispenser of all riches. I desire to hear this (from you); great indeed is my curiosity."

Vaisampayana continued, "O king, having reached king Vrishaparva's hermitage, while those fearful warriors were living in various wonderful woods, Vrikodara roaming at pleasure, with bow in hand and armed with a scimitar, found that beautiful forest, frequented by gods and *Gandharvas*. And then he beheld (some) lovely spots in the Himalayan mountains, frequented by *Devarshis* and *Siddhas* and inhabited by hosts of *Apsaras*, resounded here and there with (the warbling of) birds—the *chakora*, the *chakrabaka*, the *jibajibaka* and the cuckoo and the *Bhringaraja*, and abounding with shady trees, soft with the touch of snow and pleasing to the eye and mind, and bearing perennial fruits and flowers. And he beheld mountain streams with waters glistening like the *lapis lazuli* and with ten thousand snow-white ducks and swans and with forests of *deodar* trees forming (as it were) a trap for the clouds; and with *tugna* and *kalikaya* forests, interspersed with yellow sandal trees. And he of mighty strength, in the pursuit of the chase, roamed in the level and desert tracts of the mountain, piercing his game with unpoisoned arrows. In that forest the famous and mighty Bhimasena, possessing the strength of a hundred elephants, killed (many) large wild boars, with the force (of his arms). And endowed with terrible prowess and mighty strength, and powerful as the lion or the tiger, and capable of resisting a hundred men, and having long arms, and possessing the strength of a hundred elephants, he killed many antelopes and wild boars and buffaloes. And here and there, in that forest he pulled out trees by the roots, with great violence and broke them too, causing the earth and the woods and the (surrounding) places to resound. And then shouting and trampling on the tops of mountains, and causing the earth to resound with his roars, and striking his arms, and uttering his war-cry, and slapping and clapping his hands, Bhimasena, exempt from decay, and ever-proud and without fear, again and again leaped about in those woods. And on hearing the shouts of Bhimasena, powerful lions and elephants of huge strength, left their lairs in fright. And in that same forest, he fearlessly strolled about in search of game; and like the denizens of the woods, that most valiant of men, the mighty Bhimasena, wandered on foot in that forest. And he penetrated the vast forest, shouting strange whoops, and terrifying all creatures, endowed with strength and prowess. And then being terrified, the snakes hid (themselves) in caves, but he, overtaking them with promptitude, pursued them slowly. Then the mighty Bhimasena, like unto the Lord of the Celestials, saw a serpent of colossal proportions, living in one of the mountain fastnesses and covering the (entire) cave with its body and causing one's hair to stand on end (from fright). It had its huge body stretched like a hillock, and it possessed gigantic strength, and its body was speckled with spots and it had a turmeric-like (yellow) colour and a deep copper-coloured mouth of the form of a cave supplied with four teeth; and with glaring eyes, it was constantly licking the corners of its mouth. And it was the terror of all animated beings and it looked like the very image of the Destroyer Yama; and with the hissing noise of its breath it lay as if rebuking (an in-comer). And seeing Bhima draw so near to him, the serpent, all on a sudden, became greatly enraged, and that goat-devouring snake violently seized Bhimasena in his grip. Then by virtue of the boon that had been received by the serpent, Bhimasena with his body in the serpent's grip, instantly lost all consciousness. Unrivalled by that of others, the might of Bhimasena's arms equaled the might of ten thousand elephants combined. But Bhima, of great prowess, being thus vanquished by the snake, trembled slowly, and was unable to exert himself. And that one of mighty arms and of leonine shoulders, though possessed of strength of ten thousand elephants, yet seized by the snake, and overpowered by virtue of the boon, lost all strength. He struggled furiously to extricate himself, but did not succeed in any wise baffling this (snake)."

SECTION CLXXVIII

Vaisampayana continued, "And the powerful Bhimasena, having thus come under the power of the snake, thought of its mighty and wonderful prowess; and said unto it, 'Be thou pleased to tell me, O snake, who thou art. And, O foremost of reptiles, what wilt thou do with me? I am Bhimasena, the son of Pandu, and next by birth to Yudhishthira the just. And endued as I am with the strength of ten thousand elephants, how hast thou been able to overpower me? In fight have been encountered and slain by me innumerable lions, and tigers, and buffaloes, and elephants. And, O best of serpents, mighty *Rakshasas* and *Pisachas*, and *Nagas*, are unable to stand the force of my arms. Art thou possessed of any magic, or hast thou received any boon, that although exerting myself, I have been overcome by thee? Now I have been convinced that the strength of men is false, for, O serpent, by thee hath such mighty strength of men been baffled.'"

Vaisampayana continued, "When the heroic Bhima of noble deed had said this, the snake caught him, and coiled him all round with his body, having thus subdued that mighty-armed one, and freed his plump arms alone, the serpent spake these words, 'By good fortune it is that, myself being hungry, after long time the gods have to-day destined thee for my food; for life is dear unto every embodied being, I should relate unto thee the way in which I have come by this snake form. Hear, O best of the pious, I have fallen into this plight on account of the wrath of the *Maharshis*. Now desirous of getting rid of the curse, I will narrate unto thee all about it. Thou hast, no doubt, heard of the royal sage, *Nahusha*. He was the son of Ayu, and the perpetuator of the line of thy ancestors. Even I am that one. For having affronted the *Brahmanas* I, by (virtue of) Agastya's malediction, have come by this condition. Thou art my agnate, and lovely to behold.—so thou shouldst not be slain by me,—yet I shall to-day devour thee! Do thou behold the dispensation of Destiny! And be it a buffalo, or an elephant, none coming within my reach at the sixth division of the day, can, O best of men, escape. And, O best of the Kurus, thou hast not been taken by an animal of the lower order, having strength alone,—but this (hath been so) by reason only of the boon I have received. As I was falling rapidly from Sakra's throne placed on the front of his palace, I spake unto that worshipful sage (Agastya), "Do thou free me from this curse." Thereat filled with compassion, that energetic one said unto me, "O king, thou shall be freed after the lapse of some time." Then I fell to the earth (as a snake); but my recollection (of former life) did not renounce me. And although it be so ancient, I still recollect all that was said. And the sage said unto me, "That person who conversant with the relation subsisting between the soul and the Supreme Being, shall be able to answer the questions put by thee, shall deliver thee. And, O king, taken by thee, strong beings superior to thee, shall immediately lose their strength." I heard these words of those compassionate ones, who felt attached unto me. And then the Brahmanas vanished. Thus, O highly effulgent one, having become a serpent, I, doing exceedingly sinful acts, live in unclean hell, in expectation of the (appointed) time.' The mighty-armed Bhimasena addressed the serpent, saying, 'I am not angry, O mighty snake,—nor do I blame myself. Since in regard to happiness and misery, men sometimes possess the power of bringing and dismissing them, and sometimes do not. Therefore one should not fret one's mind. Who can baffle destiny by self-exertion? I deem destiny to be supreme, and self-exertion to be of no avail. Smitten with the stroke of destiny, the prowess of my arms lost, behold me to-day fallen unto this condition without palpable cause. But to-day I do not so much grieve for my own self being slain, as I do for my brothers deprived of their kingdom, and exiled into the forest. This Himalaya is inaccessible, and abounds with *Yakshas* and the *Rakshasas*. And searching about for me, they will be distracted. And hearing that I have been killed, (my brothers) will forego all exertion, for, firm in promise, they have hitherto been controlled by my harsh speech, I being desirous of gaining the kingdom. Or the intelligent Arjuna (alone), being versed in every lore, and incapable of being overcome by gods and *Rakshasas* and *Gandharvas*, will not be afflicted with grief. That mighty-armed and exceedingly powerful one is able single-handed to speedily pull down from his place even the celestials. What shall I say of the deceitfully gambling son of Dhritarashtra, detested of all men, and filled with haughtiness and ignorance! And I also grieve for my poor mother, affectionate to her sons, who is ever solicitous for our greatness in a large measure than is attained by our enemies. O serpent, the desire that forlorn one had in me will all be fruitless in consequence of my destruction. And gifted with manliness, the twins, Nakula and Sahadeva, following their elder brother (me), and always protected by the strength of my arms, will, owing to my destruction, be depressed and deprived of their prowess, and stricken with grief. This is what I think.' In this way Vrikodara lamented profusely. And being bound by the body of the snake, he could not exert himself.

"On the other hand, Kunti's son, Yudhishthira, (seeing) and reflecting on dreadful ill omens, became alarmed. Terrified by the blaze of the points of the horizon, jackals stationing themselves on the right of that hermitage, set up frightful and inauspicious yells. And ugly *Vartikas* as of dreadful sight, having one wing, one eye, and one leg, were seen to vomit blood, facing the sun. And the wind began to blow dryly, and violently, attracting grits. And to the right all the beasts and birds began to cry. And in the rear the black crows cried, 'Go!' 'Go!' And momentarily his (Yudhishthira's) right arm began to twitch, and his chest and left leg shook (of themselves). And indicating evil his left eye contracted spasmodically. Thereupon, O Bharata, the intelligent Yudhishthira the just, inferring some great calamity (to be imminent), asked Draupadi, saying, 'Where is Bhima?' Thereat Panchali said that Vrikodara had long gone out. Hearing this, that mighty-armed king set out with Dhaumya, after having said unto Dhananjaya, 'Thou shouldst protect Draupadi.' And he also directed Nakula and Sahadeva to protect the *Brahmanas*. And issuing from the hermitage that lord, Kunti's son, following the footprints of Bhimasena, began to search for him in that mighty forest. And on coming to the east, he found mighty leaders of elephant-herds (slain) and saw the earth marked with Bhima's (foot-prints). Then seeing thousands of deer and hundreds of lions lying in the forest, the king ascertained his course. And on the way were scattered trees pulled down by the wind caused by the thighs of that hero endued with the speed of the wind as he rushed after the deer. And proceeding, guided by those marks, to a spot filled with dry winds and abounding in leafless vegetables, brackish and devoid of water, covered with thorny plants and scattered over with gravel, stumps and shrubs and difficult of access and uneven and dangerous, he saw in a mountain cavern his younger brother motionless, caught in the folds of that foremost of snakes."

SECTION CLXXIX

Vaisampayana continued, "Yudhishthira, finding his beloved brother coiled by the body of the serpent, said these words: 'O son of Kunti, how hast thou come by this misfortune! And who is this best of serpents having a body like unto a mountain mass?' Bhimasena said, 'O worshipful one, this mighty being hath caught me for food. He is the royal sage Nahusha living in the form of a serpent.' Yudhishthira said, 'O longlived one, do thou free my brother of immeasurable prowess; we will give thee some other food which will appease thy hunger.' The serpent said, 'I have got for diet even this son of a king, come to my mouth of himself. Do thou go away. Thou shouldst not stay here. (If thou remainest here) thou too shall be my fare to-morrow. O mighty-armed one, this is ordained in respect of me, that he that cometh unto my place, becometh my food and thou too art in my quarter. After a long time have I got thy younger brother as my food; I will not let him off; neither do I like to have any other food.' Thereat Yudhishthira said, 'O serpent, whether thou art a god, or a demon, or an *Uraga*, do thou tell me truly, it is Yudhishthira that asketh thee, wherefore, O snake, hast thou taken Bhimasena? By obtaining which, or by knowing what wilt thou receive satisfaction, O snake, and what food shall I give thee? And how mayst thou free him.' The serpent said, 'O sinless one, I was thy ancestor, the son of Ayu and fifth in descent from the Moon. And I was a king celebrated under the name of Nahusha. And by sacrifices and asceticism and study of the Vedas and self-restraint and prowess I had acquired a permanent dominion over the three worlds. And when I had obtained such dominion, haughtiness possessed me. And thousands of *Brahmanas* were engaged in carrying my chair. And intoxicated by supremacy, I insulted those *Brahmanas*. And, O lord of the earth, by Agastya have I been reduced to this pass! Yet, O Pandava, to this day the memory (of my former birth) hath not forsaken me! And, O king, even by the favour of that high-souled Agastya, during the sixth division of the day have I got for meal thy younger brother. Neither will I set him free, nor do I wish for any other food. But if to-day thou answerest the questions put by me, then, I shall deliver Vrikodara!' At this Yudhishthira said, 'O serpent, ask whatever thou listest! I shall, if I can, answer thy questions with the view of gratifying thee, O snake! Thou knowest fully what should be known by *Brahmanas*. Therefore, O king of snakes, hearing (thee) I shall answer thy queries!'

"The serpent said, 'O Yudhishthira, say—Who is a *Brahmana* and what should be known? By thy speech I infer thee to be highly intelligent.'

"Yudhishthira said, 'O foremost of serpents, he, it is asserted by the wise, in whom are seen truth, charity, forgiveness, good conduct, benevolence, observance of the rites of his order and mercy is a *Brahmana*. And, O serpent, that which should be known is even the supreme *Brahma*, in which is neither happiness nor misery—and attaining which beings are not affected with misery; what is thy opinion?'

"The serpent said, 'O Yudhishthira, truth, charity, forgiveness, benevolence, benignity, kindness and the *Veda* 2 which worketh the benefit of the four orders, which is the authority in matters of religion and which is true, are seen even in the *Sudra*. As regards the object to be known and which thou allegest is without both happiness and misery, I do not see any such that is devoid of these.'

"Yudhishthira said, 'Those characteristics that are present in a *Sudra*, do not exist in a *Brahmana*; nor do those that are in a *Brahmana* exist in a *Sudra*. And a *Sudra* is not a *Sudra* by birth alone—nor a *Brahmana* is *Brahmana* by birth alone. He, it is said by the wise, in whom are seen those virtues is a *Brahmana*. And people term him a Sudra in whom those qualities do not exist, even though he be a *Brahmana* by birth. And again, as for thy assertion that the object to be known (as asserted by me) doth not exist, because nothing exists that is devoid of both (happiness and misery), such indeed is the opinion, O serpent, that nothing exists that is without (them) both. But as in cold, heat doth not exist, nor in heat, cold, so there cannot exist an object in which both (happiness and misery) cannot exist?'

"The serpent said, 'O king, if thou recognise him as a Brahmana by characteristics, then, O long-lived one, the distinction of caste becometh futile as long as conduct doth not come into play.'

"Yudhishthira said, 'In human society, O mighty and highly intelligent serpent, it is difficult to ascertain one's caste, because of promiscuous intercourse among the four orders. This is my opinion. Men belonging to all orders (promiscuously) beget offspring upon women of all the orders. And of men, speech, sexual intercourse, birth and death are common. And to this the Rishis have borne testimony by using as the beginning of a sacrifice such expressions as—*of what caste so ever we may be, we celebrate the sacrifice*. Therefore, those that are wise have asserted that character is the chief essential requisite. The natal ceremony of a person is performed before division of the umbilical cord. His mother then acts as its *Savitri* and his father officiates as priest. He is considered as a *Sudra* as long as he is not initiated in the *Vedas*. Doubts having arisen on this point, O prince of serpents, Swayambhuba Manu has declared, that the mixed castes are to be regarded as better than the (other) classes, if having gone through the ceremonies of purification, the latter do not conform to the rules of good conduct, O excellent snake! Whosoever now conforms to the rules of pure and virtuous conduct, him have I, ere now, designated as a *Brahmana*.' The serpent replied, 'O Yudhishthira, thou art acquainted with all that is fit to be known and having listened to thy words, how can I (now) eat up thy brother Vrikodara!'"

SECTION CLXXX

"Yudhishthira said, 'In this world, you are so learned in the *Vedas* and *Vedangas*; tell me (then), what one should do to attain salvation?'

"The serpent replied, 'O scion of the Bharata's race, my belief is that the man who bestows alms on proper objects, speaks kind words and tells the truth and abstains from doing injury to any creature goes to heaven.'

"Yudhishthira enquired, 'Which, O snake, is the higher of the two, truth or alms-giving? Tell me also the greater or less importance of kind behaviour and of doing injury to no creature.'

"The snake replied, 'The relative merits of these virtues, truth and alms-giving, kind speech and abstention from injury to any creature, are known (measured) by their objective gravity (utility). Truth is (sometimes) more praiseworthy than some acts of charity; some of the latter again are more commendable than true speech. Similarly, O mighty king, and lord of the earth, abstention from doing injury to any creature is seen to be important than good speech and vice-versa. Even so it is, O king, depending on effects. And now, if thou hast anything else to ask, say it all, I shall enlighten thee!' Yudhishthira said, 'Tell me, O snake, how the incorporal being's translation to heaven, its perception by the senses and its enjoyment of the immutable fruits of its actions (here below), can be comprehended.' The snake replied, 'By his own acts, man is seen to attain to one of the three conditions of human existence, of heavenly life, or of birth in the lower animal kingdom. Among these, the man who is not slothful, who injures no one and who is endowed with charity and other virtues, goes to heaven, after leaving this world of men. By doing the very contrary, O king, people are again born as men or as lower animals. O my son, it is particularly said in this connection, that the man who is swayed by anger and lust and who is given to avarice and malice falls away from his human state and is born again as a lower animal, and the lower animals too are ordained to be transformed into the human state; and the cow, the horse and other animals are observed to attain to even the divine state. 3 O my son, the sentient being, reaping the fruits of his actions, thus transmigrates through these conditions; but the regenerate and wise man reposes his soul in the everlasting Supreme Spirit. The embodied spirit, enchained by destiny and reaping the fruits of its own actions, thus undergoes birth after birth but he that has lost touch of his actions, is conscious of the immutable destiny of all born beings. 4 '

"Yudhishthira asked, 'O snake, tell me truly and without confusion how that dissociated spirit becomes cognisant of sound, touch, form, flavour, and taste. O great-minded one, dost thou not perceive them, simultaneously by the senses? Do thou, O best of snakes, answer all these queries!' The snake replied, 'O long-lived one, the thing called *Atman* (spirit), betaking itself to corporeal tenement and manifesting itself through the organs of sense, becomes duly cognisant of perceptible objects. O prince of Bharata's race, know that the senses, the mind, and the intellect, assisting the soul in its perception of objects, are called *Karanas*. O my son, the eternal spirit, going out of its sphere, and aided by the mind, acting through the senses, the receptacles of all perceptions, successively perceives these things (sound, form, flavour, &c). O most valiant of men, the mind of living creatures is the cause of all perception, and, therefore, it cannot be cognisant of more than one thing at a time. That spirit, O foremost of men, betaking itself to the space between the eyebrows, sends the high and low intellect to different objects. What the *Yogins* perceive after the action of the intelligent principle by that is manifested the action of the soul.'

"Yudhishthira said, 'Tell me the distinguishing characteristics of the mind and the intellect. The knowledge of it is ordained as the chief duty of persons meditating on the Supreme Spirit.'

"The snake replied, 'Through illusion, the soul becomes subservient to the intellect. The intellect, though known to be subservient to the soul, becomes (then) the director of the latter. The intellect is brought into play by acts of perception; the mind is self-existent. The Intellect does not cause the sensation (as of pain, pleasure, &c), but the mind does. This, my son, is the difference between the mind and the intellect. You too are learned in this matter, what is your opinion?'

"Yudhishthira said, 'O most intelligent one, you have fine intelligence and you know all that is fit to be known. Why do you ask me that question? You knew all and you performed such wonderful deeds and you lived in heaven. How could then illusion overpower you? Great is my doubt on this point.' The snake replied, 'Prosperity intoxicates even the wise and valiant men. Those who live in luxury, (soon) lose their reason. So, I too, O Yudhishthira, overpowered by the infatuation of prosperity, have fallen from my high state and having recovered my self-consciousness, am enlightening thee thus! O victorious king, thou hast done me a good turn. By conversing with thy pious self, my painful curse has been expiated. In days of yore, while I used to sojourn in heaven in a celestial chariot, reveling in my pride, I did not think of anything else, I used to exact tribute from *Brahmarshis, Devas, Yakshas, Gandharvas, Rakshasas, Pannagas* and all other dwellers of the three worlds. O lord of earth, such was the spell of my eyes, that on whatever creature, I fixed them, I instantly destroyed his power. Thousands of *Brahmarshis* used to draw my chariot. The delinquency, O king, was the cause of my fall from my high prosperity. Among them, Agastya was one day drawing my conveyance, and my feet came in contact with his body; Agastya then pronounced (this curse) on me, in anger, "Ruin seize thee, do thou become a snake." So, losing my glory, I fell down from that excellent car and while falling, I beheld myself turned into a snake, with head downwards. I thus implored that Brahmana, "May this curse be extinguished, O adorable one! You ought to forgive one who has been so foolish from infatuation." Then he kindly told me this, as I was being hurled down (from heaven), "The virtuous king Yudhishthira will save thee from this curse, and when, O king, horrible sin of pride will be extinguished in thee, thou shalt attain salvation." And I was struck with wonder on seeing (this) power of his austere virtues; and therefore, have I questioned thee about the attributes of the Supreme Spirit and of *Brahmanas*. Truth, charity, self-restraint, penance, abstention from doing injury to any creature, and constancy in virtue, these, O king, and not his race or family connections, are the means, by which a man must always secure salvation. May this brother of thine, the mighty Bhimasena, meet with good luck and may happiness abide with thee! I must go to Heaven again.'"

Vaisampayana continued, "So saying, that king, Nahusha, quitted his serpentine form, and assuming his celestial shape he went back to Heaven. The glorious and pious Yudhishthira, too, returned to his hermitage with Dhaumya and his brother Bhima. Then the virtuous Yudhishthira narrated all that, in detail, to the *Brahmanas* who had assembled (there). On hearing that, his three brothers and all the *Brahmanas* and the renowned Draupadi too were covered with shame. And all those excellent *Brahmanas* desiring the welfare of the Pandavas, admonished Bhima for his foolhardiness, telling him not to attempt such things again, and the Pandavas too were greatly pleased at seeing the mighty Bhima out of danger, and continued to live there pleasantly."

SECTION CLXXXI

(Markandeya-Samasya Parva)

Vaisampayana said, "While they were dwelling at that place, there set in the season of the rains, the season that puts an end to the hot weather and is delightful to all animated beings. Then the black clouds, rumbling loudly, and covering the heavens and the cardinal points, ceaselessly rained during day and night. These clouds, counted by hundreds and by thousands, looked like domes in the rainy season. From the earth disappeared the effulgence of the sun; its place was taken by the stainless lustre of the lightning; the earth became delightful to all, being overgrown with grass, with gnats and reptiles in their joy; it was bathed with rain and possessed with calm. When the waters had covered all, it could not be known whether the ground was at all even or uneven;—whether there were rivers or trees or hills. At the end of the hot season, the rivers added beauty to the woods being themselves full of agitated waters, flowing with great force and resembling serpents in the hissing sound they made. The boars, the stags and the birds, while the rain was falling upon them began to utter sounds of various kinds which could be heard within the forest tracts. The *chatakas*, the peacocks and the host of male *Kohilas* and the excited frogs, all ran about in joy. Thus while the Pandavas were roaming about in the deserts and sandy tracts, the happy season of rain, so various in aspect and resounding with clouds passed away. Then set in the season of autumn, thronged with ganders and cranes and full of joy; then the forest tracts were overrun with grass; the river turned limpid; the firmament and stars shone brightly., And the autumn, thronged with beasts and birds, was joyous and pleasant for the magnanimous sons of Pandu. Then were seen nights, that were free from dust and cool with clouds and beautified by myriads of planets and stars and the moon. And they beheld rivers and ponds, adorned with lilies and white lotuses, full of cool and pleasant water. And while roving by the river *Saraswati* whose banks resembled the firmament itself and were overgrown with canes, and as such abounded in sacred baths, their joy was great. And those heroes who wielded powerful bows, were specially glad to see the pleasant river *Saraswati*, with its limpid waters full to the brim. And, O Janamejaya, the holiest night, that of the full moon in the month of *Kartika* in the season of autumn, was spent by them while dwelling there! And the sons of Pandu, the best of the descendants of Bharata, spent that auspicious juncture with righteous and magnanimous saints devoted to penance. And as soon as the dark fortnight set in immediately after, the sons of Pandu entered the forest named the Kamyaka, accompanied by Dhananjaya and their charioteers and cooks."

SECTION CLXXXII

Vaisampayana said, "O son of Kuru, they, Yudhishthira and others, having reached the forest of *Kamyaka*, were hospitably received by hosts of saints and they lived together with Krishna. And while the sons of Pandu were dwelling in security in that place, many *Brahmanas* came to wait upon them. And a certain *Brahmana* said, 'He the beloved friend of Arjuna, of powerful arms and possessed of self control, descendant of *Sura*, of a lofty intellect, will come, for, O ye foremost of the descendants of Kuru, Hari knows that ye have arrived here. For, Hari has always a longing for your sight and always seeks your welfare. And Markandeya, who lived very many years devoted to great austerities, given to study and penance, will erelong come and meet you.' And the very moment that he was uttering these words, there was beheld Krishna, coming thitherward upon a car unto which were yoked the horses Saivya and Sugriva, — he the best of those that ride on cars, accompanied by Satyabhama, is like Indra by Sachi, the daughter of Pulaman. And the son of Devaki came, desirous to see those most righteous of the descendants of Kuru. And the sagacious Krishna, having alighted from the car, prostrated himself, with pleasure in his heart, before the virtuous king, in the prescribed way, and also before Bhima, that foremost of powerful men. And he paid his respects to Dhaumya, while the twin brothers prostrated themselves to him. And he embraced Arjuna of the curly hair; and spoke words of solace to the daughter of Drupada. And the descendant of the chief of the Dasaraha tribe, that chastiser of foes, when he saw the beloved Arjuna come near him, having seen him after a length of time, clasped him again and again. And so too Satyabhama also, the beloved consort of Krishna, embraced the daughter of Drupada, the beloved wife of the sons of Pandu. Then these sons of Pandu, accompanied by their wife and priests, paid their respects to Krishna, whose eyes resembled the white lotus and surrounded him on all sides. And Krishna, when united with Arjuna, the son of Pritha, the winner of riches and the terror of the demons assumed a beauty comparable to that of *Siva*, the magnanimous lord of all created beings, when he, the mighty lord, is united with Kartikeya (his son). And Arjuna, who bore a circlet of crowns on his head, gave an account of what had happened to him in the forest to Krishna, the elder brother of Gada. And Arjuna asked, saying, 'How is Subhadra, and her son

Abhimanyu?' And Krishna, the slayer of Madhu, having paid his respects in the prescribed form to the son of Pritha, and to the priest, and seating himself with them there, spoke to king Yudhishthira, in words of praise. And he said, 'O king, Virtue is preferable to the winning of kingdoms; it is, in fact, practice of austerities! By you who have obeyed with truth and candour what your duty prescribed, have been won both this world and that to come! First you have studied, while performing religious duties; having acquired in a suitable way the whole science of arms, having won wealth by pursuing the methods prescribed for the military caste, you have celebrated all the time-honoured sacrificial rites. You take no delight in sensual pleasures; you do not act, O lord of men, from motives of enjoyment, nor do you swerve from virtue from greed of riches; it is for this, you have been named the Virtuous King, O son of Pritha! Having won kingdoms and riches and means of enjoyment, your best delight has been charity and truth and practice of austerities, O King, and faith and meditation and forbearance and patience! When the population of Kuru-jangala beheld Krishna outraged in the assembly hall, who but yourself could brook that conduct, O Pandu's son, which was so repugnant both to virtue and usage? No doubt, you will, before long, rule over men in a praiseworthy way, all your desires being fulfilled. Here are we prepared to chastise the Kurus, as soon as the stipulation made by you is fully performed!' And Krishna, the foremost of the *Dasarha* tribe, then said to Dhaumya and Bhima and Yudhishthira, and the twins and Krishna, 'How fortunate that by your blessing Arjuna the bearer of the coronet, has arrived after having acquired the science of arms!' And Krishna, the leader of the *Dasarha* tribe, accompanied by friends, likewise spoke to Krishna, the daughter of Yajnasena, saying, 'How fortunate that you are united, safe and secure, with Arjuna, the winner of riches!' And Krishna also said, 'O Krishna, O daughter of Yajnasena, those sons of yours, are devoted to the study of the science of arms, are well-behaved and conduct themselves on the pattern, O Krishna, of their righteous friends. Your father and your uterine brothers proffer them a kingdom and territories; but the boys find no joy in the house of Drupada, or in that of their maternal uncles. Safely proceeding to the land of the Anartas, they take the greatest delight in the study of the science of arms. Your sons enter the town of the *Vrishnis* and take an immediate liking to the people there. And as you would direct them to conduct themselves, or as the respected Kunti would do, so does Subhadra direct them in a watchful way. Perhaps, she is still more careful of them. And, O Krishna, as Rukmini's son is the preceptor of Aniruddha, of Abhimanyu, of Sunitha, and of Bhanu; so he is the preceptor and the refuge of your sons also! And a good preceptor, would unceasingly give them lessons in the wielding of maces and swords and bucklers, in missiles and in the arts of driving cars and of riding horses, being valiant. And he, the son of Rukmini, having bestowed a very good training upon them, and having taught them the art of using various weapons in a proper way, takes satisfaction at the valorous deeds of your sons, and of Abhimanyu, O daughter of Drupada! And when your son goes out, in pursuit of (out-door) sports, each one of them is followed thither by cars and horses and vehicles and elephants.' And Krishna said to the virtuous king, Yudhishthira, 'The fighting men of the *Dasarha* tribe, and the *Kukuras*, and the *Andhakas*—let these, O king, place themselves at thy command—let them perform what thou desirest them. O lord of men, let the army of the tribe of Madhus, (resistless) like the wind, with their bows and led by Balarama whose weapon is the plough—let that army, equipped (for war), consisting of horsemen and foot soldiers and horses and cars and elephants, prepare to do your bidding. O son of Pandu! Drive Duryodhana, the son of Dhritarashtra, the vilest of sinful men, together with his followers and his hosts of friends to the path betaken by the lord of Saubha, the son of the Earth! You, O ruler of men, are welcome to stick to that stipulation which was made in the assembly-hall—but let the city of Hastina be made ready for you, when the hostile force has been slain by the soldiers of the *Dasarha* tribe! Having roamed at your pleasure in all those places where you may desire to go, having got rid of your grief and freed from all your sins— you will reach the city of Hastina—the well-known city situated in the midst of a fine territory!'—Then the magnanimous king having been acquainted with the view, thus clearly set forth by Krishna that best of men, and, having applauded the same, and having deliberated, thus spoke with joined palms unto Kesava, 'O Kesava, no doubt, thou art the refuge of the sons of Pandu; for the sons of Pandu have their protector in thee! When the time will come, there is no doubt that thou wilt do all the work just mentioned by thee; and even more than the same! As promised by us, we have spent all the twelve years in lonely forests. O Kesava, having in the prescribed way completed the period for living unrecognised, the sons of Pandu will take refuge in thee. This should be the intention of those that associate with thee, O Krishna! The sons of Pandu swerve not from the path of truth, for the sons of Pritha with their charity and their piety with their people and their wives and with their relations have their protector in thee!'"

Vaisampayana said, "O descendant of Bharata, while Krishna, the descendant of the *Vrishnis* and the virtuous king, were thus talking, there appeared then the saint Markandeya, grown grey in the practise of penances. And he had seen many thousand years of life, was of a pious soul, and devoted to great austerities. Signs of old age he had none; and deathless he was, and endued with beauty and generous and many good qualities. And he looked like one only twenty-five years old. And when the aged saint, who had seen many thousand years of life, came, all the *Brahmanas* paid their respects to him and so did Krishna together with Pandu's son. And when that wisest saint, thus honoured, took his seat in a friendly way, Krishna addressed him, in accordance with the views of the *Brahmanas* and of Pandu's sons, thus, —

"'The sons of Pandu, and the *Brahmanas* assembled here, and the daughter of Drupada, and Satyabhama, likewise myself, are all anxious to hear your most excellent words, O Markandeya! Propound to us the holy stories of events of bygone times, and the eternal rules of righteous conduct by which are guided kings and women and saints!'"

Vaisampayana continued, "When they had all taken their seats, Narada also, the divine saint, of purified soul, came on a visit to Pandu's sons. Him also, then, of great soul, all those foremost men of superior intellect, honoured in the prescribed form, by offering water to wash his feet, and the well-known oblation called the *Arghya*. Then the godlike saint, Narada, learning that they were about to hear the speech of Markandeya, expressed his assent to the arrangement. And he, the deathless, knowing what would be opportune, said smilingly, 'O saint of the *Brahmana* caste, speak what you were about to say unto the sons of Pandu!' Thus addressed, Markandeya, devoted to great austerities, replied, 'Wait a moment. A great deal will be narrated.' Thus addressed, the sons of Pandu, together with those twice-born ones, waited a moment, looking at that great saint, (bright) as the mid-day sun."

Vaisampayana continued, "Pandu's son, the king of the Kuru tribe, having observed that the great saint was willing to speak, questioned him with a view to suggesting topics to speak upon, saying, 'You who are ancient (in years), know the deeds of gods and demons, and illustrious saints, and of all the royal ones. We consider you as worthy of being worshipped and honoured; and we have long yearned after your company. And here is this son of Devaki, Krishna, who has come to us on a visit. Verily, when I look at myself, fallen away from happiness, and when I contemplate the sons of Dhritarashtra, of evil life, flourishing in every way, the idea arises in me that it is *man* who does all acts, good or bad, and that it is *he* that enjoys the fruit the acts bring forth. How then is god the agent? And, O best of those that are proficient in the knowledge of God, how is it that men's actions follow them? Is it in this world? Or is it in some subsequent existence? And, O best of righteous men among the twice-born, in what way is an embodied animated being joined by his good and evil deeds that seek him out? Is it after death? Or is it in this world? And, O descendant of Bhrigu, is what we experience in this world the result of the acts of this very life? Or will the acts of this life bear fruit in the world to come? And where do the actions of an animated being who is dead find their resting place?'

"Markandeya said, 'O best of those that can speak, this question befits thee, and is just what it should be. Thou knowest all that there is to know. But thou art asking this question, simply for the sake of form. Here I shall answer thee: listen to me with an attentive mind, as to how in this world and in that to come, a man experienceth happiness and misery. The lord of born beings, himself sprung first of all, created, for all embodied beings, bodies which were stainless, pure, and obedient to virtuous impulses, O wisest of the descendants of Kuru! The ancient men had all their desires fulfilled, were given to praiseworthy courses of life, were speakers of truth, godly and pure. All were equal to the gods, could ascend to the sky at their pleasure, and could come back again; and all went about at their pleasure. And they had their death and their life also under their own control; and they had few sufferings; had no fear; and had their wishes fulfilled; and they were free from trouble; could visit the gods and the magnanimous saints; knew by heart all righteous rules; were self-controlled and free from envy. And they lived many thousand years; and had many thousand sons. Then in course of time they came to be restricted to walking solely on the surface of the earth, overpowered by lust and wrath, dependent for subsistence upon falsehood and trick, overwhelmed by greed and senselessness. Then those wicked men, when disembodied, on account of their unrighteous and unblessed deeds, went to hell in a crooked way. Again and again, they were grilled, and, again and again they began to drag their miserable existence in this wonderful world. And their desires were unfulfilled, the objects unaccomplished, and their knowledge became unavailing. And their senses were paralysed and they became apprehensive of everything and the cause of other people's sufferings. And they were generally marked by wicked deeds, and born in low families; they became wicked and afflicted with diseases, and the terror of others. And they became short-lived and sinful and they reaped the fruit of their terrible deeds. And coveting everything, they became godless and indifferent in mind, O son of Kunti! The destiny of every creature after death is determined by his acts in this world. Thou hast asked me where this treasure of acts of the sage and the ignorant remain, and where they enjoy the fruit of their good and evil deeds! Do thou listen to the regulations on this subject! Man with his subtle original body created by God lays up a great store of virtue and vice. After death he quits his frail (outer) body and is immediately born again in another order of beings. He never remains non-existent for a single moment. In his new life his actions follow him invariably as shadow and, fructifying, makes his destiny happy or miserable. The wise man, by his spiritual insight, knows all creatures to be bound to an immutable destiny by the destroyer and incapable of resisting the fruition of his actions in good or evil fortune. This, O Yudhishthira, is the doom of all creatures steeped in spiritual ignorance. Do thou now hear of the perfect way attained by men of high spiritual perception! Such men are of high ascetic virtue and are versed in all profane and holy writ, diligent in performing their religious obligations and devoted to truth. And they pay due homage to their preceptors and superiors and practise Yoga, are forgiving, continent and energetic and pious and are generally endowed with every virtue. By the conquest of the passions, they are subdued in mind; by practising *yoga* they become free from disease, fear and sorrow; they are not troubled (in mind). In course of birth, mature or immature, or while ensconced in the womb, in every condition, they with spiritual eyes recognize the relation of their soul to the supreme Spirit. Those great-minded *Rishis* of positive and intuitive knowledge passing through this arena of actions, return again to the abode of the celestials. Men, O king, attain what they have in consequence of the grace of the gods of Destiny or of their own actions. Do thou not think otherwise. O Yudhishthira, I regard that as the highest good which is regarded so in this world. Some attain happiness in this world, but not in the next; others do so in the next, but not in this. Some, again, attain happiness in this as well as in the next world; and others neither here nor in the next world. Those that have immense wealth, shine every day with well-decorated persons. O slayer of mighty foes, being addicted to carnal pleasures, they enjoy happiness only in this world, but not in the next. But those who are engaged in spiritual meditations and the study of the Vedas, who are diligent in asceticism, and who impair the vigour of their bodies by performing their duties, who have subdued their passions, and who refrain from killing any animated being, those men, O slayer of thy enemies, attain happiness in the next world, but not in this! Those who first live a pious life, and virtuously acquire wealth in due time and then marry and perform sacrifices, attain bliss both in this and the next world. Those foolish men again who do not acquire knowledge, nor are engaged in asceticism or charity or increasing their species, or in encompassing the pleasures and enjoyments of this world, attain bliss neither in this nor in the next world. But all of you are proficient in knowledge and possessed of great power and strength and celestial vigour. For the extermination (of the wicked) and for serving the purposes of the gods, ye have come from the other world and have taken your birth in this! Ye, who are so valiant, and engaged in asceticism, self-restraining exercises, and religious ordinances, and fond of exertion, after having performed great deeds and gratified the gods and *Rishis* and the *Pitris*, ye will at last in due course attain by your own acts the supreme region—the abode of all virtuous men! O ornament of Kuru's race, may no doubts cross thy mind on account of these thy sufferings, for this affliction is for thy good!'"

SECTION CLXXXIII

Vaisampayana continued,—"The sons of Pandu said to the high-souled Markandeya, 'We long to hear of the greatness of the *Brahmanas*. Do thou tell us of it!' Thus asked, the revered Markandeya, of austere virtue and high spiritual energy, and proficient in all departments of knowledge, replied, 'A strong-limbed, handsome young prince of the race of the Haihayas, a conqueror of hostile cities, (once) went out hunting. And (while) roaming in the wilderness of big trees and thickets of grass, he saw, at no great distance from him, a *Muni* with the skin of a black antelope for his upper garment, and killed him for a deer. Pained at what he had done, and his senses paralysed with grief, he repaired to the presence of the more distinguished of the *Haihaya* chiefs. The lotus-eyed prince related to them the particulars. On hearing the account, O my son, and beholding the body of the *Muni* who had subsisted on fruits and roots, they were sorely afflicted in mind. And they all set out enquiring here and there as they proceeded, as to whose son the *Muni* might be. And they soon after reached the hermitage of Arishtanemi, son of Kasyapa. And saluting that great *Muni*, so constant in austerity, they all remained standing, while the *Muni*, on his part, busied himself about their reception. And they said unto the illustrious *Muni*, "By a freak of destiny, we have ceased to merit thy welcome: indeed, we have killed a Brahmana!" And the regenerate *Rishi* said to them, "How hath a Brahmana come to be killed by you, and say where may be he? Do ye all witness the power of my ascetic practices!" And they, having related everything to him as it had happened went back, but found not the body of the dead *Rishi* on the spot (where they had left it). And having searched for him, they returned, ashamed and bereft of all perception, as in a dream. And then, O thou conqueror of hostile cities, the *Muni* Tarkshya, addressed them, saying, "Ye princes, can this be the Brahmana of your killing? This Brahmana, endowed with occult gifts from spiritual exercises, is, indeed, my son!" Seeing that *Rishi*, O lord of the earth, they were struck with bewilderment. And they said, "What a marvel! How hath the dead come to life again? Is it the power of his austere virtue by which he hath revived again? We long to hear this, O Brahmana, if, indeed, it can be divulged?" To them, he replied, "Death, O lords of men, hath no power over us! I shall tell ye the reason briefly and intelligibly. We perform our own sacred duties; therefore, have we no fear of death; we speak well of *Brahmanas* but never think any ill of them; therefore hath death no terror for us. Entertaining our guests with food and drink, and our dependants with plenty of food, we ourselves (then) partake of what is left; therefore we are not afraid of death. We are peaceful and austere and charitable and forbearing and fond of visiting sacred shrines, and we live in sacred places; therefore we have no fear of death. And we live in places inhabited by men who have great spiritual power; therefore hath death no terror for us. I have briefly told ye all! Return ye now all together, cured of all worldly vanity. Ye have no fear of sin!" Saying *amen*, O foremost scion of Bharata's race, and saluting the great *Muni*, all those princes joyously returned to their country.'"

SECTION CLXXXIV

"Markandeya continued, 'Do ye again hear from me the glory of the *Brahmanas*! It is said that a royal sage of the name of *Vainya* was once engaged in performing the horse-sacrifice and that Atri desired to go to him for alms. But Atri subsequently gave up his desire of wealth, from religious scruples. After much thought he, of great power, became desirous of living in the woods, and, calling his wife and sons together, addressed them thus, "Let us attain the highly tranquil and complete fruition of our desires. May it, therefore, be agreeable to you to repair quickly to the forest for a life of great merit." His wife, arguing from motives of virtue also then said to him, "Hie thee to the illustrious prince Vainya, and beg of him vast riches! Asked by thee, that royal sage, engaged in sacrifice will give thee wealth. Having gone there, O regenerate *Rishi*, and received from him vast wealth, thou canst distribute it among thy sons and servants and then thou canst go whithersoever thou pleasest. This, indeed, is the higher virtue as instanced by men conversant with religion." Atri replied, "I am informed, O virtuous one, by the high-souled Gautama, that Vainya is a pious prince, devoted to the cause of truth; but there are *Brahmanas* (about his persons) who are jealous of me; and as Gautama hath told me this, I do not venture to go there, for (while) there, if I were to advise what is good and calculated to secure piety and the fulfilment of one's desires, they would contradict me with words unproductive of any good. But I approve of any counsel and will go there; Vainya will give me kine and hoards of riches."'

"Markandeya continued, 'So saying, he, of great ascetic merit, hastened to Vainya's sacrifice and reaching the sacrificial altar and making his obeisance to the king and praising him with well-meaning speeches, he spoke these words, "Blessed art thou, O king! Ruling over the earth, thou art the foremost of sovereigns! The *Munis* praise thee, and besides thee there is none so versed in religious lore!" To him the *Rishi* Gautama, of great ascetic merit, then indignantly replied saying, "Atri, do not repeat this nonsense. (It seems) thou art not in thy proper senses. In this world of ours, Mahendra the lord of all created beings (alone) is the foremost of all sovereigns!" Then,

O, great prince, Atri said to Gautama, "As Indra, the lord of all creatures, ruleth over our destinies, so doth this king! Thou art mistaken. It is thou who hast lost thine senses from want of spiritual perception!" Gautama replied, "I know I am not mistaken; it is thou who art labouring under a misconception in this matter. To secure the king's countenance, thou art flattering him in (this) assembly of the people. Thou dost not know what the highest virtue, nor dost thou feel the need for it. Thou art like a child steeped in ignorance, for what then hast thou become (so) old in years?"'

"Markandeya continued, 'While those two men were thus disputing in the presence of the *Munis*, who were engaged in Vainya's sacrifice the latter enquired, "What is the matter with them, that maketh them talk so vociferously?" Then the very pious Kasyapa learned in all religious lore, approaching the disputants asked them what was the matter. And then Gautama, addressing that assembly of great *Munis* said, "Listen, O great *Brahmanas*, to the point in dispute between us. Atri hath said that Vainya is the ruler of our destinies; great is our doubt on this point."'

"Markandeya continued, 'On hearing this, the great-mind *Munis* went instantly to Sanatkumara who was well versed in religion to clear their doubt. And then he of great ascetic merit, having heard the particulars from them addressed them these words full of religious meaning. And Sanatkumara said, "As fire assisted by the wind burneth down forests, so a Brahmana's energy in union with a Kshatriya's or a Kshatriya's joined with a Brahmana's destroyeth all enemies. The sovereign is the distinguished giver of laws and the protector of his subjects. He is (a protector of created beings) like Indra, (a propounder of morals) like Sukra, (a counsellor) like Vrihaspati and (hence he is also called) the ruler of men's destinies. Who does not think it proper to worship the individual of whom such terms as 'preserver of created beings,' 'royal,' 'emperor,' 'Kshatriya' (or saviour of the earth), 'lord of earth,' 'ruler of men,' are applied in praise? The king is (also) styled the prime cause (of social order, as being the promulgator of laws), 'the virtuous in wars,' (and therefore, preserver after peace), 'the watchman,' 'the contented,' 'the lord,' 'the guide to salvation,' 'the easily victorious,' 'the Vishnu like,' 'of effective wrath,' 'the winner of battles' and 'the cherisher of the true religion.' The *Rishis*, fearful of sin, entrusted (the temporal) power to the Kshatriyas. As among the gods in heaven the Sun dispelleth darkness by his effulgence, so doth the king completely root out sin from this earth. Therefore is the king's greatness deduced from the evidences of the sacred books, and we are bound to pronounce for that side which hath spoken in favour of the king."'

"Markandeya continued, 'Then that illustrious prince, highly pleased with the victorious party, joyfully said to Atri, who had praised him erewhile, "O regenerate *Rishi*, thou hast made and styled me the greatest and most excellent of men here, and compared me to the gods; therefore, shall I give thee vast and various sorts of wealth. My impression is that thou art omniscient. I give thee, O well-dressed and well-adorned one, a hundred millions of gold coins and also ten *bharas* of gold." Then Atri, of high austere virtues and great spiritual powers, thus welcomed (by the king), accepted all the gifts without any breach of propriety, and returned home. And then giving his wealth to his sons and subduing his self, he cheerfully repaired to the forest with the object of performing penances.'"

SECTION CLXXXV

"Markandeya continued, 'O thou conqueror of hostile cities, in this connection Saraswati too, when interrogated by that intelligent *Muni* Tarkshya, had said (this). Do thou listen to her words! Tarkshya had asked, saying, "Excellent lady, what is the best thing for a man to do here below, and how must he act so that he may not deviate from (the path of) virtue. Tell me all this, O beautiful lady, so that instructed by thee, I may not fall away from the path of virtue! When and how must one offer oblations to the (sacred) fire and when must he worship so that virtue may not be compromised? Tell me all this, O excellent lady, so that I may live without any passions, craving, or desire, in this world."'

"Markandeya continued, 'Thus questioned by that cheerful *Muni* and seeing him eager to learn and endued with high intelligence, Saraswati addressed these pious and beneficial words to the Brahmana, Tarkshya.'

"'Saraswati said, "He who is engaged in the study of the *Vedas*, and with sanctity and equanimity perceives the supreme Godhead in his proper sphere, ascends the celestial regions and attains supreme beatitude with the Immortals. Many large, beautiful, pellucid and sacred lakes are there, abounding with fish, flowers, and golden lilies. They are like shrines and their very sight is calculated to assuage grief. Pious men, distinctively worshipped by virtuous well-adorned golden-complexioned *Apsaras*, dwell in contentment on the shores of those lakes. He who giveth cows (to Brahmanas) attaineth the highest regions; by giving bullocks he reacheth the solar regions, by giving clothes he getteth to the lunar world, and by giving gold he attaineth to the state of the Immortals. He who giveth a beautiful cow with a fine calf, and which is easily milked and which doth not run away, is (destined) to live for as many years in the celestial regions as there are hairs on the body of that animal. He who giveth a fine, strong, powerful, young bullock, capable of drawing the plough and bearing burdens, reacheth the regions attained by men who give ten cows. When a man bestoweth a well-caparisoned *kapila* cow with a brazen milk-pail and with money given afterwards, that cow becoming, by its own distinguished qualities, a giver of everything reacheth the side of the man who gave her away. He who giveth away cows, reapeth innumerable fruits of his action, measured by the hairs on the body of that animal. He also saveth (from perdition) in the next world his sons and grandsons and ancestors to the seventh generation. He who presenteth to a Brahmana, sesamum made up in the form of a cow, having horns made of gold, with money besides, and a brazen milk-pail, subsequently attaineth easily to the regions of the *Vasus*. By his own acts man descends into the darksome lower regions, infested by evil spirits (of his own passions) like a ship tossed by the storm in the high seas; but the gift of kine to Brahmanas saves him in the next world. He who giveth his daughter in marriage, in the *Brahma* form, who bestoweth gifts of land on Brahmanas and who duly maketh other presents, attaineth to the regions of Purandara. O Tarkshya, the virtuous man who is constant in presenting oblations to the sacred fire for seven years, sanctifieth by his own action seven generations up and down."

"'Tarkshya said, "O beautiful lady, explain to me who ask thee, the rules for the maintenance of the sacred fire as inculcated in the *Vedas*. I shall now learn from thee the time-honoured rules for perpetually keeping up the sacred fire."'"

SECTION CLXXXVI

"Then Yudhishthira, the son of Pandu, said to the Brahmana, Markandeya, 'Do thou now narrate the history of Vaivaswata Manu.'

"Markandeya replied, 'O king, O foremost of men, there was a powerful and great *Rishi* of the name of Manu. He was the son of Vivaswan and was equal unto *Brahma* in glory. And he far excelled his father and grandfather in strength, in power, in fortune, as also in religious austerities. And standing on one leg and with uplifted hand, that lord of men did severe penance in the jujube forest called Visala. And there with head downwards and with steadfast eyes he practised the rigid and severe penance for ten thousand years. And one day, whilst he was practising austerities there with wet clothes on and matted hair on head, a fish approaching the banks of the Chirini, addressed him thus, "Worshipful sir, I am a helpless little fish, I am afraid of the large ones; therefore, do thou, O great devotee, think it worth thy while to protect me from them; especially as this fixed custom is well established amongst us that the strong fish always preys upon the weak ones. Therefore do thou think it fit to save me from being drowned in this sea of terrors! I shall requite thee for thy good offices." On hearing these words from the fish, Vaivaswata Manu was overpowered with pity and he took out the fish from the water with his own hands. And the fish which had a body glistening like the rays of the moon when taken out of the water was put back in an earthen water-vessel. And thus reared that fish O king, grew up in size and Manu tended it carefully like a child. And after a long while, it became so large in size, that there was no room for it in that vessel. And then seeing Manu (one day), it again addressed these words to him, "Worshipful sir, do thou appoint some better habitation for me." And then the adorable Manu, the conqueror of hostile cities, took it out of that vessel and carried it to a large tank and placed it there. And there again the fish grew for many a long year. And although the tank was two *yojanas* in length and one *yojana* in width, even there, O lotus-eyed son of Kunti and ruler of men, was no room for the fish to play about! And beholding Manu it said again, "O pious and adorable father, take me to the Ganga, the favourite spouse of the Ocean so that I may live there; or do as thou listest. O sinless one, as I have grown to this great bulk by thy favour I shall do thy bidding cheerfully." Thus asked the upright and continent and worshipful Manu took the fish to the river Ganga and he put it into the river with his own hands. And there, O conqueror of thy enemies, the fish again grew for some little time and then beholding Manu, it said again, "O lord, I am unable to move about in the Ganga on account of my great body; therefore, worshipful sir, do thou please take me quickly to the sea!" O son of Pritha, Manu then taking it out of the Ganga, carried it to the sea and consigned it there. And despite its great bulk, Manu transported it easily and its touch and smell were also pleasant to him. And when it was thrown into the sea by Manu, it said these words to him with a smile, "O adorable being, thou hast protected me with special care; do thou now listen to me as to what thou shouldst do in the fulness of time! O fortunate and worshipful sir, the dissolution of all this mobile and immobile world is nigh at hand. The time for the purging of this world is now ripe. Therefore do I now explain what is good for thee! The mobile and immobile divisions of the creation, those that have the power of locomotion, and those that have it not, of all these the terrible doom hath now approached. Thou shall build a strong massive ark and have it furnished with a long rope. On that must thou ascend, O great *Muni*, with the seven *Rishis* and take with thee all the different seeds which were enumerated by regenerate Brahmanas in days of yore, and separately and carefully must thou preserve them therein. And whilst there, O beloved of the *Munis*, thou shall wait for me, and I shall appear to thee like a horned animal, and thus, O ascetic, shall thou recognise me! And I shall now depart, and thou shall act according to my instructions, for, without my assistance, thou canst not save thyself from that fearful flood." Then Manu said unto the fish, "I do not doubt all that thou hast said, O great one! Even so shall I act!" And giving instructions to each other, they both went away. And Manu then, O great and powerful king and conqueror of thy enemies, procured all the different seeds as directed by the fish, and set sail in an excellent vessel on the surging sea. And then, O lord of the earth, he bethought himself of that fish. And the fish too, O conqueror of thy enemies and foremost scion of Bharata's race, knowing his mind, appeared there with horns on his head, And then, O tiger among men, beholding in the ocean that horned fish emerging like a rock in the form of which he had been before appraised, he lowered the ropy noose on its head. And fastened by the noose, the fish, O king and conqueror of hostile cities, towed the ark with great force through the salt waters. And it conveyed them in that vessel on the roaring and billow beaten sea. And, O conqueror of thy enemies and hostile cities, tossed by the tempest on the great ocean, the vessel reeled about like a drunken harlot. And neither land nor the four cardinal points of the compass, could be distinguished. And there was water every where and the waters covered the heaven and the firmament also. And, O bull of Bharata's race, when the world was thus flooded, none but Manu, the seven *Rishis* and the fish could be seen. And, O king, the fish diligently dragged the boat through the flood for many a long year and then, O descendant of Kuru and ornament of Bharata's race, it towed the vessel towards the highest peak of the Himavat. And, O Bharata, the fish then told those on the vessel to tie it to the peak of the Himavat. And hearing the words of the fish they immediately tied the boat on that peak of the mountain and, O son of Kunti and ornament of Bharata's race, know that that high peak of the Himavat is still called by the name of *Naubandhana* (the harbour). Then the fish addressing the associated *Rishis* told them these words, "I am Brahma, the Lord of all creatures; there is none greater than myself. Assuming the shape of a fish, I have saved you from this cataclysm. Manu will create (again) all beings—gods, *Asuras* and men, all those divisions of creation which have the power of locomotion and which have it not. By practicing severe austerities he will acquire this power, and with my blessing, illusion will have no power over him."

"'So saying the fish vanished instantly. And Vaivaswata Manu himself became desirous of creating the world. In this work of creation illusion overtook him and he, therefore, practised great asceticism. And endowed with ascetic merit, Manu, O ornament of Bharata's race, again set about his work of creating all beings in proper and exact order. This story which I have narrated to thee and the hearing of which destroyeth all sin, is celebrated as the Legend of the Fish. And the man who listeneth every day to this primeval history of Manu, attaineth happiness and all other objects of desire and goeth to heaven.'"

SECTION CLXXXVII

"Then the virtuous king Yudhishthira in all humility again enquired of the illustrious Markandeya, saying, 'O great *Muni*, thou hast seen many thousands of ages pass away. In this world there is none so longlived as thou! O best of those that have attained the knowledge of Supreme Spirit, there is none equal to thee in years except the great-minded *Brahma* living in the most exalted place. Thou, O Brahmana, worshippest *Brahma* at the time of the great dissolution of the universe, when this world is without sky and without the gods and *Danavas*. And when that cataclysm ceaseth and the Grandsire awaketh, thou alone, O regenerate *Rishi*, beholdest *Brahma* duly re-create the four orders of beings after having filled the cardinal points with air and consigned the waters to their proper place. Thou, O great Brahmana, hast worshipped in his presence the great Lord and Grandsire of all creatures with soul rapt in meditation and entirely swallowed up in Him! And, O Brahmana, thou hast many a time witnessed with thy eyes, the primeval acts of creation, and, plunged in severe ascetic austerities, thou hast also surpassed the *Prajapatis* themselves! Thou art esteemed as one who is nearest to Narayana, in the next world. Many a time in days of yore hast thou beheld the Supreme Creator of the universe with eyes of spiritual abstraction and renunciation, having first opened thy pure and lotus-like heart—the only place where the multiform Vishnu of universal knowledge may be seen! It is for this, O learned *Rishi*, by the grace of God neither all-destroying Death, nor dotage that causeth the decay of the body, hath any power over thee! When neither the sun, nor the moon, nor fire, nor earth, nor air, nor sky remains, when all the world being destroyed looketh like one vast ocean, when the *Gods* and *Asuras* and the great *Uragas* are annihilated, and when the great-minded *Brahma*, the Lord of all creatures, taking his seat on a lotus flower, sleepeth there, then thou alone remainest to worship him! And, O best of Brahman as thou hast seen all this that occurred before, with thy own eyes. And thou alone hast witnessed many things by the senses, and never in all the worlds hath there been any thing unknown to thee! Therefore do I long to hear any discourse explaining the causes of things!'

"Markandeya replied, 'Indeed, I shall explain all, after having bowed down to that Self-existent, Primordial Being, who is eternal and undeteriorating and inconceivable, and who is at once vested with and divested of attributes. O tiger among men, this Janardana attired in yellow robes is the grand Mover and Creator of all, the Soul and Framer of all things, and the lord of all! He is also called the Great, the Incomprehensible, the Wonderful and the Immaculate. He is without beginning and without end, pervades all the world, is Unchangeable and Undeteriorating. He is the Creator of all, but is himself uncreate and is the Cause of all power. His knowledge is greater than that of all the gods together. O best of kings and pre-eminent of men, after the dissolution of the universe, all this wonderful creation again comes into life. Four thousand years have been said to constitute the *Krita Yuga*. Its dawn also, as well as its eve, hath been said to comprise four hundred years. The *Treta-Yuga* is said to comprise three thousand years, and its dawn, as well as its eve, is said to comprise three hundred years. The *Yuga* that comes next is called *Dwapara*, and it hath been computed to consist of two thousand years. Its dawn, as well as its eve, is said to comprise two hundred years. The next *Yuga*, called *Kali*, is said to comprise one thousand years and its dawn, as well as eve, is said to comprise one hundred years. Know, O king, that the duration of the dawn is the same as that of the eve of a *Yuga*. And after the *Kali Yuga* is over, the *Krita Yuga* comes again. A cycle of the *Yugas* thus comprised a period of twelve thousand years. A full thousand of such cycles would constitute a *day of Brahma*. O tiger among men, when all this universe is withdrawn and ensconced within its home—the Creator himself—that disappearance of all things is called by the learned to be Universal Destruction. O bull of the Bharata race, towards the end of the last mentioned period of one thousand years, *i.e.*, when the period wanted to complete a cycle is short, men generally become addicted to falsehood in speech. O son of Pritha, then sacrifices and gifts and vows, instead of being performed by principals are suffered to be performed by representatives! Brahmanas then perform acts that are reserved for the *Sudras*, and the *Sudras* betake themselves to the acquisition of wealth. Then Kshatriyas also betake themselves to the practice of religious acts. In the *Kali* age, the Brahmanas also abstain from sacrifices and the study of the Vedas, are divested of their staff and deer-skin, and in respect of food become omnivorous. And, O son, the Brahmanas in that age also abstain from prayers and meditation while the Sudras betake themselves to these! The course of the world looketh contrary, and indeed, these are the signs that foreshadow the Universal Destruction. And, O lord of men, numerous *Mleccha* kings then rule over the earth! And those sinful monarchs, addicted to false speech, govern their subjects on principles that are false. The *Andhhas*, the *Sakas*, the *Pulindas*, the *Yavanas*, the *Kamvojas*, the *Valhikas* and the *Abhiras*, then become, O best of men, possessed of bravery and the sovereignty of the earth. This, O tiger among men, becometh the state of the world during the eve, O Bharata, of the *Kali* age! Not a single Brahmana then adhereth to the duties of his order. And the Kshatriyas and the Vaisyas also, O monarch, follow practices contrary to those that are proper for their own orders. And men become short-lived, weak in strength, energy, and prowess; and endued with small might and diminutive bodies, they become scarcely truthful in speech. And the human population dwindles away over large tracts of country, and the regions of the earth, North and South, and East and West, become crowded with animals and beasts of prey. And during this period, they also that utter *Brahma*, do so in vain. The *Sudras* address *Brahmanas*, saying, *Bho*, while the Brahmanas address Sudras, saying *Respected Sir*. And, O tiger among men, at the end of the *Yuga*, animals increase enormously. And, O king, odours and perfumes do not then become so agreeable to our sense of scent, and, O tiger among men, the very tastes of things do not then so well accord with our organs of taste as at other periods! And, O king, women then become mothers of numerous progeny, endued with low statures, and destitute of good behaviour and good manners. And they also make their very mouths serve the purposes of the organ of procreation. And famine ravages the habitations of men, and the highways are infested by women of ill fame, while females in general, O king, become at such periods hostile to their lords and destitute of modesty! And, O king, the very kine at such periods yield little milk, while the trees, sat over with swarms of crows, do not produce many flowers and fruits. And, O lord of the earth, regenerate classes, tainted with the sin of slaying Brahmanas, accept gifts from monarchs that are addicted to falsehood in speech. And filled with covetousness and ignorance, and bearing on their persons the outward symbols of religion, they set out on eleemosynary rounds, afflicting the people of the Earth. And people leading domestic lives, afraid of the burden of taxes, become deceivers, while Brahmanas, falsely assuming the garb of ascetics, earn wealth by trade, with nails and hair unpared and uncut. And, O tiger among men, many of the twice-born classes become, from avarice of wealth, religious mendicants of the *Brahmacharin* order. And, O monarch, men at such periods behave contrary to the *modes* of life to which they betake themselves, and addicted to intoxicating drinks and capable of violating the beds of their preceptors, their desires are all of this world, pursuing matters ministering to the flesh and the blood. And O tiger among men, at such period the asylums of ascetics become full of sinful and audacious wretches ever applauding lives of dependence. And the illustrious chastiser of Paka never showers rain according to the seasons and the seeds also that are scattered on earth, do not, O Bharata, all sprout forth. And men, unholy in deed and thought, take pleasure in envy and malice. And, O sinless one, the earth then becometh full of sin and immorality. And, O lord of the earth, he that becometh virtuous at such periods doth not live long. Indeed, the earth becometh reft of virtue in every shape. And, O tiger among men, the merchants and traders then full of guile, sell large quantities of articles with false weights and measures. And they that are virtuous do not prosper; while they that are sinful proper exceedingly. And virtue loseth her strength while sin becometh all powerful. And men that are devoted to virtue become poor and short-lived; while they that are sinful become long-lived and win prosperity. And in such times, people behave sinfully even in places of public amusements in cities and towns. And men always seek the accomplishment of their ends by means that are sinful. And having earned fortunes that are really small they become intoxicated with the pride of wealth. And O monarch, many men at such periods strive to rob the wealth that hath from trust been deposited with them in secrecy. And wedded to sinful practices, they shamelessly declare—*there is nothing in deposit*. And beasts of prey and other animals and fowl may be seen to lie down in places of public amusement in cities and towns, as well as in sacred edifices. And, O king girls of seven or eight years of age do then conceive, while boys of ten or twelve years beget offspring. And in their sixteenth year, men are overtaken with decrepitude and decay and the period of life itself is soon outrun. And O king, when men become so short-lived, more youths act like the aged; while all that is observable in youth may be noticed in the old. And women given to impropriety of conduct and marked by evil manners, deceive even the best of husbands and forget themselves with menials and slaves and even with animals. And O king, even women that are wives of heroes seek the companionship of other men and forget themselves with these during the life-time of their husbands.

"'O king, towards the end of those thousands of years constituting the four *Yugas* and when the lives of men become so short, a drought occurs extending for many years. And then, O lord of the earth, men and creatures endued with small strength and vitality, becoming hungry die by thousands. And then, O lord of men, seven blazing Suns, appearing in the firmament, drink up all the waters of the Earth that are in rivers or seas. And, O bull of the Bharata race, then also everything of the nature of wood and grass that is wet to dry, is consumed and reduced to ashes. And then, O Bharata, the fire called *Samvartaka* impelled by the winds appeareth on the earth that hath already been dried to cinders by the seven Suns. And then that fire, penetrating through the Earth and making its appearance, in the nether regions also, begetteth great terror in the hearts of the *gods*, the *Danavas* and the *Yakshas*. And, O lord of the earth, consuming the nether regions as also everything upon this Earth that fire destroyeth all things in a moment. And that fire called *Samvartaka* aided by that inauspicious wind, consumeth this world extending for hundreds and thousands of *yojanas*. And that lord of all things, that fire, blazing forth in effulgence consumeth this universe with gods and *Asuras* and *Gandharvas* and *Yakshas* and *Snakes* and *Rakshasas*. And there rise in the sky deep masses of clouds, looking like herds of elephants and decked with wreaths of lightning that are wonderful to behold. And some of those clouds are of the hue of the blue lotus; and some are of the hue of the water-lily; and some resemble in tint the filaments of the lotus and some are purple and some are yellow as turmeric and some of the hue of the crows' egg. And some are bright as the petals of the lotus and some red as vermillion. And some resemble palatial cities in shape and some herds of elephants. And some are of the form of lizards and some of crocodiles and sharks. And, O king, the clouds that gather in the sky on the occasion are terrible to behold and wreathed with lightnings, roar frightfully. And those vapoury masses, charged with rain, soon cover the entire welkin. And, O king, those masses of vapour then flood with water the whole earth with her mountains and forests and mines. And, O bull among men, urged by the Supreme Lord those clouds roaring frightfully, soon flood over the entire surface of the earth. And pouring in a great quantity of water and filling the whole earth, they quench that terrible inauspicious fire (of which I have already spoken to thee). And urged by the illustrious Lord those clouds filling the earth with their downpour shower incessantly for twelve years. And then, O Bharata, the Ocean oversteps his continents, the mountains sunder in fragments, and the Earth sinks under the increasing flood. And then moved on a sudden by the impetus of the wind, those clouds wander along the entire expanse of the firmament and disappear from the view. And then, O ruler of men, the Self-create Lord—the first Cause of everything—having his abode in the lotus, drinketh those terrible winds and goeth to sleep, O Bharata!

"'And then when the universe become one dead expanse of water, when all mobile and immobile creatures have been destroyed, when the *gods* and the *Asuras* cease to be, when the *Yakshas* and the *Rakshasas* are no more, when man is not, when trees and beasts of prey have disappeared, when the firmament itself has ceased to exist, I alone, O lord of the earth, wander in affliction. And, O best of kings, wandering over that dreadful expanse of water, my heart becometh afflicted in consequence of my not beholding any creature! And, O king, wandering without cessation, through that flood, I become fatigued, but I obtain no resting place! And some time after I behold in that expanse of accumulated waters a vast and wide-extending banian tree, O lord of earth! And I then behold, O Bharata, seated on a conch, O king, overlaid with a celestial bed and attached to a far-extended bough of that banian, a boy, O great king, of face fair as the lotus or the moon, and of eyes, O ruler of men, large as petals of a full blown lotus! And at this sight, O lord of earth, wonder filled my heart. And I asked myself, "How doth this boy alone sit here when the world itself hath been destroyed?" And, O king, although I have full knowledge of the Past, the Present, and the Future, still I failed to learn anything of this by means of even ascetic meditation. Endued with the lustre of the *Atasi* flower, and decked with the mark of *Sreevatsa*, he seemed to me to be like the abode of *Lakshmi*, herself. And that boy, of eyes like the petals of the lotus, having the mark of *Sreevatsa*, and possessed of blazing effulgence, then addressed me in words highly pleasant to the ear, saying, "O sire, I know thee to be fatigued and desirous of rest. O Markandeya of Bhrigu's race, rest thou here as long as thou wishest. O best of *Munis*, entering within my body, rest thou there. That hath been the abode assigned to thee by me. I have been pleased with thee." Thus addressed by that boy, a sense of total disregard possessed me in respect both of my long life and state of manhood. Then that boy suddenly opened his mouth, and as fate would have it, I entered his mouth deprived of the power of motion. But O king, having suddenly entered into the stomach of that boy, I behold there the whole earth teeming with cities and kingdoms. And, O best of men, while wandering through the stomach of that illustrious one, I behold the Ganga, the Satudru, the Sita, the Yamuna, and the Kausiki; the Charmanwati, the Vetravati; the Chandrabhaga, the Saraswati, the Sindhu, the Vipasa, and the Godavari; the Vaswokasara, the Nalini and the Narmada; the Tamra, and the Venna also of delightful current and sacred waters; the Suvenna, the Krishna-venna, the Irama, and the Mahanadi; the Vitasti, O great king, and that large river, the Cavery; the one also, O tiger among men, the Visalya, and the Kimpuna also. I beheld all these and many other rivers that are on the earth! And, O slayer of foes, I also beheld there the ocean inhabited by alligators and sharks, that mine of gems, that excellent abode of waters. And I beheld there the firmament also, decked with the Sun and the Moon, blazing with effulgence, and possessed of lustre of fire of the Sun. And I beheld there, O king, the earth also, graced with woods and forests. And, O monarch, I beheld there many Brahmanas also, engaged in various sacrifices; and the Kshatriyas engaged in doing good to all the orders; and the Vaisyas employed in pursuits in agriculture; and the Sudras devoted to the service of the regenerate classes. And, O king, while wandering through the stomach of that high-souled one, I also beheld the Himavat and the mountains of Hemakuta. And I also saw Nishada, and the mountains of Sweta abounding in silver. And, O king, I saw there the mountain Gandhamadana, and, O tiger among men, also Mandara and the huge mountains of Nila. And, O great king, I saw there the golden mountains of Meru and also Mahendra and those excellent mountains called the Vindhyas. And I beheld there the mountains of Malaya and of Paripatra also. These and many other mountains that are on earth were all seen by me in his stomach. And all these were decked with jewels and gems. And, O monarch, while wandering through his stomach, I also beheld lions and tigers and boars and, indeed, all other animals that are on earth, O great king! O tiger among men, having entered his stomach, as I wandered around, I also beheld the whole tribe of the *gods* with their chief Sakra, the *Sadhyas*, the *Rudras*, the *Adityas*, the *Guhyakas*, the *Pitris*, the *Snakes* and the *Nagas*, the feathery tribes, the *Vasus*, the *Aswins*, the *Gandharvas*, the *Apsaras*, the *Yakshas*, the *Rishis*, the hordes of the *Daityas* and the *Danavas*, and the *Nagas* also, O king, and the sons of *Singhika* and all the other enemies of the gods; indeed what else of mobile and immobile creatures may be seen on earth, were all seen by me, O monarch, within the stomach of that high-souled one. And, O lord, living upon fruits I dwelt within his body for many centuries wandering over the entire universe that is there. Never did I yet, O king, behold the limits of his body. And when, O lord of earth, I failed to measure the limits of that high-souled one's body, even though I wandered within him continuously in great anxiety of mind, I then, in thought and deed sought the protection of that boon-giving and pre-eminent Deity, duly acknowledging his superiority. And when I had done this, O king, I was suddenly projected (from within his body) through that high-souled one's open mouth by means, O chief of men, of a gust of wind. And, O king, I then beheld seated on the branch of that very banian that same Being of immeasurable energy, in the form of a boy with the mark of *Sreevatsa* (on his breast) having, O tiger among men, swallowed up the whole universe. And that boy of blazing effulgence and bearing the mark of *Sreevatsa* and attired in yellow robes, gratified with me, smilingly addressed me, saying, "O Markandeya, O best of *Munis*, having dwelt for some time within my body, thou hast been fatigued! I shall however speak unto thee." And as he said this to me, at that very moment I acquired a new sight, so to speak, in consequence of which I beheld myself to be possessed of true knowledge and emancipated from the illusions of the world. And, O child, having witnessed the inexhaustible power of that Being of immeasurable energy, I then worshipped his revered and well-shaped feet with soles bright as burnished copper and well-decked with toes of mild red hue, having placed them carefully on my head and joining my palms in humility and approaching him with reverence. I beheld that Divine Being who is the soul of all things and whose eyes are like the petals of the lotus. And having bowed unto him with joined hands I addressed him saying, "I wish to know thee, O Divine Being, as also this high and wonderful illusion of thine! O illustrious one, having entered into thy body through thy mouth, I have beheld the entire universe in thy stomach! O Divine Being, the gods, the *Danavas* and the *Rakshasas*, the *Yakshas*, the *Gandharvas*, and the *Nagas*, indeed, the whole universe mobile and immobile, are all within thy body! And though I have ceaselessly wandered through thy body at a quick pace, through thy grace, O God, my memory faileth me not. And, O great lord, I have come out of thy body at thy desire but not of mine! O thou of eyes like lotus leaves, I desire to know thee who art free from all faults! Why dost thou stay here in the form of a boy having swallowed up the entire universe? It behoveth thee to explain all this to me. Why, O sinless one, is the entire universe within thy body? How long also, O chastiser of foes, wilt thou stay here? Urged by a curiosity that is not improper for Brahmanas, I desire, O Lord of all the gods, to hear all this from thee, O thou of eyes like lotus leaves, with every detail and exactly as it all happens, for all I have seen, O Lord, is wonderful and inconceivable!" And thus addressed by me, that deity of deities, of blazing effulgence and great beauty, that foremost of all speakers consoling me properly, spoke unto me these words.'"

SECTION CLXXXVIII

"Markandeya continued, 'The Deity then said, "O Brahmana, the gods even do not know me truly! As however, I have been gratified with thee, I will tell thee how I created the universe! O regenerate *Rishi*, thou art devoted to thy ancestors and hast also sought my protection! Thou hast also beheld me with thy eyes, and thy ascetic merit also is great! In ancient times I called the waters by the name of *Nara*; and because the waters have ever been my *ayana* or home, therefore have I been called *Narayana* (the *water-homed*). O best of regenerate ones, I am *Narayana*, the Source of all things, the Eternal, the Unchangeable. I am the Creator of all things, and the Destroyer also of all. I am Vishnu, I am Brahma and I am Sakra, the chief of the gods. I am king Vaisravana, and I am Yama, the lord of the deceased spirits. I am Siva, I am Soma, and I am Kasyapa the lord of the created things. And, O best of regenerate ones, I am he called *Dhatri*, and he also that is called *Vidhatri*, and I am Sacrifice embodied. Fire is my mouth, the earth my feet, and the Sun and the Moon are my eyes; the Heaven is the crown of my head, the firmament and the cardinal points are my ears; the waters are born of my sweat. Space with the cardinal points are my body, and the Air is my mind. I have performed many hundreds of sacrifices with gifts in profusion. I am always present in the sacrifices of the gods; and they that are cognisant of the *Vedas* and officiate therein, make their offerings to me. On earth the Kshatriya chiefs that rule over men, in performing their sacrifices from desire of obtaining heaven, and the Vaisyas also in performing theirs from desire of winning those happy regions, all worship me at such times and by those ceremonials. It is I who, assuming the form of Sesha support (on my head) this earth bounded by the four seas and decked by Meru and Mandara. And O regenerate one, it is I who, assuming the form of a boar, had raised in days of yore this earth sunk in water. And, O best of Brahmanas, it is I who, becoming the fire that issues out of the *Equine mouth*, drink up the waters (of the ocean) and create them again. In consequence of my energy from my mouth, my arms, my thighs, and my feet gradually sprang Brahmanas and Kshatriyas and Vaisyas and Sudras. It is from me that the *Rik*, the *Sama*, the *Yajus*, and the *Atharvan* Vedas spring, and it is in me that they all enter when the time cometh. Brahmanas devoted to asceticism, they that value Peace as the highest attribute, they that have their souls under complete control, they that are desirous of knowledge, they that are freed from lust and wrath and envy, they that are unwedded to things of the earth, they that have their sins completely washed away, they that are possessed of gentleness and virtue, and are divested of pride, they that have a full knowledge of the Soul, all worship me with profound meditation. I am the flame known as *Samvartaka*, I am the Wind called by that name, I am the Sun wearing that appellation, and I am the fire that hath that designation. And, O best of Brahmanas, those things that are seen in the firmament as stars, know them to be the pores of my skin. The ocean—those mines of gems and the four cardinal points, know, O Brahmana, are my robes, my bed, and my home. By me have they been distributed for serving the purposes of the gods. And, O best of men, know also that lust, wrath, joy, fear, and the over-clouding of the intellect, are all different forms of myself. And, O Brahmana, whatever is obtained by men by the practice of truth, charity, ascetic austerities, and peace and harmlessness towards all creatures, and such other handsome deeds, is obtained because of my arrangements. Governed by my ordinance, men wander within my body, their senses overwhelmed by me. They move not according to their will but as they are moved by me. Regenerate Brahmanas that have thoroughly studied the *Vedas*, that have tranquillity in their souls, they that have subdued their wrath, obtain a high reward by means of their numerous sacrifices. That reward, however, is unattainable by men that are wicked in their deeds, overwhelmed by covetousness, mean and disreputable with souls unblessed and impure. Therefore, must thou know, O Brahmana that this reward which is obtained by persons having their souls under control and which is unobtainable by the ignorant and the foolish,—this which is attainable by asceticism alone,—is productive of high merit. And, O best of men, at those times when virtue and morality decrease and sin and immorality increase, I create myself in new forms. And, O *Muni*, when fierce and malicious *Daityas* and *Rakshasas* that are incapable of being slain by even the foremost of the gods, are born on earth, I then take my birth in the families of virtuous men, and assuming human body restore tranquillity by exterminating all evils. Moved by my own *maya*, I create gods and men, and *Gandharvas* and *Rakshasas,* and all immobile things and then destroy them all myself (when the time cometh). For the preservation of rectitude and morality I assume a human form, and when the season for action cometh, I again assume forms that are inconceivable. In the *Krita* age I become white, in the *Treta* age I become yellow, in the *Dwapara* I have become red and in the *Kali* age I become dark in hue. In the *Kali* age, the proportion of immorality becometh three-fourths, (a fourth only being that of morality). And when the end of the *Yuga* cometh, assuming the fierce form of Death, alone I destroy all the three worlds with their mobile and immobile existences. With three steps, I cover the whole Universe; I am the Soul of the universe; I am the source of all happiness; I am the humbler of all pride; I am omnipresent; I am infinite; I am the Lord of the senses; and my prowess is great. O Brahmana, alone do I set a-going the wheel of Time; I am formless; I am the Destroyer of all creatures; and I am the cause of all efforts of all my creatures. O best of *Munis*, my soul completely pervadeth all my creatures, but, O foremost of all regenerate ones, no one knoweth me. It is me that the pious and the devoted worship in all the worlds. O regenerate one, whatever of pain thou hast felt within my stomach, know, O sinless one, that all that is for thy happiness and good fortune. And whatever of mobile and immobile objects thou hast seen in the world, everything hath been ordained by my Soul which is the Spring of all existence. The grandsire of all creatures is half my body; I am called Narayana, and I am bearer of the conch-shell, the discus and the mace. O regenerate *Rishi*, for a period measured by a thousand times the length of the *Yugas*, I who am the Universal Soul sleep overwhelming all creatures in insensibility. And, O best of regenerate *Rishis*, I stay here thus for all time, in the form of a boy though I am old, until Brahma waketh up. O foremost of Brahmanas, gratified with thee, I who am *Brahma* have repeatedly granted thee boons, O thou who art worshipped by regenerate *Rishis*! Beholding one vast expanse of water and seeing that all mobile and immobile creatures have been destroyed, thou wert afflicted with melancholy. I know this, and it is for this that I showed thee the universe (within my stomach). And while thou wert within my body, beholding the entire universe, thou wert filled with wonder and deprived of thy senses. O regenerate *Rishi*, it is for this that thou wert speedily brought out by me through my mouth. I have (now) told thee of that Soul which is incapable of being comprehended by the gods and the *Asuras*. And as long as that great ascetic, the holy Brahma, doth not awake, thou, O regenerate *Rishi*, canst happily and trustfully dwell here. And when that Grandsire of all creatures awaketh up, I will then, O best of Brahmanas, alone create all creatures endued with bodies, the firmament, the earth, light, the atmosphere, water, and indeed all else of mobile and immobile creatures (that thou mayst have seen) on the earth!"'

"Markandeya continued, 'Having said so unto me that wonderful Deity vanished, O son, from my sight! I then beheld this varied and wondrous creation start into life. O king, O thou foremost of the Bharata race, I witnessed all this, so wonderful, O thou foremost of all virtuous men, at the end of the *Yuga*! And the Deity, of eyes large as lotus leaves, seen by me, in days of yore is this tiger among men, this Janardana who hath become thy relative! It is in consequence of the boon granted to me by this one that memory doth not fail me, that the period of my life, O son of Kunti, is so long and death itself is under my control. This is that ancient and supreme Lord Hari of inconceivable soul who hath taken his birth as Krishna of the Vrishni race, and who endued with mighty arms, seemeth to sport in this world! This one is *Dhatri* and *Vidhatri*, the Destroyer of all the Eternal, the bearer of the *Sreevatsa* mark on his breast, the Lord of the lord of all creatures, the highest of the high, called also Govinda! Beholding this foremost of all gods, this ever-victorious Being, attired in yellow robes, this chief of the Vrishni race, my recollection cometh back to me! This Madhava is the father and mother of all creatures! Ye bulls of the Kuru race, seek ye the refuge of this Protector!'"

Vaisampayana continued, "Thus addressed, the sons of Pritha and those bulls among men—the twins, along with Draupadi, all bowed down unto Janardana. And that tiger among men deserving of every respect thus revered by the sons of Pandu, then consoled them all with words of great sweetness."

SECTION CLXXXIX

Vaisampayana said "Yudhishthira, the son of Kunti, once more asked the great *Muni* Markandeya about the future course of the government of the Earth.

"And Yudhishthira said, 'O thou foremost of all speakers, O *Muni* of Bhrigu's race, that which we have heard from thee about the destruction and re-birth of all things at the end of the *Yuga*, is, indeed, full of wonder! I am filled with curiosity, however, in respect of what may happen in the *Kali* age. When morality and virtue will be at an end, what will remain there! What will be the prowess of men in that age, what their food, and what their amusements? What will be the period of life at the end of the *Yuga*? What also is the limit, having attained which the *Krita* age will begin anew? Tell me all in detail, O *Muni*, for all that thou narratest is varied and delightful.'

"Thus addressed, that foremost of *Munis* began his discourse again, delighting that tiger of the Vrishni race and the sons of Pandu as well. And Markandeya said, 'Listen, O monarch, to all that hath been seen and heard by me, and to all, O king of kings, that hath been known to me by intuition from the grace of the God of gods! O bull of the Bharata race, listen to me as I narrate the future history of the world during the sinful age. O bull of the Bharata race, in the *Krita* age, everything was free from deceit and guile and avarice and covetousness; and morality like a bull was among men, with all the four legs complete. In the *Treta* age sin took away one of these legs and morality had three legs. In the *Dwapara*, sin and morality are mixed half and half; and accordingly morality is said to have two legs only. In the dark age (*of Kali*), O thou best of the Bharata race, morality mixed with three parts of sin liveth by the side of men. Accordingly morality then is said to wait on men, with only a fourth part of itself remaining. Know, O Yudhishthira, that the period of life, the energy, intellect and the physical strength of men decrease in every *Yuga*! O Pandava, the Brahmanas and Kshatriyas and Vaisyas and Sudras, (in the *Kali* age) will practise morality and virtue deceitfully and men in general will deceive their fellows by spreading the net of virtue. And men with false reputation of learning will, by their acts, cause Truth to be contracted and concealed. And in consequence of the shortness of their lives they will not be able to acquire much knowledge.

And in consequence of the littleness of their knowledge, they will have no wisdom. And for this, covetousness and avarice will overwhelm them all. And wedded to avarice and wrath and ignorance and lust men will entertain animosities towards one another, desiring to take one another's lives. And Brahmanas and Kshatriyas and Vaisyas with their virtue contracted and divested of asceticism and truth will all be reduced to an equality with the Sudras. And the lowest orders of men will rise to the position of the intermediate ones, and those in intermediate stations will, without doubt, descend to the level of the lowest ones. Even such, O Yudhishthira, will become the state of the world at the end of the *Yuga*. Of robes those will be regarded the best that are made of flax, and of grain the *Paspalum frumentacea* 5 will be regarded the best. Towards this period men will regard their wives as their (only) friends. And men will live on fish and milk, goats and sheep, for cows will be extinct. And towards that period, even they that are always observant of vows, will become covetous. And opposed to one another, men will, at such a time, seek one another's lives; and divested of *Yuga*, people will become atheists and thieves. And they will even dig the banks of streams with their spades and sow grains thereon. And even those places will prove barren for them at such a time. And those men who are devoted to ceremonial rites in honour of the deceased and of the gods, will be avaricious and will also appropriate and enjoy what belongs to others. The father will enjoy what belongs to the son; and the son, what belongs to the father. And those things will also be enjoyed by men in such times, the enjoyment of which hath been forbidden in the scriptures. And the Brahmanas, speaking disrespectfully of the Vedas, will not practise vows, and their understanding clouded by the science of disputation, they will no longer perform sacrifices and the *Homa*. And deceived by the false science of reasons, they will direct their hearts towards everything mean and low. And men will till low lands for cultivation and employ cows and calves that are one year old, in drawing the plough and carrying burthens. And sons having slain their sires, and sires having slain their sons will incur no opprobrium. And they will frequently save themselves from anxiety by such deeds, and even glory in them. And the whole world will be filled with *mleccha* behaviour and notions and ceremonies, and sacrifices will cease and joy will be nowhere and general rejoicing will disappear. And men will rob the possession of helpless persons, of those that are friendless and of wisdoms also. And, possessed of small energy and strength, without knowledge and given to avarice and folly and sinful practices men will accept with joy the gifts made by wicked people with words of contempt. And, O son of Kunti, the kings of the earth, with hearts wedded to sin without knowledge and always boastful of their wisdom, will challenge one another from desire of taking one another's life. And the Kshatriyas also towards the end of such a period will become the thorns of the earth. And filled with avarice and swelling with pride and vanity and, unable and unwilling to protect (their subjects), they will take pleasure in inflicting punishments only. And attacking and repeating their attacks upon the good and the honest, and feeling no pity for the latter, even when they will cry in grief, the Kshatriyas will, O Bharata, rob these of their wives and wealth. And no one will ask for a girl (for purposes of marriage) and no one will give away a girl (for such purposes), but the girls will themselves choose their lords, when the end of the *Yuga* comes. And the kings of the earth with souls steeped in ignorance, and discontented with what they have, will at such a time, rob their subjects by every means in their power. And without doubt the whole world will be *mlecchified*. 6 And when the end of the *Yuga* comes, the right hand will deceive the left; and the left, the right. And men with false reputation of learning will contract Truth and the old will betray the senselessness of the young, and the young will betray the dotage of the old. And cowards will have the reputation of bravery and the brave will be cheerless like cowards. And towards the end of the *Yuga* men will cease to trust one another. And full of avarice and folly the whole world will have but one kind of food. And sin will increase and prosper, while virtue will fade and cease to flourish. And Brahmanas and Kshatriyas and Vaisyas will disappear, leaving, O king, no remnants of their orders. And all men towards the end of the Yuga will become members of one common order, without distinction of any kind. And sires will not forgive sons, and sons will not forgive sires. And when the end approaches, wives will not wait upon and serve their husbands. And at such a time men will seek those countries where wheat and barley form the staple food. And, O monarch, both men and women will become perfectly free in their behaviour and will not tolerate one another's acts. And, O Yudhishthira, the whole world will be *mlecchified*. And men will cease to gratify the gods by offerings of *Sraddhas*. And no one will listen to the words of others and no one will be regarded as a preceptor by another. And, O ruler of men, intellectual darkness will envelop the whole earth, and the life of man will then be measured by sixteen years, on attaining to which age death will ensue. And girls of five or six years of age will bring forth children and boys of seven or eight years of age will become fathers. And, O tiger among kings, when the end of the *Yuga* will come, the wife will never be content with her husband, nor the husband with his wife. And the possessions of men will never be much, and people will falsely bear the marks of religion, and jealousy and malice will fill the world. And no one will, at that time, be a giver (of wealth or anything else) in respect to any one else. And the inhabited regions of the earth will be afflicted with dearth and famine, and the highways will be filled with lustful men and women of evil repute. And, at such a time, the women will also entertain an aversion towards their husbands. And without doubt all men will adopt the behaviour of the *mlecchas*, become omnivorous without distinction, and cruel in all their acts, when the end of the *Yuga* will come. And, O thou foremost of the Bharatas, urged by avarice, men will, at that time, deceive one another when they sell and purchase. And without a knowledge of the ordinance, men will perform ceremonies and rites, and, indeed, behave as listeth them, when the end of the *Yuga* comes. And when the end of the *Yuga* comes, urged by their very dispositions, men will act cruelly, and speak ill of one another. And people will, without compunction, destroy trees and gardens. And men will be filled with anxiety as regards the means of living. And, O king, overwhelmed with covetousness, men will kill Brahmanas and appropriate and enjoy the possessions of their victims. And the regenerate ones, oppressed by Sudras, and afflicted with fear, and crying *Oh* and *Alas*, will wander over the earth without anybody to protect them. And when men will begin to slay one another, and become wicked and fierce and without any respect for animal life, then will the *Yuga* come to an end. And, O king, even the foremost of the regenerate ones, afflicted by robbers, will, like crows, fly in terror and with speed, and seek refuge, O perpetuator of the Kuru race, in rivers and mountains and inaccessible regions. And always oppressed by bad rulers with burthens of taxes, the foremost of the regenerate classes, O lord of the earth, will, in those terrible times, take leave of all patience and do improper acts by becoming even the servants of the Sudras. And Sudras will expound the scriptures, and Brahmanas will wait upon and listen to them, and settle their course of duty accepting such interpretations as their guides. And the low will become the high, and the course of things will look contrary. And renouncing the gods, men will worship bones and other relics deposited within walls. And, at the end of the *Yuga*, the Sudras will cease to wait upon and serve the Brahmanas. And in the asylums of great *Rishis*, and the teaching institutions of Brahmanas, and in places sacred to the gods and sacrificial compounds, and in sacred tanks, the earth will be disfigured with tombs and pillars containing bony relics and not graced with temples dedicated to the gods. All this will take place at the end of the *Yuga*, and know that these are the signs of the end of the *Yuga*. And when men become fierce and destitute of virtue and carnivorous and addicted to intoxicating drinks, then doth the *Yuga* come to an end. And, O monarch, when flowers will be begot within flowers, and fruits within fruits, then will the *Yuga* come to an end. And the clouds will pour rain unseasonably when the end of the *Yuga* approaches. And, at that time, ceremonial rites of men will not follow one another in due order, and the Sudras will quarrel with the Brahmanas. And the earth will soon be full of *mlecchas*, and the Brahmanas will fly in all directions for fear of the burthen of taxes. And all distinctions between men will cease as regards conduct and behaviour, and afflicted with honorary tasks and offices, people will fly to woody retreats, subsisting on fruits and roots. And the world will be so afflicted, that rectitude of conduct will cease to be exhibited anywhere. And disciples will set at naught the instructions of preceptors, and seek even to injure them. And preceptors impoverished will be disregarded by men. And friends and relatives and kinsmen will perform friendly offices for the sake of the wealth only that is possessed by a person. And when the end of the *Yuga* comes, everybody will be in want. And all the points of the horizon will be ablaze, and the stars and stellar groups will be destitute of brilliancy, and the planets and planetary conjunctions will be inauspicious. And the course of the winds will be confused and agitated, and innumerable meteors will flash through the sky, foreboding evil. And the Sun will appear with six others of the same kind. And all around there will be din and uproar, and everywhere there will be conflagrations. And the Sun, from the hour of his rising to that of setting, will be enveloped by Rahu. And the deity of a thousand eyes will shower rain unseasonably. And when the end of the *Yuga* comes, crops will not grow in abundance. And the women will always be sharp in speech and pitiless and fond of weeping. And they will never abide by the commands of their husbands. And when the end of the *Yuga* comes, sons will slay fathers and mothers. And women, living uncontrolled, will slay their husbands and sons. And, O king, when the end of the *Yuga* comes, *Rahu* will swallow the Sun unseasonably. And fires will blaze up on all sides. And travellers unable to obtain food and drink and shelter even when they ask for these, will lie down on the wayside refraining from urging their solicitations. And when the end of the *Yuga* comes, crows and snakes and vultures and kites and other animals and birds will utter frightful and dissonant cries. And when the end of the *Yuga* comes, men will cast away and neglect their friends and relatives and attendants. And, O monarch, when the end of the *Yuga* comes, men abandoning the countries and directions and towns and cities of their occupation, will seek for new ones, one after another. And people will wander over the earth, uttering, "O father, O son", and such other frightful and rending cries.

"'And when those terrible times will be over, the creation will begin anew. And men will again be created and distributed into the four orders beginning with Brahmanas. And about that time, in order that men may increase, Providence, according to its pleasure, will once more become propitious. And then when the Sun, the Moon, and Vrihaspati will, with the constellation *Pushya* 7 , enter the same sign, the *Krita* age will begin again. And the clouds will commence to shower seasonally, and the stars and stellar conjunctions will become auspicious. And the planets, duly revolving in their orbits, will become exceedingly propitious. And all around, there will be prosperity and abundance and health and peace. And commissioned by Time, a Brahmana of the name of *Kalki* will take his birth. And he will glorify Vishnu and possess great energy, great intelligence, and great prowess. And he will take his birth in a town of the name of *Sambhala* in an auspicious Brahmana family. And vehicles and weapons, and warriors and arms, and coats of mail will be at his disposal as soon as he will think of them. And he will be the king of kings, and ever victorious with the strength of virtue. And he will restore order and peace in this world crowded with creatures and contradictory in its course. And that blazing Brahmana of mighty intellect, having appeared, will destroy all things. And he will be the Destroyer of all, and will inaugurate a new *Yuga*. And surrounded by the Brahmanas, that Brahmana will exterminate all the *mlecchas* wherever those low and despicable persons may take refuge.'"

SECTION CLXL

"Markandeya continued, 'Having exterminated the thieves and robbers, *Kalki* will, at a great Horse-sacrifice, duly give away this earth to the Brahmanas, and having established anew the blessed rectitude ordained by the Self-create, *Kalki*, of sacred deeds and illustrious reputation, will enter a delightful forest, and the people of this earth will imitate his conduct, and when the Brahmanas will have exterminated the thieves and robbers, there will be prosperity everywhere (on earth). And as the countries of the earth will one after another be subjugated, that tiger among Brahmanas, *Kalki*, having placed deer skins and lances and tridents there, will roam over the earth, adored by foremost Brahmanas and showing his regard for them and engaged all the while in slaughtering thieves and robbers. And he will exterminate the thieves and robbers amid heart-rending cries of "*Oh, father — Oh, mother! — O son!*" and the like, and O Bharata, when sin will thus have been rooted out and virtue will flourish on arrival of the *Krita* age, men will once more betake themselves to the practice of religious rites. And in the age that will set in, viz., the *Krita*, well-planted gardens and sacrificial compounds and large tanks and educational centres for the cultivation of Brahmanic lore and ponds and temples will re-appear everywhere. And the ceremonies and rites of sacrifices will also begin to be performed. And the Brahmanas will become good and honest, and the regenerate ones, devoted to ascetic austerities, will become *Munis* and the asylums of ascetics, which had before been filled with wretches will once more be homes of men devoted to truth, and men in general will begin to honour and practise truth. And all seeds, sown on earth, will grow, and, O monarch, every kind of crop will grow in every season. And men will devotedly practise charity and vows and observances, and the Brahmanas devoted to meditation and sacrifices will be of virtuous soul and always cheerful, and the rulers of the earth will govern their kingdoms virtuously, and in the *Krita* age, the Vaisyas will be devoted to the practices of their order. And the Brahmanas will be devoted to their six-fold duties (of study, teaching, performance of sacrifices on their own account, officiating at sacrifices performed by others, charity and acceptance of gifts), and the Kshatriyas will be devoted to feats of prowess. And Sudras will be devoted to service of the three (high) orders.

"'These, O Yudhishthira, are the courses of the *Krita*, the *Treta*, the *Dwapara* and the succeeding age. I have now narrated to thee everything. I have also told thee, O son of Pandu, the periods embraced by the several *Yugas* as generally known. I have now told thee everything appertaining to both the past and the future as narrated by *Vayu* in the *Parana* (which goes by his name and) which is adored by the *Rishis*. Being immortal I have many a time beheld and otherwise ascertained the courses of the world. Indeed, all I have seen and felt I have now told thee. And, O thou of unfading glory, listen now with thy brothers to something else I will presently tell thee for clearing thy doubts about religion! O thou foremost of virtuous men, thou shouldst always fix thy soul on virtue, for, O monarch, a person of virtuous soul obtaineth bliss both here and hereafter. And, O sinless one, listen to the auspicious words that I will now speak to thee. *Never do thou humiliate a Brahmana, for a Brahmana, if angry, may by his vow destroy the three worlds.*'"

Vaisampayana continued, "Hearing these words of Markandeya, the royal head of the Kurus, endued with intelligence and possessed of great lustre, spoke these words of great wisdom, 'O *muni*, if I am to protect my subjects, to what course of conduct should I adhere? And how should I behave so that I may not fall away from the duties of my order?'

"Markandeya, hearing this, answered, 'Be merciful to all creatures, and devoted to their good. Love all creatures, scorning none. Be truthful in speech, humble, with passions under complete control, and always devoted to the protection of thy people. Practise virtue and renounce sin, and worship thou the manes and the god and whatever thou mayst have done from ignorance or carelessness, wash them off and expiate them by charity. Renouncing pride and vanity, be thou possessed to humility and good behaviour. And subjugating the whole earth, rejoice thou and let happiness be thine. This is the course of conduct that accords with virtue. I have recited to thee all that was and all that will be regarded as virtuous. There is nothing appertaining to the past or the future that is unknown to thee. Therefore, O son, take not to heart this present calamity of thine. They that are wise are never overwhelmed when they are persecuted by *Time*. O thou of mighty arms, the very dwellers of heaven cannot rise superior to Time. Time afflicts all creatures. O sinless one, let not doubt cross thy mind regarding the truth of what I have told thee, for, if thou sufferest doubt to enter thy heart, thy virtue will suffer diminution! O bull of the Bharata race, thou art born in the celebrated family of the Kurus. Thou shouldst practise that which I have told thee, in thought, word and deed.'

"Yudhishthira answered, 'O thou foremost of the regenerate ones, at thy command I will certainly act according to all the instructions thou hast given me, and which, O lord, are all so sweet to the ear. O foremost of Brahmanas, avarice and lust I have none, and neither fear nor pride nor vanity. I shall, therefore, O lord, follow all that thou hast told me.'"

Vaisampayana continued, "Having listened to the words of the intelligent Markandeya, the sons of Pandu, O king, along with the wielder of the bow called *Saranga*, and all those bulls among Brahmanas, and all others that were there, became filled with joy. And having heard those blessed words appertaining to olden time, from Markandeya gifted with wisdom, their hearts were filled with wonder."

SECTION CLXLI

Janamejaya said, "It behoveth thee to narrate to me in full the greatness of the Brahmanas even as the mighty ascetic Markandeya had expounded it to the sons of Pandu."

Vaisampayana said, "The eldest son of Pandu had asked Markandeya saying, 'It behoveth thee to expound to me the greatness of Brahmanas.' Markandeya answered him saying, 'Hear, O king, about the behaviour of Brahmanas in days of old.'

"And Markandeya continued, 'There was a king, by name Parikshit in Ayodhya and belonging to the race of Ikshvaku. And once upon a time Parikshit went a-hunting. And as he was riding alone on a horse chasing deer, the animal led him to a great distance (from the habitations of men). And fatigued by the distance he had ridden and afflicted with hunger and thirst he beheld in that part of the country whither he had been led, a dark and dense forest, and the king, beholding that forest, entered it and seeing a delightful tank within the forest, both the rider and the horse bathed in it, and refreshed by the bath and placing before his horse some stalks and fibres of the lotus, the king sat by the side of the tank. And while he was lying by the side of the tank, he heard certain sweet strains of music, and hearing those strains, he reflected, "I do not see here the foot-prints of men. Whose and whence then these strains?" And the king soon beheld a maiden of great beauty gathering flowers singing all the while, and the maiden soon came before the king, and the king thereupon asked her, "Blessed one, who art thou and whose?" And she replied, "I am a maiden." And the king said, "I ask thee to be mine." And the maiden answered, "Give me a pledge, for then only I can be thine, else not." And the king then asked about the pledge and the girl answered, "Thou wilt never make me cast my eyes on water", and the king saying, "So be it," married her, and king Parikshit having married her sported (with her) in great joy, and sat with her in silence, and while the king was staying there, his troops reached the spot, and those troops beholding the monarch stood surrounding him, and cheered by the presence of troops, the king entered a handsome vehicle accompanied by his (newly) wedded wife. And having arrived at his capital he began to live with her in privacy. And persons that were even near enough to the king could not obtain any interview with him and the minister-in-chief enquired of those females that waited upon the king, asking, "What do ye do here?" And those women replied, "We behold here a female of unrivalled beauty. And the king sporteth with her, having married her with a pledge that he would never show her water." And hearing those words, the minister-in-chief caused an artificial forest to be created, consisting of many trees with abundant flowers and fruits, and he caused to be excavated within that forest and towards one of its sides a large tank, placed in a secluded spot and full of water that was sweet as *Amrita*. The tank was well covered with a net of pearls. Approaching the king one day in private, he addressed the king saying, "This is a fine forest without water. Sport thou here joyfully!" And the king at those words of his minister entered that forest with that adorable wife of his, and the king sported with her in that delightful forest, and afflicted with hunger and thirst and fatigued and spent, the king beheld a bower of Madhavi creepers 8 and entering that bower with his dear one, the king beheld a tank full of water that was transparent and bright as nectar, and beholding that tank, the king sat on its bank with her and the king told his adorable wife, "Cheerfully do thou plunge into this water!" And she, hearing those words plunged into the tank. But having plunged into the water she appeared not above the surface, and as the king searched, he failed to discover any trace of her. And the king ordered the waters of the tank to be baled out, and thereupon he beheld a frog sitting at the mouth of a hole, and the king was enraged at this and promulgated an order saying, "Let frogs be slaughtered everywhere in my dominions! Whoever wishes to have an interview with me must come before me with a tribute of dead frogs." And accordingly when frogs began to be terribly slaughtered, the affrighted frogs represented all that had happened unto their king, and the king of the frogs assuming the garb of an ascetic came before the king Parikshit, and having approached the monarch, he said, "O king, give not thyself up to wrath! Be inclined to grace. It behoveth thee not to slay the innocent frogs." Here occurs a couple of *Slokas*. (They are these):—"O thou of unfading glory, slay not the frogs! Pacify thy wrath! The prosperity and ascetic merits of those that have their souls steeped in ignorance suffer diminution! Pledge thyself not to be angry with the frogs! What need hast thou to commit such sin! What purpose will be served by slaying the frogs!" Then king Parikshit whose soul was filled with woe on account of the death of her that was dear to him, answered the chief of the frogs who had spoken to him thus, "I will not forgive the frogs. On the other hand, I will slay them. By these wicked wretches hath my dear one been swallowed up. The frogs, therefore, always deserve to be killed by me. It behoveth thee not, O learned one, to intercede on their behalf." And hearing these words of Parikshit, the king of the frogs with his senses and mind much pained said, "Be inclined to grace, O king! I am the king of the frogs by name Ayu. She who was thy wife is my daughter of the name of Susobhana. This, indeed, is an instance of her bad conduct. Before this, many kings were deceived by her." The king thereupon said to him, "I desire to have her. Let her be granted to me by thee!" The king of the frogs thereupon bestowed his daughter upon Parikshit, and addressing her said, "Wait upon and serve the king." And having spoken these words to his daughter, he also addressed her in wrath saying, "Since thou hast deceived many Kings for this untruthful behaviour of thine, thy offspring will prove disrespectful to Brahmanas!" But having obtained her, the king became deeply enamoured of her in consequence of her companionable virtues, and feeling that he had, as it were, obtained the sovereignty of the three worlds, he bowed down to the king of the frogs and reverenced him in due form and then with utterance choked in joy and tears said, "I have been favoured indeed!" And the king of the frogs obtaining the leave of his daughter, returned to the place from which he had come and some time after the king begot three sons upon her and those sons were named Sala and Dala and Vala, and some time after, their father, installing the eldest of them of all on the throne and setting his heart on asceticism, retired into the forest. One day Sala while out a-hunting, beheld a deer and pursued it, on his car, and the prince said to his charioteer, "Drive thou fast." And the charioteer, thus addressed, replied unto the king, saying, "Do not entertain such a purpose. This deer is incapable of being caught by thee. If indeed *Vami* horses had been yoked to thy car, then couldst thou have taken it." Thereupon the king addressed his charioteer, saying, "Tell me all about *Vami* horses, otherwise I will slay thee." Thus addressed the charioteer became dreadfully alarmed and he was afraid of the king and also of Vamadeva's curse and told not the king anything and the king then lifting up his scimitar said to him, "Tell me soon, else I will slay thee." At last afraid of the king, the charioteer said, "The *Vami* horses are those belonging to Vamadeva; they are fleet as the mind." And unto his charioteer who had said so, the king said, "Repair thou to the asylum of Vamadeva." And reaching the asylum of Vamadeva the king said unto that *Rishi*, "O holy one, a deer struck by me is flying away. It behoveth thee to make it capable of being seized by me by granting me thy pair of *Vami* horses." The *Rishi* then answered him saying, "I give thee my pair of *Vami* horses. But after accomplishing thy object, my *Vami* pair you should soon return." The king then taking those steeds and obtaining the leave of the *Rishi* pursued the deer, having yoked the *Vami* pair unto his car, and after he had left the asylum he spoke unto his charioteer saying, "These jewels of steeds the Brahmanas do not deserve to possess. These should not be returned to Vamadeva." Having said this and seized the deer he returned to his capital and placed those steeds within the inner apartments of the palace.

"'Meanwhile the *Rishi* reflected, "The prince is young. Having obtained an excellent pair of animals, he is sporting with it in joy without returning it to me. Alas, what a pity it is!" And reflecting in this strain, the *Rishi* said unto a disciple of his, after the expiration of a month, "Go, O Atreya, and say to the king that if he has done with the *Vami* steeds, he should return them unto thy preceptor." And the disciple Atreya, thereupon, repairing to the king, spoke unto him as instructed, and the king replied saying, "This pair of steeds deserves to be owned by kings. The Brahmanas do not deserve to possess jewels of such value. What business have Brahmanas with horses? Return thou contentedly!" And Atreya, thus addressed by the king, returned and told his preceptor all that had happened, and hearing this sad intelligence, Vamadeva's heart was filled with wrath, and repairing in person to the king he asked him for his steeds, and the king refused to give the *Rishi* what the latter asked, and Vamadeva said, "O lord of earth, give me thou my *Vami* horses. By them hast thou accomplished a task which was almost incapable of being accomplished by thee. By transgressing the practices of Brahmanas and Kshatriyas, subject not thyself, O king, to death by means of the terrible noose of Varuna." And hearing this, the king answered, "O Vamadeva, this couple of excellent well-trained, and docile bulls are fit animals for Brahmanas. O great *Rishi*, (take them and) go with them wherever thou likest. Indeed, the very *Vedas* carry persons like thee." Then Vamadeva said, "O king, the *Vedas* do, indeed, carry persons like us. But that is in the world hereafter. In this world, however, O king, animals like these carry me and persons like me as also all others." At this the king answered, "Let four asses carry thee, or four mules of the best kind, or even four steeds endued with the speed of the wind. Go thou with these. This pair of *Vami* horses, however, deserves to be owned by Kshatriyas. Know thou, therefore, that these are not thine." At this, Vamadeva said, "O king, terrible vows have been ordained for the Brahmanas. If I have lived in their observance, let four fierce and mighty Rakshasas of terrible mien and iron bodies, commanded by me, pursue thee with desire of slaying, and carry thee on their sharp lances, having cut up thy body into four parts." Hearing this, the king said, "Let those, O Vamadeva, that know thee as a Brahmana that in thought, word, and deed, is desirous of taking life, at my command, armed with bright lances and swords prostrate thee with thy disciples before me." Then Vamadeva answered, "O king, having obtained these my *Vami* steeds, thou hadst said, '*I will return them.*' Therefore, give me back my *Vami* steeds, so thou mayst be able to protect thy life." Hearing this, the king said, "Pursuit of deer hath not been ordained for the Brahmanas. I do punish thee, however, for thy untruthfulness. From this day, too, obeying all thy commands I will, O Brahmana, attain to regions of bliss." Vamadeva then said, "A Brahmana cannot be punished in thought, word or deed.

That learned person who by ascetic austerities succeedeth in knowing a Brahmana to be so, faileth not to attain to prominence in this world."'

"Markandeya continued, 'After Vamadeva had said this, there arose, O king, (four) *Rakshasas* of terrible mien, and as they, with lances in their hands, approached the king for slaying him, the latter cried aloud, saying, "If, O Brahmana, all the descendants of Ikshvaku's race, if (my brother) Dala, if all these Vaisyas acknowledge my sway, then I will not yield up the *Vami* steeds to Vamadeva, for these men can never be virtuous." And while he was uttering those words, those *Rakshasas* slew him, and the lord of earth was soon prostrated on the ground. And the Ikshvakus, learning that their king had been slain, installed Dala on the throne, and the Brahmana Vamadeva thereupon going to the kingdom (of the Ikshvakus), addressed the new monarch, saying, "O king, it hath been declared in all the sacred books that persons should give away unto Brahmanas. If thou fearest sin, O king, give me now the *Vami* steeds without delay." And hearing these words of Vamadeva, the king in anger spoke unto his charioteer, saying, "Bring me an arrow from those I have kept, which is handsome to behold and tempered with poison, so that pierced by it Vamadeva may lie prostrate in pain, torn by the dogs." Hearing this, Vamadeva answered, "I know, O king, that thou hast a son of ten years of age, called Senajita, begotten upon thy queen. Urged by my word, slay thou that dear boy of thine without delay by means of thy frightful arrows!"'

"Markandeya continued, 'At these words of Vamadeva, O king, that arrow of fierce energy, shot by the monarch, slew the prince in the inner apartments, and hearing this, Dala said there and then, "Ye people of Ikshvaku's race, I will do ye good. I shall slay this Brahmana today, grinding him with force. Bring me another arrow of fierce energy. Ye lords of earth, behold my prowess now." And at these words of Dala, Vamadeva said, "This arrow of terrible mien and tempered with poison, that thou aimest at me, thou shall not, O ruler of men, be able to aim nor even to shoot." And thereupon the king said, "Ye men of Ikshvaku's race, behold me incapable of shooting the arrow that hath been taken up by me. I fail to compass the death of this Brahmana. Let Vamadeva who is blessed with a long life live." Then Vamadeva said, "Touching thy queen with this arrow, thou mayst purge thyself of the sin (of attempting to take the life of a Brahmana)." And king Dala did as he was directed and the queen then addressed the *Muni*, and said, "O Vamadeva, let me be able to duly instruct this wretched husband of mine from day to day, imparting unto him words of happy import; and let me always wait upon and serve the Brahmanas, and by this acquire, O Brahmana, the sacred regions hereafter." And hearing these words of the queen, Vamadeva said, "O thou of beautiful eyes, thou hast saved this royal race. Beg thou an incomparable boon. I will grant thee whatever thou mayst ask. And, O thou faultless one, rule thou, O princess, these thy kinsmen and this great kingdom of the Ikshvakus!" And hearing these words of Vamadeva the princess said, "This, O holy one, is the boon I seek, viz., that my husband may now be freed from his sin, and that thou mayst be employed in thinking of the weal of his son and kinsmen. This is the boon that I ask, O thou foremost of Brahmanas!"'

"Markandeya continued, 'Hearing these words of the queen, that *Muni*, O thou foremost of the Kuru race, said, "So be it." And thereupon king Dala became highly glad and gave unto the *Muni* his *Vami* steeds, having bowed down unto him with reverence!"'

SECTION CLXLII

Vaisampayana said, "The *Rishis*, the Brahmanas, and Yudhishthira then asked Markandeya, saying, 'How did the *Rishi* Vaka become so long lived?'

"Thus asked by them, Markandeya answered, 'The royal sage Vaka is a great ascetic and endowed with long life. Ye need not enquire into the reason of this.'

"Hearing this, O Bharata, the son of Kunti, king Yudhishthira the just, along with his brothers, then asked Markandeya saying, 'It hath been heard by us that both Vaka and Daivya are of great souls and endowed with immortality and that those *Rishis*, held in universal reverence, are the friends of the chief of the gods. O Holy One, I desire to listen to the (history of the) meeting of Vaka and Indra that is full of both joy and woe. Narrate thou that history unto us succinctly.'

"Markandeya said, 'When that horrible conflict between the gods and the *Asuras* was over, Indra became the ruler of the three worlds. The clouds showered rain copiously. And the dwellers of the world had abundance of harvests, and were excellent in disposition. And devoted to virtue, they always practised morality and enjoyed peace. And all persons, devoted to the duties of their respective orders, were perfectly happy and cheerful, and the slayer of Vala, beholding all the creatures of the world happy and cheerful, became himself filled with joy. And he of a hundred sacrifices, the chief of the *gods* seated on the back of his elephant Airavata, surveyed his happy subjects, and he cast his eyes on delightful asylums of *Rishis*, on various auspicious rivers, towns full of prosperity, and villages and rural regions in the enjoyment of plenty. And he also cast his eyes upon kings devoted to the practice of virtue and well-skilled in ruling their subjects. And he also looked upon tanks and reservoirs and wells and lakes and smaller lakes all full of water and adored by best of Brahmanas in the observance, besides, of various excellent vows, and then descending on the delightful earth, O king, the god of a hundred sacrifices, proceeded towards a blessed asylum teeming with animals and birds, situated by the side of the sea, in the delightful and auspicious regions of the East on a spot overgrown with abundance of vegetation. And the chief of the gods beheld Vaka in that asylum, and Vaka also, beholding the ruler of the Immortals, became highly glad, and he worshipped Indra by presenting him with water to wash his feet, a carpet to sit upon, the usual offering of the *Arghya*, and fruit and roots. And the boon-giving slayer of Vala, the divine ruler of those that know not old age, being seated at his ease, asked Vaka the following question, "O sinless *Muni*, thou hast lived for a hundred years! Tell me, O Brahmana, what the sorrows are of those that are immortal!"'

"Markandeya continued, 'Hearing this, Vaka answered, saying, "Life with persons that are disagreeable, separation from those that are agreeable and beloved, companionship with the wicked, these are the evils which they that are immortal have to bear. The death of sons and wives, of kinsmen and friends, and the pain of dependence on others, are some of the greatest of evils. (These may all be noticed in a deathless life). There is no more pitiable sight in the world, as I conceive, than that of men destitute of wealth being insulted by others. The acquisition of family dignity by those that have it not, the loss of family dignity by those that have it, unions and disunions,—these all are noticeable by those that lead deathless lives. How they that have no family dignity but have prosperity, win what they have not—all this, O god of a hundred sacrifices, is before thy very eyes! What can be more pitiable than the calamities and reverses sustained by the gods, the *Asuras*, the *Gandharvas*, men, the snakes, and the *Rakshasas*! They that have been of good families suffer afflictions in consequence of their subjection to persons that are ill-born and the poor are insulted by the rich. What can be more pitiable than these? Innumerable examples of such contradictory dispensations are seen in the world. The foolish and the ignorant are cheerful and happy while the learned and the wise suffer misery! Plentiful instances of misery and woe are seen among men in this world! (They that lead deathless lives are destined to behold all these and suffer on that account.)"

"'Indra then said, "O thou of great good fortune, tell me again, what the joys are of those persons that lead deathless lives,—joys that are adored by gods and *Rishis*!"'

"'Vaka answered, "If without having to associate with a wicked friend, a man cooks scanty vegetables in his own house at the eight or the twelfth part of the day, there can be nothing happier than that. 9 He in whose case the day is not counted is not called voracious. And, O Maghavan, happiness is even his own whose scanty vegetables are cooked. Earned by his own efforts, without having to depend upon any one, he that eateth even fruits and vegetables in his own house is entitled to respect. He that eateth in another's house the food given to him in contempt, even if that food be rich and sweet, doth what is despicable. This, therefore, is the opinion of the wise that fie on the food of that mean wretch who like a dog or a *Rakshasa* eateth at another's house. If after treating guests and servants and offering food to the manes a good Brahmana eateth what remains, there can be nothing happier than that. There is nothing sweeter or more sacred, O thou of a hundred sacrifices, than that food which such a person takes after serving the guest with the first portion thereof. Each mouthful (of rice) that the Brahmana eats after having served the guest, produces merit equal to what attaches to the gift of a thousand kine. And whatever sins such a one may have committed in his youth are all washed away of a certainty. The water in the hands of the Brahmana that hath been fed and honoured with a pecuniary gift (after the feeding is over) when touched with water (sprinkled by him that feeds), instantly purges off all the sins of the latter!"

"'Speaking of these and various other things with Vaka, the chief of the gods went away to heaven.'" 10

SECTION CLXLIII

Vaisampayana said, "Then the sons of Pandu again addressed Markandeya saying, 'Thou hast told us of greatness of Brahmanas. We desire now to hear of the greatness of the royal Kshatriyas!" Thus addressed by them, the great *Rishi* Markandeya spoke, 'Listen now to the greatness of the royal Kshatriyas. A certain king of the name of Suhotra belonging to the Kuru race went on a visit to the great *Rishis*. And as he was returning from that visit, he beheld king Sivi the son of Usinara, seated on his car, and as each came before the other, each saluted the other as best befitted his age and each regarding himself as the equal of the other in respect of qualities, refused to give the way to the other. And at this juncture Narada appeared there, and beholding what had happened, the celestial *Rishi* asked, "Why is it that ye both stand here blocking each other's way?" And thus questioned both of them spoke to Narada saying, "O holy one, do not speak so. The sages of old have declared that the way should be given to one who is superior or to him that is abler. We, however, that stand blocking each other's way are equal to each other in every respect. Judged properly there is no superiority amongst us." Thus addressed by them, Narada recited three *slokas*. (They are these), "O thou of the Kuru race, he that is wicked behaveth wickedly even unto him that is humble; he also that is humble behaveth with humility and honestly unto him that is wicked! He that is honest behaveth honestly even towards the dishonest. Why should he not behave honestly towards him that is honest? He that is honest regardeth the service that is done to him, as if it were a hundred times greater than it is. Is this not current amongst the gods themselves? Certainly it is the royal son of Usinara who is possessed of goodness that is greater than thine. One should conquer the mean by charity; the untruthful by truth, the man of wicked deeds by forgiveness; and the dishonest by honesty. Both of you are large-hearted. Let one amongst you stand aside, according to the indication of the above *slokas*." And having said so Narada became silent, and hearing what Narada had said the king of the Kuru race walking round *Sivi*, and praising his numerous achievements, gave him the way and went on in his course. It was even thus that Narada had described the high blessedness of the royal Kshatriyas.'"

SECTION CLXLIV

"Markandeya continued, 'Listen now to another story. One day as king Yayati, the son of Nahusha, was sitting on his throne, surrounded by the citizens, there came unto him a Brahmana desirous of soliciting wealth for his preceptor, and approaching the king, the Brahmana said, "O king, I beg of thee wealth for my preceptor according to my covenant." And the king said, "O Holy One, tell me what thy covenant is." And thereupon the Brahmana said, "O king, in this world when men are asked for alms, they entertain contempt for him that asketh it. I therefore, ask thee, O king, with what feelings thou wilt give me what I ask and upon which I have set my heart." And the king replied saying, "Having given away a thing, I never boast of it. I never also listen to solicitations for things that cannot be given. I listen, however, to prayers for things that can be given and giving them away I always become happy. I will give thee a thousand kine. The Brahmana that asks me for a gift is always dear to me. I am never angry with the person that begs of me and I am never sorry for having given away a thing!" And the Brahmana then obtained from the king a thousand kine and went away.'"

SECTION CLXLV

Vaisampayana said, "The son of Pandu again addressed the *Rishi* and said, 'Speak thou unto us of the high fortune of royal Kshatriyas!' And Markandeya said, 'There were two kings of the name of Vrishadarbha and Seduka and both of them were conversant with morals and with weapons of attack and defence. And Seduka knew that Vrishadarbha had from his boyhood an unuttered vow that he would give no other metal unto Brahmanas save gold and silver. And once on a time a Brahmana having completed his study of the *Vedas* came unto Seduka and uttering a benediction upon him begged of him wealth for his preceptor, saying, "Give me a thousand steeds." And thus addressed, Seduka said unto him, "It is not possible for me to give thee this for thy preceptor. Therefore, go thou unto king Vrishadarbha, for, O Brahmana, he is a highly virtuous king. Go and beg of him. He will grant thy request. Even this is his unuttered vow." Hearing these words that Brahmana went to Vrishadarbha and begged of him a thousand steeds, and the king thus solicited, struck the Brahmana with a whip and thereupon the Brahmana said, "Innocent as I am, why dost thou attack me thus?" And the Brahmana was on the point of cursing the king, when the latter said, "O Brahmana, dost thou curse him that doth not give thee what thou askest? Or, is this behaviour proper for a Brahmana?" And the Brahmana said, "O king of kings, sent unto thee by Seduka, I come before thee for this." The king said, "I will give thee now whatever tribute may come to me before the morning expire. How indeed, can I send away the man empty-handed who hath been whipped by me." And having said this the king gave unto that Brahmana the entire proceeds of that day and that was more than the value of a thousand horses.'"

SECTION CLXLVI

"Markandeya said, 'One day it was resolved by the gods that they should descend on the earth and try the goodness and virtue of king Sivi, the son of Usinara. And addressing each other,—"*Well*"—Agni and Indra came to the earth. And Agni took the form of a pigeon flying away from Indra who pursued him in the form of a hawk, and that pigeon fell upon the lap of king Sivi who was seated on an excellent seat. And the priest thereupon addressing the king said, "Afraid of the hawk and desirous of saving its life, this pigeon hath come to thee for safety. The learned have said that the falling of a pigeon upon one's body forebodeth a great danger. Let the king that understands omens give away wealth for saving himself from the danger indicated." And the pigeon also addressed the king and said, "Afraid of the hawk and desirous of saving my life I have come to thee for protection. I am a *Muni*. Having assumed the form of a pigeon, I come to thee as a seeker of thy protection. Indeed, I seek thee as my life. Know me as one possessed of Vedic lore, as one leading the *Brahmacharya* mode of life, as one possessed also of self-control and ascetic virtues. And know me further as one that has never spoken disagreeably unto his preceptor, as one possessed of every virtue indeed, as one that is sinless. I repeat the Vedas, I know their prosody; indeed, I have studied all the Vedas letter by letter. I am not a pigeon. Oh, do not yield me up to the hawk. The giving up of a learned and pure Brahmana can never be a good gift." And after the pigeon said so, the hawk addressed the king, and said, "Creatures do not come into the world in the same particular order. In the order of creation, thou mayst, in a former birth, have been begotten by this pigeon. It is not proper for thee, O king, to interfere with my food by protecting this pigeon (even though he might have been thy father)." And thus addressed, the king said, "Hath any one, before this, seen birds thus speak the pure speech of man? Knowing what this pigeon sayeth, and this hawk also, how can we act to-day according to virtue? He that giveth up an affrighted creature seeking protection, unto its foe, doth not obtain protection when he is in need of it himself. Indeed, the very clouds do not shower rain seasonably for him, and the seeds though scattered do not grow for him. He that giveth up an afflicted creature seeking protection unto its foe, hath to see his offspring die in childhood. The ancestor of such a person can never dwell in heaven; indeed, the very gods decline to accept the libations of clarified butter poured by him into the fire. He that giveth up an affrighted creature seeking protection, unto its foe, is struck with the thunder-bolt by the gods with Indra at their head. The food that he eateth is unsanctified, and he, of a narrow soul, falleth from heaven very soon. O hawk, let the people of the Sivi tribe place before thee a bull cooked with rice instead of this pigeon. And let them also carry to the place where thou livest in joy, meat in abundance." And hearing this, the hawk said, "O king, I do not ask for a bull, nor, indeed, any other meat, nor meat more in quantity than that of this pigeon. It hath been given to me by the gods. The creature, therefore, is my food today in consequence of its death that hath been ordained. Therefore, O monarch, give it up to me." Thus addressed by the hawk, the king said, "Let my men see and carefully carry the bull to thee with every limb entire. Let that bull be the ransom of this creature afflicted with fright and let it be carried to thee before my eyes. Oh, slay not this pigeon! I will yield up my very life, yet I would not give up this pigeon. Dost thou not know, O hawk, that this creature looketh like a sacrifice with the *Soma* juice? O blessed one, cease to take so much trouble for it. I cannot, by any means, yield up the pigeon to thee. Or, O hawk, if it pleases thee, command me to do some such thing which I may do for thee, which may be agreeable to thee, and upon doing which the men of the Sivi tribe may yet in joy bless me in terms of applause. I promise thee that I will do what thou mayst did me do." And at this appeal of the king, the hawk said, "O king, if thou givest me as much flesh as would be equal to the weight of the pigeon, cutting it off thy right thigh; then can the pigeon be properly saved by thee; then wouldst thou do what would be agreeable to me and what the men of the Sivi tribe would speak of in terms of praise." And the king agreed to this and he cut off a piece of flesh from his right thigh and weighed it against the pigeon. But the pigeon weighed heavier. And thereupon the king cut off another piece of his flesh, but the pigeon still weighed heavier, and then the king cut off pieces of flesh from all parts of his body and placed them on the scale. But the pigeon still weighed heavier, and then the king himself ascended the scale and he felt no grief at this and beholding this, the hawk disappeared there saying—(The pigeon hath been) *Saved*,—And the king asked the pigeon saying, "O pigeon, let the Sivis know who the hawk is. None but the lord of the universe could do as he did. O Holy One, answer thou this question of mine!" And the pigeon then said, "I am the smoke-bannered Agni called also Vaiswanara. The hawk is none other than Sachi's lord armed with the thunder-bolt. O son of Suratha, thou art a bull among men. We came to try thee. These pieces of flesh, O king, that thou hast cut off with thy sword from thy body for saving me have caused gashes in thy body. I will make these marks auspicious and handsome and they will be of the colour of gold and emit a sweet perfume, and earning great fame and respected by the gods and the *Rishis* thou shall long rule these subjects of thine, and a son will spring from thy flank who shall be called *Kapataroman*. O king, thou shalt obtain this son of the name of *Kapataroman* from out of thy own body and thou wilt behold him become the foremost of the *Saurathas*, blazing with renown, possessed of bravery and great personal beauty!"'"

SECTION CLXLVII

Vaisampayana said, "And the son of Pandu once more addressed Markandeya, saying, 'Tell us again of the great good fortune of kings.' And Markandeya said, 'There came unto the horse-sacrifice of king Ashtaka of Viswamitra's race, many kings. And there came unto that sacrifice the three brothers also of that king, viz., Pratardana, Vasumanas, and Sivi, the son of Usinara. And after the sacrifice was completed, Ashtaka was proceeding on his car along with his brothers when they all beheld Narada coming that way and they saluted the celestial *Rishi* and said unto him, "Ride thou on this car with us." And Narada, saying, *So be it*, mounted on the car, and one among those kings having gratified the holy and celestial *Rishi* Narada, said, "O Holy One, I desire, to ask thee something." And the *Rishi* said, "Ask." And the person, thus permitted, said, "All four of us are blessed with long lives and have indeed every virtue. We shall, therefore, be permitted to go to a certain heaven and dwell there for a long period. Who amongst us, however, O king, shall fall down first?" Thus questioned the *Rishi* said, "This Ashtaka shall first come down." And thereupon the enquirer asked, "For what cause?" And the *Rishi* answered, "I lived for a few days in the abode of Ashtaka. He carried me (one day) on his car out of the town and there I beheld thousands of kine distinguished from one another by difference of hue. And beholding those kine I asked Ashtaka whose they were and Ashtaka answered me, saying, *'I have given away these kine.'* By this answer he gave expression to his own praise. It is for this answer of his that Ashtaka shall have to come down." And after Narada had said so, one of them again enquired, saying, "Three of us then will stay in heaven. Amongst us three, who shall fall down first?" And the *Rishi* answered, "Pratardana." And the enquirer asked, "For what cause?" And the *Rishi* answered, "I lived for some days in the abode of Pratardana also. And he carried me on his car one day. And while doing so, a Brahmana asked him saying, *'Give me a horse!'* And Pratardana replied, *'After returning, I will give thee one!'* And thereupon the Brahmana said, *'Let it be given to me soon.'* And as the Brahmana spoke those words, the king gave unto him the steed that had been yoked on the right-hand wheel of the car. And there came unto him another Brahmana desirous of obtaining a steed. And the king having spoken to him in the same way, gave him the steed that had been yoked on the left wheel of his car. And having given away the horse unto him, the king proceeded on his journey. And then there came unto the king another Brahmana desirous of obtaining a horse. And the king soon gave him the horse on the left front of his car, unyoking the animal. And having done so, the king proceeded on his journey. And then there came unto the king another Brahmana desirous of obtaining a horse. And the king said unto him, '*Returning, I will give thee a horse.*' But the Brahmana said, '*Let the steed be given to me soon.*' And the king gave him the only horse he had. And seizing the yoke of the car himself, the king began to draw it. And as he did so, he said, '*There is now nothing for the Brahmanas.*' The king had given away, it is true, but he had done so with detraction. And for that speech of his, he shall have to fall down from heaven." And after the *Rishi* had said so, of the two that remained, one asked, "Who amongst us two shall fall down?" And the *Rishi* answered, "Vasumanas." And the enquirer asked, "For what reason?" And Narada said, "In course of my wanderings I arrived at the abode of Vasumanas. And at that time the Brahmanas were performing the ceremony of *Swastivachana* for the sake of a flowery car. 11 And I approached the king's presence. And after the Brahmanas had completed the ceremony, the flowery car became visible to them. And I praised that car, and thereupon the king told me, '*Holy one, by thee hath this car been praised. Let this car, therefore, be thine.*' And after this I went to Vasumanas another time when I was in need of a (flowery) car. And I admired the car, and the king said, '*It is thine.*' And I went to the king a third time and admired the car again. And even then the king exhibiting the flowery car to the Brahmanas, cast his eyes on me, and said, '*O holy one, thou hast praised the flowery car sufficiently.*" And the king only said these words, without making me a gift of that car. And for this he will fall down from heaven."

"'And one among them said, "Of the one who is to go with thee, who will go and who will fall down?" And Narada answered, saying, "Sivi will go, but I will fall down." "For what reason?" asked the enquirer. And Narada said, "I am not the equal of Sivi. For one day a Brahmana came unto Sivi and addressing him, said, 'O Sivi, I came to thee for food.' And Sivi replied unto him, saying. 'What shall I do? Let me have thy orders.' And the Brahmana answered, 'This thy son known by the name of Vrihadgarbha should be killed. And, O king, cook him for my food.' And hearing this, I waited to see what would follow. And Sivi then killed his son and cooking him duly and placing that food in a vessel and taking it upon his head, he went out in search of the Brahmana and while Sivi was thus seeking, for the Brahmana, some one told him, 'The Brahmana thou seekest, having entered thy city, is setting fire to thy abode and he is also setting fire, in wrath, to thy treasury, thy arsenal, the apartments of the females and thy stables for horses and elephants.' And Sivi heard all this, without change of colour, and entering his city spoke unto the Brahmana, 'O holy one, the food has been cooked.' And the Brahmana hearing this spoke not a word and from surprise he stood with downcast looks. And Sivi with a view to gratifying the Brahmana said, 'O holy one, eat thou this.' And the Brahmana looking at Sivi for a moment said, 'Eat it thyself.' And thereupon Sivi said, 'Let it be so.' And Sivi cheerfully taking the vessel from his head desired to eat it and thereupon the Brahmana caught hold of Sivi's hand and addressing him said, 'Thou hast conquered wrath. There is nothing that thou canst not give unto the Brahmanas.' And saying this, that Brahmana adored Sivi, and then as Sivi cast his eyes before him, he beheld his son standing like a child of the *gods*, decked in ornaments and yielding a fragrance from his body and the Brahmana, having accomplished all this, made himself visible and it was *Vidhatri* himself who had thus come in that guise to try that royal sage, and after *Vidhatri* had disappeared, the counsellors addressed the king, saying, 'Thou knowest everything. For what didst thou do all this?' And Sivi answered, 'It was not for fame, nor for wealth, nor from desire of acquiring objects of enjoyment that I did all this. This course is not sinful. It is for this that I do all this. The path which is trodden by the virtuous is laudable. My heart always inclineth towards such a course. This high instance of Sivi's blessedness I know, and I have, therefore, narrated it duly!'"""

SECTION CLXLVIII

Vaisampayana said, "The sons of Pandu and those *Rishis* then asked Markandeya, 'Is there anybody that is blessed with longer life than thou?' And Markandeya answered them, saying, 'There is without doubt, a royal sage of the name of Indradyumna and his virtue having diminished, he fell from heaven, crying, "My achievements are lost!" And he came unto me and asked, "Dost thou know me?" And I answered him, saying, "From our anxiety to acquire religious merit we do not confine ourselves to any home. We live but for a night in the same village or town. A person like us, therefore, cannot possibly know thy pursuits. The fasts and vows we observe render us weak in body and unable to follow any worldly pursuits on our own behalf. Hence, one like us cannot possibly know thee." He then asked me, "Is there any one who is longer lived than thou?" I answered him, saying, "There liveth on the Himavat an owl of the name of Pravarakarna. He is older than I. He may know thee. The part of the Himavat where he dwelleth is far off from here." And at this Indradyumna became a horse and carried me to where that owl lived and the king asked the owl, saying, "Dost thou know me?" And the owl seemed to reflect for a moment and then said unto the king, "I do not know thee." And the royal sage Indradyumna thereupon asked the owl, "Is there any one who is older than thou?" And thus asked the owl answered, saying, "There is a lake of the name of Indradyumna. In that lake dwelleth a crane of the name of Nadijangha. He is older than we. Ask thou him." And at this king Indradyumna taking both myself and the owl went to that lake where the crane Nadijangha dwelt. And that crane was asked by us, "Dost thou know the king Indradyumna?" And the crane thereupon seemed to reflect a little and then said, "I do not know king Indradyumna." And the crane was asked by us, "Is there any one who is older than thou?" And he answered us, saying, "There dwelleth in this very lake a tortoise of the name of Akupara. He is older than I. He may know something of this king. Therefore, enquire ye of Akupara." And then that crane gave information to the tortoise, saying, "It is intended by us to ask thee something. Please come to us." And hearing this the tortoise came out of the lake to that part of the bank where we all were and as he came there we asked him, saying, "Dost thou know this king Indradyumna?" And the tortoise reflected for a moment. And his eyes were filled with tears and his heart was much moved and he trembled all over and was nearly deprived of his senses. And he said with joined hands, "Alas, do I not know this one? He had planted the sacrificial stake a thousand times at the time of kindling the sacrificial fire. This lake was excavated by the feet of the cows given away by this king unto the Brahmanas on the completion of the sacrifice. I have lived here ever since." And after the tortoise had said all this, there came from the celestial regions a car. And an aerial voice was heard which said, addressing Indradyumna, "Come thou and obtain the place thou deservest in heaven! Thy achievements are great! Come thou cheerfully to thy place! Here also are certain *slokas*: The report of virtuous deeds spreadeth over the earth and ascendeth to heaven. As long as that report lasts, so long is the doer said to be in heaven. The man whose evil deeds are bruited about, is said to fall down and live, as long as that evil report lasts in the lower regions. Therefore should man be virtuous in his acts if he is to gain Heaven. And he should seek refuge in virtue, abandoning a sinful heart."

"'And hearing these words, the king said, "Let the car stay here as long as I do not take these old persons to the places whence I brought them.' And having brought me and the owl Pravarakarna to our respective places, he went away, riding on that car, to the place that was fit for him. Being longlived, I witness all this."'"

Vaisampayana continued, "It was thus that Markandeya narrated all this unto the son of Pandu. And after Markandeya finished, the sons of Pandu said, 'Blessed be thou! Thou hadst acted properly in causing king Indradyumna who had fallen from Heaven to regain his sphere!' And Markandeya answered them, saying, 'Devaki's son, Krishna, also had thus raised the royal sage Nriga who had sunk in hell and caused him to regain Heaven!'"

SECTION CLXLIX

Vaisampayana said, "King Yudhishthira, hearing from the illustrious Markandeya the story of the royal sage Indradyumna's regaining of Heaven, again asked the *Muni*, saying, 'O great *Muni*, tell me in what condition should a man practise charity in order to gain admission into the regions ŏf Indra? Is it by practising charity while leading a domestic mode of life, or in boyhood, or in youth, or in old age? O, tell me about the respective merits reaped from the practice of charity in these different stages of life.'

"Markandeya said, 'Life that is futile is of four kinds. Charity also that is futile is of sixteen kinds. His life is vain who hath no son; and his also who is out of pale of virtue: and his too who liveth on the food of other; and, lastly, his who cooketh for himself without giving therefrom unto the *Pitris*, the gods, and the guests, and who eateth of it before these all. The gift to one that has fallen away from the practice of virtuous vows, as also the gift of wealth that has been earned wrongly, are both in vain. The gift to a fallen Brahmana, that to a thief, that also to a preceptor that is false, is in vain. The gift to an untruthful man, to a person that is sinful, to one that is ungrateful, to one that officiates at sacrifices performed by all classes of people residing in a village, to one that sells the *Vedas*, 12 to a Brahmana that cooks for Sudra, to one that too by birth is a Brahmana but who is destitute of the occupations of his order, is in vain. The gift to one that has married a girl after the accession of puberty, to females, to one that sports with snakes, and to one that is employed in menial offices, is also in vain. These sixteen kinds of gifts are productive of no merits. That man who with mind clouded with darkness giveth away from fear or anger, enjoyeth the merit of such gift while he is in the womb of his mother. The man who (under other circumstances) maketh gifts unto the Brahmanas, enjoyeth the fruit thereof while he is in old age. Therefore, O king, the man who wishes to win the way of heaven, should under all conditions, make gifts unto Brahmanas of everything that he wishes to give away.'

"Yudhishthira said, 'By what means do Brahmanas, who accept gifts from all the four orders, save others as well as themselves?"

"Markandeya said, 'By *Japa*, 13 and *Mantras*, 14 and *Homa* 15 and the study of the *Vedas*, the Brahmanas construct a *Vedic* boat 16 wherewith they save both others and themselves. The gods themselves are pleased with that man who gratifieth the Brahmanas. Indeed, a man may attain heaven at the command of a Brahmana. Thou wilt, O king, without doubt ascend to regions of everlasting bliss, in consequence of thy worship of the *Pitris* and the gods, and thy reverence for the Brahmanas, even though thy body is filled with phlegmatic humours and withal so dull and inert! He that desires virtue and heaven should adore the Brahmanas. One should feed Brahmanas with care on occasions of *Sraddhas*, although those among them that are cursed or fallen should be excluded. They also should be carefully excluded that are either excessively fair or excessively black, that have diseased nails, that are lepers, that are deceitful, that are born in bastardy of widows or of women having husbands alive; and they also that support themselves by the profession of arms. That *Sraddha* which is censurable, consumeth the performer thereof like fire consuming fuel. If they that are to be employed in *Sraddhas* happen to be dumb, blind, or deaf, care should be taken to employ them along with Brahmanas conversant with the Vedas. O Yudhishthira, listen now unto whom thou shouldst give. He that knoweth all the *Vedas* should give only to that able Brahmana who is competent to rescue both the giver and himself, for he, indeed, is to be regarded as able who can rescue both the giver and himself. O son of Pritha, the sacred fires do not receive such gratification from libations of clarified butter, from offerings of flowers and sandal and other perfumed pastes as from the entertainment of guests. Therefore, do thou strive to entertain guests, O son of Pandu! O king, they that give unto guests water to wash their feet, butter to rub over their (tired) legs, light during the hours of darkness, food, and shelter, have not to go before Yama. The removal (after worship) of the flowery offerings unto the gods, the removal of the remnants of a Brahmana's feast, waiting (upon a Brahmana) with perfumed pastes, and the massaging of a Brahmana's limbs, are, each of them, O foremost of kings, productive of greater merit than the gift of kine. A person, without doubt, rescueth himself by the gift of a *Kapila* cow. Therefore, should one give away a *Kapila* cow decked with ornaments unto Brahmanas. O thou of the Bharata race, one should give unto a person of good lineage and conversant with the Vedas; unto a person that is poor; unto one leading a domestic mode of life but burdened with wife and children; unto one that daily adoreth the sacred fire; and unto one that hath done thee no service. Thou shouldst always give unto such persons but not to them that are in affluence. What merit is there, O thou foremost of the Bharata race, by giving unto one that is affluent? One cow must be given unto one Brahmana. A single cow must not be given unto many. For if the cow so given away (unto many) be sold, the giver's family is lost for three generations. Such a gift would not assuredly rescue the giver nor the Brahmana that takes it. He who giveth eighty *Ratis* of pure gold, earneth the merit of giving away a hundred pieces of gold for ever. He that giveth away a strong bull capable also of drawing the plough, is certainly rescued from all difficulties and finally goeth to heaven. He that giveth away land unto a learned Brahmana, hath all his desires fulfilled. The tired traveller, with weakened limbs and feet besmeared with dust, asks for the name of him that may give him food. There are men who answer him by telling him the name. That wise man who informs these toil-worn ones of the name of the person who may give them food, is, without doubt, regarded as equal in merit unto the giver himself of food. Therefore, abstaining from other kinds of gift, give thou food. There is no merit (arising out of gifts) that is so great as that of giving food. The man that according to the measure of his might gives well-cooked and pure food unto the Brahmanas, acquires, by that act of his, the companionship of Prajapati (*Brahma*). There is nothing superior to food. Therefore, food is regarded as the first and foremost of all things (to be given away). It hath been said that food itself is *Prajapati*. And *Prajapati* is regarded as the Year. And the Year is sacrifice. And everything is established in sacrifice, for it is from sacrifice that all creatures, mobile and immobile, take their origin. For this reason, it hath been heard by us, food is the foremost of all things. They that give away lakes and large pieces of water, and tanks and wells, and shelter and food and they that have sweet words for all, have not to hear the admonitions of Yama. With him who gives rice, and wealth earned by his labour, unto Brahmana of good behaviour, the earth is satisfied. And she poureth upon him showers of wealth. The giver of food walketh first, after him the speaker of truth and he that giveth unto persons that do not solicit. But the three go to the same place.'"

Vaisampayana continued, "Hearing all this, Yudhishthira, along with his younger brothers, impelled by curiosity, again addressed the high-souled Markandeya, saying, 'O great *Muni*, what is the distance of Yama's region from that of men? What is its measurement? How also do men pass it over? And by what means? O, tell me all this!'

"Markandeya said, 'O king, O them foremost of virtuous men, this question of thine appertains to a great mystery. It is sacred and much applauded by the *Rishis*. Appertaining as it also does to virtue, I will speak of it to thee. The distance of Yama's region from the abode of men is, O king, eighty-six thousand *Yojanas*! The way is over space, without water, and very terrible to behold. Nowhere on that road is the shade of a tree, nowhere any water, and nowhere any resting place in which the traveller, when fatigued, may rest for some moments. And men and women and all on earth that have life, are forcibly led along this way by the messengers of Yama. Those creatures that obey the mandates of the grim king, and they, O king, that have given horses and other good conveyances unto Brahmanas, proceed along this way on those animals and vehicles. And they that have given umbrellas proceed along this way with umbrellas warding off the sun's rays. And they that have given food, proceed without hunger, while they that have not given food proceed afflicted with hunger. And they that have given robes, proceed along this way attired in robes while they that have given none, proceed naked. And they that have given gold, proceed in happiness, themselves decked in ornaments. And they that have given land, proceed with every desire completely gratified. And they that have given grain, proceed without being afflicted with any want. And they that have given houses, proceed happily on cars. And those men that have given something to drink, proceed with cheerful hearts unafflicted with thirst. And they that have given lights, proceed happily lighting the way before them. And they that have given kine, proceed along the way happily, freed from all their sins. And they that have fasted for a month, proceed on cars drawn by swans. And they who have fasted for six nights, proceed on cars drawn by peacocks. And, O son of Pandu, he that fasteth three nights upon only one meal without a second during this period goeth into a region free from disease and anxiety. And water hath this excellent property that it produceth happiness in the region of Yama. And they that give water find for themselves a river there of the name of Pushpodaka. And the givers of water on the earth drink cool and ambrosial draughts from that stream. And they that are of evil deeds have pus ordained for them. Thus, O great king, that river serveth all purposes. Therefore, O king, adore thou duly these Brahmanas (that are with thee). Weak in limbs owing to the way he has walked, and besmeared with the dust of the high-road, the traveller enquireth for the name of him who giveth food, and cometh in hope to his house. Adore thou him with reverent attention, for he indeed is a guest, and he is a Brahmana. The gods with Indra at their head follow him as he proceedeth. And if he is adored, the gods with Indra become gratified, and if he is not adored, the celestials with their chief become cheerless. Therefore, O thou foremost of kings, worship thou these Brahmanas duly. I have thus spoken to thee upon a hundred subjects. What dost thou desire to hear from me again?'

"Yudhishthira said, 'O master, conversant thou art with virtue and morality, and so I desire to repeatedly listen to thee as thou speakest on sacred subjects appertaining to virtue and morals.'

"Markandeya said, 'O king, I will now speak on another sacred subject appertaining to eternal interests and capable of washing off all sins. Listen thou with rapt attention. O thou foremost of the Bharatas, the merit equal to that of giving away a *Kapila* cow in (the *tirtha* called) *Jyeshtha-Pushkara* arises from washing the feet of Brahmanas. As long as the earth remains wet with water which a Brahmana hath touched with his feet, so long do *Pitris* drink water of cups made of lotus-leaves. If the guest is welcomed (with enquiries about his welfare), the deities of fire become glad; and if he is offered a seat, it is the god of a hundred sacrifices, who is gratified. If his feet are washed, it is the *Pitris* who are delighted; and if he is fed it is *Prajapati* that is pleased. One should with collected soul, give a cow when (during her throes) the feet and head of her calf are visible, before her delivery is complete. A cow with her calf in the air in course of falling from the uterus to the earth, is to be regarded as equal to the earth herself. He, therefore, that giveth away such a cow, reapeth the merit of giving away the earth. And he that giveth away such a cow, is adored in heaven for as many thousands of *Yugas* as there are bristles on the bodies of the animal and her young one together. And, O Bharata, he that having accepted a thing in gift giveth it away immediately unto a person that is virtuous and honest, reapeth very great merit. Without doubt, he reapeth the fruit of giving away the whole earth to her utmost limits and with her oceans and seas and caves, her mountains and forests and woods. That Brahmana who eateth in silence from a plate, keeping his hands between his knees, succeedeth in rescuing others. And those Brahmanas that abstain from drink and who are never spoken of by others as having any faults and who daily read the *Samhitas*, are capable of rescuing others. Libations of butter and edible offerings should all be presented to a Brahmana who is learned in the *Vedas*. And as libations of clarified butter poured into fire never go in vain, so gift to virtuous Brahmanas learned in the *Vedas* can never go in vain. The Brahmanas have anger for their weapon; they never fight with arms of iron and steel. Indeed the Brahmanas slay with anger like Indra slaying the Asuras with his thunder-bolt. Thus prelection appertaining to virtue and morality is now over. Hearing this, the *Munis* of the forest of *Naimisha* were filled with delight. And those ascetics were also freed from grief and anger by listening to it. And they were also purged of all their sins in consequence of this. And, O king, those human beings that listen to it become freed from the obligation of rebirth.'

"Yudhishthira said, 'O thou of great wisdom, what purification is there by which a Brahmana may always keep himself pure? I desire to hear of it from thee, O thou foremost of all virtuous men!'

"Markandeya answered, 'There are three kinds of purity, viz., purity in speech, purity in deed, and purity achieved by use of water. He that has recourse to these three different kinds of purity, attains, without doubt, to heaven. That Brahmana who adoreth the goddess *Sandhya* in the morning and the evening, and who recites meditatively the sacred goddess *Gayairi* who is the mother of the *Vedas*, sanctified by the latter, is freed from all his sins. Even if he accepts in gift the entire earth with her oceans, he doth not, on that account, suffer the least unhappiness. And those heavenly bodies in the sky including the sun that may be inauspicious and hostile towards him soon become auspicious and favourable towards him in consequence of these acts of his, while those stars that are auspicious and favourable become more auspicious and more favourable in consequence of such conduct of his. And terrible Rakshasas subsisting on animal food, of gigantic and fierce mien, all become unable to prevail over a Brahmana who practiseth these purifications. The Brahmanas are even like blazing fires. They incur no fault in consequence of teaching, of officiating at sacrifices, and of accepting gifts from others. Whether the Brahmana be cognisant of the *Vedas* or ignorant of them, whether they be pure or impure, they should never be insulted, for Brahmanas are like fires. As the fire that blazeth up in the place set apart for the cremation of the dead is never regarded impure on that account, so the Brahmana, be he learned or ignorant, is always pure. He is great and a very god! Cities that are adorned with walls and gates and palaces one after another, lose their beauty if they are bereft of Brahmanas. That, indeed, O king, is a city where Brahmanas accomplished in the *Vedas*, duly observing the duties of their order and possessed of learning and ascetic merit, reside. O son of Pritha, that spot, be it a wood or pasture land, where learned Brahmanas reside, hath been called a city. And that place, O king, becometh a *tirtha* also. By approaching a king that offereth protection, as also a Brahmana possessed of ascetic merit, and by offering worship unto both, a man may purge off his sins immediately. The learned have said that ablutions in the sacred *tirthas*, recitation of the names of holy ones, and converse with the good and virtuous, are all acts worthy of applause. They that are virtuous and honest always regard themselves as sanctified by the holy companionship of persons like themselves and by the water of pure and sacred converse. The carrying of three staffs, the vow of silence, matted hair on head, the shaving of the crown, covering one's person with barks and deerskins, the practice of vows, ablutions, the worship of fire, abode in the woods, emaciating the body, all these are useless if the heart be not pure. The indulgence of the six senses is easy, if purity be not sought in the object of enjoyment. Abstinence, however, which of itself is difficult, is scarcely easy without purity of the objects of enjoyment. O king of kings, among the six senses, the mind alone that is easily moved is the most dangerous!

Those high-souled persons that do not commit sins in word, deed, heart and soul, are said to undergo ascetic austerities, and not they that suffer their bodies to be wasted by fasts and penances. He that hath no feeling of kindness for relatives cannot be free from sin even if his body be pure. That hard-heartedness of his is the enemy of his asceticism. Asceticism, again, is not mere abstinence from the pleasures of the world. He that is always pure and decked with virtue, he that practises kindness all his life, is a *Muni* even though he may lead a domestic life. Such a man is purged of all his sins. Fasts and other penances cannot destroy sins, however much they may weaken and dry up the body that is made of flesh and blood. The man whose heart is without holiness, suffers torture only by undergoing penances in ignorance of their meaning. He is never freed from sins of such acts. The fire he worshippeth doth not consume his sins. It is in consequence of holiness and virtue alone that men attain to regions of blessedness, and fasts and vows become efficacious. Subsistence on fruits and roots, the vow of silence, living upon air, the shaving of the crown, abandonment of a fixed home, the wearing of matted locks on the head, lying under the canopy of heaven, daily fasts, the worship of fire, immersion in water, and lying on the bare ground,—these alone cannot produce such a result. They only that are possessed of holiness succeed, by knowledge and deeds, to conquer disease, decrepitude and death, and acquire a high status. As seeds that have been scorched by fire do not sprout forth, so the pains that have been burnt by knowledge cannot effect the soul. This inert body that is only like a block of wood when destitute of souls, is, without doubt, short lived like froth in the ocean. He that obtaineth a view of his soul, the soul that resideth in every body, by help of one or half of a rhythmic line (of the *Vedas*), hath no more need for anything. Some obtaining a knowledge of identity with the Supreme Soul from but two letters (of the *Vedas*) and some from hundreds and thousands of rhythmic lines, acquire salvation, for the knowledge of one's identity with the Supreme Soul is the sure indication of salvation. The men of old, distinguished for their knowledge, have said, neither this world nor that hereafter nor bliss can be his who is disturbed by doubts. And belief of one's identity with the Supreme Soul is the indication of salvation. He that knoweth the true meaning of the Vedas, understandeth their true use. Such a man is affrighted at the Vedic ritual like a man at sight of a forest conflagration. Giving up dry disputation, have recourse to *Sruti* and *Smriti*, and seek thou, with the aid of thy reason, the knowledge of the Undecaying One that is without a second. One's search (after this knowledge) becometh futile from defect of means. Therefore, should one carefully strive to obtain that knowledge by aid of the *Vedas*. The *Vedas* are the Supreme Soul; they are His body; they are the Truth. The soul that is bounded by the animal organism is incompetent to know Him in whom all the *Vedas* merge. That Supreme Soul, however, is capable of being known by the pure intellect. The existence of the *gods* as stated in the *Vedas*, the efficacy of acts, and the capacity for action of being furnished with bodies, are noticeable in every *Yuga*. Independence of these and annihilation are to be sought from purity of the senses. Therefore, the suspension of the function of the senses is the true fasting. One may attain to heaven by asceticism, one may obtain objects of enjoyment by the practice of charity and may have his sins purged off by ablutions in *tirthas*. But complete emancipation cannot be had except by knowledge.'"

Vaisampayana continued, "Thus addressed, O great king, by the *Rishi*, Yudhishthira of great fame then said, 'O holy one, I desire to listen to the rules about that charity which is meritorious.'

"Markandeya said, 'O great king, O Yudhishthira, the rules about charity which thou wishest to hear from me are always highly regarded by me. Listen now to the mysteries of charity as expounded in the *sruti* and the *smritis*! A man that performs a *sraddha* in the conjunction called *Gajacchaya* at a place that is fanned by the leaves of the *Aswattha* tree enjoys the fruits thereof, O Yudhishthira, for a hundred thousand *kalpas*. O king, he that foundeth a *dharmasala* and established there a person to look after all comers, is crowned with the merits of all the sacrifices. He that giveth away a horse at a *tirtha* where the current of the river runneth in a direction opposite to its general course, reapeth merit that is inexhaustible. The guest that comes to one's house for food is none other than Indra himself. If he is entertained with food, Indra himself conferreth on the best merit that is inexhaustible. As men cross seas by vessels, so are the givers mentioned above are saved from all their sins. So what is given unto Brahmanas produceth, like gift of curds, inexhaustible merits. A gift on particular lunations produceth merit that is twice as much as a gift on other days. That in a particular season produceth merit ten times greater that in other seasons. That in a particular year produceth merit a hundred times greater than in other years. And lastly, a gift on the last day of the last month of the year produceth merit that is inexhaustible. A gift also that is made while the Sun is on the solstitial points, one again that is made on the last day of the Sun's path through Libra, Aries, Gemini, Virgo, and Pisces, a gift again during eclipses of the Moon and the Sun, produce merit that is inexhaustible. The learned have also said that gifts made during the seasons produce merit that is ten times, those made during the change of seasons, a hundred times—and those made during the days when *Rahu* is visible, a thousand times—greater than what is produced by gifts at other time; while a gift made on the last day of the Sun's course through Libra and Aries produces merit that knows no diminution. O king, no one can enjoy landed possessions unless he giveth away land, and no one can go on cars and vehicles unless he giveth away these. Indeed a person on rebirth obtaineth the fruition of whatever objects he hath in view at the time of making a gift to a Brahmana. Gold hath sprung from Fire; the Earth from Vishnu; and the cows from the Sun. He, therefore, that giveth away gold, land, and kine attaineth all the regions of Agni, Vishnu, and the Sun. There is nothing so eternal as a gift. Where, therefore, in the three worlds is anything that is more auspicious? It is for this, O king, that they who have great intelligence say that there is nothing higher and greater in the three worlds than gift!'"

SECTION CC

Vaisampayana said, "Having, O great king, heard from the illustrious Markandeya the history of the attainment of heaven by the royal sage Indradyumna, Yudhishthira, that bull of the Bharata race, once more asked that sinless *Muni* endued with great ascetic merit and long life, saying, 'Thou knowest, O virtuous one, the entire host of the gods, the *Danavas*, and the *Rakshasas*. Thou art acquainted also with various royal genealogies and many eternal lines of *Rishis*! O best of Brahmanas, there is nothing in this world that thou dost not know! Thou knowest also, O *Muni*, many delightful stories about *men*, *Snakes* and *Rakshasas*; about gods, *Gandharvas*, and *Yakshas*, and about *Kinnaras* and *Apsaras*! I desire now to hear from thee, O best of Brahmanas, as to why Kuvalaswa—that unvanquished king of Ikshavaku's race changed his name, assuming another, viz., *Dhundhumara*. O thou best of Bhrigu's line, I desire to know in detail why the name of Kuvalaswa of great intelligence underwent such a change!'"

Vaisampayana continued, "Thus addressed by Yudhishthira, the great *Muni* Markandeya, O Bharata, then began the history of Dhundhumara!"

"Markandeya said, 'O royal Yudhishthira, listen to me, I will tell thee all! The story of Dhundhumara is a moral one. Listen to it then! Listen now, O king, to the story of how the royal Kuvalaswa of Ikshvaku's race came to be known as Dhundhumara. O son, O Bharata, there was a celebrated *Rishi* of the name of Utanka and, O thou of the Kuru race, Utanka had his hermitage in a delightful wilderness. And, O great king, the *Rishi* Utanka underwent ascetic austerities of the severest kind and the lord Utanka underwent those penances for numberless years with the object of obtaining the favours of Vishnu, and gratified with his penances that illustrious Lord presented himself before Utanka. And beholding the Deity, the *Rishi* in all humility began to gratify him with many hymns, and Utanka said, "O thou of great effulgence all creatures with the gods, *Asuras* and human beings, all things that are mobile or immobile, even *Brahma* himself, the Vedas, and all things that are capable of being known, have, O lord, been created by thee! The firmament is thy head, O god, and the sun and the moon are thy eyes! And, O Unfading One, the winds are thy breath and fire thy energy! The directions of the horizon constitute thy arms and the great ocean thy stomach! And, O god, the hills and mountains constitute thy thigh and the sky thy hips, O slayer of Madhu! The earth constitutes thy feet, and the plants the bristles on thy body. And, O lord, Indra and Soma and Agni and Varuna, indeed all the gods, the *Asuras* and the great Snakes all wait upon thee with humility, adoring thee with various hymns! O Lord of the Universe, created things are pervaded by thee. The great *Rishis* of high energy and ever plunged in ascetic meditation, always adore thee. When thou art gratified, the universe is in peace. And when thou art angry, terror pervadeth every soul. Thou art, O Lord, the great dispeller of all terrors and thou art the One Supreme Male Being! Thou art the cause of happiness of both gods and human beings! And, O Lord, by three steps of thine thou didst cover the three worlds! And it was by thee that the *Asuras* in the height of their power were destroyed! It is owing to thy prowess, O God, that the celestials obtained peace and happiness and, O thou of great effulgence, it was thy anger that destroyed hundred great *Daitya* chiefs. Thou art the Creator and destroyer of all creatures in the world. It is by adoring thee that the gods have obtained happiness." It was thus, O Yudhishthira, that the high-souled Utanka praised the Lord of the senses. And Vishnu, therefore, said unto Utanka, "I am gratified with thee. Ask thou the boon that thou desirest." And Utanka said, "This indeed hath been a great boon to me, in that I have been able to behold Hari, that eternal Being, that divine Creator, that Lord of the universe!" Thus addressed Vishnu said, "I am gratified with this absence of all desires on thy part and with thy devotion, O thou best of men! But, O Brahmanas, O regenerate one, thou shouldst of a certainty accept some boon from me!" Thus requested by Hari to accept a boon Utanka then, O thou best of Bharatas, with joined hands begged a boon saying, "O illustrious one, O thou of eyes like lotus leaves, if thou hast been gratified with me, then let my heart always rest on virtue, truth, and self-content. And, O Lord, let my heart always turn to thee in devotion." And hearing these words of Utanka, the holy one said, "O regenerate one, all this shall happen to thee through my grace. And there will also appear in thee a *yoga* power endued with which thou shalt achieve a great thing for the dwellers of Heaven, as also for the triple world. Even now a great *Asura* of the name of Dhundhu is undergoing ascetic penances of fierce austerity with the object of destroying the triple world. Hear now as to who will slay that *Asura*. O son, there will appear a king of invincible energy and great prowess and he will be born in the race of Ikshvaku and will be known by the name of Vrihadaswa who will have a son of the name of Kuvalaswa endued with great holiness and self-control and celebrity. And that best of kings will be furnished with *yoga* power springing from me and urged and commended by thee, O regenerate *Rishi*, that king will be the slayer of the Asura Dhundhu." And having said these words unto that Brahmana, Vishnu disappeared there and then.'"

SECTION CCI

"Markandeya said, 'O king, after the death of Ikshvaku, a highly virtuous king of the name of *Sasada*, ascending the throne of Ayodhya ruled this earth. And from *Sasada* was descended Kakutstha of great energy. And Kakutstha had a son of name Anenas. And Anenas had a son named Prithu and Prithu had a son named Viswagaswa and from Viswagaswa sprang Adri and from Adri sprang Yuvanaswa and from Yuvanaswa sprang Sravastha and it was by this Sravastha that the city called *Sravasthi* was built and from Sravastha was descended Vrihadaswa and from Vrihadaswa sprang Kuvalaswa and Kuvalaswa had twentyone thousand sons and all these sons were fierce and powerful and skilled in learning. And Kuvalaswa excelled his father in every quality. And when the time came, his father Vrihadaswa installed him—the brave and highly virtuous Kuvalaswa—on the throne. And having thus made over the royal dignity to his son, that slayer of foes—king Vrihadaswa of great intelligence—retired into the woods for asceticism.'

"Markandeya continued, 'O king, when the royal sage Vrihadaswa was about to retire into the woods, that best of Brahmanas, Utanka heard of it. And Utanka who was possessed of great energy and immeasurable soul, approached that foremost of all wielders of weapons and best of men. And approaching him, the *Rishis* began to persuade him to give up asceticism. And Utanka said, "O king, to protect (the people) is thy duty. It behoveth thee to do that duty of thine. Let us be free from all anxiety through thy grace. Possessed as thou art of a great soul, protected by thee, the earth will be freed from all dangers. Therefore, it behoveth thee, not to retire into the woods. Great merit attaches to the act of protecting people in this world. Such merit can never be acquired in the woods. Let not thy heart, therefore, turn to this course. The merit, great king, that was acquired in days of old by great royal sages by protecting their subjects was so great that nothing equal to it could be seen. The king should always protect his subjects. It behoveth thee, therefore, to protect thy people. O lord of the earth, I cannot (at present) perform my ascetic devotions peacefully. Close to my asylum there is a sea of sands known by the name of *Ujjalaka*. And it occupies a level country and is without any water. And it extends many *yojanas* in length and breadth and in that desert dwells a chief of the *Danavas* called Dhundhu by name. And Dhundhu is the son of Madhu and Kaitabha, and is fierce and terrible and possessed of great prowess. And endued with immeasurable energy, that *Danava*, O king, dwelleth under the ground, and, O king, it behoveth thee to retire into the woods, having first slain that *Asura*. That *Asura* is now lying still in the observance of an ascetic penance of great austerity and, O king, the object he hath in view is sovereignty over the celestials as also of the three worlds. And, O king, having obtained a boon from the Grandsire of all creatures, that *Asura* hath become incapable of being slain by the gods and *Daityas* and *Rakshasas* and *Gandharvas*. Slay though him, O king, and blessed be thou and let not thy heart turn to any other course. By slaying him thou wilt without doubt, achieve a great thing and thou wilt also obtain eternal and undying fame. And O king, when at the end of every year that wicked *Asura* lying covered with sands, wakes up and begins to breathe, then the whole earth with her mountains, forests and woods begins to tremble. And his breath raiseth up clouds of sands, and shroudeth the very sun, and for seven days continually the earth tremble all over, and sparks and flames of fire mixed with smoke spread far around and for all this, O king, I cannot rest in peace in my asylum. Slay thou him, O king, for the good of the world. Indeed, when that *Asura* is slain the triple world will be in peace and happiness. That thou art competent, O king, to slay that *Asura*, I fully believe. Thy energy will be enhanced by Vishnu with the addition of his own. In days of old, O king, Vishnu gave this boon that the king who should slay this fierce and great *Asura* would be pervaded by the invincible energy of Vishnu himself. Bearing that invincible *Vaishnava* energy in thyself, slay thou, O great king, that *Daitya* of fierce prowess. Possessed as Dhundhu is of mighty energy, no one, O king, that is endued with small energy himself will be capable of consuming him, even if he were to strive for a hundred years."'"

SECTION CCII

"Markandeya said, 'Thus addressed by Utanka, that unvanquished royal sage, with joined hands, O thou foremost of the Kuru race, replied unto Utanka, saying, "This visit of thine, O Brahmana, will not be in vain. This my son, O holy one, known by the name of Kuvalaswa is endued with steadiness and activity. In prowess also he is unequaled on earth. Without doubt he will accomplish all this that is agreeable to thee, aided by all his brave sons endued with arms like unto iron maces. Give me leave to retire, O Brahmana, for I have now given up my weapons." Thus addressed by the king, that *Muni* of immeasurable energy replied unto him, saying, "So be it." And the royal sage Vrihadaswa then, having commended his son to obey the behest of the high-souled Utanka saying, "Let it be done by thee," himself retired into an excellent forest.'

"Yudhishthira said, 'O holy one, O thou possessed of the wealth of asceticism, who was this *Daitya* of great energy? Whose son and whose grandson was he? I desire to know all this; O thou possessed of the wealth of asceticism I never heard of this mighty *Daitya* before. I desire to know all this truly, O holy one, and with all particulars in detail, O thou of great wisdom and ascetic wealth!'

"Markandeya said, 'O monarch, know everything as it happened, O ruler of men, as I narrate the particulars truly, O thou of great wisdom! When the world became one broad expanse of water and creatures mobile and immobile were destroyed, when, O bull of the Bharata race, the entire creation came to its end, He who is the Source and Creator of the Universe, viz., the Eternal and unfading Vishnu, He who is called by *Munis* crowned with ascetic success as the Supreme Lord of the Universe, that Being of great holiness, then lay in *Yoga* sleep on the wide hood of the Snake Sesha of immeasurable energy, and the Creator of the Universe, that highly-blessed and holy Hari, knowing no deterioration, lay on the hood of that Snake encircling the whole Earth and as the Deity lay asleep on that bed, a lotus, endued with great beauty and effulgence equal unto that of the Sun, sprang from his navel. And from that lotus possessed of effulgence like unto the Sun's, sprang the Grandsire *Brahma*, that lord of the worlds who is the four *Vedas*, who hath four forms and four faces, who is invincible in consequence of his own energy and who is endued with mighty strength and great prowess and as the Lord Hari of wondrous frame, possessed of great lustre and decked with a crown and the *Kaustubha* gem and attired in purple silk, lay stretched for many a *yojana* on that excellent bed furnished by the hood of the snake itself extending far and wide, blazing, O king, in his beauty and the lustre of his own body like a thousand Suns concentrated in one mass. He was beheld some time after by two *Danavas* of great prowess named Madhu and Kaitabha and beholding Hari (in that posture) and the Grandsire with eyes like lotus-leaves seated on that lotus, both Madhu and Kaitabha wandered much and they began to terrify and alarm Brahma of immeasurable prowess, and the illustrious Brahma alarmed by their continued exertions trembled on his seat, and at his trembling the stalk of the lotus on which he was seated began to tremble and when the lotus-stalk trembled, Kesava awoke. And awakened from his slumber, Govinda beheld those *Danavas* of mighty energy, and beholding them the Deity said unto them, "Welcome, ye mighty ones! I am gratified with you! Therefore, I will grant you excellent boons!" And thereupon both those proud and mighty *Danavas*, O king, laughingly replied unto Hrishikesa, saying, "Ask boons of us, O Divine one! O thou that art the Supreme Deity, we are disposed to grant thee a boon. Indeed, we will grant thee a boon! Therefore, ask thou of us anything that cometh to thy mind." Thus addressed by them the holy one spoke, "Ye brave ones, I will accept a boon from you. There is a boon that I desire. Both of you are possessed of mighty energy. There is no male person like unto any of you. O ye of unbaffled prowess, submit ye to be slain by me. Even that is what I desire to accomplish for the good of the world." Hearing these words of the Deity, both Madhu and Kaitabha said, "We have never before spoken an untruth; no, not even in jest; what shall we say of other occasions! O thou foremost of male Beings, know that we have ever been firm in truth and morality. In strength, in forms, in beauty, in virtue, in asceticism, in charity, in behaviour, in goodness, in self control, there is no one equal unto either of us. A great danger, O Kesava, hath approached us. Accomplish thou, therefore, what thou hast said. No one can prevail over Time. But, O Lord, there is one thing that we desire to be done by thee. O thou best and foremost of all Deities, thou must slay us at a spot that is absolutely uncovered. And, O thou of excellent eyes, we also desire

to become thy sons. This is the boon that we desire, know then, O chief of the gods! Let not that, O Deity, be false which thou hadst at first promised to us." The Holy One then replied unto them saying, "Yes, I will do as ye desire. Everything will be as ye wish!"

"Markandeya continued, 'Then Govinda began to reflect but uncovered space found he none and when he could not discover any spot that was uncovered on earth or in the sky, that foremost Deity then beheld his thighs to be absolutely uncovered. And there, O king, the illustrious Deity cut off the heads of Madhu and Kaitabha with his keenedged discus!'"

SECTION CCIII

"Markandeya said, 'The illustrious Dhundhu, O king, was the son of Madhu and Kaitabha, and possessed of great energy and prowess, he underwent ascetic penances of great austerity and he stood erect on one leg and reduced his body to a mass of only veins and arteries, and Brahma, gratified with him, gave him a boon. And the boon he had asked of the lord Prajapati was in these words, "Let no one among the gods, the *Danavas*, the *Rakshas*, the Snakes, the *Gandharvas* and the *Rakshasas* be capable of slaying me. Even this is the boon that I ask of thee." And the Grandsire replied unto him saying, "Let it be as thou wishest. Go thy way." And thus addressed by the Grandsire, the *Danava* placed the feet of the Deity on his head and having thus touched with reverence the Deity's feet he went away and possessed of mighty energy and prowess. Dhundhu, having obtained the boon hastily approached Vishnu remembering the death of his father at the hands of that Deity, and the wrathful Dhundhu having vanquished the gods with the *Gandharvas* began to distress all the celestials with Vishnu at their head. And at last O bull of the Bharata race, that wicked souled *Asura* arriving at a sea of sands known by the name of Ujjalaka, began to distress to the utmost of his might the asylum of Utanka. And endued with fierce energy, Dhundhu, the son of Madhu and Kaitabha, lay in his subterranean cave underneath the sands in the observance of fierce ascetic and severe austerities with the object of destroying the triple world, and while the *Asura* lay breathing near the asylum of Utanka that *Rishi* possessed of the splendour of fire, king Kualaswa with his troops, accompanied by the Brahmana Utanka, as also by all his sons set out for that region, O bull of the Bharata race! And after that grinder of foes, the royal Kuvalaswa, had set out, accompanied by his twenty-one thousand sons all of whom were exceedingly powerful, the illustrious Lord Vishnu filled him with his own energy at the command of Utanka and impelled by the desire of benefiting the triple world and while that invincible hero was proceeding on his way a loud voice was heard in the sky repeating the words, "This fortunate and unslayable one will become the destroyer of Dhundhu to-day." And the gods began to shower upon him celestial flowers. And the celestial kettle drums began to sound their music although none played upon them. And during the march of that wise one, cool breezes began to blow and the chief of the celestials poured

gentle showers wetting the dust on the roads and, O Yudhishthira, the cars of the celestials could be seen high over the spot where the mighty *Asura* Dhundhu was. The gods and *Gandharvas* and great *Rishis* urged by curiosity, came there to behold the encounter between Dhundhu and Kuvalaswa and, O thou of the Kuru race, filled by Narayana with his own energy, king Kuvalaswa, aided by his sons, soon surrounded that sea of sands and the king ordered that wilderness to be excavated and after the king's sons had excavated that sea of sands for seven days, they could see the mighty *Asura* Dhundhu. And, O bull of the Bharata race, the huge body of that *Asura* lay within those sands, effulgent in its own energy like the Sun himself. And Dhundhu, O king, was lying covering the western region of the desert and surrounded on all sides by the sons of Kuvalaswa, the *Danava* was assaulted with sharp-pointed shafts and maces and heavy and short clubs and axes and clubs, with iron spikes and darts and bright and keen-edged swords, and thus assaulted, the mighty *Danava* rose from his recumbent posture in wrath. And enraged, the *Asura* began to swallow those various weapons that were hurled at him and he vomited from his mouth fiery flames like unto those of the fire called *Samvarta* that appeareth at the end of the *Yuga* and by those flames of his, the *Asura* consumed all the sons of the king and, O tiger among men, like the Lord Kapila of old consuming the sons of king Sagara, the infuriated *Asura* overwhelming the triple world with the flames vomited from his mouth, achieved that wonderful feat in a moment. And, O thou best of the Bharatas, when all those sons of king Kuvalaswa were consumed by the fire emitted by the *Asura* in wrath, the monarch, possessed as he was of mighty energy, then approached the *Danava* who, like unto a second Kumbhakarna of mighty energy, had come to the encounter after waking from his slumbers. From the body of the king, O monarch, then began to flow a mighty and copious stream of water and that stream soon extinguished, O king, the fiery flames emitted by the *Asura*. And, O great king, the royal Kuvalaswa, filled with *Yoga* force, having extinguished those flames by the water that issued from his body, consumed that *Daitya* of wicked prowess with the celebrated weapon called *Brahma* for relieving the triple world of its fears, and the royal sage Kuvalaswa, having consumed that great *Asura*, that foe of the celestials and slayer of all enemies, by means of that weapon became like unto a second chief of the triple world and the high-souled king Kuvalaswa having slain the *Asura* Dhundhu, became from that time known by the name of *Dhundhumara* and from that time he came to be regarded as invincible in battle, and the gods and the great *Rishis* who had come to witness that encounter were so far gratified with him that they addressed him saying, "Ask thou a boon of us!" And thus solicited by the gods, the king bowed to them and filled with joy, the king said unto them, with joined hands these words, "Let me be always able to give wealth unto

superior Brahmanas! Let me be invincible as regards all foes! Let there be friendship between myself and Vishnu! Let me have no ill-feeling towards any creature! Let my heart always turn to virtue! And let me (finally) dwell in heaven for ever!" And the gods and the *Rishis* and Utanka, hearing this were exceedingly gratified and all of them said, "Let it be as thou wishest!" And, O king, having also blessed him with many other speeches, the gods and the great *Rishis* then went away to their respective abodes. And, O Yudhishthira, after the slaughter of all his sons, king Kuvalaswa had still three sons left, and, O thou of the Bharata race, they were called *Dridaswa* and *Kapilaswa* and *Chandraswa*. It is from them, O king, that the illustrious line of kings belonging to Ikshvaku's race, all possessed of immeasurable prowess, hath sprung.

"'It was thus, O best of king, that that great *Daitya* of the name Dhundhu, the son of Madhu and Kaitabha was slain by Kuvalaswa and it was for this also that king came to be called by the name of *Dhundhumara*. And indeed, the name he assumed was no empty one but was literally true.

"'I have now told thee all that thou hadst asked me, viz., all about that person in consequence of whose act the story of Dhundhu's death hath become famous. He that listeneth to this holy history connected with the glory of Vishnu, becometh virtuous and obtaineth children. By listening to this story on particular lunations, one becometh blessed with long life and great good fortune. And freed from every anxiety one ceaseth to have any fear of diseases.'"

SECTION CCIV

Vaisampayana said, "O thou foremost of the Bharata race, king Yudhishthira then asked the illustrious Markandeya a difficult question about morality, saying, 'I desire to hear, O holy one, about the high and excellent virtue of women. I desire to hear from thee, O Brahmana, discourse about the subtle truths of morality. O regenerate *Rishi*, O best of men, the Sun, the Moon, the Wind, the Earth, the Fire, the father, the mother, the preceptor—these and other objects ordained by the gods, appear to us as Deities embodied! All these that are reverend ones are worthy of our best regard. So also is the woman who adoreth one lord. The worship that chaste wives offer unto their husbands appeareth to me to be fraught with great difficulty. O adorable one, it behoveth thee to discourse to us of the high and excellent virtue of chaste wives—of wives who restraining all their senses and keeping their hearts under complete control regard their husbands as veritable gods. O holy and adorable one, all this appears to me to be exceedingly difficult of accomplishment. O regenerate one, the worship that sons offer to their mothers and fathers and that wives offer to their husbands, both seem to me to be highly difficult. I do not behold anything that is more difficult than the severe virtue of chaste women. O Brahmana, the duties that women of good behaviour discharge with care and the conduct that is pursued by good sons towards their fathers and mothers appear to me to be most difficult of performance. Those women that are each devoted to but one lord, they that always speak the truth, they that undergo a period of gestation for full ten months—there is nothing, O Brahmana, that is more difficult than that is done by these. O worshipful one, women bring forth their offspring with great hazard to themselves and great pain and rear their children, O bull among Brahmanas, with great affection! Those persons also who being always engaged in acts of cruelty and thereby incurring general hatred, succeed yet in doing their duties accomplish what, in my opinion, is exceedingly difficult. O regenerate one, tell me the truths of the duties of the Kshatriya order. It is difficult, O twice-born one, for those high-souled ones to acquire virtue who by the duties of their order are obliged to do what is cruel. O holy one, thou art capable of answering all questions; I desire to hear thee discourse on all this. O thou foremost of Bhrigu's race, I desire to listen to all this, waiting respectfully on thee, O thou of excellent vows!'

"Markandeya said, 'O thou foremost of the Bharata race, I will discourse to thee on all this truly, however difficult of answer thy question may be. Listen to me, therefore, as I speak unto thee. Some regard the mother as superior and some the father. The mother, however, that bringeth forth and reareth up offspring what is more difficult. Fathers also, by ascetic penances, by worship of the gods, by adorations addressed to them, by bearing cold and heat, by incantations and other means desire to have children. And having by these painful expedients obtained children that are so difficult of acquisition, they then, O hero, are always anxious about the future of their sons and, O Bharata, both the father and the mother desire to see in their sons fame and achievements and prosperity and offspring and virtue. That son is virtuous who realises these hopes of his parents. And, O great king, that son with whom the father and the mother are gratified, achieveth eternal fame and eternal virtue both here and thereafter. As regards women again, neither sacrifice nor *sraddhas,* nor fasts are of any efficacy. By serving their husbands only they can win heaven. O king, O Yudhishthira, remembering this alone, listen thou with attention to the duties of chaste women.'"

SECTION CCV

"Markandeya said, 'There was, O Bharata, a virtuous ascetic of the name of Kausika and endued with wealth of asceticism and devoted to the study of the *Vedas*, he was a very superior Brahmana and that best of Brahmanas studied all the *Vedas* with the *Angas* and the *Upanishadas* and one day he was reciting the *Vedas* at the foot of a tree and at that time there sat on the top of that tree a female crane and that she-crane happened at that time to befoul the Brahmana's body and beholding that crane the Brahmana became very angry and thought of doing her an injury and as the Brahmana cast his angry glances upon the crane and thought also of doing her an injury, she fell down on the ground and beholding the crane thus fallen from the tree and insensible in death, the Brahmana was much moved by pity and the regenerate one began to lament for the dead crane saying, "Alas, I have done a bad deed, urged by anger and malice!"'

"Markandeya continued, 'Having repeated these words many times, that learned Brahmana entered a village for procuring alms. And, O bull of the Bharata race, in course of his eleemosynary round among the houses of persons of good lineage, the Brahmana entered one such house that he knew from before. And as he entered the house, he said, "*Give.*" And he was answered by a female with the word, "*Stay.*" And while the housewife was engaged, O king, in cleaning the vessel from which alms are given, her husband, O thou best of the Bharatas, suddenly entered the house, very much afflicted with hunger. The chaste housewife beheld her husband and disregarding the Brahmana, gave her lord water to wash his feet and face and also a seat and after that the black-eyed lady, placing before her lord savoury food and drink, humbly stood beside him desirous of attending to all his wants. And, O Yudhishthira, that obedient wife used every day to eat the orts of her husband's plate and, always conducting herself in obedience to the wishes of the lord, that lady ever regarded her husband, and all her heart's affections inclined towards her lord. Of various and holy behaviour and skilful in all domestic duties and attentive to all her relatives, she always did what was agreeable and beneficial to her husband and she also, with rapt senses attended to the worship of the gods and the wants of guests and servants and her mother-in-law and father-in-law.

"'And while the lady of handsome eyes was still engaged in waiting upon her lord, she beheld that Brahmana waiting for alms and beholding him, she remembered that she had asked him to wait. And remembering all this, she felt abashed. And then that chaste woman possessed of great fame, took something for alms and went out, O thou foremost of the Bharatas, for giving it unto that Brahmana. And when she came before him, the Brahmana said, "O best of women, O blessed one, I am surprised at thy conduct! Having requested me to wait saying, '*Stay*' thou didst not dismiss me!"'

"Markandeya continued, 'O lord of men, beholding that Brahmana filled with wrath and blazing with his energy, that chaste woman began to conciliate him and said, "O learned one, it behoveth thee to forgive me. My husband is my supreme god. He came hungry and tired and was being served and waited upon by me." Hearing this, the Brahmana said, "With thee Brahmanas are not worthy of superior regard. Exaltest thou thy husband above them? Leading a domestic life, dost thou disregard Brahmanas? Indra himself boweth down unto them, what shall I say of men on earth. Proud woman, dost thou not know it, hast thou never heard it, that the Brahmanas are like fire and may consume the entire earth?" At these words of that Brahmana the woman answered, "I am no she-crane, O regenerate *Rishi*! O thou that art endued with the wealth of asceticism, cast off this anger of thine. Engaged as thou are, what canst thou do to me with these angry glances of thine? I do not disregard Brahmanas. Endued with great energy of soul, they are like unto the gods themselves. But, O sinless one, this fault of mine it behoveth thee to forgive. I know the energy and high dignity of Brahmanas that are possessed of wisdom. The waters of the ocean have been made brackish and undrinkable by the wrath of the Brahmanas. I know also the energy of *Munis* of souls under complete control and endued with blazing ascetic merit. The fire of their wrath to this day hath not been extinguished in the forest of Dandaka. It was for his having disregarded the Brahmanas that the great *Asura*—the wicked and evil-minded Vatapi was digested when he came in contact with Agastya. It hath been heard by us that the powers and merits of high-souled Brahmanas are great. But, O Brahmana, as regenerate ones of high souls are great in wrath, so are they equally great in forgiveness. Therefore, O sinless one, it behoveth thee to forgive me in the matter of this my offence. O Brahmana, my heart inclineth to that merit which springeth from the service of my husband, for I regard my husband as the highest among all the gods. O best of Brahmanas, I practise that virtue which consists in serving my husband whom I regard as the highest Deity. Behold, O regenerate one, the merit that attaches to the service of one's husband! I know that thou hast burnt a she-crane with thy wrath! But, O best of regenerate ones, the anger that a person cherishes is the greatest of foes which that person hath. The gods know him for a Brahmana who hath cast off anger and passion. The gods know him for a Brahmana who always speaketh the truth here, who always gratifieth his preceptor, and who, though injured himself, never returneth the injury. The gods know him for a Brahmana who hath his senses under control, who is virtuous and pure and devoted to the study of the Vedas, and who hath mastery over anger and lust. The gods know him for a Brahmana who, cognisant of morals and endued with mental energy, is catholic in religion and looketh upon all equal unto himself. The gods know him for a Brahmana who studieth himself and teacheth others, who performeth sacrifices himself and officiateth at the sacrifices of others, and who giveth away to the best of his means. The gods know that bull among the regenerate ones for a Brahmana who, endued with liberality of soul, practiseth the *Brahmacharya* vow and is devoted to study,—in fact who is vigilantly devoted to the study of the *Vedas*. Whatever conduceth to the happiness of the Brahmanas is always recited before these. Ever taking pleasure in truth, the hearts of such men never find joy in untruth. O thou best of regenerate ones, it hath been said that the study of the Vedas, tranquillity of soul, simplicity of behaviour, and repression of the senses, constitute the eternal duties of the Brahmana. Those cognisant with virtue and morals have said that truth and honesty are the highest virtue. Virtue that is eternal is difficult of being understood. But whatever it is, it is based on *truth*. The ancients have declared that virtue dependeth on *sruti*. But, O foremost of regenerate ones, virtue as exposed in *sruti* appears to be of various kinds. It is, therefore, too subtle of comprehension. Thou, O holy one, art cognisant of virtue, pure, and devoted to the study of the *Vedas*. I think, however, O holy one, that thou dost not know what virtue in reality is. Repairing to the city of Mithila, enquire thou of a virtuous fowler there, if indeed, O regenerate one, thou art not really acquainted with what constitutes the highest virtue. There liveth in Mithila a fowler who is truthful and devoted to the service of his parents and who hath senses under complete control. Even he will discourse to thee on virtue. Blessed be thou, O best of regenerate ones, if thou likest, repair thither. O faultless one, it behoveth thee to forgive me, if what I have said be unpalatable, for they that are desirous of acquiring virtue are incapable of injuring women!"

"'At these words of the chaste woman, the Brahmana replied, saying, "I am gratified with thee. Blessed be thou; my anger hath subsided, O beautiful one! The reproofs uttered by thee will be of the highest advantage to me. Blessed be thou, I shall now go and accomplish what is so conducive, O handsome one, to my benefit!"

"Markandeya continued, 'Dismissed by her, Kausika, that best of regenerate ones, left her house, and, reproaching himself, returned to his own abode.'"

SECTION CCVI

"Markandeya said, 'Continually reflecting upon that wonderful discourse of the woman, Kausika began to reproach himself and looked very much like a guilty person and meditating on the subtle ways of morality and virtue, he said to himself, "I should accept with reverence what the lady hath said and should, therefore, repair to Mithila. Without doubt there dwelleth in that city a fowler of soul under complete control and fully acquainted with the mysteries of virtue and morality. This very day will I repair unto that one endued with wealth of asceticism for enquiring of him about virtue." His faith in her was assured by her knowledge of the death of the she-crane and the excellent words of virtuous import she had uttered. Kausika thus reflecting with reverence upon all she had said, set out for Mithila, filled with curiosity. And he traversed many forests and villages and towns and at last reached Mithila that was ruled over by Janaka and he beheld the city to be adorned with the flags of various creeds. And he beheld that beautiful town to be resounding with the noise of sacrifices and festivities and furnished with splendid gateways. It abounded with palatial residences and protected by walls on all sides; it had many splendid buildings to boast of. And that delightful town was also filled with innumerable cars. And its streets and roads were many and well-laid and many of them were lined with shops. And it was full of horses and cars and elephants and warriors. And the citizens were all in health and joy and they were always engaged in festivities. And having entered that city, that Brahmana beheld there many other things. And there the Brahmana enquired about the virtuous fowler and was answered by some twice-born persons. And repairing to the place indicated by those regenerate ones, the Brahmana beheld the fowler seated in a butcher's yard and the ascetic fowler was then selling venison and buffalo meat and in consequence of the large concourse of buyers gathered round that fowler, Kausika stood at a distance. But the fowler, apprehending that the Brahmana had come to him, suddenly rose from his seat and went to that secluded spot where the Brahmana was staying and having approached him there, the fowler said, "I salute thee, O holy one! Welcome art thou, O thou best of Brahmanas! I am the fowler. Blessed be thou! Command me as to what I may do for thee. The word that the chaste woman said unto thee, viz., *Repair thou to Mithila,* are known to me. I also know for what purpose thou hast come hither." Hearing these words of the fowler that Brahmana was filled with surprise. And he began to reflect inwardly, saying, "This indeed, is the second marvel that I see!" The fowler then said unto the Brahmana, saying, "Thou art now standing in place that is scarcely proper for thee, O sinless one. If it pleasest thee, let us go to my abode, O holy one!"'

"Markandeya continued, '"*So be it*," said the Brahmana unto him, gladly. And thereupon, the fowler proceeded towards his home with the Brahmana walking before him. And entering his abode that looked delightful, the fowler reverenced his guest by offering him a seat. And he also gave him water to wash his feet and face. And accepting these, that best of Brahmanas sat at his ease. And he then addressed the fowler, saying, "It seems to me that this profession doth not befit thee. O fowler, I deeply regret that thou shouldst follow such a cruel trade." At these words of the Brahmana the fowler said, "This profession is that of my family, myself having inherited it from my sires and grandsires. O regenerate one, grieve not for me owing to my adhering to the duties that belong to me by birth. Discharging the duties ordained for me beforehand by the Creator, I carefully serve my superiors and the old. O thou best of Brahmanas! I always speak the truth, never envy others; and give to the best of my power. I live upon what remaineth after serving the gods, guests, and those that depend on me. I never speak ill of anything, small or great. O thou best of Brahmanas, the actions of a former life always follow the doer. In this world there are three principal professions, viz., agriculture, rearing of cattle, and trade. As regards the other world, the three *Vedas*, knowledge, and the science of morals are efficacious. Service (of the other three orders) hath been ordained to be the duty of the Sudra. Agriculture hath been ordained for the Vaisyas, and fighting for the Kshatriyas, while the practice of the *Brahmacharya* vow, asceticism, recitation of *mantras*, and truthfulness have been ordained for the Brahmanas. Over subjects adhering to their proper duties, the king should rule virtuously; while he should set those thereto that have fallen away from the duties of their order. Kings should ever be feared, because they are the lords of their subjects. They restrain those subjects of theirs that fall away from their duties as they restrain the motions of the deer by means of their shafts. O regenerate *Rishi*, there existeth not in the kingdom of Janaka a single subject that followeth not the duties of his birth. O thou best of the Brahmanas, all the four orders here rigidly adhere to their respective duties. King Janaka punisheth him that is wicked, even if he be his own son; but never doth he inflict pain on him that is virtuous. With good and able spies employed under him, he looketh upon all with impartial eyes. Prosperity, and kingdom, and capacity to punish, belong,

O thou best of Brahmanas, to the Kshatriyas. Kings desire high prosperity through practice of the duties that belong to them. The king is the protector of all the four orders. As regards myself, O Brahmana, I always sell pork and buffalo meat without slaying those animals myself. I sell meat of animals, O regenerate *Rishi*, that have been slain by others. I never eat meat myself; never go to my wife except in her season; I always fast during the day, and eat, O regenerate one, in the night. Even though the behaviour of his order is bad, a person may yet be himself of good behaviour. So also a person may become virtuous, although he may be slayer of animals by profession. It is in consequence of the sinful acts of kings that virtue decreaseth greatly, and sin beginneth to prosper. And when all this taketh place the subjects of the kingdom begin to decay. And it is then, O Brahmana, that ill-looking monsters, and dwarfs, and hunch-backed and large-headed wights, and men that are blind or deaf or those that have paralysed eyes or are destitute of the power of procreation, begin to take their birth. It is from the sinfulness of kings that their subjects suffer numerous mischiefs. But this our king Janaka casteth his eyes upon all his subjects virtuously, and he is always kind unto them who, on their part, ever adhere to their respective duties. Regarding myself, I always with good deeds please those that speak well, as also those that speak ill of me. Those kings that live in the observance of their own proper duties, who are always engaged in the practice of acts that are good and honest, who are of souls under complete control and who are endued with readiness and alacrity, may not depend upon anything else for supporting their power. Gift of food to the best of one's power, endurance of heat and cold, firmness in virtue, and a regard and tenderness for all creatures,—these attributes can never find place in a person, without an innate desire being present in him of separating himself from the world. One should avoid falsehood in speech, and should do good without solicitation. One should never cast off virtue from lust, from wrath, or from malice. One should never joy immoderately at a good turn or grieve immoderately at a bad one. One should never feel depressed when overtaken by poverty, nor when so overtaken abandon the path of virtue. If at any time one doth what is wrong, he should never do its like again. One should always urge his soul to the doing of that which he regardeth as beneficial. One should never return wrong for wrong, but should act honestly by those that have wronged him. That wretched man who desireth to do what is sinful, slayeth himself. By doing what is sinful, one only imitates them that are wicked and sinful. Disbelieving in virtue they that mock the good and the pure saying, *'There is no virtue'* undoubtedly meet with destruction. A sinful man swelleth up like a leather bag puffed up with wind. The thoughts of these wretches filled with pride and folly are feeble and unprofitable. It is the heart, the inner soul, that discovereth the fool like the sun that discovereth forms during the day. The food cannot always shine in the world by means of self-praise. The learned man, however, even if he be destitute of beauty, displayeth his lustre by refraining from speaking ill of others and well of himself. No example, however, can be met with, in this world, of a person shining brilliantly on account of attributes to be found in him in their reputed measure. If one repenteth of a wrong done by him, that repentance washeth off his sin. The resolution of never doing it again saveth him from future sin, even as, O thou best of Brahmanas, he may save himself from sin by any of those expiations obtained in the scriptures. Even this, O regenerate one, is the *sruti* that may be seen in respect of virtue. He that having before been virtuous, committeth a sin, or committeth it unknowingly may destroy that sin. For virtue, O Brahmana, driveth off the sin that men commit from ignorance. A man, after having committed a sin, should cease to regard himself any longer as a man. No man can conceal his sins. The gods behold what one does, also the Being that is within every one. He that with piety and without detraction hideth the faults of the honest and the wise like holes in his own attire, surely seeketh his salvation. If a man seeketh redemption after having committed a sin, without doubt he is purged of all his sins and looketh pure and resplendent like the moon emerged from the clouds. A man that seeketh redemption is washed of all his sins, even as the sun, upon rising, dispelleth all darkness. O best of Brahmanas, it is temptation that constitutes the basis of sin. Men that are ignorant commit sin, yielding to temptation alone. Sinful men generally cover themselves with a virtuous exterior, like wells whose mouths are covered by long grass. Outwardly they seem to possess self-control and holiness and indulge in preaching virtuous texts which, in their mouth are of little meaning. Indeed, everything may be noticed in them except conduct that is truly virtuous!'"

"Markandeya continued, 'At these words, O best of men, of the fowler, that Brahmana endued with great wisdom, then asked the fowler, saying, "How shall I know what is virtuous conduct? Blessed be thou, I desire to hear this, O thou foremost of virtuous men, from thee. Therefore, O thou of exalted soul, tell me all about it truly." Hearing these words, the fowler replied, saying, "O best of Brahmanas, Sacrifices, Gift, Asceticism, the Vedas, and Truth—these five holy things are ever present in conduct that is called virtuous. Having subjugated lust and wrath, pride, avarice, and crookedness, they that take pleasure in virtue because it is virtue, are regarded as really virtuous and worthy of the approbation of persons that are virtuous. These persons who are devoted to sacrifices, and study of the Vedas have no independent behaviour. They follow only the practices of the honest and the good. This indeed, is the second attribute of the virtuous. Waiting upon superiors, Truth, Freedom from anger, and Gift, these four,

O Brahmana, are inseparably connected with behaviour that is virtuous. For the reputation that a person acquires by setting his heart on virtuous behaviour and adhering to it rigidly is incapable of acquisition except by practising the four virtues named above. The essence of the *Vedas* is Truth: the essence of Truth is self-control, and the essence of self-control is abstention from the pleasures of the world. These all are to be noticed in behaviour that is virtuous. They that follow those deluded fools that mock the forms of faith prevailing among men, are dragged into destruction for walking in such a sinful path. They, however, that are virtuous and engaged in the observance of vows, who are devoted to the *srutis* and the virtue of abstention from the pleasure of the world, they in fact who tread in virtue's path and follow the true religion, they that are obedient to the mandates of their preceptors, and who reflect upon the sense of the scriptures with patience and carefulness,—it is these that are said to be possessed of behaviour that is virtuous; it is these, O Brahmana, that are said to properly guide their higher intelligence. Forsaking those that are atheists, those that transgress virtue's limits, those that are of wicked souls, those that live in sinfulness, betake thyself to knowledge reverencing those that are virtuous. Lust and temptation are even like sharks in the river of life; the waters are the five senses. Do thou cross over to the other side of this river in the boat of patience and resignation, avoiding the shoals of corporeal existence (repeated births in this world). The supreme virtue consisting in the exercise of the intelligent principle and abstraction, when gradually super-added to virtuous conduct, becomes beautiful like dye on white fabrics. Truthfulness and abstention from doing injury to any one, are virtues highly beneficial to all creatures. Of these, that latter is a cardinal virtue, and is based on truth. Our mental faculties have their proper play when their foundation is laid in truth, and in the exercise of virtue truth is of the highest value. Purity of conduct is the characteristic of all good men. Those that are distinguished for holy living are good and virtuous. All creatures follow the principles of conduct which are innate in their nature. The sinful being who has no control over self acquires lust, anger and other vices. It is the immemorial rule that virtuous actions are those that are founded on justice, and it is also ordained by holy men that all iniquitous conduct is sin. Those who are not swayed by anger, pride, haughtiness and envy, and those who are quiet and straight-forward, are men of virtuous conduct. Those who are diligent in performing the rites enjoined in the three *Vedas*, who are wise, and of pure and virtuous conduct, who exercise self-restraint and are full of attention to their superior, are men of virtuous conduct. The actions and conduct of such men of great power, are very difficult of attainment. They are sanctified by the purification of their own actions, and consequently sin in them dies out of itself. This virtue of good conduct is wonderful, ancient, immutable and eternal; and wise men observing this virtue with holiness, attain to heaven. These men who believe in the existence of the Deity, who are free from false pride, and versed in holy writ, and who respect regenerate (twice-born) men, go to heaven. Among holy men, virtue is differentiated in three ways—that great virtue which is inculcated in the *Vedas*, the other which is inculcated in the *dharmashastras* (the minor scriptures), and virtuous conduct. And virtuous conduct is indicated by acquisition of knowledge, pilgrimage to sacred places, truthfulness, forbearance, purity and straight-forwardness. Virtuous men are always kind to all creatures, and well-disposed towards regenerate men. They abstain from doing injury to any creature, and are never rude in speech. Those good men who know well the consequences of the fruition of their good and evil deeds, are commended by virtuous men. Those who are just and good-natured, and endowed with virtue, who wish well of all creatures, who are steadfast in the path of virtue, and have conquered heaven, who are charitable, unselfish and of unblemished character, who succour the afflicted, and are learned and respected by all, who practise austerities, and are kind to all creatures, are commended as such by the virtuous. Those who are charitably disposed attain prosperity in this world, as also the regions of bliss (hereafter). The virtuous man when solicited for assistance by good men bestow alms on them by straining to the utmost, even to the deprivation of the comforts of his wife and servants. Good men having an eye to their own welfare, as also virtue and the ways of the world, act in this way and thereby grow in virtue through endless ages. Good persons possessing the virtues of truthfulness, abstention from doing injury to any one, rectitude, abstention from evil towards any one, want of haughtiness, modesty, resignation, self-restraint, absence of passion, wisdom, patience, and kindness towards all creatures, and freedom from malice and lust, are the witnesses of the world. These three are said to constitute the perfect way of the virtuous, viz., a man must not do wrong to any body, he must bestow alms, and must always be truthful. Those high-souled good men of virtuous conduct, and settled convictions, who are kind to all and are full of compassion, depart with contentment from this world to the perfect way of virtue. Freedom from malice, forbearance, peace of mind, contentment, pleasant speech, renunciation of desire and anger, virtuous conduct and actions regulated according to the ordinances of holy writ, constitute the perfect way of the virtuous. And those who are constant in virtue follow these rules of virtuous conduct, and having reached the pinnacle of knowledge, and discriminating between the various phases of human conduct, which are either very virtuous or the reverse, they escape from the great danger. Thus, O great Brahmana, having introduced the subject of virtuous conduct, have I described to thee all this, according to my own knowledge and to what I have heard on the subject."'"

SECTION CCVII

"Markandeya continued, 'The pious fowler, O Yudhishthira, then said to that Brahmana, "Undoubtedly my deeds are very cruel, but, O Brahmana, Destiny is all-powerful and it is difficult to evade the consequence of our past actions. And this is the *karmic evil* arising out of sin committed in a former life. But, O Brahmana, I am always assiduous in eradicating the evil. The Deity takes away life, the executioner acts only as a secondary agent. And we, O good Brahmana, are only such agents in regard to our *karma*. Those animals that are slain by me and whose meat I sell, also acquire *karma*, because (with their meat), gods and guests and servants are regaled with dainty food and the *manes* are propitiated. It is said authoritatively that herbs and vegetables, deer, birds and wild animals constitute the food of all creatures. And, O Brahmana, king Sivi, the son of Usinara, of great forbearance attained to heaven, which is hard to reach, giving away his own flesh. And in days of yore, O Brahmana, two thousand animals used to be killed every day in the kitchen of king Rantideva; and in the same manner two thousand cows were killed every day; and, O best of regenerate beings, king Rantideva acquired unrivalled reputation by distributing food with meat every day. For the performance of the fourmonthly rites animals ought to be sacrificed daily. 'The sacred fire is fond of animal food,' this saying has come down to us. And at sacrifices animals are invariably killed by regenerate Brahmanas, and these animals being purged of sin, by incantation of hymns, go to heaven. If, O Brahmana, the sacred fire had not been so fond of animal food in ancient times, it could never have become the food of any one. And in this matter of animal food, this rule has been laid down by *Munis*:—Whoever partakes of animal food after having first offered it duly and respectfully to the gods and the *manes*, is not polluted by the act. And such a man is not at all considered to have partaken of animal food, even, as a Brahmacharin having intercoursed with his wife during the menstrual period, is nevertheless considered to be a good Brahmana. After consideration of the propriety and impropriety of the matter, this rule has been laid down. King Saudasa, O Brahmana, when under a curse, often used to prey upon men; what is thy opinion of this matter? And, O good Brahmana, knowing this to be the consequence of my own actions, I obtain my livelihood from this profession. The forsaking of one's own occupation is considered, O Brahmana, to be a sin, and the act of sticking to one's own profession is without doubt a meritorious act. The *Karma* of a former existence never forsakes any creature. And in determining the various consequences of one's *Karma*, this rule was not lost sight of by the Creator. A person having his being under the influence of evil *Karma*, must always consider how he can atone for his *Karma*, and extricate himself from an evil doom, and the evil *Karma* may be expiated in various ways. Accordingly, O good Brahmana, I am charitable, truthful, assiduous in attending on my superior, full of respect towards regenerate Brahmanas, devoted to and free from pride and (idle) excessive talk. Agriculture is considered to be a praiseworthy occupation, but it is well-known that even there, great harm is done to animal life; and in the operation of digging the earth with the plough, numberless creatures lurking in the ground as also various other forms of animal life are destroyed. Dost thou not think so? O good Brahmana, *Vrihi* and other seeds of rice are all living organisms. What is thy opinion on this matter? Men, O Brahmana, hunt wild animals and kill them and partake of their meat; they also cut up trees and herbs; but, O Brahmana, there are numberless living organisms in trees, in fruits, as also in water; dost thou not think so? This whole creation, O Brahmana, is full of animal life, sustaining itself with food derived from living organisms. Dost thou not mark that fish preys upon fish, and that various species of animals prey upon other species, and there are species the members of which prey upon each other? Men, O Brahmana, while walking about hither and thither, kill numberless creatures lurking in the ground by trampling on them, and even men of wisdom and enlightenment destroy animal life in various ways, even while sleeping or reposing themselves. What hast thou to say to this?—The earth and the air all swarm with living organisms, which are unconsciously destroyed by men from mere ignorance. Is not this so? The commandment that people should not do harm to any creature, was ordained of old by men, who were ignorant of the true facts of the case. For, O Brahmana, there is not a man on the face of this earth, who is free from the sin of doing injury to creatures. After full consideration, the conclusion is irresistible that there is not a single man who is free from the sin of doing injury to animal life. Even the sage, O good Brahmana, whose vow is to do harm to no creature, doth inflict injury to animal life. Only, on account of greater needfulness, the harm is less. Men of noble birth and great qualities perpetrate wicked acts in defiance of all, of which they are not at all ashamed. Good men acting in an exemplary way are not commended by other good men; nor are bad men acting in a contrary way praised by their wicked compeers; and friends are not agreeable to friends, albeit endowed with high qualities; and foolish pedantic men cry down the virtues of their preceptors. This reversal of the natural order of things, O good Brahmana, is seen everywhere in this world. What is thy opinion as to the virtuousness or otherwise of this state of things? There is much that can be said of the goodness or badness of our actions. But whoever is addicted to his own proper occupation surely acquires great reputation."'"

SECTION CCVIII

"Markandeya continued, 'O Yudhishthira, the virtuous fowler, eminent in pity, then skilfully addressed himself again to that foremost of Brahmanas, saying, "It is the dictum of the aged that the ways of righteousness are subtle, diverse and infinite. When life is at stake and in the matter of marriage, it is proper to tell an untruth. Untruth sometimes leads to the triumph of truth, and the latter dwindles into untruth. Whichever conduces most to the good of all creatures is considered to be truth. Virtue is thus perverted; mark thou its subtle ways. O best of virtuous men, man's actions are either good or bad, and he undoubtedly reaps their fruits. The ignorant man having attained to an abject state, grossly abuses the gods, not knowing that it is the consequence of his own evil *karma*. The foolish, the designing and the fickle, O good Brahmana, always attain the very reverse of happiness or misery. Neither learning nor good morals, nor personal exertion can save them. And if the fruits of our exertion were not dependent on anything else, people would attain the object of their desire, by simply striving to attain it. It is seen that able, intelligent and diligent persons are baffled in their efforts, and do not attain the fruits of their actions. On the other hand, persons who are always active in injuring others and in practising deception on the world, lead a happy life. There are some who attain prosperity without any exertion. And there are others, who with the utmost exertion, are unable to achieve their dues. Miserly persons with the object of having sons born to them worship the gods, and practise severe austerities, and those sons having remained in the womb for ten months at length turn out to be very infamous issue of their race; and others begotten under the same auspices, decently pass their lives in luxury with heaps of riches and grain accumulated by their ancestors. The diseases from which men suffer, are undoubtedly the result of their own *karma*. They then behave like small deer at the hands of hunters, and they are racked with mental troubles. And, O Brahmana, as hunters intercept the flight of their game, the progress of those diseases is checked by able and skilful physicians with their collections of drugs. And, thou best of the cherishers of religion, thou hast observed that those who have it in their power to enjoy (the good things of this earth), are prevented from doing so from the fact of their suffering from chronic bowel-complaints, and that many others that are strong and powerful, suffer from misery, and are enabled with great difficulty to obtain a livelihood; and that every man is thus helpless, overcome by misery and illusion, and again and again tossed and overpowered by the powerful current of his own actions (*karma*). If there were absolute freedom of action, no creature would die, none would be subject to decay, or await his evil doom, and everybody would attain the object of his desire. All persons desire to out distance their neighbours (in the race of life), and they strive to do so to the utmost of their power; but the result turns out otherwise. Many are the persons born under the influence of the same star and the same auspices of good luck; but a great diversity is observable in the maturity of their actions. No person, O good Brahmana, can be the dispenser of his own lot. The actions done in a previous existence are seen to fructify in our present life. It is the immemorial tradition that the soul is eternal and everlasting, but the corporeal frame of all creatures is subject to destruction here (below). When therefore life is extinguished, the body only is destroyed, but the spirit, wedded to its actions, travels elsewhere."

"'The Brahmana replied, "O best of those versed in the doctrine of *karma*, and in the delivery of discourses, I long to know accurately how the soul becomes eternal." The fowler replied, "The spirit dies not, there being simply a change of tenement. They are mistaken, who foolishly say that all creatures die. The soul betakes itself to another frame, and its change of habitation is called its death. In the world of men, no man reaps the consequences of another man's *karma*. Whatever one does, he is sure to reap the consequences thereof; for the consequences of the *karma* that is once done, can never be obviated. The virtuous become endowed with great virtues, and sinful men become the perpetrators of wicked deeds. Men's actions follow them; and influenced by these, they are born again." The Brahmana enquired, "Why does the spirit take its birth, and why does its nativity become sinful or virtuous, and how, O good man, does it come to belong to a sinful or virtuous race?" The fowler replied, "This mystery seems to belong to the subject of procreation, but I shall briefly describe to you, O good Brahmana, how the spirit is born again with its accumulated load of *karma*, the righteous in a virtuous, and the wicked in a sinful nativity. By the performance of virtuous actions it attains to the state of the gods, and by a combination of good and evil, it acquires the human state; by indulgence in sensuality and similar demoralising practices it is born in the lower species of animals, and by sinful acts, it goes to the infernal regions. Afflicted with the miseries of birth and dotage, man is fated to rot here below from the evil consequences of his own actions. Passing through thousands of births as also the infernal regions, our spirits wander about, secured by the fetters of their own *karma*. Animate beings become miserable in the next world on account of these actions done by themselves and from the reaction of those miseries, they assume lower births and then they accumulate a new series of actions, and they consequently suffer misery over again, like sickly men partaking of unwholesome food; and although they are thus afflicted, they consider themselves to be happy and at ease and consequently their fetters are not loosened and new *karma* arises; and suffering from diverse miseries they turn about in this world like a wheel. If casting off their fetters they purify themselves by their actions and practise austerities and religious meditations, then, O best of Brahmanas, they attain the Elysian regions by these numerous acts and by casting off their fetters and by the purification of *karma*, men attain those blissful regions where misery is unknown to those who go there. The sinful man who is addicted to vices, never comes to the end of his course of iniquities. Therefore must we strive to do what is virtuous and forbear from doing what is unrighteous. Whoever with a heart full of gratefulness and free from malice strives to do what is good, attains wealth, virtue, happiness and heaven (hereafter). Those who are purified of sins, wise, forbearing, constant in righteousness, and self-restrained enjoy continuous felicity in this as well as in the next world. Man must follow the standard of virtue of the good and in his acts imitate the example of the righteous. There are virtuous men, versed in holy writ and learned in all departments of knowledge. Man's proper duty consists in following his own proper avocation, and this being the case these latter do not become confused and mixed up. The wise man delights in virtue and lives by righteousness. And, O good Brahmana, such a man with the wealth of righteousness which he hereby acquires, waters the root of the plant in which he finds most virtue. The virtuous man acts thus and his mind is calmed. He is pleased with his friends in this world and he also attains happiness hereafter. Virtuous people, O good man, acquire dominion over all and the pleasure of beauty, flavour, sound and touch according to their desire. These are known to be the rewards of virtue. But the man of enlightened vision, O great Brahmana, is not satisfied with reaping the fruits of righteousness. Not content with that, he with the light of spiritual wisdom that is in him, becomes indifferent to pain and pleasure and the vice of the world influenceth him not. Of his own free will he becometh indifferent to worldly pursuits but he forsaketh not virtue. Observing that everything worldly is evanescent, he trieth to renounce everything and counting on more chance he deviseth means for the attainment of salvation. Thus doth he renounce the pursuits of the world, shunneth the ways of sin, becometh virtuous and at last attaineth salvation. Spiritual wisdom is the prime requisite of men for salvation, resignation and forbearance are its roots. By this means he attaineth all the objects of this desire. But subduing the senses and by means of truthfulness and forbearance, he attaineth, O good Brahmana, the supreme asylum of *Brahma*." The Brahmana again enquired, "O thou most eminent in virtue and constant in the performance of the religious obligations, you talk of senses; what are they; how may they be subdued; and what is the good of subduing them; and how doth a creature reap the fruits thereof? O pious man, I beg to acquaint myself with the truth of this matter."""

SECTION CCIX

"Markandeya continued, 'Hear, O king Yudhishthira what the virtuous fowler, thus interrogated by that Brahmana, said to him in reply. The fowler said, "Men's minds are at first bent on the acquisition of knowledge. That acquired, O good Brahmana, they indulge in their passions and desires, and for that end, they labour and set about tasks of great magnitude and indulge in much-desired pleasures of beauty, flavour, &c. Then follows fondness, then envy, then avarice and then extinction of all spiritual light. And when men are thus influenced by avarice, and overcome by envy and fondness, their intellect ceases to be guided by righteousness and they practise the very mockery of virtue. Practising virtue with hypocrisy, they are content to acquire wealth by dishonourable means with the wealth thus acquired the intelligent principle in them becomes enamoured of those evil ways, and they are filled with a desire to commit sins. And when, O good Brahmana, their friends and men of wisdom remonstrate with them, they are ready with specious answers, which are neither sound nor convincing. From their being addicted to evil ways, they are guilty of a threefold sin. They commit sin in thought, in word, as also in action. They being addicted to wicked ways, all their good qualities die out, and these men of wicked deeds cultivate the friendship of men of similar character, and consequently they suffer misery in this world as well as in the next. The sinful man is of this nature, and now hear of the man of virtue. He discerns these evils by means of his spiritual insight, and is able to discriminate between happiness and misery, and is full of respectful attention to men of virtue, and from practising virtues, his mind becomes inclined to righteousness." The Brahmana replied, "Thou hast given a true exposition of religion which none else is able to expound. Thy spiritual power is great, and thou dost appear to me to be like a great *Rishi*." The fowler replied, "The great Brahmanas are worshipped with the same honours as our ancestors and they are always propitiated with offerings of food before others. Wise men in this world do what is pleasing to them, with all their heart. And I shall, O good Brahmana, describe to thee what is pleasing to them, after having bowed down to Brahmanas as a class. Do thou learn from me the Brahmanic philosophy. This whole universe unconquerable everywhere and abounding in great elements, is Brahma, and there is nothing higher than this. The earth, air, water, fire and sky are the great elements. And form, odour, sound, touch and taste are their characteristic properties. These latter too have their properties which are also correlated to each other. And of the three qualities, which are gradually characterised by each, in order of priority is consciousness which is called the mind. The seventh is intelligence and after that comes egoism; and then the five senses, then the soul, then the moral qualities called *sattwa, rajas* and *tamas*. These seventeen are said to be the unknown or incomprehensible qualities. I have described all this to thee, what else dost thou wish to know?"'"

SECTION CCX

"Markandeya continued, 'O Bharata, the Brahmana, thus interrogated by the virtuous fowler, resumed again this discourse so pleasing to the mind. The Brahmana said, "O best of the cherishers of religion, it is said that there are five great elements; do thou describe to me in full the properties of any one of the five." The fowler replied, "The earth, water, fire, air and sky all have properties interlapping each other. I shall describe them to thee. The earth, O Brahmana, has five qualities, water four, fire three and the air and sky together three also. Sound, touch, form, odour and taste— these five qualities belong to earth, and sound, touch, form and taste, O austere Brahmana, have been described to thee as the properties of water, and sound, touch and form are the three properties of fire and air has two properties sound and touch, and sound is the property of sky. And, O Brahmana, these fifteen properties inherent in five elements, exist in all substances of which this universe is composed. And they are not opposed to one another; they exist, O Brahmana, in proper combination. When this whole universe is thrown into a state of confusion, then every corporeal being in the fulness of time, assumes another *corpus*. It arises and perishes in due order. And there are present the five elementary substances of which all the mobile and immobile world is composed. Whatever is perceptible by the senses, is called *vyakta* (knowable or comprehensible) and whatever is beyond the reach of the senses and can only be perceived by guesses, is known to be *avyakta* (not *vyakta*). When a person engages in the discipline of self-examination, after having subdued the senses which have of their own proper objective play in the external conditions of sound, form, &c, then he beholds his own spirit pervading the universe, and the universe reflected in itself. He who is wedded to his previous *karma*, although skilled in the highest spiritual wisdom, is cognisant only of his soul's objective existence, but the person whose soul is never affected by the objective conditions around, is never subject to ills, owing to its absorption in the elementary spirit of Brahma. When a person has overcome the domination of illusion, his manly virtues consisting of the essence of spiritual wisdom, turn to the spiritual enlightenment which illumines the intelligence of sentient beings. Such a person is styled by the omnipotent, intelligent Spirit as one who is without beginning and without end, self-existent, immutable, incorporeal and incomparable. This, O Brahmana, that thou hast enquired of me is only the result of self discipline. And this self-discipline can only be acquired by subduing the senses. It cannot be otherwise, heaven and hell are both dependent on our senses. When subdued, they lead to heaven; when indulged in, they lead to perdition. This subjugation of the senses is the highest means of attaining spiritual light. Our senses are at the (cause) root of our spiritual advancement as also at the root of our spiritual degradation. By indulging in them, a person undoubtedly contracts vices, and by subduing these, he attains salvation. The self-restrained person who acquires mastery over the six senses inherent in our nature, is never tainted with sin, and consequently evil has no power over him. Man's corporeal self has been compared to a chariot, his soul to a charioteer and his senses to horses. A dexterous man drives about without confusion, like a quiet charioteer with well-broken horses. That man is an excellent driver who knows how to patiently wield the reins of those wild horses, — the six senses inherent in our nature. When our senses become ungovernable like horses on the high road, we must patiently rein them in; for with patience, we are sure to get the better of them. When a man's mind is overpowered by any one of these senses running wild, he loses his reason, and becomes like a ship tossed by storms upon the high ocean. Men are deceived by illusion in hoping to reap the fruits of those six things, whose effects are studied by persons of spiritual insight, who thereby reap the fruits of their clear perception."'"

SECTION CCXI

"Markandeya continued, 'O Bharata, the fowler having expounded these abstruse points, the Brahmana with great attention again enquired of him about these subtle topics. The Brahmana said, "Do thou truly describe to me, who now duly ask thee, the respective virtues of the qualities of *sattwa*, *rajas*, and *tamas*." The fowler replied, "Very well, I shall tell thee what thou hast asked. I shall describe separately their respective virtues, do thou listen. Of them *tamas* is characterised by illusion (spiritual), *rajas* incites (men to action), *sattwa* is of great grandeur, and on that account, it is said to be the greatest of them. He who is greatly under the influence of spiritual ignorance, who is foolish, senseless and given to dreaming, who is idle, unenergetic and swayed by anger and haughtiness, is said to be under the influence of *tamas*. And, O Brahmana *rishi*, that excellent man who is agreeable in speech, thoughtful, free from envy, industrious in action from an eager desire to reap its fruits, and of warm temperament, is said to be under the influence of *rajas*. And he who is resolute, patient, not subject to anger, free from malice, and is not skilful in action from want of a selfish desire to reap its fruits, wise and forbearing, is said to be under the influence of *sattwa*. When a man endowed with the *sattwa* quality, is influenced by worldliness, he suffers misery; but he hates worldliness, when he realises its full significance. And then a feeling of indifference to worldly affairs begins to influence him. And then his pride decreases, and uprightness becomes more prominent, and his conflicting moral sentiments are reconciled. And then self-restraint in any matter becomes unnecessary. A man, O Brahmana, may be born in the Sudra caste, but if he is possessed of good qualities, he may attain the state of *Vaisya* and similarly that of a *Kshatriya*, and if he is steadfast in rectitude, he may even become a Brahmana. I have described to thee these virtues, what else dost thou wish to learn?"'"

SECTION CCXII

"'The Brahmana enquired, "How is it that fire (vital force) in combination with the earthly element (matter), becomes the corporeal tenement (of living creatures), and how doth the vital air (the breath of life) according to the nature of its seat (the muscles and nerves) excite to action (the corporeal frame)?"' Markandeya said, 'This question, O Yudhishthira, having been put to the Brahmana by the fowler, the latter, in reply, said to that high-minded Brahmana. (The fowler said):—"The vital spirit manifesting itself in the seat of consciousness, causes the action of the corporeal frame. And the soul being present in both of them acts (through them). The past, the present and the future are inseparably associated with the soul. And it is the highest of a creature's possessions; it is of the essence of the Supreme Spirit and we adore it. It is the animating principle of all creatures, and it is the eternal *pumsha* (spirit). It is great and it is the intelligence and the *ego*, and it is the subjective seat of the various properties of elements. Thus while seated here (in a corporeal frame) it is sustained in all its relations external or internal (to matter or mind) by the subtle ethereal air called *prana*, and thereafter, each creature goes its own way by the action of another subtle air called *Samana*. And this latter transforming itself into *Apana* air, and supported by the head of the stomach carries the refuse matter of the body, urine &c, to the kidneys and intestines. That same air is present in the three elements of effort, exertion and power, and in that condition it is called *Udana* air by persons learned in physical science, and when manifesting itself by its presence at all the junctional points of the human system, it is known by the name *Vyana*. And the internal heat is diffused over all the tissues of our system, and supported by these kinds of air, it transforms our food and the tissues and the humours of our system. And by the coalition of *Prana* and other airs, a reaction (combination) ensues, and the heat generated thereby is known as the internal heat of the human system which causes the digestion of our food. The *Prana* and the *Apana* air are interposed within the *Samana* and the *Udana* air. And the heat generated by their coalition causes the growth of the body (consisting of the seven substances, bones, muscles, &c). And that portion of its seat extending to as far as the rectum is called *Apana*; and from that arteries arise in the five airs *Prana*, &c. The *Prana* air, acted on by the heat strikes against the extremity of the *Apana* region and then recoiling, it reacts on the heat. Above the navel is the region of undigested food and below it the region of digestion. And the *Prana* and all other airs of the system are seated in the navel. The arteries issuing from the heart run upwards and downwards, as also in oblique directions; they carry the best essence of our food, and are acted upon by the ten *Prana* airs. This is the way by which patient *Yogins* who have overcome all difficulties, and who view things with an impartial and equal eye, with their souls seated in the brain, find the Supreme Spirit, the *Prana* and the *Apana* airs are thus present in the body of all creatures. Know that the spirit is embodied in corporeal disguise, in the eleven allotropous conditions (of the animal system), and that though eternal, its normal state is apparently modified by its accompaniments,—even like the fire purified in its pan,—eternal, yet with its course altered by its surroundings; and that the divine thing which is kindred with the body is related to the latter in the same way as a drop of water to the sleek surface of a lotus-leaf on which it rolls. Know that *sattwa, rajas* and *tamas*, are the attributes of all life and that life is the attribute of spirit, and that the latter again is an attribute of the Supreme Spirit. Inert, insensible matter is the seat of the living principle, which is active in itself and induces activity in others. That thing by which the seven worlds are incited to action is called the most high by men of high spiritual insight. Thus in all these elements, the eternal spirit does not show itself, but is perceived by the learned in spiritual science by reason of their high and keen perception. A pure-minded person, by purification of his heart, is able to destroy the good and evil effect of his actions and attains eternal beatitude by the enlightenment of his inward spirit. That state of peace and purification of heart is likened to the state of a person who in a cheerful state of mind sleeps soundly, or the brilliance of a lamp trimmed by a skillful hand. Such a pure-minded person living on spare diet perceives the Supreme Spirit reflected in his own, and by practising concentration of mind in the evening and small hours of the night, he beholds the Supreme Spirit which has no attributes, in the light of his heart, shining like a dazzling lamp, and thus he attains salvation. Avarice and anger must be subdued by all means, for this act constitutes the most sacred virtue that people can practise and is considered to be the means by which men can cross over to the other side of this sea of affliction and trouble. A man must preserve his righteousness from being overcome by the evil consequences of anger, his virtues from the effects of pride, his learning from the effects of vanity, and his own spirit from illusion. Leniency is the best of virtues, and forbearance is the best of powers, the knowledge of our spiritual nature is the best of all knowledge, and truthfulness is the best of all religious obligations. The telling of truth is good, and the knowledge of truth may also be good, but what conduces to the greatest good of all creatures, is known as the highest truth. He whose actions are performed not with the object of securing any reward or blessing, who has sacrificed all to the requirements of his renunciation, is a real *Sannyasin* and is really wise. And as communion with Brahma cannot be taught to us, even by our spiritual preceptor,—he only giving us a clue to the mystery—renunciation of the material world is called *Yoga*. We must not do harm to any creature and must live in terms of amity with all, and in this our present existence, we must not avenge ourselves on any creature. Self-abnegation, peace of mind, renunciation of hope, and equanimity,— these are the ways by which spiritual enlightenment can always be secured; and the knowledge of self (one's own spiritual nature) is the best of all knowledge. In this world as well as hereafter, renouncing all worldly desires and assuming a stoic indifference, wherein all suffering is at rest, people should fulfil their religious duties with the aid of their intelligence. The *muni* who desires to obtain *moksha* (salvation), which is very difficult to attain, must be constant in austerities, forbearing, self-restrained, and must give up that longing fondness which binds him to the things of this earth. They call these the attributes of the Supreme Spirit. The *gunas* (qualities or attributes) that we are conscious of, reduce themselves to *agunas* (non-gunas) in Him; He is not bound by anything, and is perceptible only by the expansion and development of our spiritual vision; as soon as the illusion of ignorance is dispelled, this supreme unalloyed beatitude is attained. By foregoing the objects of both pleasure and pain and by renouncing the feelings which bind him to the things of this earth, a man may attain Brahma (Supreme Spirit or salvation). O good Brahmana, I have now briefly explained to thee all this, as I have heard. What else dost thou wish to know?"'"

SECTION CCXIII

"Markandeya said, 'When, O Yudhishthira, all this mystery of salvation was explained to that Brahmana, he was highly pleased and he said addressing the fowler, "All this that thou hast explained, is rational, and it seems to me that there is nothing in connection with the mysteries of religion which thou dost not know." The fowler replied, "O good and great Brahmana, thou shalt perceive with thine own eyes, all the virtue that I lay claim to, and by reason of which I have attained this blissful state. Rise, worshipful sir, and quickly enter this inner apartment. O virtuous man, it is proper that thou shouldst see my father and my mother."' Markandeya continued, 'Thus addressed the Brahmana went in, and beheld a fine beautiful mansion. It was a magnificent house divided in four suites of rooms, admired by gods and looking like one of their palaces; it was also furnished with seats and beds, and redolent of excellent perfumes. His revered parents clad in white robes, having finished their meals, were seated at ease. The fowler, beholding them, prostrated himself before them with his head at their feet. His aged parents then addressed him thus, "Rise, O man of piety, rise, may righteousness shield thee; we are much pleased with thee for thy piety; mayst thou be blessed with a long life, and with knowledge, high intelligence, and fulfilment of thy desires. Thou art a good and dutiful son, for, we are constantly and reasonably looked after by thee, and even amongst the celestials thou hast not another divinity to worship. By constantly subduing thyself, thou hast become endowed with the self-restraining power of Brahmanas and all thy grandsires and ancestors are constantly pleased with thee for thy self-restraining virtues and for thy piety towards us. In thought, word or deed thy attention to us never flags, and it seems that at present thou hast no other thought in thy mind (save as to how to please us). As Rama, the son of Jamadagni, laboured to please his aged parents, so hast thou, O Son, done to please us, and even more." Then the fowler introduced the Brahmana to his parents and they received him with the usual salutation of welcome, and the Brahmana accepting their welcome, enquired if they, with their children and servants, were all right at home, and if they were always enjoying good health at that time (of life). The aged couple replied, "At home, O Brahmana, we are all right, with all our servants. Hast thou, adorable sir, reached this place without any difficulty?"' Markandeya continued, 'The Brahmana replied, "Yes, I have." Then the fowler addressing himself to the Brahmana said to him, "These my parents, worshipful sir, are the idols that I worship; whatever is due to the gods, I do unto them. As the thirty-three gods with Indra at their head are worshipped by men, so are these aged parents of mine worshipped by me. As Brahmanas exert themselves for the purpose of procuring offering for their gods, so do I act with diligence for these two (idols of mine). These my father and mother, O Brahmana, are my supreme gods, and I seek to please them always with offering of flowers, fruits and gems. To me they are like the three sacred fires mentioned by the learned; and, O Brahmana, they seem to me to be as good as sacrifices or the four *Vedas*. My five life-giving airs, my wife and children and friends are all for them (dedicated to their service). And with my wife and children I always attend on them. O good Brahmana, with my own hands I assist them in bathing and also wash their feet and give them food and I say to them only what is agreeable, leaving out what is unpleasant. I consider it to be my highest duty to do what is agreeable to them even though it be not strictly justifiable. And, O Brahmana, I am always diligent in attending on them. The two parents, the sacred fire, the soul and the spiritual preceptor, these five, O good Brahmana, are worthy of the highest reverence from a person who seeks prosperity. By serving them properly, one acquires the merit of perpetually keeping up the sacred fire. And it is the eternal and invariable duty of all householders."''"

SECTION CCXIV

"Markandeya continued, 'The virtuous fowler, having introduced his (both) parents to that Brahmana as his highest *gurus,* again spoke to him as follows, "Mark thou the power of this virtue of mine, by which my inner spiritual vision is extended. For this, thou wast told by that self-restrained, truthful lady, devoted to her husband, 'Hie thee to Mithila; for there lives a fowler who will explain to thee, the mysteries of religion.'" The Brahmana said, "O pious man, so constant in fulfilling thy religious obligations, bethinking myself of what that truthful good-natured lady so true to her husband, hath said, I am convinced that thou art really endowed with every high quality." The fowler replied, "I have no doubt, my lord, that what that lady, so faithful to her husband, said to thee about me, was said with full knowledge of the facts. I have, O Brahmana, explained to thee all this as a matter of favour. And now, good sir, listen to me. I shall explain what is good for thee. O good Brahmana, of irreproachable character, thou hast wronged thy father and thy mother, for thou hast left home without their permission, for the purpose of learning the *Vedas.* Thou hast not acted properly in this matter, for thy ascetic and aged parents have become entirely blind from grief at thy loss. Do thou return home to console them. May this virtue never forsake thee. Thou art high-minded, of ascetic merit, and always devoted to thy religion but all these have become useless to thee. Do thou without delay return to console thy parents. Do have some regard for my words and not act otherwise; I tell thee what is good for thee, O Brahmana *Rishi.* Do thou return home this very day." The Brahmana replied, "This that thou hast said, is undoubtedly true; mayst thou, O pious man, attain prosperity; I am much pleased with thee." The fowler said, "O Brahmana, as thou practisest with assiduousness those divine, ancient, and eternal virtues which are so difficult of attainment even by pure-minded persons, thou appearest (to me) like a divine being. Return to the side of thy father and mother and be quick and diligent in honouring thy parents; for, I do not know if there is any virtue higher than this." The Brahmana replied, "By a piece of singular good luck have I arrived here, and by a piece of similar good luck have I thus been associated with thee. It is very difficult to find out, in our midst, a person who can so well expound the mysteries of religion; there is scarcely one man among thousands, who is well versed in the science of religion. I am very glad, O great man, to have secured thy friendship; mayst thou be prosperous. I was on the point of falling into hell, but was extricated by thee. It was destined to be so, for thou didst (unexpectedly) come in my way. And, O great man, as the fallen King Yayati was saved by his virtuous grandsons (daughter's sons), so have I know been saved by thee. According to thy advice, I shall honour my father and my mother; for a man with an impure heart can never expound the mysteries of sin and righteousness. As it is very difficult for a person born in the Sudra class to learn the mysteries of the eternal religion, I do not consider thee to be a Sudra. There must surely be some mystery in connection with this matter. Thou must have attained the Sudra's estate by reason of the fruition of thine own past *karma*. O magnanimous man, I long to know the truth about this matter. Do thou tell it to me with attention and according to thy own inclination."

"'The fowler replied, "O good Brahmana, Brahmanas are worthy of all respect from me. Listen, O sinless one, to this story of a previous existence of mine. O son of an excellent Brahmana, I was formerly a Brahmana, well-read in the *Vedas*, and an accomplished student of the *Vedangas*. Through my own fault I have been degraded to my present state. A certain king, accomplished in the science of *dhanurveda* (science of archery), was my friend; and from his companionship, O Brahmana, I, too became skilled in archery; and one day the king, in company with his ministers and followed by his best warriors, went out on a hunting expedition. He killed a large number of deer near a hermitage. I, too, O good Brahmana, discharged a terrible arrow. And a *rishi* was wounded by that arrow with its head bent out. He fell down upon the ground, and screaming loudly said, 'I have harmed no one, what sinful man has done this?' And, my lord, taking him for a deer, I went up to him and found that he was pierced through the body by my arrow. On account of my wicked deed I was sorely grieved (in mind). And then I said to that *rishi* of severe ascetic merit, who was loudly crying, lying upon the ground, 'I have done this unwittingly, O *rishi*.' And also this I said to the *muni*: 'Do thou think it proper to pardon all this transgression.' But, O Brahmana, the *rishi*, lashing himself into a fury, said to me, 'Thou shalt be born as a cruel fowler in the Sudra class.'"'"

SECTION CCXV

"'The fowler continued, "Thus cursed by that *rishi*, I sought to propitiate him with these words: 'Pardon me, O *muni*, I have done this wicked deed unwittingly. It behooves thee to pardon all that. Do thou, worshipful sir, soothe yourself.' The *rishi* replied, 'The curse that I have pronounced can never be falsified, this is certain. But from kindness towards thee, I shall do thee a favour. Though born in the Sudra class thou shalt remain a pious man and thou shalt undoubtedly honour thy parents; and by honouring them thou shalt attain great spiritual perfection; thou shalt also remember the events of thy past life and shalt go to heaven; and on the expiation of this curse, thou shalt again become a Brahmana.' O best of men, thus, of old was I cursed by that *rishi* of severe power, and thus was he propitiated by me. Then, O good Brahmana, I extricated the arrow from his body, and took him into the hermitage, but he was not deprived of his life (recovered). O good Brahmana, I have thus described to thee what happened to me of old, and also how I can go to heaven hereafter." The Brahmana said, "O thou of great intelligence, all men are thus subject to happiness or misery, thou shouldst not therefore grieve for that. In obedience to the customs of thy (present) race, thou hast pursued these wicked ways, but thou art always devoted to virtue and versed in the ways and mysteries of the world. And, O learned man, these being the duties of thy profession, the stain of evil *karma* will not attach to thee. And after dwelling here for some little time, thou shalt again become a Brahmana; and even now, I consider thee to be a Brahmana, there is no doubt about this. For the Brahmana who is vain and haughty, who is addicted to vices and wedded to evil and degrading practices, is like a Sudra. On the other hand, I consider a Sudra who is always adorned with these virtues,—righteousness, self-restraint, and truthfulness,—as a Brahmana. A man becomes a Brahmana by his character; by his own evil *karma* a man attains an evil and terrible doom. O good man, I believe that sin in thee has now died out. Thou must not grieve for this, for men, like thee who art so virtuous and learned in the ways and mysteries of the world, can have no cause for grief."

"'The fowler replied, "The bodily afflictions should be cured with medicines, and the mental ones with spiritual wisdom. This is the power of knowledge. Knowing this, the wise should not behave like boys. Men of low intelligence are overpowered with grief at the occurrence of something which is not agreeable to them, or non-occurrence of something which is good or much desired. Indeed, all creatures are subject to this characteristic (of grief or happiness). It is not merely a single creature or class that is subject to misery. Cognisant of this evil, people quickly mend their ways, and if they perceive it at the very outset they succeed in curing it altogether. Whoever grieves for it, only makes himself uneasy. Those wise men whose knowledge has made them happy and contented, and who are indifferent to happiness and misery alike, are really happy. The wise are always contented and the foolish always discontented. There is no end to discontentment, and contentment is the highest happiness. People who have reached the perfect way, do not grieve, they are always conscious of the final destiny of all creatures. One must not give way to discontent 17 for it is like a virulent poison. It kills persons of undeveloped intelligence, just as a child is killed by an enraged snake. That man has no manliness whose energies have left him and who is overpowered with perplexity when an occasion for the exercise of vigour presents itself. Our actions are surely followed by their consequences. Whoever merely gives himself up to passive indifference (to worldly affairs) accomplishes no good. Instead of murmuring one must try to find out the way by which he can secure exemption from (spiritual) misery; and the means of salvation found, he must then free himself from sensuality. The man who has attained a high state of spiritual knowledge is always conscious of the great deficiency (instability) of all matter. Such a person keeping in view the final doom (of all), never grieves. I too, O learned man, do not grieve; I stay here (in this life) biding my time. For this reason, O best of men, I am not perplexed (with doubts)". The Brahmana said, "Thou art wise and high in spiritual knowledge and vast is thy intelligence. Thou who art versed in holy writ, art content with thy spiritual wisdom. I have no cause to find fault with thee. Adieu, O best of pious men, mayst thou be prosperous, and may righteousness shield thee, and mayst thou be assiduous in the practice of virtue."'

"Markandeya continued, 'The fowler said to him, "Be it so." And the good Brahmana walked round him 18 and then departed. And the Brahmana returning home was duly assiduous in his attention to his old parents. I have thus, O pious Yudhishthira, narrated in detail to thee this history full of moral instruction, which thou, my good son, didst ask me to recite,—the virtue of women's devotion to their husbands and that of filial piety.' Yudhishthira replied, 'O most pious Brahmana and best of *munis*, thou hast related to me this good and wonderful moral story; and listening to thee, O learned man, my time has glided away like a moment; but, O adorable sir, I am not as yet satiated with hearing this moral 19 discourse.'"

SECTION CCXVI

Vaisampayana continued, "The virtuous king Yudhishthira, having listened to this excellent religious discourse, again addressed himself to the *rishi* Markandeya saying, 'Why did the fire-god hide himself in water in olden times, and why is it that Angiras of great splendour officiating as fire-god, used to convey 20 oblations during his dissolution. There is but one fire, but according to the nature of its action, it is seen to divide itself into many. O worshipful sir, I long to be enlightened on all these points, — How the Kumara 21 was born, how he came to be known as the son of Agni (the fire-god) and how he was begotten by Rudra or Ganga and Krittika. O noble scion of Bhrigu's race, I desire to learn all this accurately as it happened. O great *muni*, I am thrilled with great curiosity.' Markandeya replied, 'In this connection this old story is cited by the learned, as to how the carrier of oblations (the fire-god) in a fit of rage, sought the waters of the sea in order to perform a penance, and how the adorable Angiras transforming himself into the fire-god, 22 destroyed darkness and distressed the world with his scorching rays. In olden times, O long-armed hero, the great Angiras performed a wonderful penance in his hermitage; he even excelled the fire-god, the carrier of oblations, in splendour and in that state he illumined the whole universe. At that time the fire-god was also performing a penance and was greatly distressed by his (Angirasa's) effulgence. He was greatly depressed, but did not know what to do. Then that adorable god thought within himself, "Brahma has created another fire-god for this universe. As I have been practising austerities, my services as the presiding deity of fire have been dispensed with;" and then he considered how he could re-establish himself as the *god* of fire. He beheld the great *muni* giving heat to the whole universe like fire, and approached him slowly with fear. But Angiras said to him, "Do thou quickly re-establish yourself as the fire animating the universe, thou art well-known in the three stable worlds and thou wast first created by Brahma to dispel darkness. Do thou, O destroyer of darkness, quickly occupy thine own proper place." Agni replied, "My reputation has been injured now in this world. And thou art become the fire-god, and people will know thee, and not me, as fire. I have relinquished my god-hood of fire, do thou become the primeval fire and I shall officiate as the second or Prajapatyaka fire." Angiras replied, "Do thou become the fire-god and the destroyer of darkness and do thou attend to thy sacred duty of clearing people's way to heaven, and do thou, O lord, make me speedily thy first child.'" Markandeya continued, 'Hearing these words of Angiras, the fire-god did as desired, and, O king, Angiras had a son named Vrihaspati. Knowing him to be the first son of Angiras by Agni, the gods, O Bharata, came and enquired about the mystery. And thus asked by the gods he then enlightened them, and the gods then accepted the explanation of Angiras. In this connection, I shall describe to thee religious sorts of fire of great effulgence which are here variously known in the Brahmanas 23 by their respective uses.'"

SECTION CCXVII

"Markandeya continued, 'O ornament of Kuru's race, he (Angiras) who was the third son of Brahma had a wife of the name of Subha. Do thou hear of the children he had by her. His son Vrihaspati, O king, was very famous, large-hearted and of great bodily vigour. His genius and learning were profound, and he had a great reputation as a counsellor. Bhanumati was his first-born daughter. She was the most beautiful of all his children. Angiras's second daughter was called Raga. 24 She was so named because she was the object of all creature's love. Siniwali was the third daughter of Angiras. Her body was of such slender make that she was visible at one time and invisible at another; and for this reason she was likened to *Rudra's* daughter. Archismati was his fourth daughter, she was so named from her great refulgence. And his fifth daughter was called *Havishmati*, so named from her accepting *havis* or oblations. The sixth daughter of Angiras was called Mahismati the pious. O keen-witted being, the seventh daughter of Angiras is known by the name of Mahamati, who is always present at sacrifices of great splendour, and that worshipful daughter of Angiras, whom they call unrivalled and without portion, and about whom people utter the words *kuhu kuhu* (wonder), is known by the name of Kuhu.'"

SECTION CCXVIII

"Markandeya continued, 'Vrihaspati had a wife (called Tara) belonging to the lunar world. By her, he had six sons partaking of the energy of fire, and one daughter. The fire in whose honour oblations of clarified butter are offered at the Paurnamasya and other sacrifices, was a son of Vrihaspati called Sanju; he was of great ascetic merit. At the *Chaturmasya* (four-monthly) and *Aswamedha* (horse) sacrifices, animals are offered first in his honour, and this powerful fire is indicated by numerous flames. Sanju's wife was called Satya, she was of matchless beauty and she sprang from Dharma (righteousness) for the sake of truth. The blazing fire was his son, and he had three daughters of great religious merit. The fire which is honoured with the first oblations at sacrifices is his first son called Bharadwaja. The second son of Sanju is called Bharata in whose honour oblations of clarified butter are offered with the sacrificial ladle (called Sruk) at all the full moon (*Paurnamasaya*) sacrifices. Beside these three sons of whom Bharata is the senior, he had a son named Bharata and a daughter called Bharati. The Bharata fire is the son of *Prajapati* Bharata *Agni* (fire). And, O ornament of Bharata's race, because he is greatly honoured, he is also called the great. Vira is Bharadwaja's wife; she gave birth to Vira. It is said by the Brahmanas that he is worshipped like *Soma* (with the same hymns) with offerings of clarified butter. He is joined with Soma in the secondary oblation of clarified butter and is also called Rathaprabhu, Rathadhwana and Kumbhareta. He begot a son named Siddhi by his wife Sarayu, and enveloped the sun with his splendour and from being the presiding genius of the fire sacrifice he is ever mentioned in the hymns in praise of fire. And the fire *Nischyavana* praises the earth only; he never suffers in reputation, splendour and prosperity. The sinless fire Satya blazing with pure flame is his son. He is free from all taint and is not defiled by sin, and is the regulator of time. That fire has another name Nishkriti, because he accomplished the *Nishkriti* (relief) of all blatant creatures here. When properly worshipped he vouchsafes good fortune. His son is called Swana, who is the generator of all diseases; he inflicts severe sufferings on people for which they cry aloud, and moves in the intelligence of the whole universe. And the other fire (Vrihaspati's third son) is called Viswajit by men of spiritual wisdom. The fire, which is known as the internal heat by which the food of all creatures is digested, is the fourth son of Vrihaspati known through all the worlds, O Bharata, by the name of Viswabhuk. He is self-restrained, of great religious merit, and is a *Brahmacharin* and he is worshipped by Brahmanas at the Paka-sacrifices. The sacred river Gomati was his wife and by her all religious-minded men perform their rites. And that terrible water-drinking sea fire called Vadava is the fifth son of Vrihaspati. This Brahmic fire has a tendency to move upwards and hence it is called *Urdhvabhag*, and is seated in the vital air called *Prana*. The sixth son is called the great Swishtakrit; for by him oblations became *swishta* (*su*, excellently, and *ishta*, offered) and the *udagdhara* oblation is always made in his honour. And when all creatures are claimed, the fire called Manyauti becomes filled with fury. This inexorably terrible and highly irascible fire is the daughter of Vrihaspati, and is known as *Swaha* and is present in all matter. (By the respective influence of the three qualities of *sattwa, rajas* and *tamas,* Swaha had three sons). By reason of the first she had a son who was equaled by none in heaven in personal beauty, and from this fact he was surnamed by the gods as the *Kama*-fire. 25 (By reason of the second) she had a son called the *Amogha* or invincible fire, the destroyer of his enemies in battle. Assured of success he curbs his anger and is armed with a bow and seated on a chariot and adorned with wreaths of flowers. (From the action of the third quality) she had a son, the great *Uktha* (the means of salvation) praised by (akin to) three Ukthas. 26 He is the originator of the great word 27 and is therefore known as the Samaswasa or the means of rest (salvation).'"

SECTION CCXIX

"Markandeya continued, 'He (*Uktha*) performed a severe penance lasting for many years, with the view of having a pious son equal unto *Brahma* in reputation. And when the invocation was made with the *vyahriti* hymns and with the aid of the five sacred fires, *Kasyapa, Vasistha, Prana,* the son of *Prana, Chyavana,* the son of *Angiras,* and *Suvarchaka*—there arose a very bright energy (force) full of the animating (creative) principle, and of five different colours. Its head was of the colour of the blazing fire, its arms were bright like the sun and its skin and eyes were golden-coloured and its feet, O Bharata, were black. Its five colours were given to it by those five men by reason of their great penance. This celestial being is therefore described as appertaining to five men, and he is the progenitor of five tribes. After having performed a penance for ten thousand years, that being of great ascetic merit produced the terrible fire appertaining to the *Pitris* (manes) in order to begin the work of creation, and from his head and mouth respectively he created Vrihat and Rathantara (day and night) who quickly steal away (life, &c.). He also created Siva from his navel, Indra from his might and wind and fire from his soul, and from his two arms sprang the hymns *Udatta* and *Anudatta*. He also produced the mind, and the five senses, and other creatures. Having created these, he produced the five sons of the *Pitris*. Of these *Pranidhi* was the son of *Vrihadratha*. Vrihadratha was the son of Kasyapa. Bhanu was the godson of Chyavana, Saurabha, the son of Suvarchaka, and Anudatta, the son of Prana. These twenty-five beings are reputed (to have been created by him). Tapa also created fifteen other gods who obstruct sacrifices 28 . They are Subhima, Bhima, Atibhima, Bhimavala, Avala, Sumitra, Mitravana, Mitasina, Mitravardhana and Mitradharaman, 29 and Surapravira, Vira, Suveka, Suravarchas and Surahantri. These gods are divided into three classes of five each. Located here in this world, they destroy the sacrifices of the gods in heaven; they frustrate their objects and spoil their oblations of clarified butter. They do this only to spite the sacred fires carrying oblations to the gods. If the officiating priests are careful, they place the oblations in their honour outside of the sacrificial altar. To that particular place where the sacred fire may be placed, they cannot go. They carry the oblation of their votaries by means of wings. When appeased by hymns, they do not frustrate the sacrificial rites. Vrihaduktha, another son of Tapa, belongs to the Earth. He is worshipped here in this world by pious men performing *Agnihotra* sacrifices. Of the son of Tapa who is known as Rathantara, it is said by officiating priests that the sacrificial oblation offered in his honour is offered to Mitravinda. The celebrated Tapa was thus very happy with his sons.'"

SECTION CCXX

"Markandeya continued, 'The fire called Bharata was bound by severe rules of asceticism. Pushtimati is another name of his fire; for when he is satisfied he vouchsafes *pushti* (development) to all creatures, and for this reason he is called *Bharata* (or the Cherisher). And that other fire, by name Siva, is devoted to the worship of Sakti (the forces of the presiding deity of the forces of Nature), and because he always relieves the sufferings of all creatures afflicted with misery, he is called Siva (the giver of good). And on the acquisition of great ascetic wealth by *Tapa*, an intelligent son named Puranda was born to inherit the same. Another son named Ushma was also born. This fire is observed in the vapour of all matter. A third son Manu was born. He officiated as Prajapati. The Brahmanas who are learned in the Vedas, then speak of the exploits of the fire Sambhu. And after that the bright Avasathya fire of great refulgence is spoken of by the Brahmanas. Tapa thus created the five Urjaskara fires, all bright as gold. These all share the *Soma* drink in sacrifices. The great sun-god when fatigued (after his day's labours) is known as the Prasanta fire. He created the terrible *Asuras* and various other creatures of the earth. Angiras, too created the *Prajapati* Bhanu, the son of Tapa. He is also called Vrihadbhanu (the great Bhanu) by Brahmanas learned in the *Vedas*. Bhanu married Supraja, and Brihadbhanu the daughter of Surya (the sun-god). They gave birth to six sons; do thou hear of their progeny. The fire who gives strength to the weak is called Valada (or the giver of strength). He is the first son of Bhanu, and that other fire who looks terrible when all the elements are in a tranquil state is called the Manjuman fire; he is the second son of Bhanu. And the fire in whose honour oblations of clarified butter are enjoined to be made here at the *Darsa* and *Paurnamasya* sacrifices and who is known as Vishnu in this world, is (the third son of Bhanu) called Angiras, or Dhritiman. And the fire to whom with Indra, the *Agrayana* oblation is enjoined to be made is called the Agrayana fire. He is the (fourth) son of Bhanu. The fifth son of Bhanu is Agraha who is the source of the oblations which are daily made for the performance of the *Chaturmasya* (four-monthly) rites. And Stuva is the sixth son of Bhanu. Nisa was the name of another wife of that Manu who is known by the name of Bhanu. She gave birth to one daughter, the two Agnishtomas, and also five other fire-gods. The resplendent fire-god who is honoured with the first oblations in company with the presiding deity of the clouds is called Vaiswanara. And that other fire who is called the lord of all the worlds is Viswapati, the second son of Manu. And the daughter of Manu is called Swistakrit, because by oblations unto her one acquires great merit. Though she was the daughter of Hiranyakasipu, she yet became his wife for her evil deeds. She is, however, one of the Prajapatis. And that other fire which has its seats in the vital airs of all creatures and animates their bodies, is called Sannihita. It is the cause of our perceptions of sound and form. That divine spirit whose course is marked with black and white stains, who is the supporter of fire, and who, though free from sin, is the accomplisher of desired *karma*, whom the wise regard as a great *Rishi*, is the fire Kapila, the propounder of the *Yoga* system called Sankhya. The fire through whom the elementary spirits always receive the offerings called *Agra* made by other creatures at the performance of all the peculiar rites in this world is called Agrani. And these other bright fires famous in the world, were created for the rectification of the *Agnihotra* rites when marred by any defects. If the fires interlap each other by the action of the wind, then the rectification must be made with the *Ashtakapala* rites in honour of the fire Suchi. And if the southern fire comes in contact with the two other fires, then rectification must be made by the performance of the *Ashtakapala* rites in honour of the fire Viti. If the fires in their place called Nivesa come in contact with the fire called Devagni, then the *Ashtakapala* rites must be performed in honour of the fire Suchi for rectification. And if the perpetual fire is touched by a woman in her monthly course, then for rectification the *Ashtakapala* rites must be performed in honour of the fire called Dasyuman. If at the time of the performance of this *Agnihotra* rites the death of any creature is spoken of, or if animals die, then rectification must be made with the performance of the *Ashtakapala* rites in honour of the Suraman fire. The Brahmana, who while suffering from a disease is unable to offer oblations to the sacred fire for three nights, must make amends for the same by performing the *Ashtakapala* rites in honour of the northern fire. He who has performed the *Darsa* and the *Paurnamasya* rites must make the rectification with the performance of the *Ashtakapala* rites in honour of the Patikrit fire. If the fire of a lying-in room comes in contact with the perpetual sacred fire, then rectification must be made with the performance of *Ashtakapala* rites in honour of the Agniman fire.'"

SECTION CCXXI

"Markandeya continued, 'Mudita, the favourite wife of the fire Swaha, used to live in water. And Swaha who was the regent of the earth and sky begot in that wife of his a highly sacred fire called Advanta. There is a tradition amongst learned Brahmanas that this fire is the ruler and inner soul of all creatures. He is worshipful, resplendent and the lord of all the great *Bhutas* here. And that fire, under the name of Grihapati, is ever worshipped at all sacrifices and conveys all the oblations that are made in this world. That great son of Swaha—the great Adbhuta fire is the soul of the waters and the prince and regent of the sky and the lord of everything great. His (son), the Bharata fire, consumes the dead bodies of all creatures. His first Kratu is known as Niyata at the performance of the *Agnishtoma* sacrifice. That powerful prime fire (*Swaha*) is always missed by the gods, because when he sees Niyata approaching him he hides himself in the sea from fear of contamination. Searching for him in every direction, the gods could not (once) find him out and on beholding Atharvan the fire said to him, "O valiant being, do thou carry the oblations for the gods! I am disabled from want of strength. Attaining the state of the red-eyed fire, do thou condescend to do me this favour!" Having thus advised Atharvan, the fire went away to some other place. But his place of concealment was divulged by the finny tribe. Upon them the fire pronounced this curse in anger, "You shall be the food of all creatures in various ways." And then that carrier of oblations spoke unto *Atharvan* (as before). Though entreated by the gods, he did not agree to continue carrying their oblations. He then became insensible and instantly gave up the ghost. And leaving his material body, he entered into the bowels of the earth. Coming into contact with the earth, he created the different metals. Force and scent arose from his pus; the *Deodar* pine from his bones; glass from his phlegm; the *Marakata* jewel from his bile; and the black iron from his liver. And all the world has been embellished with these three substances (wood, stone and iron). The clouds were made from his nails, and corals from his veins. And, O king, various other metals were produced from his body. Thus leaving his material body, he remained absorbed in (spiritual) meditation. He was roused by the penance of Bhrigu and Angiras. The powerful fire thus gratified with penance, blazed forth intensely. But on beholding the *Rishi* (Atharvan), he again sought his watery refuge. At this extinction of the fire, the whole world was frightened, and sought the protection of Atharvan, and the gods and others began to worship him. Atharvan rummaged the whole sea in the presence of all those beings eager with expectation, and finding out the fire, himself began the work of creation. Thus in olden times the fire was destroyed and called back to life by the adorable Atharvan. But now he invariably carries the oblations of all creatures. Living in the sea and travelling about various countries, he produced the various fires mentioned in the *Vedas*.

"'The river Indus, the five rivers (of the Punjab), the Sone, the Devika, the Saraswati, the Ganga, the Satakumbha, the Sarayu, the Gandaki, the Charmanwati, the Mahi, the Medha, the Medhatithi, the three rivers Tamravati, the Vetravati, and the Kausiki; the Tamasa, the Narmada, the Godavari, the Vena, the Upavena, the Bhima, the Vadawa, the Bharati, the Suprayoga, the Kaveri, the Murmura, the Tungavenna, the Krishnavenna and the Kapila, these rivers, O Bharata, are said to be the mothers of the fires! The fire called Adbhuta had a wife of the name of Priya, and Vibhu was the eldest of his sons by her. There are as many different kinds of *Soma sacrifices* as the number of fires mentioned before. All this race of fires, first-born of the spirit of Brahma, sprang also from the race of Atri. Atri in his own mind conceived these sons, desirous of extending the creation. By this act, the fires came out of his own Brahmic frame. I have thus narrated to thee the history of the origin of these fires. They are great, resplendent, and unrivalled in power, and they are the destroyers of darkness. Know that the powers of those fires are the same as those of the Adbhuta fire as related in the Vedas. For all these fires are one and same. This adorable being, the first born fire, must be considered as one. For like the *Jyotishtoma* sacrifice he came out of Angiras body in various forms. I have thus described to thee the history of the great race of Agni (fires) who when duly worshipped with the various hymns, carry the oblations of all creatures to the gods.'"

SECTION CCXXII

"Markandeya continued, 'O sinless scion of Kuru's race, I have described to thee the various branches of the race of Agni. Listen now to the story of the birth of the intelligent Kartikeya. I shall tell thee of that wonderful and famous and highly energetic son of the Adbhuta fire begotten of the wives of the *Brahmarshis*. In ancient times the *gods* and *Asuras* were very active in destroying one another. And the terrible *Asuras* always succeeded in defeating the gods. And Purandara (Indra) beholding the great slaughter of his armies by them and anxious to find out a leader for the celestial host, thought within himself, "I must find out a mighty person who observing the ranks of the celestial army shattered by the *Danavas* will be able to reorganize it with vigour." He then repaired to the Manasa mountains and was there deeply absorbed in thought of nature, when he heard the heart-rending cries of a woman to the effect, "May some one come quick and rescue me, and either indicate a husband for me, or be my husband himself." Purandara said to her, "Do not be afraid, lady!" And having said these words, he saw Kesin (an *Asura*) adorned with a crown and mace in hand standing even like a hill of metals at a distance and holding that lady by the hand. Vasava addressed then that *Asura* saying, "Why art thou bent on behaving insolently to this lady? Know that I am the god who wields the thunderbolt. Refrain thou from doing any violence to this lady." To him Kesin replied, "Do thou, O Sakra, leave her alone. I desire to possess her. Thinkest thou, O slayer of Paka, that thou shalt be able to return home with thy life?" With these words Kesin hurled his mace for slaying Indra. Vasava cut it up in its course with his thunderbolt. Then Kesin, furious with rage, hurled a huge mass of rock at him. Beholding that, he of a hundred sacrifices rent it asunder with his thunderbolt, and it fell down upon the ground. And Kesin himself was wounded by that falling mass of rock. Thus sorely afflicted, he fled leaving the lady behind. And when the *Asura* was gone, Indra said to that lady, "Who and whose wife art thou, O lady with a beautiful face, and what has brought thee here?"'"

SECTION CCXXIII

"'The lady replied, "I am a daughter of Prajapati (the lord of all creatures, Brahma) and my name is Devasena. My sister Daityasena has ere this been ravished by Kesin. We two sisters with our maids habitually used to come to these Manasa mountains for pleasures with the permission of Prajapati. And the great *Asura* Kesin used daily to pay his court to us. Daityasena, O conqueror of Paka, listened to him, but I did not. Daityasena was, therefore, taken away by him, but, O illustrious one, thou hast rescued me with thy might. And now, O lord of the celestials, I desire that thou shouldst select an invincible husband for me." To this Indra replied, "Thou art a cousin of mine, thy mother being a sister of my mother Dakshayani, and now I desire to hear thee relate thine own prowess." The lady replied, "O hero with long arms, I am *Avala* 30 (weak) but my husband must be powerful. And by the potency of my father's boon, he will be respected by *gods* and *Asuras* alike." Indra said, "O blameless creature, I wish to hear from thee, what sort of power thou wishest thy husband to possess." The lady replied, "That manly and famous and powerful being devoted to Brahma, who is able to conquer all the celestials, *Asuras, Yakshas, Kinnaras, Uragas, Rakshasas*, and the evil-minded *Daityas* and to subdue all the worlds with thee, shall be my husband."'

"Markandeya continued, 'On hearing her speech, Indra was grieved and deeply thought within himself, "There is no husband for this lady, answering to her own description." And that god adorned with sun-like effulgence, then perceived the Sun rising on the Udaya hill, 31 and the great Soma (Moon) gliding into the Sun. It being the time of the new Moon, he of a hundred sacrifices, at the *Raudra* 32 moment, observed the gods and *Asuras* fighting on the Sunrise hill. And he saw that the morning twilight was tinged with red clouds. And he also saw that the abode of Varuna had become blood-red. And he also observed Agni conveying oblations offered with various hymns by Bhrigu, Angiras, and others and entering the disc of the Sun. And he further saw the twenty four *Parvas* adorning the Sun, and the terrible Soma also present in the Sun under such surroundings. And observing this union of the Sun and the Moon and that fearful conjunction of theirs, Sakra thought within himself, "This terrific conjunction of the

Sun and the Moon forebodeth a fearful battle on the morrow. And the river Sindhu (Indus) too is flowing with a current of fresh blood and the jackals with fiery laces are crying to the Sun. This great conjunction is fearful and full of energy. This union of the Moon (Soma) with the Sun and Agni is very wonderful. And if Soma giveth birth to a son now, that son may become the husband of this lady. And Agni also hath similar surroundings now, and he too is a god. If the two begetteth a son, that son may become the husband of this lady." With these thoughts that illustrious celestial repaired to the regions of Brahma, taking Devasena 33 with him. And saluting the Grandsire he said unto him, "Do thou fix a renowned warrior as husband of this lady." Brahma replied, "O slayer of *Asuras*, it shall be as thou hast intended. The issue of that union will be mighty and powerful accordingly. That powerful being will be the husband of this lady and the joint leader of thy forces with thee." Thus addressed, the lord of the celestials and the lady bowed unto him and then repaired to the place where those great Brahmanas, the powerful celestial *Rishis*, Vasistha and others, lived. And with Indra at their head, the other gods also, desirous of drinking the Soma beverage, repaired to the sacrifices of those *Rishis* to receive their respective shares of the offerings. Having duly performed the ceremonies with the bright blazing fire, those great-minded persons offered oblations to the celestials. And the *Adbhuta* fire, that carrier of oblations, was invited with *mantras*. And coming out of the solar disc, that lordly fire duly repaired thither, restraining speech. And, O chief of Bharata's race, that fire entering the sacrificial fire that had been ignited and into which various offerings were made by the *Rishis* with recitations of hymns, took them with him and made them over to the dwellers of heaven. And while returning from that place, he observed the wives of those high-souled *Rishis* sleeping at their ease on their beds. And those ladies had a complexion beautiful like that of an altar of gold, spotless like moon-beams, resembling fiery flames and looking like blazing stars. And seeing those wives of the illustrious Brahmanas with eager eyes, his mind became agitated and he was smitten with their charms. Restraining his heart he considered it improper for him to be thus agitated. And he said unto himself, "The wives of these great Brahmanas are chaste and faithful and beyond the reach of other people's desires. I am filled with desire to possess them. I cannot lawfully cast my eyes upon them, nor ever touch them when they are not filled with desire. I shall, therefore, gratify myself daily with only looking at them by becoming their *Garhapatya* (house-hold) fire."'

"Markandeya continued, 'The *Adbhuta* fire, thus transforming himself into a house-hold one, was highly gratified with seeing those gold-complexioned ladies and touching them with his flames. And influenced by their charms he dwelt there for a long time, giving them his heart and filled with an intense love for them. And baffled in all his efforts to win the hearts of those Brahmana ladies, and his own heart tortured by love, he repaired to a forest with the certain object of destroying himself. A little while before, Swaha, the daughter of Daksha, had bestowed her love'on him. The excellent lady had been endeavouring for a long time to detect his weak moments; but that blameless lady did not succeed in finding out any weakness in the calm and collected fire-god. But now that the god had betaken himself to a forest, actually tortured by the pangs of love, she thought, "As I too am distressed with love, I shall assume the guise of the wives of the seven *Rishis*, and in that disguise I shall seek the fire-god so smitten with their charms. This done, he will be gratified and my desire too will be satisfied."'"

SECTION CCXXIV

"Markandeya continued, 'O lord of men, the beautiful Siva endowed with great virtues and an unspotted character was the wife of Angiras (one of the seven *Rishis*). That excellent lady (Swaha) at first assuming the disguise of Siva, sought the presence of Agni unto whom she said, "O Agni, I am tortured with love for thee. Do thou think it fit to woo me. And if thou dost not accede to my request, know that I shall commit self-destruction. I am Siva the wife of Angiras. I have come here according to the advice of the wives of the other *Rishis*, who have sent me here after due deliberation."

"'Agni replied, "How didst thou know that I was tortured with love and how could the others, the beloved wives of the seven *Rishis*, of whom thou hast spoken, know this?"

"'Swaha replied, "Thou art always a favourite with us, but we are afraid of thee. Now having read thy mind by well-known signs, they have sent to thy presence. I have come here to gratify my desire. Be thou quick, O Agni, to encompass the object of thy desire, my sisters-in-law are awaiting me. I must return soon."

"Markandeya continued, 'Then Agni, filled with great joy and delight, married Swaha in the guise of Siva, and that lady joyfully cohabiting with him, held the *semen virile* in her hands. And then she thought within herself that those who would observe her in that disguise in the forest, would cast an unmerited slur upon the conduct of those Brahmana ladies in connection with Agni. Therefore, to prevent this, she should assume the disguise of a bird, and in that state she should more easily get out of the forest.'

"Markandeya continued, 'Then assuming the disguise of a winged creature, she went out of the forest and reached the White Mountain begirt with clumps of heath and other plants and trees, and guarded by strange seven-headed serpents with poison in their very looks, and abounding with *Rakshasas*, male and female *Pisachas*, terrible spirits, and various kinds of birds and animals. That excellent lady quickly ascending a peak of those mountains, threw that *semen* into a golden lake. And then assuming successively the forms of the wives of the high-souled seven *Rishis*, she continued to dally with Agni. But on account of the great ascetic merit of

Arundhati and her devotion to her husband (Vasishtha), she was unable to assume her form. And, O chief of Kuru's race, the lady Swaha on the first lunar day threw six times into that lake the *semen* of Agni. And thrown there, it produced a male child endowed with great power. And from the fact of its being regarded by the *Rishis* as *cast off*, the child born therefrom came to be called by the name of *Skanda*. And the child had six faces, twelve ears, as many eyes, hands, and feet, one neck, and one stomach. And it first assumed a form on the second lunar day, and it grew to the size of a little child on the third. And the limbs of Guha were developed on the fourth day. And being surrounded by masses of red clouds flashing forth lightning, it shone like the Sun rising in the midst of a mass of red clouds. And seizing the terrific and immense bow which was used by the destroyer of the *Asura* Tripura for the destruction of the enemies of the gods, that mighty being uttered such a terrible roar that the three worlds with their mobile and immobile divisions became struck with awe. And hearing that sound which seemed like the rumbling of a mass of big clouds, the great *Nagas*, *Chitra* and *Airavata*, were shaken with fear. And seeing them unsteady that lad shining with sun-like refulgence held them with both his hands. And with a dart in (another) hand, and with a stout, red-crested, big cock fast secured in another, that long-armed son of Agni began to sport about making a terrible noise. And holding an excellent conch-shell with two of his hands, that mighty being began to blow it to the great terror of even the most powerful creatures. And striking the air with two of his hands, and playing about on the hill-top, the mighty Mahasena of unrivalled prowess, looked as if he were on the point of devouring the three worlds, and shone like the bright Sun-god at the moment of his ascension in the heavens. And that being of wonderful prowess and matchless strength, seated on the top of that hill, looked on with his numerous faces directed towards the different cardinal points, and observing various things, he repeated his loud roars. And on hearing those roars various creatures were prostrate with fear. And frightened and troubled in mind they sought protection. And all those persons of various orders who then sought the protection of that god are known as his powerful Brahmana followers. And rising from his seat, that mighty god allayed the fears of all those people, and then drawing his bow, he discharged his arrows in the direction of the White Mountain. And with those arrows the hill Krauncha, the son of Himavat, was rent asunder. And that is the reason why swans and vultures now migrate to the Sumeru mountains. The Krauncha hill, sorely wounded, fell down uttering fearful groans. And seeing him fallen, the other hills too began to scream. And that mighty being of unrivalled prowess, hearing the groans of the afflicted, was not at all moved, but himself uplifting his mace, yelled forth his war-whoop. And that high-souled being then hurled his mace of great lustre and quickly rent in twain one of the peaks of the White Mountain. And the White Mountain being thus pierced by him was greatly afraid of him and dissociating himself from the earth fled with the other mountains. And the earth was greatly afflicted and bereft of her ornaments on all sides. And in this distress, she went over to *Skanda* and once more shone with all her might. And the mountains too bowed down to *Skanda* and came back and stuck into the earth. And all creatures then celebrated the worship of *Skanda* on the fifth day of the lunar month.'"

SECTION CCXXV

"Markandeya continued, 'When that powerful, high-souled, and mighty being was born, various kinds of fearful phenomena occurred. And the nature of males and females, of heat and cold, and of such other pairs of contraries, was reversed. And the planets, the cardinal points and the firmaments became radiant with light and the earth began to rumble very much. And the *Rishis* even, seeking the welfare of the world, while they observed all these terrific prodigies on all sides, began with anxious hearts to restore tranquillity in the universe. And those who used to live in that Chitraratha forest said, "This very miserable condition of ours hath been brought about by Agni cohabiting with the six wives of the seven *Rishis*." Others again who had seen the goddess assume the disguise of a bird said, "This evil hath been brought about by a bird." No one ever imagined that Swaha was the authoress of that mischief. But having heard that the (new born) male child was hers, she went to Skanda and gradually revealed to him the fact that she was his mother. And those seven *Rishis*, when they heard that a son of great power had been born (to them), divorced their six wives with the exception of the adorable Arundhati, because all the dwellers of that forest protested that those six persons had been instrumental in bringing forth the child. Swaha too, O king, said again and again to the seven *Rishis*, saying, "Ye ascetics, this child is mine, your wives are not his mother."

"'The great *Muni* Viswamitra had, after the conclusion of the sacrifices of the seven *Rishis*, followed unseen the god of fire, while the latter was tortured with lust. He, therefore, knew everything as it happened and he was the first to seek the protection of Mahasena. And he offered divine prayers to Mahasena and all the thirteen auspicious rites appertaining to childhood, such as the natal and other ceremonies, were all performed by the great *Muni* in respect of that child. And for the good of the world he promulgated the virtues of the six-faced Skanda, and performed ceremonies in honour of the cock, the goddess *Sakti*, and the first followers of Skanda. And for this reason he became a great favourite of the celestial youth. That great *Muni* then informed the seven *Rishis* of the transformations of Swaha and told them that their wives were perfectly innocent. But though thus informed the seven *Rishis* abandoned their spouses unconditionally.'"

"Markandeya continued, 'The celestials having heard of the prowess of Skanda, all said to Vasava, "O Sakra, do thou kill Skanda without delay for his prowess is unbearable. And if thou dost not exterminate him, he will conquer the three worlds with ourselves, and overpowering thee, will himself become the mighty lord of the celestials." Perplexed in mind, Sakra replied unto them, "This child is endowed with great prowess. He can himself destroy the Creator of the Universe, in battle putting forth his might. I venture not, therefore, to do away with him." To this the gods replied, "Thou hast no manliness in thee, in that thou talkest in this manner. Let the great Mothers of the Universe repair to-day to Skanda. They can master at will any degree of energy. Let them kill this child." "It shall be so."—the mothers replied. And then they went away. But on beholding that he was possessed of great might, they became dispirited, and considering that he was invincible, they sought his protection and said unto him, "Do thou, O mighty being, become our (adopted) son. We are full of affection for thee and desirous of giving thee suck. Lo, the milk oozes from our breasts!" On hearing these words, the mighty Mahasena became desirous of sucking their breasts and he received them with due respect and acceded to their request. And that mightiest of mighty creatures then beheld his father Agni come towards him. And that god, who is the doer of all that is good, was duly honoured by his son, and in company with the Mothers, he stayed there by the side of Mahasena to tend him. And that lady amongst the Mothers who was born of Anger 34 with a spike in hand kept watch over Skanda even like a mother guarding her own offspring, and that irascible red-coloured daughter of the Sea, who lived herself on blood, hugged Mahasena in her breast and nursed him like a mother. And Agni transforming himself into a trader with a goat's mouth and followed by numerous children began to gratify that child of his with toys in that mountain abode of his.'"

SECTION CCXXVI

"Markandeya continued, 'The planets with their satellites, the *Rishis* and the Mothers, Agni and numerous other blazing courtiers and many other dwellers of heaven of terrible mien, waited on Mahasena along with the Mothers. And the illustrious sovereign of the gods, desirous of victory but believing success to be doubtful mounted his elephant Airavata and attended by the other gods advanced towards Skanda. That mighty being followed by all the celestials was armed with his thunderbolt. And with the object of slaying Mahasena, he marched with terrible celestial army of great splendour, sounding their shrill war-cry and furnished with various sorts of standards, with warriors encased in various armour and armed with numerous bows and riding on various animals. When Mahasena beheld the gloriously decked Sakra, attired in his best clothes, advancing with the determination of slaying him, he (too on his part) advanced to meet that chief of the celestials. O Partha, the mighty Vasava, the lord of the celestials, then uttered a loud shout, to encourage his warriors and marching rapidly with the view of killing Agni's son and praised by Tridasas 35 and great *Rishis*, he at length reached the abode of Kartikeya. And then he shouted out with other gods; and Guha too in response to this, uttered a fearful war-cry resembling the roaring of the sea. On hearing that noise, the celestial army behaved like an agitated sea, and was stunned and fixed to the spot. And that son of *Pavaka* (the Fire-god) beholding the gods come near to him with the object of killing him, was filled with wrath, and gave out rising flame of fire from within his mouth. And these flames destroyed the celestial forces struggling on the ground. Their heads, their bodies, their arms and riding animals were all burnt in that conflagration and they appeared all on a sudden like stars displaced from their proper spheres. Thus afflicted, the god renounced all allegiance to the thunder-bolt, and sought the protection of Pavaka's son; and thus peace was again secured. When he was thus forsaken by the gods, Sakra hurled his thunder-bolt at Skanda. It pierced him on the right side; and, O great king, it passed through the body of that high-souled being. And from being struck with the thunder-bolt, there arose from Skanda's body another being—a youth with a club in hand, and adorned with a celestial amulet. And because he was born on account of the piercing of the thunder-bolt, he was named Visakha. And Indra, when he beheld that another person looking like the fierce destroying Fire-god had come into being was frightened out of his wits and besought the protection of Skanda, with the palms of his hands joined together (as a mark of respect). And that excellent being Skanda, bade him renounce all fear, with his arm. The gods were then transported with joy, and their hands too struck up.'"

SECTION CCXXVII

"Markandeya continued, 'Now hear of those terrible and curious-looking followers of Skanda. A number of male children came into being when Skanda was struck with the thunder-bolt,—those terrific creatures that steal (spirit away) little children, whether born, or in the womb and a number of female children too of great strength were born to him. Those children adopted Visakha as their father. That adorable and dexterous Bhadrasakha, having a face like that of a goat was at the time (of the battle) surrounded by all his sons and daughters whom he guarded carefully in the presence of the great mothers. And for this reason the inhabitants of this earth call Skanda the father of *Kumaras* (little children). Those persons who desire to have sons born to them, worship in their places the powerful *Rudra* in the form of the Fire-god, and *Uma* in the form of *Swaha*. And by that means they are blessed with sons. The daughters begotten by the Fire-god, *Tapa*, went over to Skanda, who said to them, "What can I do for you?" Those girls replied, "Do us this favour; by thy blessing, may we become the good and respected mothers of all the world!" He replied, "Be it so." And that liberal-minded being repeated again and again, "Ye shall be divided into Siva and Asiva." 36   And the mothers then departed, having first established Skanda's sonship, Kaki, Halima, Malini, Vrinhila, Arya, Palala and Vaimitra, these were the seven mothers of Sisu. They had a powerful, red-eyed, terrific, and very turbulent son named Sisu born by the blessing of Skanda. He was reputed as the eighth hero, born of the mothers of Skanda. But he is also known as the ninth, when that being with the face of a goat, is included. Know that the sixth face of Skanda was like that of a goat. That face, O king, is situated in the middle of the six, and is regarded constantly by the mother. That head by which Bhadrasakha created the divine energy, is reputed to be the best of all his heads. O ruler of men, these virtuous wonderful events happened on the fifth day of the bright half of the lunar month, and on the sixth, a very fierce and terrific battle was fought at that place."

SECTION CCXXVIII

"Markandeya continued, 'Skanda was adorned with a golden amulet and wreath, and wore a crest and a crown of gold; his eyes were golden-coloured, and he had a set of sharp teeth; he was dressed in a red garment and looked very handsome; he had a comely appearance, and was endowed with all good characteristics and was the favourite of the three worlds. He granted boons (to people who sought them) and was brave, youthful, and adorned with bright ear-rings. Whilst he was reposing himself, the goddess of fortune, looking like a lotus and assuming a personal embodiment, rendered her allegiance to him. When he became thus possessed of good fortune, that famous and delicate-looking creature appeared to all like the moon at its full. And high-minded Brahmanas worshipped that mighty being, and the *Maharshis* (great *rishis*) then said as follows to Skanda, "O thou born of the golden egg, mayst thou be prosperous and mayst thou become an instrument of good to the universe! O best of the gods, although thou wast born only six nights (days) ago, the whole world has owned allegiance to thee (within this short time), and thou hast also allayed their fears. Therefore do thou become the Indra (lord) of the three worlds and remove their cause of apprehension." Skanda replied, "You gentlemen of great ascetic wealth (tell me) what Indra does with all three worlds and how that sovereign of the celestials protects the hosts of gods unremittingly." The *Rishis* replied, "Indra is the giver of strength, power, children and happiness to all creatures and when propitiated, that Lord of the celestials bestows on all the objects of their desire. He destroys the wicked and fulfils the desires of the righteous; and that Destroyer of Vala assigns to all creatures their various duties. He officiates for the sun and the moon in places where there is no sun or moon; he even when occasion requires it, acts for (serves the purposes of) fire, air, earth, and water. These are the duties of Indra; his capacities are immense. Thou too art mighty; therefore great hero, do thou become our Indra."

"'Sakra said, "O mighty being, do thou make us happy, by becoming our lord. Excellent being, thou art worthy of the honour; therefore shall we anoint thee this very day."

"'Skanda replied, "Do thou continue to rule the three worlds with self-possession, and with thy heart bent on conquest. I shall remain thy humble servant. I covet not thy sovereignty."

"'Sakra replied, "Thy prowess is unrivalled, O hero, do thou therefore vanquish the enemies of the gods. People have been struck with wonder at thy prowess. More specially as I have been bereft of my prowess, and defeated by thee, now if I were to act as Indra, I should not command the respect of all creatures, and they would be busy in bringing about dissensions between us; and then, my lord, they would become the partisans of one or other of us. And when they formed themselves into two distinct factions, war as before would be the result of that defection. And in that war, thou wouldst undoubtedly defeat me without difficulty and thyself become the lord of all worlds."

"'Skanda replied, "Thou, O Sakra, art my sovereign, as also of the three worlds; mayst thou be prosperous! Tell me if I can obey any commands of thine."

"'Indra replied, "At thy bidding, O powerful being, I shall continue to act as Indra. And if thou hast said this deliberately and in earnest, then hear me how thou canst gratify thy desire of serving me. Do thou, O mighty being, take the leadership of the celestial forces accordingly."

"'Skanda replied, "Do thou anoint me as leader, for the destruction of the Danavas, for the good of the celestials, and for the well-being of cows and Brahmanas."'

"Markandeya continued, 'Thus anointed by Indra and all other gods, and honoured by the *Maharshis*, he looked grand at the moment. The golden umbrella 37 held (over his head) looked like a halo of blazing fire. That famous god, the Conqueror of Tripura, himself fastened the celestial wreath of gold, of Viswakarma's manufacture, round his neck. And, O great man and conqueror of thine enemies, that worshipful god with the emblem of the bull, had gone there previously with Parvati. He honoured him with a joyous heart. The Fire-god is called Rudra by Brahmanas, and from this fact Skanda is called the son of Rudra. The White Mountain was formed from discharges of Rudra's *semen virile* and the sensual indulgences of the

Fire-god with the Krittikas took place on that same White Mountain. And as Rudra was seen by all the dwellers of heaven to heap honours on the excellent Guha (Skanda), he was for that reason reputed as the son of Rudra. This child had his being by the action of Rudra entering into the constitution of the Fire-god, and for this reason, Skanda came to be known as the son of Rudra. And, O Bharata, as Rudra, the Fire-god, Swaha, and the six wives (of the seven Rishis) were instrumental to the birth of the great god Skanda, he was for that reason reputed as the son of Rudra.'

"'That son of Fire-god was clad in a pair of clean red cloths, and thus he looked grand and resplendent like the Sun peeping forth from behind a mass of red clouds. And the red cock given to him by the Fire-god, formed his ensign; and when perched on the top of his chariot, it looked like the image of the all-destroying fire. And the presiding deity of the power which conduces to the victory of the god, and which is the director of the exertions of all creatures, and constitutes their glory, prop and refuge, advanced before him. And a mysterious charm entered into his constitution, the charm which manifests its powers on the battlefield. Beauty, strength, piety, power, might, truthfulness, rectitude, devotion to Brahmanas, freedom from illusion or perplexity, protection of followers, destruction of foes, and care of all creatures,—these, O lord of men, are the inborn virtues of Skanda. Thus anointed by all the gods, he looked pleased and complacent; and dressed in his best style, he looked beautiful like the moon at its full. The much-esteemed incantation of *Vedic* hymns, the music of the celestial band, and the songs of gods and *Gandharvas* then rang on all sides. And surrounded by all the well-dressed *Apsaras*, and many other gay and happy-looking *Pisachas* and hosts of gods, that anointed (by gods) son of Pavaka disported himself in all his grandeur. To the dwellers of heaven, the anointed Mahasena appeared like the Sun rising after extinction of darkness. And then the celestial forces looking upon him as their leader, surrounded him on all sides in thousands. That adorable being followed by all creatures then assumed their commands, and praised and honoured by them, he encouraged them in return.

"'The Performer of a thousand sacrifices then thought of Devasena, whom he has rescued before. And considering that this being (Skanda) was undoubtedly destined to be the husband of this lady by Brahma himself, he had her brought there, dressed her with the best apparel. And the vanquisher of Vala then said to Skanda, "O foremost of gods, this lady was, even before thy birth, destined to be thy bride by that Self-existent Being. 38 Therefore do thou duly accept her lotus-like beautiful right hand with invocation of the (marital) hymns." Thus told, he duly married her. And Vrihaspati learned in hymns performed the necessary prayers and oblations. She who is called Shashthi, Lakshmi, Asa, Sukhaprada, Sinivali, Kuhu, Saivritti, and Aparajita, is known among men as Devasena, the wife of Skanda. When Skanda became united to Devasena in indissoluble bonds of matrimony, then the gods of prosperity in her own personal embodiment began to serve him with diligence. As Skanda attained celebrity on the fifth lunar day, that day is called *Sripanchami* (or the auspicious fifth day) and as he attained his object on the sixth, that lunar day is considered to be of great moment.'"

SECTION CCXXIX

"Markandeya continued, 'Those six ladies, the wives of the seven *Rishis* when they learned that good fortune had smiled on Mahasena and that he had been made leader of the celestial forces, 39 repaired to his camp. Those virtuous ladies of high religious merit had been disowned by the *Rishis*. They lost no time in visiting that leader of the celestial forces and then addressed him thus, "We, O son, have been cast out by our god-like husbands, without any cause. Some people spread the rumour that we gave birth to thee. Believing in the truth of this story, they became greatly indignant, and banished us from our sacred places. It behooves thee now to save us from this infamy. We desire to adopt thee as our son, so that, O mighty being, eternal bliss may be secured to us by that favour. Do thou thus repay the obligation thou owest to us."

"'Skanda replied, "O ladies of faultless character, do you accordingly become my mothers. I am your son and ye shall attain all the objects of your desire."

"Markandeya continued, 'Then Sakra having expressed a wish to say something to Skanda, the latter enquired, "What is it?" Being told by Skanda to speak it out, Vasava said, "The lady Abhijit, the younger sister of Rohini, being jealous of her seniority, has repaired to the woods to perform austerities. And I am at a loss to find out a substitute for the fallen star. May good luck attend on thee, do thou consult with *Brahma* (for the purpose of filling up the room) of this great asterism." Dhanishtha and other asterisms were created by *Brahma*, and Rohini used to serve the purpose of one such; and consequently their number was full. And in accordance with Sakra's advice, Krittika was assigned a place in the heavens, and that star presided over by *Agni* shines as if with seven heads. Vinata also said to Skanda, "Thou art as a son to me, and entitled to offer me the funeral cakes (at my funeral obsequies). I desire, my son, to live with thee always."

"'Skanda replied, "Be it so, all honour to thee! Do thou guide me with a mother's affection, and honoured by thy daughter-in-law, thou shalt always live with me."'

"Markandeya continued, 'Then the great mothers spoke as follows to Skanda, "We have been described by the learned as the mothers of all creatures. But we desire to be thy mothers, do thou honour us."

"'Skanda replied, "Ye are all as mothers to me, and I am your son. Tell me what I can do to please you."

"'The mothers replied, "The ladies (Brahmi, Maheswari, &c.) were appointed as mothers of the world in bygone ages. We desire, O great god, that they be dispossessed of that dignity, and ourselves installed in their place, and that we, instead of them, be worshipped by the world. Do thou now restore to us those of our progeny, of whom we have been deprived, by them on thy account."

"'Skanda replied, "Ye shall not recover those that have been once given away, but I can give you other offspring if ye like."

"'The mothers replied, "We desire that living with thee and assuming different shapes we be able to eat up the progeny of those mothers and their guardians. Do thou grant us this favour."

"'Skanda said, "I can grant you progeny, but this topic on which ye have just now dilated is a very painful one. May ye be prosperous! All honour to you, ladies, do ye vouchsafe to them your protecting care."

"'The mothers replied, "We shall protect them, O Skanda, as thou desirest. Mayst thou be prosperous! But, O mighty being, we desire to live with thee always."

"'Skanda replied, "So long as children of the human kind do not attain the youthful state in the sixteenth year of their age, ye shall afflict them with your various forms, and I too shall confer on you a fierce inexhaustible spirit. And with that ye shall live happily, worshipped by all."'

"Markandeya continued, 'And then a fiery powerful being came out of the body of Skanda for the purpose of devouring the progeny of mortal beings. He fell down upon the ground, senseless and hungry. And bidden by Skanda, that genius of evil assumed a terrific form. Skandapasmara is the name by which it is known among good Brahmanas. Vinata is called the terrific Sakuni *graha* (spirit of evil). She who is known as *Putana Rakshasi* by the learned is the *graha* called Putana; that fierce and terrible looking *Rakshasa* of a hideous appearance is also called the *pisacha*, Sita Putana. That fierce-looking spirit is the cause of abortion in women. Aditi is also known by the name of Revati; her evil spirit is called Raivata, and that terrible *graha* also afflicts children. Diti, the mother of the Daityas (*Asuras*), is also called Muhkamandika, and that terrible creature is very fond of the flesh of little children. Those male and female children, O Kaurava, who are said to have been begotten by Skanda, are spirit of evil and they destroy the foetus in the womb. They (the *Kumaras*) are known as the husbands of those very ladies, and children are seized unawares by these cruel spirits. And, O king, *Surabhi* who is called the mother of bovine kind by the wise is best ridden by the evil spirit Sakuni, who in company with her, devours children on this earth. And Sarama, the mother of dogs, also habitually kills human beings while still in the womb. She who is the mother of all trees has her abode in a *karanja* tree. She grants boons and has a placid countenance and is always favourably disposed towards all creatures. Those persons who desire to have children, bow down to her, who is seated in a *karanja* tree. These eighteen evil spirits fond of meat and wine, and others of the same kind, invariably take up their abode in the lying-in-room for ten days. Kadru introduces herself in a subtle form into the body of a pregnant woman and there she causes the destruction of the foetus, and the mother is made to give birth to a *Naga* (serpent). And that mother of the Gandharvas takes away the foetus, and for this reason, conception in woman turns out to be abortive. The mother of the *Apsaras* removes the foetus from the womb, and for this reason such conceptions are said to be stationary by the learned. The daughter of the Divinity of the Red Sea is said to have nursed Skanda,—she is worshipped under the name of Lohitayani on Kadamva trees. Arya acts the same part among female beings, as Rudra does among male ones. She is the mother of all children and is distinctly worshipped for their welfare. These that I have described are the evil spirits presiding over the destinies of young children, and until children attain their sixteenth year, these spirits exercise their influence for evil, and after that, for good. The whole body of male and female spirits that I have now described are always denominated by men as the spirits of Skanda. They are propitiated with burnt offerings, ablutions, unguents, sacrifices and other offerings, and particularly by the worship of Skanda. And, O king, when they are honoured and worshipped with due reverence, they bestow on men whatever is good for them, as also valour and long life. And now having bowed down to Maheswara, I shall describe the nature of those spirits who influence the destinies of men after they have attained their sixteenth year.

"'The man who beholds gods while sleeping, or in a wakeful state soon turns mad, and the spirit under whose influence these hallucinations take place is called the celestial spirit. When a person beholds his dead ancestors while he is seated at ease, or lying in his bed, he soon loses his reason, and the spirit which causes this illusion of sensible perception, is called the ancestral spirit. The man who shows disrespect to the *Siddhas* and who is cursed by them in return, soon runs mad and the evil influence by which this is brought about, is called the *Siddha* spirit. And the spirit by whose influence a man smells sweet odour, and becomes cognisant of various tastes (when there are no odoriferous or tasteful substances about him) and soon becomes tormented, is called the *Rakshasa* spirit. And the spirit by whose action celestial musicians (*Gandharvas*) blend their existence into the constitution of a human being, and make him run mad in no time, is called the *Gandharva* spirit. And that evil spirit by whose influence men are always tormented by *Pisachas*, is called the *Pisacha* spirit. When the spirit of *Yakshas* enters into the system of a human being by some accident, he loses his reason immediately, and such a spirit is called the *Yaksha* spirit. The man who loses his reason on account of his mind being demoralised with vices, runs mad in no time, and his illness must be remedied according to methods prescribed in the *Sastras*. Men also run mad from perplexity, from fear, as also on beholding hideous sights. The remedy lies in quieting their minds. There are three classes of spirits, some are frolicsome, some are gluttonous, and some sensual. Until men attain the age of three score and ten, these evil influences continue to torment them, and then fever becomes the only evil spirit that afflicts sentient beings. These evil spirits always avoid those who have subdued their senses, who are self-restrained, of cleanly habits, god-fearing and free from laziness and contamination. I have thus described to thee, O king, the evil spirits that mould the destinies of men. Thou who art devoted to Maheswara art never troubled by them.'"

SECTION CCXXX

"Markandeya continued, 'When Skanda had bestowed these powers, Swaha appeared to him and said, "Thou art my natural son,—I desire that thou shalt grant exquisite happiness to me."

"'Skanda replied, "What sort of happiness dost thou wish to enjoy?"

"'Swaha replied, "O mighty being, I am the favourite daughter of Daksha, by name Swaha; and from my youthful days I have been in love with Hutasana (the Fire-god); but that god, my son, does not understand my feelings. I desire to live for ever with him (as his wife)."

"'Skanda replied, "From this day, lady, all the oblations that men of virtuous character, who swerve not from the path of virtue, will offer to their gods or ancestors with incantation of purifying hymns by Brahmanas, shall always be offered (through Agni) coupled with the name of Swaha, and thus, excellent lady, wilt thou always live associated with Agni, the god of fire."'

"Markandeya continued, 'Thus addressed and honoured by Skanda, Swaha was greatly pleased; and associated with her husband Pavaka (the Fire-god), she honoured him in return.

"'Then *Brahma*, the lord of all creatures, said to Mahasena, "Do thou go and visit thy father Mahadeva, the conqueror of Tripura. Rudra coalescing with Agni (the Fire-god) and Uma with Swaha have combined to make thee invincible for the well-being of all creatures. And the semen of the high-souled Rudra cast into the reproductive organ of Uma was thrown back upon this hill, and hence the twin Mujika and Minjika came into being. A portion of it fell into the Blood Sea, another portion, into the rays of the sun, another upon the earth and thus was it distributed in five portions. Learned men ought to remember that these thy various and fierce-looking followers living on the flesh of animals were produced from the *semen*." "Be it so," so saying, the high-souled Mahasena with fatherly love, honoured his father Maheswara.'

"Markandeya continued, 'Men who are desirous of acquiring wealth, should worship those five classes of spirits with the sun flower, and for alleviation of diseases also worship must be rendered to them. The twin

Mujika and Minjika begotten by Rudra must always be respected by persons desiring the welfare of little children; and persons who desire to have children born to them must always worship those female spirits who live on human flesh and are produced in trees. Thus all *Pisachas* are said to be divided into innumerable classes. And now, O king, listen to the origin of the bells and standards of Skanda. Airavata (Indra's elephant) is known to have had two bells of the name of Vaijayanti, and the keen-witted Sakra had them brought to him, and personally gave them to Guha. Visakha took one of those bells and Skanda the other. The standards of both Kartikeya and Visakha were of a red colour. That mighty god Mahasena was pleased with the toys that had been given to him by the gods. Surrounded by hosts of gods and *Pisachas* and seated on the Golden Mountain, he looked splendid in all the grandeur of prosperity. And that mountain covered with fine forests, also looked grand in his companionship, just as the Mandara hill abounding with excellent caves shines with the rays of the sun. The White Mountain was adorned with whole tracts of wood-land covered with blossoming Santanaka flowers and with forests of Karavira, Parijata, Jaba and Asoke trees,—as also with wild tracts overgrown with Kadamva trees; and it abounded with herds of celestial deer and flocks of celestial birds. And the rumbling of clouds serving the purpose of musical instruments sounded like the murmur of an agitated sea, and celestial Gandharvas and Apsaras began to dance. And there arose a great sound of joy from the merriment of all creatures. Thus the whole world with Indra himself seemed to have been transferred to the White Mountain. And all the people began to observe Skanda with satisfaction in their looks, and they did not at all feel tired of doing so.'

"Markandeya continued, 'When that adorable son of the Fire-god was anointed as leader of the celestial army, that grand and happy lord, Hara (Mahadeva) riding with Parvati in a chariot shining with sunlike refulgence repaired to a place called Bhadravata. His excellent chariot was drawn by a thousand lions and managed by *Kala*. They passed through blank space, and seemed as if they were about to devour the sky; and striking terror into the heart of all creatures in the mobile divisions of the worlds, those maned beasts flitted through the air, uttering fearful growls. And that lord of all animals (Mahadeva) seated in that chariot with Uma, looked like the sun with flames of lightning illuminating masses of clouds begirt with Indra's bow (rainbow). He was preceded by that adorable Lord of riches riding on the backs of human beings with his attendant Guhyakas riding in his beautiful car Pushpaka. And Sakra too riding on his elephant Airavata and accompanied by other gods brought up the rear of Mahadeva, the granter of boons, marching in this way at the head of the celestial army. And the great *Yaksha Amogha* with his attendants—the *Jambhaka Yakshas* and other *Rakshasas* decorated with garlands of flowers—obtained a place in the right wing of his army; and many gods of wonderful fighting powers in company with the *Vasus* and the *Rudras*, also marched with the right division of his army. And the terrible-looking Yama too in company with Death marched with him (followed by hundreds of terrible diseases); and behind him was carried the terrible, sharp-pointed, well-decorated trident of Siva, called Vijaya. And Varuna, the adorable lord of waters with his terrible *Pasa*, 40 and surrounded by numerous aquatic animals, marched slowly with the trident. And the trident Vijaya was followed by the *Pattisa* 41 of Rudra guarded by maces, balls, clubs and other excellent weapons. And the *Pattisa*, O king, was followed by the bright umbrella of Rudra and the Kamandalu served by the *Maharshis*; and on it progressed in the company of Bhrigu, Angiras and others. And behind all these rode Rudra in his white chariot, re-assuring the gods with the exhibition of his powers. And rivers and lakes and seas, *Apsaras, Rishis*, Celestials, *Gandharvas* and serpents, stars, planets, and the children of gods, as also many women, followed him in his train. These handsome-looking ladies proceeded scattering flowers all around; and the clouds marched, having made their obeisance to that god (Mahadeva) armed with the *Pinaka* bow. And some of them held a white umbrella over his head, and Agni (the Fire god) and Vayu (the god of winds) busied themselves with two hairy fans (emblems of royalty). And, O king, he was followed by the glorious Indra accompanied by the *Rajarshis*, and singing the praise of that god with the emblem of the bull. And Gauri, Vidya, Gandhari, Kesini, and the lady called Mitra in company with Savitri, all proceeded in the train of Parvati, as also all the Vidyas (presiding deities of all branches of knowledge) that were created by the learned. The *Rakshasa* spirit who delivers to different battalions the commands which are implicitly obeyed by Indra and other gods, advanced in front of the army as standard-bearer. And that foremost of *Rakshasas,* by name Pingala, the friend of Rudra, who is always busy in places where corpses are burnt, and who is agreeable to all people, marched with them merrily, at one time going ahead of the army, and falling behind again at another, his movements being uncertain. Virtuous actions are the offerings with which the god Rudra is worshipped by mortals. He who is also called Siva, the omnipotent god, armed with the Pinaka bow, is Maheswara. He is worshipped in various forms.

"'The son of Krittika, the leader of the celestial army, respectful to Brahmanas, surrounded by the celestial forces, also followed that lord of the gods. And then Mahadeva said these weighty words to Mahasena, "Do thou carefully command the seventh army corps of the celestial forces."

"'Skanda replied, "Very well, my lord! I shall command the seventh army corps. Now tell me quickly if there is anything else to be done."

"'Rudra said, "Thou shall always find me in the field of action. By looking up to me and by devotion to me shalt thou attain great welfare."'

"Markandeya continued, 'With these words Maheswara received him in his embrace, and then dismissed him. And, O great king, after the dismissal of Skanda, prodigies of various kinds occurred to disturb the equanimity of the gods.

"'The firmament with the stars was in a blaze, and the whole universe in a state of utter confusion. The earth quaked and gave forth a rumbling sound, and darkness overspread the whole world. Then observing this terrible catastrophy, Sankara with the estimable Uma, and the celestials with the great *Maharshis*, were much exercised in mind. And when they had fallen into this state of confusion, there appeared before them a fierce and mighty host armed with various weapons, and looking like a mass of clouds and rocks. Those terrible and countless beings, speaking different languages directed their movements towards the point where Sankara and the celestials stood. They hurled into the ranks of the celestial army flights of arrows in all directions, masses of rock, maces, *sataghnis, prasas* and *parighas*. The celestial army was thrown into a state of confusion by a shower of these terrible weapons and their ranks were seen to waver. The *Danavas* made a great havoc by cutting up their soldiers, horses, elephants, chariots and arms. And the celestial troops then seemed as if they were about to turn their backs upon the enemy. And numbers of them fell, slain by the *Asuras*, like large trees in a forest burnt in a conflagration. Those dwellers of heaven fell with their heads separated from their bodies, and having none to lead them in that fearful battle, they were slaughtered by the enemy. And then the god Purandara (Indra), the slayer of Vala, observing that they were unsteady and hard-pressed by the *Asuras*, tried to rally them with this speech, "Do not be afraid, ye heroes, may success attend your efforts! Do ye all take up your arms, and resolve upon manly conduct, and ye will meet with no more misfortune, and defeat those wicked and terrible-looking *Danavas*. May ye be successful! Do ye fall upon the *Danavas* with me."

"'The dwellers of heaven were re-assured on hearing this speech from Sakra; and under his leadership, they again rushed against the *Danavas*. And then the thirty-three crores of gods and all the powerful *Marutas* and the *Sadhyas* with the *Vasus* returned to the charge. And the arrows which they angrily discharged against the enemy drew a large quantity of blood from the bodies of the *Daityas* and of their horses and elephants. And those sharp arrows passing through their bodies fell upon the ground, looking like so many snakes falling from the sides of a hill. And, O king, the *Daityas* pierced by those arrows fell fast on all sides, looking like so many detached masses of clouds. Then the *Danava* host, struck with panic at that charge of the celestials on the field of battle, wavered at that shower of various weapons. Then all the gods loudly gave vent to their joy, with arms ready to strike; and the celestial bands too struck up various airs. Thus took place that encounter, so fearful to both sides: for all the battle-field was covered with blood and strewn with the bodies of both gods and *Asuras*. But the gods were soon worsted all on a sudden, and the terrible *Danavas* again made a great havoc of the celestial army. Then the *Asuras* drums struck up and their shrill bugles were sounded; and the *Danava* chiefs yelled their terrific war-cry.

"'Then a powerful *Danava*, taking a huge mass of rock in his hands, came out of that terrible *Daitya* army. He looked like the sun peering forth from against a mass of dark clouds. And, O king, the celestials, beholding that he was about to hurl that mass of rock at them, fled in confusion. But they were pursued by Mahisha, who hurled that hillock at them. And, O lord of the world, by the falling of that mass of rock, ten thousand warriors of the celestial army were crushed to the ground and breathed their last. And this act of Mahisha struck terror into the hearts of the gods, and with his attendant *Danavas* he fell upon them like a lion attacking a herd of deer. And when Indra and the other celestials observed that Mahisha was advancing to the charge, they fled, leaving behind their arms and colours. And Mahisha was greatly enraged at this, and he quickly advanced towards the chariot of Rudra; and reaching near, he seized its pole with his hands. And when Mahisha in a fit of rage had thus seized the chariot of Rudra, all the Earth began to groan and the great *Rishis* lost their senses. And *Daityas* of huge proportions, looking like dark clouds, were boisterous with joy, thinking that victory was assured to them. And although that adorable god (Rudra) was in that plight, yet he did not think it worth while to kill Mahisha in battle; he remembered that Skanda would deal the deathblow to that evil-minded *Asura*. And the fiery Mahisha, contemplating with satisfaction the prize (the chariot of Rudra) which he had secured, sounded his war-cry, to the great alarm of the gods and the joy of the *Daityas*. And when the gods were in that fearful predicament, the mighty Mahasena, burning with anger, and looking grand like the Sun advanced to their rescue. And that lordly being was clad in blazing red and decked with a wreath of red flowers. And cased in armour of gold he rode in a gold-coloured chariot bright as the Sun and drawn by chestnut horses. And at his sight the army of the daityas was suddenly dispirited on the field of battle. And, O great king, the mighty Mahasena discharged a bright *Sakti* for the destruction of

Mahisha. That missile cut off the head of Mahisha, and he fell upon the ground and died. And his head massive as a hillock, falling on the ground, barred the entrance to the country of the Northern Kurus, extending in length for sixteen *Yojanas* though at present the people of that country pass easily by that gate.

"'It was observed both by the gods and the *Danavas* that Skanda hurled his *sakti* again and again on the field of battle, and that it returned to his hands, after killing thousands of the enemy's forces. And the terrible *Danavas* fell in large numbers by the arrows of the wise Mahasena. And then a panic seized them, and the followers of Skanda began to slay and eat them up by thousands and drink their blood. And they joyously exterminated the *Danavas* in no time, just as the sun destroys darkness, or as fire destroys a forest, or as the winds drive away the clouds. And in this manner the famous Skanda defeated all his enemies. And the gods came to congratulate him, and he, in turn, paid his respects to Maheswara. And that son of Krittika looked grand like the sun in all the glory of his effulgence. And when the enemy was completely defeated by Skanda and when Maheswara left the battle-field, Purandara embraced Mahasena and said to him, "This Mahisha, who was made invincible by the favour of Brahma hath been killed by thee. O best of warriors, the gods were like grass to him. O strong-limbed hero, thou hast removed a thorn of the celestials. Thou hast killed in battle hundreds of Danavas equal in valour to Mahisha who were all hostile to us, and who used to harass us before. And thy followers too have devoured them by hundreds. Thou art, O mighty being, invincible in battle like Uma's lord; and this victory shall be celebrated as thy first achievement, and thy fame shall be undying in the three worlds. And, O strong-armed god, all the gods will yield their allegiance to thee." Having spoken thus to Mahasena, the husband of Sachi left the place accompanied by the gods and with the permission of the adorable three-eyed god (Siva). And Rudra returned to Bhadravata, and the celestials too returned to their respective abodes. And Rudra spoke, addressing the gods, "Ye must render allegiance to Skanda just as ye do unto me." And that son of the Fire-god, having killed the Danavas hath conquered the three worlds, in one day, and he hath been worshipped by the great *Rishis*. The Brahmana who with due attention readeth this story of the birth of Skanda, attaineth to great prosperity in this world and the companionship of Skanda hereafter.'

"Yudhishthira said, 'O good and adorable Brahmana, I wish to know the different names of that high-souled being, by which he is celebrated throughout the three worlds.'"

Vaisampayana continued, "Thus addressed by the Pandava in that assembly of *Rishis*, the worshipful Markandeya of high ascetic merit replied,

'Agneya (Son of Agni), Skanda (Cast-off), Diptakirti (Of blazing fame), Anamaya (Always hale), Mayuraketu (Peacock-bannered), Dharmatman (The virtuous-souled), Bhutesa (The lord of all creatures), Mahishardana (The slayer of Mahisha), Kamajit (The subjugator of desires), Kamada (The fulfiller of desires), Kanta (The handsome), Satyavak (The truthful in speech), Bhuvaneswara (The lord of the universe), Sisu (The child), Sighra (The quick), Suchi (The pure), Chanda (The fiery), Diptavarna (The bright-complexioned), Subhanana (Of beautiful face), Amogha (Incapable of being baffled), Anagha (The sinless), Rudra (The terrible), Priya (The favourite), Chandranana (Of face like the moon), Dipta-sasti (The wielder of the blazing lance), Prasantatman (Of tranquil soul), Bhadrakrit (The doer of good), Kutamahana (The chamber of even the wicked), Shashthipriya (True favourite of Shashthi), Pavitra (The holy), Matrivatsala (The reverencer of his mother), Kanya-bhartri (The protector of virgins), Vibhakta (Diffused over the universe), Swaheya (The son of Swaha), Revatisuta (The child of Revati), Prabhu (The Lord), Neta (The leader), Visakha (Reared up by Visakha), Naigameya (Sprang from the Veda), Suduschara (Difficult of propitiation), Suvrata (Of excellent vows), Lalita (The beautiful), Valakridanaka-priya (Fond of toys), Khacharin (The ranger of skies), Brahmacharin (The chaste), Sura (The brave), Saravanodbhava (Born in a forest of heath), Viswamitra priya (The favourite of Viswamitra), Devasena-priya (The lover of Devasena), Vasudeva-priya (The beloved of Vasudeva), and Priya-krit (The doer of agreeable things)—these are the divine names of Kartikeya. Whoever repeateth them, undoubtedly secureth fame, wealth, and salvation.'

"Markandeya continued, 'O valiant scion of Kuru's race, I shall now with due devotion pray to that unrivalled, mighty, six-faced, and valiant Guha who is worshipped by gods and *Rishis*, enumerating his other titles of distinction: do thou listen to them: Thou art devoted to *Brahma*, begotten of Brahma, and versed in the mysteries of *Brahma*. Thou art called *Brahmasaya*, and thou art the foremost of those who are possessed of *Brahma*. Thou art fond of *Brahma*, thou art austere like the Brahmanas and art versed in the great mystery of *Brahma* and the leader of the Brahmanas. Thou art *Swaha*, thou art *Swadha*, and thou art the holiest of the holy, and art invoked in hymns and celebrated as the six-flamed fire. Thou art the year, thou art the six seasons, thou art the months, the (lunar) half months, the (solar) declinations, and the cardinal points of space. Thou art lotus-eyed. Thou art possessed of a lily-like face. Thou hast a thousand faces and a thousand arms. Thou art the ruler of the universe, thou art the great Oblation, and thou art the animating spirit of all the gods and the *Asuras*. Thou art the great leader of armies. Thou art *Prachanda* (furious), thou art the Lord, and thou art the great master and the conqueror of thine enemies. Thou art *Sahasrabhu* (multiform), *Sahasratusti* (a thousand times content), *Sahasrabhuk* (devourer of everything), and *Sahasrapad* (of a thousand legs), and thou art the earth itself. Thou art possessed of infinite forms and thousand heads and great strength. According to thine own inclinations thou hast appeared as the son of Ganga, Swaha, Mahi, or Krittika. O six-faced god, thou dost play with the cock and assume different forms according to thy will. Thou art Daksha, Soma, the Maruta, Dharma, Vayu, the prince of mountains, and Indra, for all time. Thou art mighty, the most eternal of all eternal things, and the lord of all lords. Thou art the progenitor of Truth, the destroyer of Diti's progeny (*Asuras*), and the great conqueror of the enemies of the celestials. Thou art the personation of virtue and being thyself vast and minute, thou art acquainted with the highest and lowest points of virtuous acts, and the mysteries of *Brahma*. O foremost of all gods and high-souled lord of the Universe, this whole creation is over-spread with thy energy! I have thus prayed to thee according to the best of my power. I salute thee who art possessed of twelve eyes and many hands. Thy remaining attributes transcend my powers of comprehension!'

"'The Brahmana who with due attention readeth this story of the birth of Skanda, or relateth it unto Brahmanas, or hears it narrated by regenerate men, attaineth to wealth, long life, fame, children, as also victory, prosperity and contentment, and the companionship of Skanda.'"

SECTION CCXXXI

(Draupadi-Satyabhama Samvada)

Vaisampayana said, "After those Brahmanas and the illustrious sons of Pandu had taken their seats, Draupadi and Satyabhama entered the hermitage. And with hearts full of joy the two ladies laughed merrily and seated themselves at their ease. And, O king, those ladies, who always spake sweetly to each other, having met after a long time, began to talk upon various delightful topics arising out of the stories of the Kurus and the Yadus. And the slender-waisted Satyabhama, the favourite wife of Krishna and the daughter of Satrajit, then asked Draupadi in private, saying, 'By what behaviour is it, O daughter of Drupada, that thou art able to rule the sons of Pandu—those heroes endued with strength and beauty and like unto the *Lokapalas* themselves? Beautiful lady, how is it that they are so obedient to thee and are never angry with thee? Without doubt the sons of Pandu, O thou of lovely features, are ever submissive to thee and watchful to do thy bidding! Tell me, O lady, the reason of this. Is it practice of vows, or asceticism, or incantation or drug at the time of the bath (in season) or the efficacy of science, or the influence of youthful appearance, or the recitation of particular formulae, or *Homa*, or collyrium and other medicaments? Tell me now, O princess of Panchala, of that blessed and auspicious thing by which, O Krishna, Krishna may ever be obedient to me.'

"When the celebrated Satyabhama, having said this, ceased, the chaste and blessed daughter of Drupada answered her, saying, 'Thou askedest me, O Satyabhama, of the practices of women that are wicked. How can I answer thee, O lady, about the cause that is pursued by wicked females? It doth not become thee, lady, to pursue the questions, or doubt me, after this, for thou art endued with intelligence and art the favourite wife of Krishna. When the husband learns that his wife is addicted to incantations and drugs, from that hour he beginneth to dread her like a serpent ensconced in his sleeping chamber. And can a man that is troubled with fear have peace, and how can one that hath no peace have happiness? A husband can never be made obedient by his wife's incantations. We hear of painful diseases being transmitted by enemies. Indeed, they that desire to slay others, send poison in the shape of customary gifts, so that the man that taketh the powders so sent, by tongue or skin, is, without doubt, speedily deprived of life. Women have sometimes caused dropsy and leprosy, decrepitude and impotence and idiocy and blindness and deafness in men. These wicked women, ever treading in the path of sin, do sometimes (by these means) injure their husbands. But the wife should never do the least injury to her lord. Hear now, O illustrious lady, of the behaviour I adopt towards the high-souled sons of Pandu. Keeping aside vanity, and controlling desire and wrath, I always serve with devotion the sons of Pandu with their wives. Restraining jealousy, with deep devotion of heart, without a sense of degradation at the services I perform, I wait upon my husbands. Ever fearing to utter what is evil or false, or to look or sit or walk with impropriety, or cast glances indicative of the feelings of the heart, do I serve the sons of Pritha—those mighty warriors blazing like the sun or fire, and handsome as the moon, those endued with fierce energy and prowess, and capable of slaying their foes by a glance of the eye. Celestial, or man, or Gandharva, young or decked with ornaments, wealthy or comely of person, none else my heart liketh. I never bathe or eat or sleep till he that is my husband hath bathed or eaten or slept,—till, in fact, our attendants have bathed, eaten, or slept. Whether returning from the field, the forest, or the town, hastily rising up I always salute my husband with water and a seat. I always keep the house and all household articles and the food that is to be taken well-ordered and clean. Carefully do I keep the rice, and serve the food at the proper time. I never indulge in angry and fretful speech, and never imitate women that are wicked. Keeping idleness at distance I always do what is agreeable. I never laugh except at a jest, and never stay for any length of time at the house-gate. I never stay long in places for answering calls of nature, nor in pleasure-gardens attached to the house. I always refrain from laughing loudly and indulging in high passion, and from everything that may give offence. Indeed, O Satyabhama, I always am engaged in waiting upon my lords. A separation from my lords is never agreeable to me. When my husband leaveth home for the sake of any relative, then renouncing flowers and fragrant paste of every kind, I begin to undergo penances. Whatever my husband drinketh not, whatever my husband eateth not, whatever my husband enjoyeth not, I ever renounce. O beautiful lady, decked in ornaments and ever controlled by the instruction imparted to me, I always devotedly seek the good of my lord. Those duties that my mother-in-law had told me of in respect of relatives, as also the duties of alms-giving, of offering worship to the gods, of oblations to the diseased, of boiling food in pots on auspicious days for offer to ancestors and guests of reverence and service to those that deserve our regards, and all else that is known to me, I always discharge day and night, without idleness of any kind. Having with my whole heart recourse to humility and approved rules I serve my meek and truthful lords ever observant of virtue, regarding them as poisonous snakes capable of being excited at a trifle. I think that to be eternal virtue for women which is based upon a regard for the husband. The husband is the wife's god, and he is her refuge. Indeed, there is no other refuge for her. How can, then, the wife do the least injury to her lord? I never, in sleeping or eating or adorning any person, act against the wishes of my lord, and always guided by my husbands, I never speak ill of my mother-in-law. O blessed lady, my husbands have become obedient to me in consequence of my diligence, my alacrity, and the humility with which I serve superiors. Personally do I wait every day with food and drink and clothes upon the revered and truthful Kunti—that mother of heroes. Never do I show any preference for myself over her in matters of food and attire, and never do I reprove in words that princess equal unto the Earth herself in forgiveness. Formerly, eight thousand Brahmanas were daily fed in the palace of Yudhishthira from off plates of gold. And eighty thousand Brahmanas also of the *Snataka* sect leading domestic lives were entertained by Yudhishthira with thirty serving-maids assigned to each. Besides these, ten thousand *yatis* with the vital seed drawn up, had their pure food carried unto them in plates of gold. All these Brahmanas that were the utterers of the *Veda*, I used to worship duly with food, drink, and raiment taken from stores only after a portion thereof had been dedicated to the Viswadeva. 42 The illustrious son of Kunti had a hundred thousand well-dressed serving-maids with bracelets on arms and golden ornaments on necks, and decked with costly garlands and wreaths and gold in profusion, and sprinkled with sandal paste. And adorned with jewels and gold they were all skilled in singing and dancing. O lady, I knew the names and features of all those girls, as also what they are and what they were, and what they did not. Kunti's son of great intelligence had also a hundred thousand maid-servants who daily used to feed guests, with plates of gold in their hands. And while Yudhishthira lived in Indraprastha a hundred thousand horses and a hundred thousand elephants used to follow in his train. These were the possessions of Yudhishthira while he ruled the earth. It was I however, O lady, who regulated their number and framed the rules to be observed in respect of them; and it was I who had to listen to all complaints about them. Indeed, I knew everything about what the maid-servants of the palace and other classes of attendants, even the cow-herds and the shepherds of the royal establishment, did or did not. O blessed and illustrious lady, it was I alone amongst the Pandavas who knew the income and expenditure of the king and what their whole wealth was. And those bulls among the Bharatas, throwing upon me the burden of looking after all those that were to be fed by them, would, O thou of handsome face, pay their court to me. And this load, so heavy and incapable of being borne by persons of evil heart, I used to bear day and night, sacrificing my ease, and all the while affectionately devoted to them. And while my husbands were engaged in the pursuit of virtue, I only supervised their treasury inexhaustible like the ever-filled receptacle of Varuna. Day and night bearing hunger and thirst, I used to serve the Kuru princes, so that my nights and days were equal to me. I used to wake up first and go to bed last. This, O Satyabhama, hath ever been my charm for making my husbands obedient to me! This great art hath ever been known to me for making my husbands obedient to me. Never have I practised the charms of wicked women, nor do I ever wish to practise them.'"

Vaisampayana continued, "Hearing those words of virtuous import uttered by Krishna, Satyabhama, having first reverenced the virtuous princess of Panchala, answered saying, 'O princess of Panchala, I have been guilty, O daughter of Yajnasena, forgive me! Among friends, conversations in jest arise naturally, and without premeditation.'"

SECTION CCXXXII

"Draupadi said, 'I shall now indicate to thee, for attracting the heart of thy husbands a way that is free from deceit. By adopting it duly, dear friend, thou will be able to draw away thy lord from other females. In all the worlds, including that of the celestials, there is no god equal, O Satyabhama, unto the husband. When he is gratified with thee, thou mayst have (from thy husband) every object of desire; when he is angry, all these may be lost. It is from her husband that the wife obtaineth offspring and various articles of enjoyment. It is from thy husband that thou mayst have handsome beds and seats, and robes and garlands, and perfumes, and great fame and heaven itself hereafter. One cannot obtain happiness here by means that are easy. Indeed, the woman that is chaste, obtains weal with woe. Always adore Krishna, therefore, with friendship and love physical sufferings. And do thou also act in a way, by offering handsome seats and excellent garlands and various perfumes and prompt service, that he may be devoted to thee, thinking, *"I am truly loved by her!"* Hearing the voice of thy lord at the gate, rise thou up from thy seat and stay in readiness within the room. And as soon as thou seest him enter thy chamber, worship him by promptly offering him a seat and water to wash his feet. And even when he commands a maidservant to do anything, get thou up and do it thyself. Let Krishna understand this temper of thy mind and know that thou adorest him with all thy heart. And, O Satyabhama, whatever thy lord speaketh before thee, do not blab of it even if it may not deserve concealment,—for if any of thy co-wives were to speak of it unto Vasudeva, he might be irritated with thee. Feed thou by every means in thy power those that are dear and devoted to thy lord and always seek his good. Thou shouldst, however, always keep thyself aloof from those that are hostile to and against thy lord and seek to do him injury, as also from those that are addicted to deceit. Foregoing all excitement and carelessness in the presence of men, conceal thy inclinations by observing silence, and thou shouldst not stay or converse in private even with thy sons, Pradyumna and Samva. Thou shouldst form attachments with only such females as are high-born and sinless and devoted to their lords, and thou shouldst always shun women that are wrathful, addicted to drinks, gluttonous, thievish, wicked and fickle. Behaviour such as this is reputable and productive of prosperity; and while it is capable of neutralising hostility, it also leadeth to heaven. Therefore, worship thou thy husband, decking thyself in costly garlands and ornaments and smearing thyself with unguents and excellent perfumes.'"

SECTION CCXXXIII

Vaisampayana said, "Then Kesava, the slayer of Madhu, also called Janardana, having conversed on various agreeable themes with the illustrious sons of Pandu and with those Brahmanas that were headed by Markandeya and having bid them farewell, mounted his car and called for Satyabhama. And Satyabhama then, having embraced the daughter of Drupada, addressed her in these cordial words expressive of her feelings towards her: 'O Krishna, let there be no anxiety, no grief, for thee! Thou hast no cause to pass thy nights in sleeplessness, for thou wilt surely obtain back the earth subjugated by thy husbands, who are all equal unto the gods. O thou of black eyes, women endued with such disposition and possessed of such auspicious marks, can never suffer misfortune long. It hath been heard by me that thou shall, with thy husbands, certainly enjoy this earth peacefully and freed from all thorns! And, O daughter of Drupada, thou shalt certainly behold the earth ruled by Yudhishthira after the sons of Dhritarashtra have been slain and the deeds of their hostility avenged! Thou wilt soon behold those wives of the Kurus, who, deprived of sense by pride, laughed at thee while on thy way to exile, themselves reduced to a state of helplessness and despair! Know them all, O Krishna, that did thee any injury while thou wert afflicted, to have already gone to the abode of Yama. Thy brave sons, Prativindhya by Yudhishthira and Sutasoma by Bhima, and Srutakarman by Arjuna, and Satanika by Nakula, and Srutasena begot by Sahadeva, are well and have become skilled in weapons. Like Abhimanyu they are all staying at Dwaravati, delighted with the place. And Subhadra also, cheerfully and with her whole soul, looketh after them like thee, and like thee joyeth in them and deriveth much happiness from them. Indeed, she grieveth in their griefs and joyeth in their joys. And the mother of Pradyumna also loveth them with her whole soul. And Kesava with his sons Bhanu and others watcheth over them with especial affection. And my mother-in-law is ever attentive in feeding and clothing them. And the Andhakas and Vrishnis, including Rama and others, regard them with affection. And, O beautiful lady, their affection for thy sons is equal unto what they feel for Pradyumna.'

"Having said these agreeable and truthful and cordial words, Satyabhama desired to go to Vasudeva's car. And the wife of Krishna then walked round the queen of the Pandavas. And having done so the beautiful Satyabhama mounted the car of Krishna. And the chief of the Yadavas, comforting Draupadi with a smile and causing the Pandavas to return, set out for his own city, with swift horses (yoked unto his car)."

SECTION CCXXXIV

(Ghosha-yatra Parva)

Janamejaya said, "While those foremost of men—the sons of Pritha—were passing their days in the forest exposed to the inclemencies of the winter, the summer, the wind and the sun, what did they do, O Brahmana, after they had reached the lake and woods going by the name of Dwaita?"

Vaisampayana said, "After the sons of Pandu had arrived at that lake, they chose a residence that was removed from the habitations of men. And they began to roam through delightful woods and ever charming mountains and picturesque river-valleys. And after they had taken up their residence there, many venerable ascetics endued with Vedic lore often came to see them. And those foremost of men always received those *Veda*-knowing *Rishis* with great respect. And one day there came unto the Kaurava princes a certain Brahmana who was well known on earth for his powers of speech. And having conversed with the Pandavas for a while, he went away as pleased him to the court of the royal son of Vichitravirya. Received with respect by that chief of the Kurus, the old king, the Brahmana took his seat; and asked by the monarch he began to talk of the sons of Dharma, Pavana, Indra and of the twins, all of whom having fallen into severe misery, had become emaciated and reduced owing to exposure to wind and sun. And that Brahmana also talked of Krishna who was overwhelmed with suffering and who then had become perfectly helpless, although she had heroes for her lords. And hearing the words of that Brahmana, the royal son of Vichitravirya became afflicted with grief, at the thought of those princes of royal lineage then swimming in a river of sorrow. His inmost soul afflicted with sorrow and trembling all over with sighs, he quieted himself with a great effort, remembering that everything had arisen from his own fault. And the monarch said, 'Alas, how is it that Yudhishthira who is the eldest of my sons, who is truthful and pious and virtuous in his behaviour, who hath not a foe, who had formerly slept on beds made of soft *Ranku* skins, sleepeth now on the bare ground! Alas, wakened formerly by *Sutas* and *Magadhas* and other singers with his praises, melodiously recited every morning, that prince of the Kuru race, equal unto Indra himself, is now waked from the bare ground towards the small hours of the night by a multitude of birds! How doth Vrikodara, reduced by exposure to wind and sun and filled with wrath, sleep, in the presence of the princess of Panchala, on the bare ground, unfit as he is to suffer such lot! Perhaps also, the intelligent Arjuna, who is incapable of bearing pain, and who, though obedient to the will of Yudhishthira, yet feeleth himself to be pierced over all by the remembrance of his wrongs, sleepeth not in the night! Beholding the twins and Krishna and Yudhishthira and Bhima plunged in misery, Arjuna without doubt, sigheth like a serpent of fierce energy and sleepeth not from wrath in the night! The twins also, who are even like a couple of blessed celestials in heaven sunk in woe though deserving of bliss, without doubt pass their nights in restless wakefulness restrained (from avenging their wrongs) by virtue and truth! The mighty son of the Wind-god, who is equal to the Wind-god himself in strength, without doubt, sigheth and restraineth his wrath, being tied through his elder brother in the bonds of truth! Superior in battle to all warriors, he now lieth quiet on the ground, restrained by virtue and truth, and burning to slay my children, he bideth his time. The cruel words that Dussasana spoke after Yudhishthira had been deceitfully defeated at dice, have sunk deep into Vrikodara's heart, and are consuming him, like a burning bundle of straw consuming a fagot of dry wood! The son of Dharma never acteth sinfully; Dhananjaya also always obeyeth him; but Bhima's wrath, in consequence of a life of exile, is increasing like a conflagration assisted by the wind! That hero, burning with rage such as that, squeezeth his hands and breatheth hot and fierce sighs, as if consuming therewith my sons and grandsons! The wielder of the *Gandiva* and Vrikodara, when angry, are like Yama and Kala themselves; scattering their shafts, which are like unto thunder-bolts, they exterminate in battle the ranks of the enemy. Alas Duryodhana, and Sakuni, and the *Suta's* son, and Dussasana also of wicked soul, in robbing the Pandavas of their kingdom by means of dice, seem to behold the honey alone without marking the terrible ruin. A man having acted rightly or wrongly, expecteth the fruit of those acts. The fruit, however, confounding him, paralyses him fully. How can man, thereof, have salvation? If the soil is properly tilled, and the seed sown therein, and if the god (of rain) showereth in season, still the crop may not grow. This is what we often hear. Indeed, how could this saying be true unless, as I think, it be that everything here is dependent on Destiny? The gambler Sakuni hath behaved deceitfully towards the son of Pandu, who ever acteth honestly. From affection for my wicked sons I also have acted similarly. Alas, it is owing to this that the hour of destruction hath come for the Kurus! Oh, perhaps, what is inevitable must happen! The wind, impelled or not, will move. The woman that conceives will bring forth. Darkness will be dispelled at dawn, and day disappear at evening!

Whatever may be earned by us or others, whether people spend it or not, when the time cometh, those possessions of ours do bring on misery. Why then do people become so anxious about earning wealth? If, indeed, what is acquired is the result of fate, then should it be protected so that it may not be divided, nor lost little by little, nor permitted to flow out at once, for if unprotected, it may break into a hundred fragments. But whatever the character of our possessions, our acts in the world are never lost. Behold what the energy of Arjuna is, who went into the abode of Indra from the woods! Having mastered the four kinds of celestial weapons he hath come back into this world! What man is there who, having gone to heaven in his human form, wisheth to come back? This would never have been but because he seeth innumerable Kurus to be at the point of death, afflicted by Time! The bowman is Arjuna, capable of wielding the bow with his left hand as well! The bow he wieldeth is the *Gandiva* of fierce impetus. He hath, besides, those celestial weapons of his! Who is there that would bear the energy of these three!'

"Hearing these words of the monarch, the son of Suvala, going unto Duryodhana, who was then sitting with Karna, told them everything in private. And Duryodhana, though possessed of little sense, was filled with grief at what he heard."

SECTION CCXXXV

Vaisampayana said, "Hearing those words of Dhritarashtra, Sakuni, when the opportunity presented itself, aided by Karna, spoke unto Duryodhana these words, 'Having exiled the heroic Pandavas by thy own prowess, O Bharata, rule thou this earth without a rival like the slayer of Samvara ruling the heaven! O monarch, the kings of the east, the south, the west, and the north, have all been made tributary to thee! O lord of earth, that blazing Prosperity which had before paid her court to the sons of Pandu, hath now been acquired by thee along with thy brothers! That blazing Prosperity, O king, which we not many days ago saw with heavy hearts in Yudhishthira at Indraprastha, is today seen by us to be owned by thee, she having, O mighty-armed monarch, been snatched by thee from the royal Yudhishthira by force of intellect alone. O slayer of hostile heroes, all the kings of the earth now living in subjection to thee, await thy commands, as they did before under Yudhishthira, awaiting his. O monarch, the goddess Earth with her boundless extent with girth of seas, with her mountains and forests, and towns and cities and mines, and decked with woodlands and hills is now thine! Adored by the Brahmanas and worshipped by the kings, thou blazest forth, O king, in consequence of thy prowess, like the Sun among the gods in heaven! Surrounded by the Kurus, O king, like Yama by the Rudra, or Vasava by the Maruts, thou shinest, O monarch, like the Moon among the stars! Let us, therefore, O king, go and look at the sons of Pandu—them who are now divested of prosperity, them who never obeyed commands, them who never owed subjection! It hath been heard by us, O monarch, that the Pandavas are now living on the banks of the lake called *Dwaitavana*, with a multitude of Brahmanas, having the wilderness for their home. Go thither, O king, in all thy prosperity, scorching the son of Pandu with a sight of thy glory, like the Sun scorching everything with his hot rays! Thyself a sovereign and they divested of sovereignty, thyself in prosperity and they divested of it, thyself possessing affluence and they in poverty, behold now, O king, the sons of Pandu. Let the sons of Pandu behold thee like Yayati, the son of Nahusha, accompanied by a large train of followers and enjoying bliss that is great. O king, that blazing Prosperity which is seen by both one's friends and foes, is regarded as well-bestowed! What happiness can be more complete than that which he enjoyeth who while himself in prosperity, looketh upon his foes in adversity, like a person on the hill top looking down upon another crawling on the earth? O tiger among kings, the happiness that one derives from beholding his foes in grief, is greater than what one may derive from the acquisition of offering or wealth or kingdom! What happiness will not be his who, himself in affluence, will cast his eyes on Dhananjaya attired in barks and deer-skins? Let thy wife dressed in costly robes look at the woeful Krishna clad in barks and deer-skins, and enhance the latter's grief! Let the daughter of Drupada reproach herself and her life, divested as she is of wealth, for the sorrow that she will feel upon beholding thy wife decked in ornaments will be far greater than what she had felt in the midst of the assembly (when Dussasana had dragged her there)!'"

Vaisampayana continued, "Having thus spoken unto the king, Karna and Sakuni both remained silent, O Janamejaya, after their discourse was over."

SECTION CCXXXVI

Vaisampayana said, "Having heard these words of Karna, king Duryodhana became highly pleased. Soon after, however, the prince became melancholy and addressing the speaker said, 'What thou tellest me, O Karna, is always before my mind. I shall not, however, obtain permission to repair to the place where the Pandavas are residing. King Dhritarashtra is always grieving for those heroes. Indeed, the king regarded the sons of Pandu to have become more powerful than before in consequence of their ascetic austerities. Or, if the king understands our motives, he will never, having regard to the future, grant us permission, for, O thou of great effulgence, we can have no other business in the woods of *Dwaitavana* than the destruction of the Pandavas in exile! Thou knowest the words that Kshatri spoke to me, to thyself, and to the son of Suvala, at the time of the match at dice! Reflecting upon all those words as also upon all those lamentations (that he and others indulged in), I cannot make up my mind as to whether I should or should not go! I shall certainly be highly pleased if I cast my eyes on Bhima and Phalguna passing their days in pain with Krishna in the woods. The joy that I may feel in obtaining the sovereignty of the entire earth is nothing to that which will be mine upon beholding the sons of Pandu attired in barks of trees and deer-skins. What joy can be greater, O Karna, that will be mine upon beholding the daughter of Drupada dressed in red rags in the woods? If king Yudhishthira and Bhima, the sons of Pandu, behold me graced with great affluence, then only shall I have attained the great end of my life! I do not, however, see the means by which I may repair to those woods, by which, in fact, I may obtain the king's permission to go thither! Contrive thou, therefore, some skilful plan, with Suvala's son and Dussasana, by which we may go to those woods! I also, making up my mind today as to whether I should go or not, approach the presence of the king tomorrow. And when I shall be sitting with Bhishma—that best of the Kurus—thou wilt, with Sakuni propose the pretext which thou mayst have contrived. Hearing then the words of Bhishma and of the king on the subject of our journey, I will settle everything beseeching our grandfather.'

"Saying 'So be it,' they then all went away to their respective quarters. And as soon as the night had passed away, Karna came to the king. And coming to him, Karna smilingly spoke unto Duryodhana, saying, 'A plan hath been contrived by me. Listen to it, O lord of men! Our herds are now waiting in the woods of *Dwaitavana* in expectation of thee! Without doubt, we may all go there under the pretext of supervising our cattle stations, for, O monarch, it is proper that kings should frequently repair to their cattle stations. If this be the motive put forth, thy father, O prince, will certainly grant thee permission!' And while Duryodhana and Karna were thus conversing laughingly, Sakuni addressed them and said, 'This plan, free from difficulties, was what I also saw for going thither! The king will certainly grant us permission, or even send us thither of his own accord. Our herds are now all waiting in the woods of *Dwaitavana* expecting thee. Without doubt, we may all go there under the pretext of supervising our cattle stations!'

"They then all three laughed together, and gave their hands unto one another. And having arrived at that conclusion, they went to see the chief of Kurus."

SECTION CCXXXVII

Vaisampayana said, "They then all saw king Dhritarashtra, O Janamejaya, and having seen him, enquired after his welfare, and were, in return, asked about their welfare. Then a cow-herd named Samanga, who had been instructed beforehand by them, approaching the king, spoke unto him of the cattle. Then the son of Radha and Sakuni, O king, addressing Dhritarashtra, that foremost of monarchs, said, 'O Kaurava, our cattle-stations are now in a delightful place. The time for their tale as also for marking the calves hath come. And, O monarch, this also is an excellent season for thy son to go ahunting! It behoveth thee, therefore, to grant permission to Duryodhana to go thither.'

"Dhritarashtra replied, 'The chase of the deer, as also the examination of cattle is very proper, O child! I think, indeed, that the herdsmen are not to be trusted. But we have heard that those tigers among men, the Pandavas, are now staying in the vicinity of those cattle stations. I think, therefore, ye should not go thither yourselves! Defeated by deceitful means they are now living in the deep forest in great suffering. O Radheya, they are mighty warriors and naturally able, they are now devoted to ascetic austerities. King Yudhishthira will not suffer his wrath to be awakened, but Bhimasena is naturally passionate. The daughter of Yajnasena is energy's self. Full of pride and folly, ye are certain to give offence. Endued with ascetic merit she will certainly consume you, or perhaps, those heroes, armed with swords and weapons! Nor, if from force of numbers, ye seek to injure them in any respect, that will be a highly improper act, although, as I think, ye will never be able to succeed. The mighty-armed Dhananjaya hath returned thence to the forest. While unaccomplished in arms, Vivatsu had subjugated the whole earth before. A mighty warrior as he is and accomplished in arms now, will he not be able to slay you all? Or, if in obedience to my words, ye behave carefully having repaired thither, ye will not be able to live happily there in consequence of the anxiety ye will feel owing to a state of continued trustlessness. Or, some soldier of yours may do some injury to Yudhishthira, and that unpremeditated act will be ascribed to your fault. Therefore, let some faithful men proceed there for the work of tale. I do not think it is proper for thee, Bharata, to go thither thyself.'

"Sakuni said, 'The eldest of the sons of Pandu is cognisant of morality. He pledged in the midst of the assembly, O Bharata, that he would live for twelve years in the forest. The other sons of Pandu are all virtuous and obedient to Yudhishthira. And Yudhishthira himself, the son of Kunti, will never be angry with us. Indeed, we desire very much to go on a hunting expedition, and will avail of that opportunity for supervising the tale of our cattle. We have no mind to see the sons of Pandu. We will not go to that spot where the Pandavas have taken up their residence, and consequently no exhibition of misconduct can possibly arise on our part.'"

Vaisampayana continued, "Thus addressed by Sakuni, that lord of men, Dhritarashtra, granted permission, but not very willingly, to Duryodhana and his counsellors to go to the place. And permitted by the monarch the Bharata prince born of Gandhari started, accompanied by Karna and surrounded by a large host. And he was also accompanied by Dussasana and Suvala's son of great intelligence and by many other brothers of his and by ladies in thousands. And as the mighty-armed prince started for beholding the lake that was known by the name of *Dwaitavana*, the citizens (of Hastina), also accompanied by their wives began to follow him to that forest. Eight thousand cars, thirty thousand elephants, nine thousand horses, and many thousands of foot-soldiers, and shops and pavilions and traders, bards and men trained in the chase by hundreds and thousands followed the prince. And as the king started, followed by this large concourse of people, the uproar that was caused there resembled, O king, the deep tumult of the ranging winds in the rainy season. And reaching the lake *Dwaitavana* with all his followers and vehicles, king Duryodhana took up his quarters at the distance of four miles from it."

SECTION CCXXXVIII

Vaisampayana said, "King Duryodhana then moving from forest to forest, at last approached the cattle-stations, and encamped his troops. And his attendants, selecting a well-known and delightful spot that abounded in water and trees and that possessed every convenience constructed an abode for him. And near enough to the royal residence they also erected separate abodes for Karna and Sakuni and the brothers of the king. And the king beheld his cattle by hundreds and thousands and examining their limbs and marks supervised their tale. And he caused the calves to be marked and took note of those that required to be tamed. And he also counted those kine whose calves had not yet been weaned. And completing the task of tale by marking and counting every calf that was three years old, the Kuru prince, surrounded by the cowherds, began to sport and wander cheerfully. And the citizens also and the soldiers by thousands began to sport, as best pleased them, in those woods, like the celestials. And the herdsmen, well skilled in singing and dancing and instrumental music, and virgins decked in ornaments, began to minister to the pleasures of Dhritarashtra's son. And the king surrounded by the ladies of the royal household began cheerfully to distribute wealth and food and drinks of various kinds amongst those that sought to please him, according to their desires.

"And the king, attended by all his followers, began also to slay hyenas and buffaloes and deer and gayals and bears and boars all around. And the king, piercing by his shafts those animals by thousands in deep forest, caused the deer to be caught in the more delightful parts of the woods. Drinking milk and enjoying, O Bharata, various other delicious articles and beholding, as he proceeded, many delightful forests and woods swarming with bees inebriate with floral honey and resounding with the notes of the peacock, the king at last reached the sacred lake of *Dwaitavana*. And the spot which the king reached swarmed with bees inebriate with floral honey, and echoed with the mellifluous notes of the blue-throated jay and was shaded by *Saptacchadas* and *punnagas* and *Vakulas*. And the king graced with high prosperity proceeded thither like the thunder-wielding chief of the celestials himself. And, O thou best of the Kuru race, King Yudhishthira the just, endued with high intelligence, was then, O monarch, residing in the vicinity of that lake at will and celebrating with his wedded wife, the daughter of Drupada, the diurnal sacrifice called *Rajarshi*, according to the ordinance sanctioned for the celestials and persons living in the wilderness. And, O monarch, having reached that spot, Duryodhana commanded his men by thousands, saying, 'Let pleasure-houses be constructed soon.' Thus commanded, those doers of the king's behests replying to the Kuru chief with the words, 'So be it,' went towards the banks of the lake for constructing pleasure-houses. And as the picked soldiers of Dhritarashtra's son, having reached the region of the lake, were about to enter the gates of the wood, a number of *Gandharvas* appeared and forbade them to enter. For, O monarch, the king of the *Gandharvas* accompanied by his followers, had come thither beforehand, from the abode of *Kuvera*. And the king of the *Gandharvas* had also been accompanied by the several tribes of *Apsaras*, as also by the sons of the celestials. And intent upon sport, he had come to that place for merriment, and occupying it, had closed it against all comers. And the attendants of the (Kuru) king, finding the lake closed by the king of the *Gandharvas*, went back, O monarch, to where the royal Duryodhana was. And Duryodhana having heard these words, despatched a number of his warriors difficult of being subjugated in battle, commanding them to drive away the *Gandharvas*. And those warriors who formed the vanguard of the Kuru army, hearing these words of the king, went back to the lake of *Dwaitavana* and addressing the *Gandharvas*, said, 'The mighty king Duryodhana—the son of Dhritarashtra—is coming, hither for sport. Stand ye aside, therefore!' Thus addressed by them, O king, the *Gandharvas* laughed and replied unto those men in these harsh words: 'Your wicked king Duryodhana must be destitute of sense. How else could he have thus commanded us that are dwellers of heaven, as if indeed, we were his servants? Without forethought, ye also are doubtless on the point of death; for senseless idiots as ye are, ye have dared to bring us his message! Return ye soon to where that king of the Kurus is, or else go this very day to the abode of Yama.' Thus addressed by the *Gandharvas*, the advanced guard of the king's army ran back to the place where the royal son of Dhritarashtra was."

SECTION CCXXXIX

Vaisampayana said, "Those soldiers then, O king, all went back to Duryodhana and repeated to him every word that the *Gandharvas* had said. And, O Bharata, finding that his soldiers had been opposed by the *Gandharvas*, Dhritarashtra's son, endued with energy, was filled with rage. And the king addressed his soldiers, saying, 'Punish these wretches who desire to oppose my will, even if they have come hither to sport, accompanied by all the celestials with him of a hundred sacrifices.' And hearing these words of Duryodhana, the sons and officers of Dhritarashtra all endued with great strength, as also warriors by thousands, began to arm themselves for battle. And filling the ten sides with loud leonine roars and rushing at those *Gandharvas* that had been guarding the gates, they entered the forest. And as the Kuru soldiers entered the forest, other *Gandharvas* came up and forbade them to advance. And though gently forbidden by the *Gandharvas* to advance, the Kuru soldiers, without regarding them in the least, began to enter that mighty forest. And when those rangers of the sky found that the warriors of Dhritarashtra along with their king could not be stopped by words they all went to their king Chitrasena and represented everything unto him. And when Chitrasena, the king of the Gandharvas, came to know all this he became filled with rage, alluding to the Kuru, and commanded his followers saying, 'Punish these wretches of wicked behaviour.' And, O Bharata, when the *Gandharvas* were so commanded by Chitrasena, they rushed weapons in hand, towards the Dhritarashtra ranks. And beholding the *Gandharvas* impetuously rushing towards them with upraised weapons, the Kuru warriors precipitously fled in all directions at the very sight of Duryodhana. And beholding the Kuru soldiers all flying from the field with their backs to the foe, the heroic Radheya alone fled not. And seeing the mighty host of the Gandharvas rushing towards him, Radheya checked them by a perfect shower of arrows. And the *Suta's* son, owing to his extreme lightness of hand, struck hundreds of *Gandharvas* with *Kshurapras* and arrows and *Bhallas* and various weapons made of bones and steel. And that mighty warrior, causing the heads of numerous *Gandharvas* to roll down within a short time, made the ranks of Chitrasena to yell in anguish. And although they were slaughtered in great numbers by Karna endued with great intelligence, yet the *Gandharvas* returned to the charge by hundreds and thousands. And in consequence of the swarms of Chitrasena's warriors rushing impetuously to the field the earth itself became soon covered by the *Gandharva* host. Then king Duryodhana, and Sakuni, the son of Suvala, and Dussasana, and Vikarna, and other sons of Dhritarashtra, seated on cars the clatter of whose wheels resembled the roars of Garuda, returned to the charge, following the lead of Karna, and began to slaughter that host. And desirous of supporting Karna, these princes invested the Gandharva army, with a large number of cars and a strong body of horses. Then the whole of the *Gandharva* host began to fight with the Kauravas. And the encounter that took place between the contending hosts was fierce in the extreme and might make one's hair stand on end. The *Gandharvas*, at last, afflicted with the shafts of the Kuru army, seemed to be exhausted. And the Kauravas beholding the *Gandharvas* so afflicted sent up a loud sound.

"And seeing the *Gandharva* host yielding to fear, the angry Chitrasena sprang from his seat, resolved to exterminate the Kuru army. And conversant with various modes of warfare, he waged on the fight, aided by his weapons of illusion. And the Kaurava warriors were then all deprived of their senses by the illusion of Chitrasena. And then, O Bharata, it seemed that every warrior of the Kuru army was fallen upon and surrounded by ten *Gandharvas*. And attacked with great vigour, the Kuru host was greatly afflicted and struck with panic. O king, all of them that liked to live, fled from the field. But while the entire Dhritarashtra host broke and fled, Karna, that offspring of the Sun, stood there, O king, immovable as a hill. Indeed, Duryodhana and Karna and Sakuni, the son of Suvala, all fought with the *Gandharvas*, although every one of them was much wounded and mangled in the encounter. All the *Gandharvas* then, desirous of slaying Karna, rushed together by hundreds and thousands towards Karna. And those mighty warriors, desirous of slaying the *Suta's* son, surrounded him on all sides, with swords and battle-axes and spears. And some cut down the yoke of his car, and some his flagstaff, and some the shaft of his car, and some his horses, and some his charioteer. And some cut down his umbrella and some the wooden fender round his car and some the joints of his car. It was thus that many thousands of Gandharvas, together attacking his car, broke it into minute fragments. And while his car was thus attacked, Karna leaped therefrom with sword and shield in hand, and mounting on Vikarna's car, urged the steeds for saving himself."

SECTION CCXL

Vaisampayana said, "After that great warrior Karna had been routed by the *Gandharvas*, the whole of the Kuru army, O monarch, fled from the field in the very sight of Dhritarashtra's son. And beholding all his troops flying from the field of battle with their back to the foe, king Duryodhana refused to fly. Seeing the mighty host of the *Gandharvas* rushing towards him, that represser of foes poured down upon them a thick shower of arrows. The *Gandharvas*, however, without regarding that arrowy shower, and desirous also of slaying him, surrounded that car of his. And by means of their arrows, they cut off into fragments the yoke, the shaft, the fenders, the flagstaff, the three-fold bamboo poles, and the principal turret of his car. And they also slew his charioteer and horses, hacking them to pieces. And when Duryodhana, deprived of his car, fell on the ground, the strong-armed Chitrasena rushed towards him and seized him in such a way that it seemed his life itself was taken. And after the Kuru king had been seized, the *Gandharvas*, surrounding Dussasana, who was seated on his car, also took him prisoner. And some *Gandharvas* seized Vivinsati and Chitrasena, and some Vinda and Anuvinda, while others seized all the ladies of royal household. And the warriors of Duryodhana, who were routed by the *Gandharvas*, joining those who had fled first, approached the Pandavas (who were living in the vicinity). And after Duryodhana had been made captive, the vehicles, the shops, the pavilions, the carriages, and the draught animals, all were made over to the Pandavas for protection. And those soldiers said, 'The mighty-armed son of Dhritarashtra, possessed of great strength and handsome mien, is being taken away captive by the *Gandharvas*! Ye sons of Pritha, follow them! Dussasana, Durvishasa, Durmukha, and Durjaya, are all being led away as captives in chains by the Gandharvas, as also all the ladies of the royal household!'

"Crying thus, the followers of Duryodhana, afflicted with grief and melancholy, approached Yudhishthira, desirous of effecting the release of the king. Bhima then answered those old attendants of Duryodhana, who, afflicted with grief and melancholy, were thus soliciting (the aid of Yudhishthira), saying, 'What we should have done with great efforts, arraying ourselves in line of battle, supported by horses and elephants hath, indeed, been done by the *Gandharvas*! They that come hither for other purposes, have been overtaken by consequences they had not foreseen! Indeed, this is the result of the evil counsels of a king who is fond of deceitful play! It hath been heard by us that the foe of a person who is powerless, is overthrown by others. The Gandharvas have, in an extraordinary way illustrated before our eyes the truth of this saying! It seems that there is still fortunately some person in the world who is desirous of doing us good who hath, indeed, taken upon his own shoulders our pleasant load, although we are sitting idly! The wretch had come hither to cast his eyes on us,—himself in prosperity while ourselves are sunk in adversity and emaciated by ascetic austerities and are exposed to wind, cold and heat. They that imitate the behaviour of that sinful and wretched Kaurava, are now beholding his disgrace! He that had instructed Duryodhana to do this, had certainly acted sinfully. That the sons of Kunti are not wicked and sinful, I tell it before you all!'

"And while Bhima, the son of Kunti, was speaking thus in a voice of sarcasm, king Yudhishthira told him, 'This is not time for cruel words!'"

SECTION CCXLI

"Yudhishthira said, 'O child, why dost thou use language such as this, towards the frightened Kurus, who are now in adversity and who have come to us, solicitous of protection! O Vrikodara, disunions and disputes do take place amongst those that are connected in blood. Hostilities such as these do go on. But the honour of the family is never suffered to be interfered with. If any stranger seeketh to insult the honour of a family, they that are good never tolerate such insult coming from the stranger. The wicked-souled king of the Gandharvas knoweth that we are living here from some time. Yet disregarding us, he hath done this deed which is so disagreeable to us! O exalted one, from this forcible seizure of Duryodhana and from this insult to the ladies of our house by a stranger, our family honour is being destroyed. Therefore, ye tigers among men, arise and arm yourselves without delay for rescuing those that have sought our protection and for guarding the honour of our family. Ye tigers among men, let Arjuna and the twins and thyself also that art brave and unvanquished, liberate Duryodhana, who is even now being taken away a captive! Ye foremost of warriors, these blazing cars, furnished with golden flagstaffs and every kind of weapons belonging to Dhritarashtra's sons, are ready here. With Indrasena and other charioteers skilled in arms, for guiding them, ride ye on these everfurnished cars of deep rattle! And riding on these, exert ye with activity for fighting with the Gandharvas to liberate Duryodhana. Even an ordinary Kshatriya (amongst those that are here), would to the height of his power, protect one that hath come hither for refuge! What then, O Vrikodara, shall I say of thee! Entreated for assistance in such words as *"O hasten to my aid!"* Who is there (amongst those standing around me) that is high-souled enough to assist even his foe, beholding him seeking shelter with joined hands? The bestowal of a boon, sovereignty, and the birth of a son are sources of great joy. But, ye sons of Pandu, the liberation of a foe from distress is equal to all the three put together! What can be a source of greater joy to you than that Duryodhana sunk in distress seeketh his very life as depending on the might of your arms? O Vrikodara, if the vow in which I am engaged had been over, there is little doubt that I would myself have run to his aid. Strive thou by all means, O Bharata, to liberate Duryodhana by the arts of conciliation. If, however, the king of the Gandharvas cannot be managed by the arts of conciliation, then must thou try to rescue Suyodhana by lightly skirmishing with the foe. But if the chief of the Gandharvas do not let the Kurus off even then, they must be rescued by crushing the foe by all means. O Vrikodara, this is all I can tell thee now, for my vow hath been begun and is not ended yet!'"

Vaisampayana continued, "Hearing these words of Ajatasatru, Dhananjaya pledged himself, from respect for these commands of his superior, to liberate the Kauravas. And Arjuna said, 'If the Gandharvas do not set the Dhartarashtras free peacefully, the Earth shall this day drink the blood of the king of the Gandharvas!' And hearing that pledge of the truth-speaking Arjuna, the Kauravas then, O king, regained (the lost) tenor of their minds."

SECTION CCXLII

Vaisampayana said, "Hearing the words of Yudhishthira, those bulls among men, headed by Bhimasena, rose up with faces beaming in joy. And those mighty warriors, O Bharata, then began to case themselves in impenetrable mail that were besides variegated with pure gold, and armed themselves with celestial weapons of various kinds. And the Pandavas thus cased in mail, and mounted on those chariots furnished with flagstaffs and armed with bows and arrows, looked like blazing fires. And those tigers among warriors, riding upon those well furnished cars drawn by fleet horses, proceeded to that spot without losing a moment. And beholding those mighty warriors—the sons of Pandu—thus proceeding together (for the liberation of Duryodhana), the Kuru army sent forth a loud shout. And soon did those rangers of the sky flushed with victory, and those impetuous warriors, the sons of Pandu, fearlessly encounter each other in that forest. The Gandharvas were flushed with success, and beholding the four brave sons of Pandu coming to battle seated on their cars, they all turned back towards the advancing combatants. And, the dwellers of the Gandhamadana, beholding the Pandavas looking like blazing guardians of the world provoked to ire, stood arrayed in order of battle. And, O Bharata, in accordance with words of king Yudhishthira of great wisdom, the encounter that took place was a skirmish. But when Arjuna—that persecutor of foes—saw that the foolish soldiers of the king of Gandharvas could not be made to understand what was good for them by means of a light skirmish, he addressed those invincible rangers of the skies in a conciliatory tone and said, 'Leave ye my brother king Suyodhana.' Thus addressed by the illustrious son of Pandu, the Gandharvas, laughing aloud, replied unto him saying, 'O child, there is but one in the world whose behests we obey and living under whose rule we pass our days in happiness: O Bharata, we always act as that one only person commandeth us! Besides that celestial chief there is none that can command us!' Thus addressed by the Gandharvas, Dhananjaya, the son of Kunti, replied unto them, saying, 'This contact with other people's wives and this hostile encounter with human beings are acts that are both censurable in the king of the Gandharvas and not proper for him. Therefore, leave ye these sons of Dhritarashtra all endued with mighty energy. And liberate ye also these ladies, at the command of king Yudhishthira the just.

If, ye Gandharvas, ye do not set the sons of Dhritarashtra free peacefully, I shall certainly rescue Suyodhana (and his party) by exerting my prowess.' And speaking unto them thus, Pritha's son, Dhananjaya, capable of wielding the bow with his left hand also, then rained a shower of sharp pointed sky-ranging shafts upon those rangers of the firmament. Thus attacked, the mighty Gandharvas then encountered the sons of Pandu with a shower of arrows equally thick, and the Pandavas also replied by attacking those dwellers of heaven. And the battle then, O Bharata, that ranged between the active and agile Gandharvas and the impetuous son of Pandu was fierce in the extreme."

SECTION CCXLIII

Vaisampayana said, "Then those Gandharvas decked in golden garlands and accomplished in celestial weapons, showing their blazing shafts, encountered the Pandavas from every side. And as the sons of Pandu were only four in number and the Gandharvas counted by thousands, the battle that ensued appeared to be extraordinary. And as the cars of Karna and Duryodhana had formerly been broken into a hundred fragments by the Gandharvas, so were the cars of the four heroes attempted to be broken. But those tigers among men began to encounter with their showers of arrows thousands upon thousands of Gandharvas rushing towards them. Those rangers of skies endued with great energy, thus checked on all sides by that arrowy down-pour, succeeded not in even coming near to the sons of Pandu. Then Arjuna whose ire had been provoked, aiming at the angry Gandharvas, prepared to hurl against them his celestial weapons. And in that encounter, the mighty Arjuna, by means of his *Agneya* weapon, sent ten hundreds of thousands of Gandharvas to the abode of Yama. And that mighty bowman, Bhima, also, that foremost of all warriors in battle, slew, by means of his sharp arrows, Gandharvas by hundreds. And the mighty sons of Madri also, battling with vigour, encountered hundreds of Gandharvas, O king, and slaughtered them all. And as Gandharvas were being thus slaughtered by the mighty warriors with their celestial weapons, they rose up to the skies, taking with them the sons of Dhritarashtra. But Dhananjaya, the son of Kunti, beholding them rise up to the skies, surrounded them on every side by a wide net of arrows. And confined within that arrowy net like birds within a cage, they showered in wrath upon Arjuna maces and darts and broad-swords. But Arjuna who was conversant with the most efficacious weapons, soon checked that shower of maces and darts and broad-swords, and in return began to mangle the limbs of the Gandharvas with his crescent-shaped arrows. And heads and legs and arms began to drop down from above resembling a shower of stones. And at that sight, the foe was struck with panic. And as the Gandharvas were being slaughtered by the illustrious son of Pandu, they began to shower from the skies a heavy downpour of shafts upon Arjuna, who was on the surface of the earth. But that chastiser of foes, Arjuna, endued with mighty energy checked that shower of arrows by means of his own weapons and began, in return, to wound them. Then Arjuna of the Kuru race shot his well-known weapons called *Sthunakarna, Indrajala, Saura, Agneya* and *Saumya*. And the Gandharvas consumed by the fiery weapons of Kunti's son, began to suffer heavily, like the sons of Diti, while being scorched by Sakra's thunder-bolt. And when they attacked Arjuna from above, they were checked by his net of arrows. And while they attacked him from all sides on the surface of the earth, they were checked by his crescent-shaped arrows. And beholding the Gandharvas put in fear by Kunti's son, Chitrasena rushed, O Bharata, at Dhananjaya, armed with a mace. And as the king of the Gandharvas was rushing at Arjuna from above with that mace in hand, the latter cut with his arrows that mace wholly made of iron into seven pieces. And beholding that mace of his cut into many pieces by Arjuna of great activity, with his arrows, Chitrasena, by means of his science, concealed himself from the view of the Pandava and began to fight with him. The heroic Arjuna, however, by means of his own celestial weapons checked all the celestial weapons that were aimed at him by the Gandharvas. And when the chief of the Gandharvas saw that he was checked by the illustrious Arjuna with those weapons of his he entirely disappeared from sight by help of his powers of illusion. And Arjuna, observing that the chief of the Gandharvas was striking at him concealed from sight, attacked his assailant with celestial weapon inspired with proper *Mantras*. And the multiform Dhananjaya filled with wrath, prevented the disappearance of his foe by means of his weapon known by the name of *Sabda-veda*. And assailed with those weapons by the illustrious Arjuna, his dear friend, the king of the Gandharvas, showed himself unto him. And Chitrasena said, 'Behold in me thy friend battling with thee!' And beholding his friend Chitrasena exhausted in the battle, that bull among the sons of Pandu withdrew the weapons he had shot. And the other sons of Pandu beholding Arjuna withdraw his weapons, checked their flying steeds and the impetus of their weapons and withdrew their bows. And Chitrasena and Bhima and Arjuna and the twins enquiring about one another's welfare, sat awhile on their respective cars."

SECTION CCXLIV

Vaisampayana said, "Then that mighty bowman of blazing splendour, Arjuna, smilingly said unto Chitrasena in the midst of the Gandharva host, 'What purpose dost thou serve, O hero, in punishing the Kauravas? O, why also hath Suyodhana with his wives been thus punished?'

"Chitrasena replied, 'O Dhananjaya, without stirring from my own abode I became acquainted with the purpose of the wicked Duryodhana and the wretched Karna in coming hither. The purpose was even this,—knowing that ye are exiles in the forest and suffering great afflictions as if ye had none to take care of you, himself in prosperity, this wretch entertained the desire of beholding you plunged in adversity and misfortune. They came hither for mocking you and the illustrious daughter of Drupada. The lord of the celestials also, having ascertained this purpose of theirs, told me, "Go thou and bring Duryodhana hither in chains along with his counsellors. Dhananjaya also with his brother should always be protected by thee in battle, for he is thy dear friend and disciple." At these words of the lord of the celestials I came hither speedily. This wicked prince hath also been put in chains. I will now proceed to the region of the celestials, whither I will lead this wicked wight at the command of the slayer of Paka!'

"Arjuna answered, saying, 'O Chitrasena, if thou wishest to do what is agreeable to me, set Suyodhana free, at the command of king Yudhishthira the just, for he is our brother!'

"Chitrasena said, 'This sinful wretch is always full of vanity. He deserveth not to be set free. O Dhananjaya, he hath deceived and wronged both king Yudhishthira the just and Krishna. Yudhishthira the son of Kunti as yet knoweth not the purpose on which the wretch came hither. Let the king, therefore, do what he desires after knowing everything!'"

Vaisampayana continued, "After this, all of them went to king Yudhishthira the just. And going unto the king, they represented unto him everything about Duryodhana's conduct. And Ajatasatru, hearing everything that the Gandharvas had said, liberated all the Kauravas and applauded the Gandharvas. And the king said, 'Fortunate it is for us that though gifted with great strength, ye did not yet slay the wicked son of

Dhritarashtra along with all counsellors and relatives. This, O sir, hath been an act of great kindness done to me by the Gandharvas. The honour also of my family is saved by liberating this wicked wight. I am glad at seeing you all. Command me what I am to do for you. And having obtained all you wish, return ye soon whence ye came!'

"Thus addressed by the intelligent son of Pandu, the Gandharvas became well-pleased and went away with the Apsaras. And the lord of the celestials then, coming to that spot, revived those Gandharvas that had been slain in the encounter with the Kurus, by sprinkling the celestial *Amrita* over them. And the Pandavas also, having liberated their relatives along with the ladies of the royal household, and having achieved that difficult feat (the defeat of the Gandharvas host) became well-pleased. And those illustrious and mighty warriors worshipped by the Kurus along with their sons and wives, blazed forth in splendour like flaming fires in the sacrificial compound. And Yudhishthira then addressing the liberated Duryodhana in the midst of his brothers, from affection, told him these words: 'O child, never again do such a rash act. O Bharata, a rash wight never cometh by happiness. O son of the Kuru race, pleased be thou with all thy brothers. Go back to thy capital as pleaseth thee, without yielding thyself to despondency or cheerlessness!'"

Vaisampayana continued, "Thus dismissed by the son of Pandu, king Duryodhana then saluted king Yudhishthira the just and overwhelmed with shame, and his heart rent in twain, mechanically set out for his capital, like one destitute of life. And after the Kaurava prince had departed, the brave Yudhishthira, the son of Kunti, along with his brothers, was worshipped by the Brahmanas, and surrounded by those Brahmanas endued with the wealth of asceticism, like Sakra himself by the celestials, he began to pass his days happily in the woods of Dwaita."

SECTION CCXLV

Janamejaya said, "After his defeat and capture by the foe and his subsequent liberation by the illustrious sons of Pandu by force of arms, it seemeth to me that the entry into Hastinapura of the proud, wicked, boastful, vicious, insolent, and wretched Duryodhana, engaged in insulting the sons of Pandu and bragging of his own superiority, must have been exceedingly difficult. Describe to me in detail, O Vaisampayana, the entry into the capital, of that prince overwhelmed with shame and unmanned by grief!"

Vaisampayana said, "Dismissed by the king Yudhishthira the just, Dhritarashtra's son Suyodhana, bending his head down in shame and afflicted with grief and melancholy, set out slowly. And the king, accompanied by his four kinds of forces, proceeded towards his city, his heart rent in grief and filled with thoughts of his defeat along the way in a region that abounded in grass and water. The king encamped on a delightful piece of ground as pleased him best, with his elephants and cars and cavalry and infantry stationed all around. And as the king Duryodhana was seated on an elevated bedstead endued with the effulgence of fire, himself looking like the moon under an eclipse, towards the small hours of the morning Karna, approaching him, said, 'Fortunate it is, O son of Gandhari, that thou art alive! Fortunate it is, that we have once more met! By good luck it is that thou hast vanquished the Gandharvas capable of assuming any form at will. And, O son of the Kuru race, it is by good luck alone, that I am enabled to see thy brothers—mighty warriors all—come off victorious from that encounter, having subjugated their foes! As regards myself, assailed by all the Gandharvas, I fled before thy eyes, unable to rally our flying host. Assailed by the foe with all his might, my body mangled with their arrows, I sought safety in flight. This however, O Bharata, seemed to me to be a great marvel that I behold you all come safe and sound in body, with your wives, troops, and vehicles, out of that super-human encounter. O Bharata, there is another man in this world who can achieve what thou, O king, hast achieved in battle to-day with thy brothers.'"

Vaisampayana continued, "Thus addressed by Karna, king Duryodhana replied unto the ruler of the Angas in a voice choked with tears."

SECTION CCXLVI

"Duryodhana said, 'O Radheya, thou knowest not what hath happened. Therefore, I do not resent thy words. Thou thinkest the hostile Gandharvas to have been vanquished by me with my own energy. O thou of mighty arms, my brothers, indeed had for a long time, aided by me fought with the Gandharvas. The slaughtered, indeed, on both sides were great. But when those brave Gandharvas, resorting to their many powers of illusion, ascended the skies and began to fight with us thence, our encounter with them ceased to be an equal one. Defeat then was ours and even captivity. And afflicted with sorrow, we along with our attendants and counsellors and children and wives and troops and vehicles were being taken by them through the skies. It was then that some soldiers of ours and some brave officers repaired in grief unto the sons of Pandu—those heroes that never refuse succour to those that ask for it. And having gone to them they said, "Here is king Duryodhana, the son of Dhritarashtra, who with his younger brothers and friends and wives is being led away a captive by the Gandharvas along the sky. Blest be ye. Liberate the king along with the women of the royal household! Suffer no insult to be offered unto all the ladies of the Kuru race." And when they had spoken thus, the eldest of Pandu's sons, who is endued with a virtuous soul then conciliated his brothers and commanded them to liberate us. Then those bulls among men, the Pandavas, overtaking the Gandharvas, solicited our release in soft words, although fully able to effect it by force of arms. And when the Gandharvas, addressed in such conciliatory words, refused to set us at liberty, then Arjuna and Bhima and the twins endued with mighty energy, shot showers of arrows at the Gandharvas. Then the Gandharvas, abandoning the fight, fled through the sky, dragging our melancholy selves after them, filled with joy. Then we beheld a network of arrows spread all around by Dhananjaya, who was also shooting celestial weapons upon the foe. And seeing the points of the horizon covered by Arjuna with a thick network of sharp arrows, his friend, the chief of the Gandharvas, showed himself. And Chitrasena and Arjuna, embracing each other, enquired after each other's welfare. And the other sons of Pandu also embraced the chief of the Gandharvas and were embraced by him. And enquiries of courtesy passed between them also. And the brave Gandharvas then abandoning their weapons and mail mingled in a friendly spirit with the Pandavas. And Chitrasena and Dhananjaya worshipped each other with regard.'"

SECTION CCXLVII

"Duryodhana said, 'That slayer of hostile heroes, Arjuna, then approaching Chitrasena, smilingly addressed him in these manly words: "O hero, O foremost of the Gandharvas, it behoveth thee to set my brothers at liberty. They are incapable of being insulted as long as the sons of Pandu are alive." Thus addressed by the illustrious son of Pandu, the chief of the Gandharvas, O Karna, disclosed unto the Pandavas the object we had in view in proceeding to that place, viz., that we came there for casting our eyes on the sons of Pandu with their wife, all plunged in misery. And while the Gandharva was disclosing those counsels of ours, overwhelmed with shame I desired the earth to yield me a crevice, so that I might disappear there and then. The Gandharvas then, accompanied by the Pandavas, went to Yudhishthira, and, disclosing unto him also counsels, made us over, bound as we were, to him. Alas, what greater sorrow could be mine than that I should thus be offered as a tribute unto Yudhishthira, in the very sight of the women of our household, myself in chains and plunged in misery, and under the absolute control of my enemies. Alas, they, who have ever been persecuted by me, they unto whom I have ever been a foe released me from captivity, and wretch that I am, I am indebted to them for my life. If, O hero, I had met with my death in that great battle, that would have been far better than that I should have obtained my life in this way. If I had been slain by the Gandharvas, my fame would have spread over the whole earth, and I should have obtained auspicious regions of eternal bliss in the heaven of Indra. Listen to me therefore, ye bulls among men, as to what I intend to do now. I will stay here forgoing all food, while ye all return home. Let all my brothers also go to Hastinapura. Let all our friends, including Karna, and all our relatives headed by Dussasana, return now to the capital. Insulted by the foe, I myself will not repair thither. I who had before wrested from the foe his respect, I who had always enhanced the respect of my friends, have now become a source of sorrow unto friends and of joy unto enemies. What shall I now say unto the king, going to the city named after the elephant? What will Bhishma and Drona, Kripa, and Drona's son, Vidura and Sanjaya, Vahuka and Somadatta and other revered seniors,—what will the principal men of the other orders and men of independent professions, say to me and what shall I say unto them in reply? Having hitherto stayed over the heads of my enemies, having hitherto trod upon their breasts, I have fallen away from my position. How shall I ever speak with them? Insolent men having obtained prosperity and knowledge and affluence, are seldom blest for any length of time like myself puffed up with vanity. Alas, led by folly I have done a highly improper and wicked act, for which, fool that I am, I have fallen into such distress. Therefore, will I perish by starving, life having become insupportable to me. Relieved from distress by the foe, what man of spirit is there who can drag on his existence? Proud as I am, shorn of manliness, the foe hath laughed at me, for the Pandavas possessed of prowess have looked at me plunged in misery!'"

Vaisampayana continued, "While giving way to such reflections Duryodhana spoke unto Dussasana thus: 'O Dussasana, listen to these words of mine, O thou of the Bharata race! Accepting this installation that I offer thee, be thou king in my place. Rule thou the wide earth protected by Karna and Suvala's sons. Like Indra himself looking after the Maruts, cherish thou thy brothers in such a way that they may all confide in thee. Let thy friends and relatives depend on thee like the gods depending on him of a hundred sacrifices. Always shouldst thou bestow pensions on Brahmanas, without idleness, and be thou ever the refuge of thy friends and relatives. Like Vishnu looking after the celestials, thou shouldst always look after all consanguineous relatives. Thou shouldst also ever cherish thy superiors. Go, rule thou the earth gladdening thy friends and reproving thy foes.' And clasping his neck, Duryodhana said, 'Go!' Hearing these words of his, Dussasana in perfect cheerlessness and overwhelmed with great sorrow, his voice choked in tears, said, with joined hands and bending his head unto his eldest brother, 'Relent!' And saying this he fell down on earth with heavy heart. And afflicted with grief that tiger among men, shedding his tears on the feet of his brother again said, 'This will never be! The earth may split, the vault of heaven may break in pieces, the sun may cast off his splendour, the moon may abandon his coolness, the wind may forsake its speed, the Himavat may be moved from its site, the waters of the ocean may dry up, and fire may abandon its heat, yet I, O king, may never rule the earth without thee.' And Dussasana repeatedly said, 'Relent, O king! Thou alone shall be king in our race for a hundred years.' And having spoken thus unto the king, Dussasana began to weep melodiously catching, O Bharata, the feet of his eldest brother deserving of worship from him.

"And beholding Dussasana and Duryodhana thus weeping, Karna in great grief approached them both and said, 'Ye Kuru princes, why do you thus yield to sorrow like ordinary men, from senselessness? Mere weeping can never ease a sorrowing man's grief. When weeping can never remove one's griefs, what do you gain by thus giving way to sorrow? Summon patience to your aid to not gladden the foe by such conduct. O king, the Pandavas only did their duty in liberating thee. They that reside in the dominions of the king, should always do what is agreeable to the king. Protected by thee, the Pandavas are residing happily in thy dominion. It behoveth thee not to indulge in such sorrow like an ordinary person. Behold, thy uterine brothers are all sad and cheerless at seeing thee resolved to put an end to thy life by forgoing food. Blest be thou! Rise up and come to thy city and console these thy uterine brothers.'"

SECTION CCXLVIII

"Karna continued, 'O king, this conduct of thine to-day appeareth to be childish. O hero, O slayer of foes, what is to be wondered at in this that the Pandavas liberated thee when thou wert vanquished by the foe? O son of the Kuru race, those that reside in the territories of the king, especially those (amongst them) that lead the profession of arms, should always do what is agreeable to the king whether they happen to be known to their monarch or unknown to him. It happened often that foremost men who crush the ranks of the hostile host, are vanquished by them, and are rescued by their own troops. They that leading the profession of arms, reside in the king's realm should always combine and exert themselves to the best of their power, for the king. If, therefore, O king, the Pandavas, who live in the territories, have liberated thee, what is there to be regretted at in this? That the Pandavas, O best of kings, did not follow thee when thou didst march forth to battle at the head of thy troops, has been an improper act on their part. They had before this come under thy power, becoming thy slaves. They are, therefore, bound to aid thee now, being endued with courage and might and incapable of turning away from the field of battle. Thou art enjoying all the rich possessions of the Pandavas. Behold them yet alive, O king! They have not resolved to die, forgoing all food. Blest be thou! Rise up, O king! It behoveth thee not to indulge in great sorrow long. O king, it is the certain duty of those that reside in the king's realm to do what is agreeable to the king. Where should the regret be in all this? If thou, O king, dost not act according to my words I shall stay here employed in reverentially serving thy feet. O bull among men, I do not desire to live deprived of thy company. O king, if thou resolvest to slay thyself by forgoing food, thou wilt simply be an object of laughter with other kings.'"

Vaisampayana continued, "Thus addressed by Karna, king Duryodhana, firmly resolved to leave the world, desired not to rise from where he sat."

SECTION CCXLIX

Vaisampayana said, "Beholding king Duryodhana, incapable of putting up with an insult, seated with the resolution of giving up life by forgoing food, Sakuni, the son of Suvala, said these words to comfort him. Sakuni said, 'O son of the Kuru race, you have just heard what Karna hath said. His words are, indeed fraught with wisdom. Why wouldst thou abandoning from foolishness the high prosperity that I won for thee, cast off thy life today, O king, yielding to silliness? It seemeth to me to-day that thou hast never waited upon the old. He that cannot control sudden accession of joy or grief, is lost even though he may have obtained prosperity, like an unburnt earthen vessel in water. That king who is entirely destitute of courage, who hath no spark of manliness, who is the slave of procrastination, who always acts with indiscretion, who is addicted to sensual pleasures, is seldom respected by his subjects. Benefited as thou has been, whence is this unreasonable grief of thine? Do not undo this graceful act done by the sons of Pritha, by indulging in such grief. When thou shouldst joy and reward the Pandavas, thou art grieving, O king? Indeed, this behaviour of thine is inconsistent. Be cheerful, do not cast away thy life; but remember with a pleased heart the good they have done thee. Give back unto the sons of Pritha their kingdom, and win thou both virtue and renown by such conduct. By acting in this way, thou mayst be grateful. Establish brotherly relations with the Pandavas by being friends, and give them their paternal kingdom, for then thou wilt be happy!'"

Vaisampayana continued, "Hearing these words of Sakuni, and seeing the brave Dussasana lying prostrate before him unmanned by fraternal love, the king raised Dussasana and, clasping him in his well round arms, smelt his head from affection. And hearing these words of Karna and Sauvala, king Duryodhana lost heart more than ever, and he was overwhelmed with shame and utter despair overtook his soul. And hearing all that his friends said, he answered with sorrow, 'I have nothing more to do with virtue, wealth, friendship, affluence, sovereignty, and enjoyments. Do not obstruct my purpose, but leave me all of you. I am firmly resolved to cast away my life by forgoing food. Return to the city, and treat my superiors there respectfully.'

"Thus addressed by him, they replied unto that royal grinder of foes, saying, 'O monarch, the course that is thine, is also ours, O Bharata. How can we enter the city without thee?'"

Vaisampayana continued, "Though addressed in all manner of ways by his friends and counsellors and brothers and relatives, the king wavered not from his purpose. And the son of Dhritarashtra in accordance with his purpose spread *Kusa* grass on the earth, and purifying himself by touching water, sat down upon that spot. And clad in rags and *Kusa* grass he set himself to observe the highest vow. And stopping all speech, that tiger among kings, moved by the desire of going to heaven, began to pray and worship internally suspending all external intercourse.

"Meanwhile the fierce *Daityas* and the *Danavas* who had been defeated of old by the celestials and had been dwelling in the nether regions having ascertained Duryodhana's purpose and knowing that if the king died their party would be weakened, commenced a sacrifice with fire for summoning Duryodhana to their presence. And *mantra* knowing persons then commenced with the help of formulae declared by Brihaspati and Usanas, those rites that are indicated in the *Atharva Veda* and the *Upanishads* and which are capable of being achieved by *mantras* and prayers. And Brahmins of rigid vows, well-versed in the *Vedas* and the branches, began, with rapt soul, to pour libations of clarified butter and milk into the fire, uttering *mantras*. And after those rites were ended, a strange goddess, O king, with mouth wide open, arose (from the sacrificial fire), saying, 'What am I to do?' And the Daityas with well-pleased hearts, commanded her, saying, 'Bring thou hither the royal son of Dhritarashtra, who is even now observing the vow of starvation for getting rid of his life.' Thus commanded, she went away saying, 'So be it.' And she went in the twinkling of an eye to that spot where Suyodhana was. And taking up the king back to the nether regions, and having brought him thus in a moment, she apprised the *Danavas* of it. And the *Danavas* beholding the king brought into their midst in the night, united together, and all of them with well-pleased hearts and eyes expanded in delight addressed these flattering words to Duryodhana."

SECTION CCL

"The Danavas said, 'O Suyodhana, O great king! O perpetuator of the race of Bharata, thou art ever surrounded by heroes and illustrious men. Why hast thou, then, undertaken to do such a rash act as the vow of starvation? The suicide ever sinketh into hell and becometh the subject of calumnious speech. Nor do intelligent persons like thee ever set their hands to acts that are sinful and opposed to their best interests and striking at the very root of their purposes. Restrain this resolve of thine, therefore, O king, which is destructive of morality, profit, and happiness, of fame, prowess, and energy, and which enhanceth the joy of foes. O exalted king, know the truth, the celestial origin of thy soul, and the maker of thy body, and then summon thou patience to thy aid. In days of old, O king, we have obtained thee, by ascetic austerities from Maheswara. The upper part of thy body is wholly made of an assemblage of *Vajras,* and is, therefore, invulnerable to weapons of every description, O sinless one. The lower part of thy body, capable of captivating the female heart by its comeliness was made of flowers by the goddess herself—the wife of Mahadeva. Thy body is thus, O best of kings, the creation of Maheswara himself and his goddess. Therefore, O tiger among kings, thou art of celestial origin, not human. Other brave Kshatriyas of mighty energy headed by Bhagadatta, and all acquainted with celestial weapons, will slay thy foes. Therefore, let this grief of thine cease. Thou hast no cause for fear. For aiding thee, many heroic *Danavas* have been born on the earth. Other Asuras will also possess Bhishma and Drona and Karna and others. Possessed by those Asuras, these heroes will cast away their kindness and fight with thy foes. Indeed, when the *Danavas* will enter their heart and possess them completely, flinging all affections to a distance, becoming hard-hearted, these warriors will strike every body opposed to them in battle without sparing sons, brothers, fathers, friends, disciples, relatives, even children and old men. Blinded by ignorance and wrath, and impelled by that destiny which hath been ordained by the Creator, these tigers among men, with hearts steeped in sin, will, O thou foremost of the Kurus, depopulate the earth by hurling and shooting all kinds of weapons, with great manliness and strength and always addressing one another boastfully with words such as these, *"Thou shall not escape from me today with life."* And these illustrious sons of Pandu also, five in number, will fight with these. And, endued with mighty strength and favoured by Fate, they will compass the destruction of these. And, O king, many *Daityas* and *Rakshasas* also that have been born in the Kshatriya order, will fight with great prowess in the battle with thy foes, using maces and clubs and lances and various weapons of a superior kind. And, O hero, with respect to the fear that is in thy heart rising from Arjuna, we have already settled the means for slaying Arjuna. The soul of the slain Naraka hath assumed the form of Karna. Recollecting his former hostility he will encounter both Kesava and Arjuna. And that mighty warrior and foremost of smiters, proud of his prowess will vanquish Arjuna in battle as also all thy enemies. The wielder of the thunder-bolt, knowing all this, and desirous of saving Arjuna, will in disguise take away from Karna his ear-rings and coat of mail. We also have for that reason appointed hundreds upon hundreds and thousands upon thousands of *Daityas* and *Rakshasas*, viz., those that are known by the name of *Samsaptakas*. 43 These celebrated warriors will slay the heroic Arjuna. Therefore, grieve not, O king. Thou wilt rule the whole earth, O monarch, without a rival. Do not yield to despondency. Conduct such as this does not suit thee. O thou of the Kuru race, if thou diest, our party becometh weak. Go thou, O hero, and let not thy mind be directed to any other course of action. Thou art ever our refuge as, indeed, the Pandavas are the refuge of the gods.'"

Vaisampayana continued, "Having addressed him thus, those *Daityas* embraced that elephant among kings, and those bulls among the *Danavas* cheered that irrepressible one like a son. And, O Bharata, pacifying his mind by soft speech, they permitted him to depart, saying, 'Go and attain victory!' And when they had given leave to the mighty-armed one, that very goddess carried him back to the spot where he had sat down, intent upon putting an end to his life. And having set that hero down and paid him homage, the goddess vanished, taking the king's permission. O Bharata, when she had gone, king Duryodhana considered all (that had happened) as a dream. He then thought within himself, 'I shall defeat the Pandavas in battle.' And Suyodhana thought that Karna and the Samsaptaka army were both able (to destroy) and intent upon destroying that slayer of foes, Partha. Thus, O bull of the Bharata race, the hope was strengthened of the wicked minded son of Dhritarashtra, of conquering the Pandavas. And Karna also, his soul and faculties possessed by the inmost soul of Naraka, had at that time cruelly determined to slay Arjuna. And those heroes—the Samsaptakas also—having their sense possessed by the *Rakshasas*, and influenced by the qualities of emotion and darkness, were desirous of slaying Phalguna. And, O king, others with Bhishma, Drona, and Kripa at their head, having their faculties influenced by the Danavas, were not so affectionate towards the sons of Pandu as they had been. But king Suyodhana did not tell any one of this.

"When the night passed away, Karna, that offspring of the Sun, with joined hands, smilingly addressed these wise words to king Duryodhana, 'No dead man conquereth his foes: it is when he is alive that he can see his good. Where is the good of the dead person; and, O Kauravya, where is his victory? Therefore, this is no time for grief, or fear or death.' And having, with his arms embraced that mighty-armed one, he further said, 'Rise up, O king! Why dost thou lie down? Why dost thou grieve, O slayer of foes? Having afflicted thy enemies by thy prowess, why dost thou wish for death? Or (perhaps) fear hath possessed thee at the sight of Arjuna's prowess. I truly promise unto thee that I will slay Arjuna in battle. O lord of men, I swear by my weapon that when the three and ten years shall have passed away, I will bring the sons of Pritha under thy subjection.' Thus addressed by Karna, and remembering the words of the *Daityas* and supplications made by them (his brothers), Suyodhana rose up. And having heard those words of the *Daityas* that tiger among men, with a firm resolve in his heart arrayed his army, abounding in horses and elephants and cars and infantry. And, O monarch, immensely swarming with white umbrellas, and pennons, and white *Chamaras*, and cars, and elephants, and foot-soldiers, that mighty army, as it moved like the waters of the Ganga, looked graceful like the firmament, at a season when the clouds have dispersed and the signs of autumn have been but partially developed. And, O foremost of kings, eulogised like a monarch by the best of the Brahmanas blessing with victory, that lord of men Suyodhana, Dhritarashtra's son, receiving honours paid with innumerable joined palms, and flaming in exceeding splendour, went in the front, accompanied by Karna, and that gambler, the son of Suvala. And all his brothers with Dussasana at their head, and Bhurisrava, and Somadatta, and the mighty king Vahlika, followed that lion among kings on his way, with cars of various forms, and horses, and the best of elephants. And, O prince among monarchs, in a short time, those perpetuators of the Kuru race entered their own city."

SECTION CCLI

Janamejaya said, "When the high-souled sons of Pritha were living in the forest, what did those foremost of men and mighty archers—the sons of Dhritarashtra—do? And what did the offspring of the Sun, Karna, and the mighty Sakuni, and Bhishma, and Drona, and Kripa do? It behoveth thee to relate this unto me."

Vaisampayana said, "When, O mighty king, in this manner the Pandavas had gone, leaving Suyodhana, and when, having been liberated by Pandu's sons, he had come to Hastinapura, Bhishma said these words to the son of Dhritarashtra, 'O child, I had told thee before, when thou wert intent upon going to the hermitage that thy journey did not please me. But thou didst do so. And as a consequence, O hero, wert thou forcibly taken captive by the enemy, and wert delivered by the Pandavas versed in morality. Yet art thou not ashamed. Even in the presence of thee, O son of Gandhari, together with thy army, did the Suta's son, struck with panic, fly from the battle of the Gandharvas, O king. And, O foremost of kings, O son of the monarch! while thou with thy army wert crying distressfully, thou didst witness the prowess of the high-souled Pandavas, and also, O mighty-armed one, of the wicked son of the Suta, Karna. O best of kings, whether in the science of arms, or heroism, or morality, Karna, O thou devoted to virtue, is not a fourth part of the Pandavas. Therefore, for the welfare of this race, the conclusion of peace is, I think, desirable with the high-souled Pandavas.'

"Having been thus addressed by Bhishma, Dhritarashtra's son the king, laughed a good deal, and then suddenly sailed out with the son of Suvala. Thereupon, knowing that he was gone, those mighty bowmen with Karna, and Dussasana at their head, followed the highly powerful son of Dhritarashtra. And seeing them gone, Bhishma, the grandfather of the Kurus, hung down his head from shame, and then, O king, went to his own quarters. And, O mighty monarch, when Bhishma had left, that lord of men, Dhritarashtra's son came there again, and began to consult with his counsellors, 'What is it that is good for me? What remaineth to be done? And how we can most effectively bring about the good we shall discuss to-day.' Karna said, 'O Kuru's son, Duryodhana, do thou lay to heart the words that I say. Bhishma always blameth us, and praiseth the Pandavas.

And from the ill-will he beareth towards thee, he hateth me also. And, O lord of men, in thy presence he ever crieth me down. I shall never, O Bharata, bear these words that Bhishma had said in thy presence in relation to this matter, extolling the Pandavas, and censuring thee, O represser of foes! Do thou, O king, enjoin on me, together with servants, forces, and cars. I shall, O monarch, conquer the earth furnished with mountains and woods and forests. The earth had been conquered by the four powerful Pandavas. I shall, without doubt, conquer it for thee single-handed. Let that wretch of the Kuru race, the exceedingly wicked-minded Bhishma, see it,—he who vilifies those that do not deserve censure, and praises those that should not be praised. Let him this day witness my might, and blame himself. Do thou, O king, command me. Victory shall surely be thine. By my weapon, O monarch, I swear this before thee.'

"O king, O bull of the Bharata race, hearing those words of Karna, that lord of men, experiencing the highest delight, spoke unto Karna, saying, 'I am blessed. I have been favoured by thee,—since thou, endued with great strength, art ever intent on my welfare. My life hath borne fruit, to-day. As thou, O hero, intendest to subdue all our enemies, repair thou. May good betide thee! Do thou command me (what I am to do).' O subduer of foes, having been thus addressed by Dhritarashtra's intelligent son, Karna ordered all the necessaries for the excursion. And on an auspicious lunar day, at an auspicious moment, and under the influence of a star presided over by an auspicious deity, that mighty bowman, having been honoured by twice-born ones, and been bathed with auspicious and holy substances and also worshipped by speech set out, filling with the rattle of his car the three worlds, with their mobile and immobile objects."

SECTION CCLII

Vaisampayana continued, "Then, O bull among the Bharatas, that mighty bowman, Karna, surrounded by a large army, besieged the beautiful city of Drupada. And he, after a hard conflict, brought the hero under subjection, and, O best of monarchs, made Drupada contribute silver and gold and gems, and also pay tribute. And, O foremost of kings, having subdued him, (Karna) brought under subjection those princes that were under him (Drupada) and made them pay tribute. Then going to the north, he subdued the sovereigns (of that quarter) and having effected the defeat of Bhagadatta, Radha's son ascended that mighty mountain Himavat, all along fighting his foes. And ranging all sides, he conquered and brought under subjection all the kings inhabiting the Himavat, and made them pay dues. Then descending from the mountain and rushing to the east, he reduced the Angas, and the Bangas, and the Kalingas, and the Mandikas, and the Magadhas, the Karkakhandas; and also included with them the Avasiras, Yodhyas, and the Ahikshatras. Having (thus) conquered the eastern quarter Karna then presented himself before Batsa-bhumi. And having taken Batsa-bhumi, he reduced Kevali, and Mrittikavati, and Mohana and Patrana, and Tripura, and Kosala, —and compelled all these to pay tribute. Then going to the south, Karna vanquished the mighty charioteers (of that quarter) and in Dakshinatya, the Suta's son entered into conflict with Rukmi. After having fought dreadfully, Rukmi spake to the Suta's son saying, 'O foremost of monarchs, I have been pleased with thy might and prowess. I shall not do thee wrong: I have only fulfilled the vow of a Kshatriya. Gladly will I give thee as many gold coins as thou desirest.' Having met with Rukmi, Karna repaired to Pandya and the mountain, Sri. And by fighting, he made Karala, king Nila, Venudari's son, and other best of kings living in the southern direction pay tribute. Then going to Sisupala's son, the son of the Suta defeated him and that highly powerful one also brought under his sway all the neighbouring rulers. And, O bull of the Bharata race, having subjugated the Avantis and concluded peace with them, and having met with the Vrishnis, he conquered the west. And, having come to the quarter of Varuna, he made all the Yavana and Varvara kings pay tribute. And, having conquered the entire earth—east, west, north and south—that hero without any aid brought under subjection all the nations of the Mlechchhas, the mountaineers, the Bhadras, the Rohitakas, the Agneyas and the Malavas. And, having conquered the mighty charioteers, headed by the Nagnajitas, the Suta's son brought the *Sasakas* and the *Yavanas* under his sway. Having thus conquered and brought under his subjection the world, the mighty charioteer and tiger among men came (back) to Hastinapura. That lord of men, Dhritarashtra's son, accompanied by his father and brothers and friends, came to that mighty bowman, who had arrived, and duly paid homage unto Karna crowned with martial merit. And the king proclaimed his feats, saying, 'What I have not received from either Bhishma, or Drona, or Kripa, or Vahlika, I have received from thee. May good betide thee! What need of speaking at length! Hear my words, O Karna! In thee, O chief of men, I have my refuge. O mighty-armed one, O tiger among men, without doubt all the Pandavas and the other kings crowned with prosperity, come not to a sixteenth part of thee. Do thou, O mighty bowman, O Karna, see Dhritarashtra, and the illustrious Gandhari, as the bearer of the thunderbolt did Aditi.'

"Then, O king, there arose in the city of Hastinapura a clamour, and sounds of *Oh!* and *Alas!* and, O lord of men, some of the kings praised him (Karna), while others censured him, while others, again, remained silent. Having thus, O foremost of monarchs, in a short time conquered this earth furnished with mountains and forests and skies, and with oceans, and fields, and filled with high and low tracts, and cities, and replete also with islands, O lord of earth, and brought the monarchs under subjection,—and having gained imperishable wealth, the Suta's son appeared before the king. Then, O represser of foes, entering into the interior of the palace that hero saw Dhritarashtra with Gandhari, O tiger among men, that one conversant with morality took hold of his feet even like a son. And Dhritarashtra embraced him affectionately, and then dismissed him. Ever since that time, O monarch, O Bharata, king Duryodhana and Sakuni, the son of Suvala, thought that Pritha's sons had already been defeated in battle by Karna."

SECTION CCLIII

Vaisampayana continued, "O king, O lord of men, that slayer of hostile heroes, the Suta's son, said these words to Duryodhana, 'O Kaurava Duryodhana, do thou lay unto thy heart the words that I shall tell thee; and, O represser of foes, after having heard my words, it behoveth thee to act accordingly every way. Now, O best of monarchs, O hero, hath the earth been rid of foes. Do thou rule her even like the mighty-minded Sakra himself, having his foes destroyed.'"

Vaisampayana continued, "Having been thus addressed by Karna, the king again spake unto him, saying, 'O bull among men, nothing whatever is unattainable to him who hath thee for refuge, and to whom thou art attached and on whose welfare thou art entirely intent. Now, I have a purpose, which do thou truly listen to. Having beheld that foremost of sacrifices, the mighty *Rajasuya*, performed by the Pandavas, a desire hath sprung up in me (to celebrate the same). Do thou, O Suta's son, fulfil this desire of mine.' Thus addressed, Karna spake thus unto the king, 'Now that all the rulers of the earth have been brought under thy subjection, do thou summon the principal Brahmanas, and, O best of Kurus, duly procure the articles required for the sacrifice. And, O represser of foes, let Ritwijas as prescribed, and versed in the Vedas, celebrate thy rites according to the ordinance, O king. And, O bull of the Bharata race, let thy great sacrifice also, abounding in meats and drinks, and grand with parts, commence.'

"O king, having been thus addressed by Karna, Dhritarashtra's son summoned the priest, and spake unto him these words, 'Do thou duly and in proper order celebrate for me that best of sacrifices, the *Rajasuya* furnished with excellent *Dakshinas*.' Thus accosted, that best of Brahmanas spake unto the king, saying, 'O foremost of the Kauravas, while Yudhishthira is living, that best of sacrifices cannot be performed in thy family, O Prince of kings! Further, O monarch, thy father Dhritarashtra, endued with long life, liveth. For this reason also, O best of kings, this sacrifice cannot be undertaken by thee. There is, O lord, another great sacrifice, resembling the Rajasuya. Do thou, O foremost of kings, celebrate that sacrifice. Listen to these words of mine. All these rulers of the earth, who have, O king, become tributary to thee, will pay thee tribute in gold, both pure and impure. Of that gold, do thou, O best of monarchs, now make the (sacrificial) plough, and do thou, O Bharata, plough the sacrificial compound with it. At that spot, let there commence, O foremost of kings, with due rites, and without any disturbance the sacrifice, sanctified with *mantras* abounding in edibles. The name of that sacrifice worthy of virtuous persons, is Vaishnava. No person save the ancient Vishnu hath performed it before. This mighty sacrifice vies with that best of sacrifices—the *Rajasuya* itself. And, further, it liketh us—and it is also for thy welfare (to celebrate it). And, moreover, it is capable of being celebrated without any disturbance. (By undertaking this), thy desire will be fufilled.'

"Having been thus addressed by those Brahmanas, Dhritarashtra's son, the king, spake these words to Karna, his brothers and the son of Suvala, 'Beyond doubt, the words of the Brahmanas are entirely liked by me. If they are relished by you also, express it without delay.' Thus appealed, they all said unto the king, 'So be it.' Then the king one by one appointed persons to their respective tasks; and desired all the artisans to construct the (sacrificial) plough. And, O best of kings, all that had been commanded to be done, was gradually executed."

SECTION CCLIV

Vaisampayana continued, "Then all the artisans, the principal counsellors, and the highly wise Vidura said unto Dhritarashtra's son, 'All the preparations for the excellent sacrifice have been made, O king; and the time also hath come, O Bharata. And the exceedingly precious golden plough hath been constructed.' Hearing this, O monarch, that best of kings, Dhritarashtra's son commanded that prince among sacrifices to be commenced. Then commenced that sacrifice sanctified by *mantras*, and abounding in edibles, and the son of Gandhari was duly initiated according to the ordinance. And Dhritarashtra, and the illustrious Vidura, and Bhishma, and Drona, and Kripa, and Karna, and the celebrated Gandhari experienced great delight. And, O foremost of kings, Duryodhana despatched swift messengers to invite the princes and the Brahmanas. And mounting fleet vehicles they went to the (respective) directions assigned to them. Then to a certain messenger on the point of setting out, Dussasana said, 'Go thou speedily to the woods of *Dwaita*; and in that forest duly invite the Brahmanas and those wicked persons, the Pandavas.' Thereupon, he repaired thither, and bowing down to all the Pandavas, said, 'Having acquired immense wealth by his native prowess, that best of kings and foremost of Kurus, Duryodhana, O monarch, is celebrating a sacrifice. Thither are going from various directions the kings and the Brahmanas. O king, I have been sent by the high-souled Kaurava. That king and lord of men, Dhritarashtra's son, invites you. It behoveth you, therefore, to witness the delightful sacrifice of that monarch.'

"Hearing these words of the messenger, that tiger among kings, the royal Yudhishthira, said, 'By good luck it is that that enhancer of the glory of his ancestors, king Suyodhana is celebrating this best of sacrifices. We should certainly repair thither; but we cannot do now; for till (the completion of) the thirteenth year, we shall have to observe our vow.' Hearing this speech of Yudhishthira the just, Bhima said these words, 'Then will king Yudhishthira the just go thither, when he will cast him (Duryodhana) into the fire kindled by weapons. Do thou say unto Suyodhana. *"When after the expiration of the thirteenth year, that lord of men, the Pandava, will, in the sacrifice of battle, pour upon the Dhritarashtras, the clarified butter of his ire, then will I come!"'* But the other Pandavas, O king, did not say anything unpleasant. The messenger (on his return) related unto Dhritarashtra's son all as it had fallen out. Then there came to the city of Dhritarashtra many foremost of men, lords of various countries, and highly virtuous Brahmanas. And duly received in order according to the ordinance, those lords of men experienced great delight and were all well-pleased. And that foremost among monarchs— Dhritarashtra—surrounded by all the Kauravas, experienced the height of joy, and spake unto Vidura, saying, 'Do thou, O Kshatta, speedily so act that all persons in the sacrificial compound may be served with food, be refreshed and satisfied.' Thereupon, O represser of foes, assenting to that order, the learned Vidura versed in morality, cheerfully entertained all the orders in proper measure with meat and beverages to eat and drink, and fragrant garland and various kinds of attire. And having constructed pavilions (for their accommodation), that hero and foremost of kings, duly entertained the princes and the Brahmanas by thousands, and also bestowing upon them wealth of various kinds, bade them farewell. And having dismissed all the kings, he entered Hastinapura, surrounded by his brothers, and in company with Karna and Suvala's son."

SECTION CCLV

Vaisampayana said, "While, O great king, Duryodhana was entering (the city), the panegyrists eulogized the prince of unfailing prowess. And others also eulogized that mighty bowman and foremost of kings. And sprinkling over him fried paddy and sandal paste the citizens said, 'By good luck it is, O king, that thy sacrifice hath been completed without obstruction.' And some, more reckless of speech, that were present there, said unto that lord of the earth, 'Surely this thy sacrifice cannot be compared with Yudhishthira's: nor doth this come up to a sixteenth part of that (sacrifice).' Thus spake unto that king some that were reckless of consequences. His friends, however, said, 'This sacrifice of thine hath surpassed all others. Yayati and Nahusha, and Mandhata and Bharata, having been sanctified by celebrating such a sacrifice, have all gone to heaven.' Hearing such agreeable words from his friends, that monarch, O bull of the Bharata's race, well-pleased, entered the city and finally his own abode. Then, O king, worshipping the feet of his father and mother and of others headed by Bhishma, Drona and Kripa, and of the wise Vidura, and worshipped in turn by his younger brothers, that delighter of brothers sat down upon an excellent seat, surrounded by the latter. And the Suta's son, rising up, said, 'By good luck it is, O foremost of the Bharata race, that this mighty sacrifice of thine hath been brought to a close. When, however, the sons of Pritha shall have been slain in battle and thou wilt have completed the *Rajasuya* sacrifice, once again, O lord of men, shall I honour thee thus.' Then that mighty king, the illustrious son of Dhritarashtra, replied unto him, 'Truly hath this been spoken by thee. When, O foremost of men, the wicked-minded Pandavas have been slain, and when also the grand *Rajasuya* hath been celebrated by me, then thou shalt again, O hero, honour me thus.' And having said this, O Bharata, the Kaurava embraced Karna, and began, O mighty king, to think of the *Rajasuya*, that foremost of sacrifices. And that best of kings also addressed the Kurus around him, saying, 'When shall I, ye Kauravas, having slain all the Pandavas, celebrate that costly and foremost of sacrifices, the *Rajasuya*.' Then spake Karna unto him, saying, 'Hear me, O elephant among kings! So long as I do not slay Arjuna, I shall not allow any one to wash my feet, nor shall I taste meat. And I shall observe the *Asura* vow 44 and whoever may solicit me (for any thing), I never shall say, "*I have it not.*"' When Karna had thus vowed to slay Phalguna in battle, those mighty charioteers and bowmen, the sons of Dhritarashtra, sent up a loud cheer; and Dhritarashtra's sons thought that the Pandavas had already been conquered. Then that chief of kings, the graceful Duryodhana, leaving those bulls among men, entered his apartment, like the lord Kuvera entering the garden of Chitraratha. And all those mighty bowmen also, O Bharata, went to their respective quarters.

"Meanwhile those mighty bowmen, the Pandavas, excited by the words the messenger had spoken, became anxious, and they did not (from that time) experience the least happiness. Intelligence, further, O foremost of kings, had been brought by spies regarding the vow of the Suta's son to slay Vijaya. Hearing this, O lord of men, Dharma's son became exceedingly anxious. And considering Karna of the impenetrable mail to be of wonderful prowess, and remembering all their woes, he knew no peace. And that high-souled one filled with anxiety, made up his mind to abandon the woods about *Dwaitavana* abounding with ferocious animals.

"Meanwhile the royal son of Dhritarashtra began to rule the earth, along with his heroic brothers as also with Bhishma and Drona and Kripa. And with the assistance of the Suta's son crowned with martial glory, Duryodhana remained ever intent on the welfare of the rulers of the earth, and he worshipped the foremost of Brahmanas by celebrating sacrifices with profuse gifts. And that hero and subduer of foes, O king, was engaged in doing good to his brothers, concluding for certain in his mind that giving and enjoying are the only use of riches."

SECTION CCLVI

Janamejaya said, "After having delivered Duryodhana, what did the mighty sons of Pandu do in that forest? It behoveth thee to tell me this."

Vaisampayana said, "Once on a time, as Yudhishthira lay down at night in the *Dwaita* woods, some deer, with accents choked in tears, presented themselves before him in his dreams. To them standing with joined hands, their bodies trembling all over that foremost of monarchs said, 'Tell me what ye wish to say. Who are ye? And what do ye desire?' Thus accosted by Kunti's son—the illustrious Pandava, those deer, the remnant of those that had been slaughtered, replied unto him, saying, 'We are, O Bharata, those deer that are still alive after them that had been slaughtered. We shall be exterminated totally. Therefore, do thou change thy residence. O mighty king, all thy brothers are heroes, conversant with weapons; they have thinned the ranks of the rangers of the forest. We few—the remnants,—O mighty-minded one, remain like seed. By thy favour, O king of kings, let us increase.' Seeing these deer, which remained like seed after the rest had been destroyed trembling and afflicted with fear, Yudhishthira the just was greatly affected with grief. And the king, intent on the welfare of all creatures, said unto them, 'So be it. I shall act as ye have said.' Awaking after such a vision, that excellent king, moved by pity towards the deer, thus spake unto his brothers assembled there, 'Those deer that are alive after them that have been slaughtered, accosted me at night, after I had awakened, saying, "*We remain like the cues of our lines. Blest be thou! Do thou have compassion on us.*" And they have spoken truly. We ought to feel pity for the dwellers of the forest. We have been feeding on them for a year together and eight months. Let us, therefore, again (repair) to the romantic Kamyakas, that best of forests abounding in wild animals, situated at the head of the desert, near lake Trinavindu. And there let us pleasantly pass the rest of our time.' Then, O king, the Pandavas versed in morality, swiftly departed (thence), accompanied by the Brahmanas and all those that lived with them, and followed by Indrasena and other retainers. And proceeding along the roads walked (by travellers), furnished with excellent corn and clear water, they at length beheld the sacred asylum of Kamyaka endued with ascetic merit. And as pious men enter the celestial regions, those foremost of the Bharata race, the Kauravas, surrounded by those bulls among Brahmanas entered that forest."

SECTION CCLVII

Vaisampayana continued, "Dwelling in the woods, O bull of the Bharata race, the high-souled Pandavas spent one and ten years in a miserable plight. And although deserving of happiness, those foremost of men, brooding over their circumstances, passed their days miserably, living on fruits and roots. And that royal sage, the mighty-armed Yudhishthira, reflecting that the extremity of misery that had befallen his brothers, was owing to his own fault, and remembering those sufferings that had arisen from his act of gambling, could not sleep peacefully. And he felt as if his heart had been pierced with a lance. And remembering the harsh words of the Suta's son, the Pandava, repressing the venom of his wrath, passed his time in humble guise, sighing heavily. And Arjuna and both the twins and the illustrious Draupadi, and the mighty Bhima—he that was strongest of all men—experienced the most poignant pain in casting their eyes on Yudhishthira. And thinking that a short time only remained (of their exile), those bulls among men, influenced by rage and hope and by resorting to various exertions and endeavours, made their bodies assume almost different shapes.

"After a little while, that mighty ascetic, Vyasa, the son of Satyavati, came there to see the Pandavas. And seeing him approach, Kunti's son, Yudhishthira, stepped forward, and duly received that high-souled one. And having gratified Vyasa by bowing down unto him, Pandu's son of subdued senses, after the *Rishi* had been seated, sat down before him, desirous of listening to him. And beholding his grandsons lean and living in the forest on the produce of the wilderness, that mighty sage, moved by compassion, said these words, in accents choked in tears, 'O mighty-armed Yudhishthira, O thou best of virtuous persons, those men that do not perform ascetic austerities never attain great happiness in this world. People experience happiness and misery by turns; for surely, O bull among men, no man ever enjoyeth unbroken happiness. A wise man endued with high wisdom, knowing that life hath its ups and downs, is neither filled with joy nor with grief. When happiness cometh, one should enjoy it; when misery cometh, one should bear it, as a sower of crops must bide his season. Nothing is superior to asceticism: by asceticism one acquireth mighty fruit. Do thou know, O Bharata, that there is nothing that asceticism cannot achieve. Truth, sincerity, freedom from anger, justice, self-control, restraint of the faculties, immunity from malice, guilelessness, sanctity, and mortification of the senses, these, O mighty monarch, purify a person of meritorious acts. Foolish persons addicted to vice and bestial ways, attain to brutish births in after life and never enjoy happiness. The fruit of acts done in this world is reaped in the next. Therefore should one restrain his body by asceticism and the observance of vows. And, O king, free from guile and with a cheerful spirit, one should, according to his power, bestow gifts, after going down to the recipient and paying him homage. A truth-telling person attaineth a life devoid of trouble. A person void of anger attaineth sincerity, and one free from malice acquireth supreme contentment. A person who hath subdued his senses and his inner faculties, never knoweth tribulation; nor is a person of subdued senses affected by sorrow at the height of other's prosperity. A man who giveth everyone his due, and the bestower of boons, attain happiness, and come by every object of enjoyment; while a man free from envy reapeth perfect ease. He that honoureth those to whom honour is due, attaineth birth in an illustrious line; and he that hath subdued his senses, never cometh by misfortune. A man whose mind followeth good, after having paid his debt to nature, is on this account, born again endued with a righteous mind.'

"Yudhishthira said, 'O eminently virtuous one, O mighty sage, of the bestowal of gifts and the observance of asceticism, which is of greater efficacy in the next world, and which, harder of practice?'

"Vyasa said, 'There is nothing, O child, in this world harder to practise than charity. Men greatly thirst after wealth, and wealth also is gotten with difficulty. Nay, renouncing even dear life itself, heroic men, O magnanimous one, enter into the depths of the sea and the forest for the sake of wealth. For wealth, some betake themselves to agriculture and the tending of kine, and some enter into servitude. Therefore, it is extremely difficult to part with wealth that is obtained with such trouble. Since nothing is harder to practise than charity, therefore, in my opinion, even the bestowal of boons is superior to everything. Specially is this to be borne in mind that well-earned gains should, in proper time and place, be given away to pious men. But the bestowal of ill-gotten gains can never rescue the giver from the evil of rebirth. It hath been declared, O Yudhishthira, that by bestowing, in a pure spirit, even a slight gift in due time and to a fit recipient, a man attaineth inexhaustible fruit in the next world. In this connection is instanced the old story regarding the fruit obtained by *Mudgala*, for having given away only a *drona* 45 of corn.'"

SECTION CCLVIII

"Yudhishthira said, 'Why did that high-souled one give away a drona of corn? And, O eminently pious one, to whom and in what prescribed way did he give it? Do thou tell me this. Surely, I consider the life of that virtuous person as having borne fruit with whose practices the possessor himself of the six attributes, witnessing everything, was well pleased.'

"Vyasa said, 'There lived, O king, in Kurukshetra a virtuous man (sage), Mudgala by name. And he was truthful, and free from malice, and of subdued senses. And he used to lead the *Sila* and *Unchha* modes of life. 46 And although living like a pigeon, yet that one of mighty austerities entertained his guests, celebrated the sacrifice called *Istikrita*, and performed other rites. And that sage together with his son and wife, ate for a fortnight, and during the other fortnight led the life of a pigeon, collecting a *drona* of corn. And celebrating the *Darsa* and *Paurnamasya* sacrifices, that one devoid of guile, used to pass his days by taking the food that remained after the deities and the guests had eaten. And on auspicious lunar days, that lord of the three worlds, Indra himself, accompanied by the celestials used, O mighty monarch, to partake of the food offered at his sacrifice. And that one, having adopted the life of a *Muni*, with a cheerful heart entertained his guests also with food on such days. And as that high-souled one distributed his food with alacrity, the remainder of the *drona* of corn increased as soon as a guest appeared. And by virtue of the pure spirit in which the sage gave away, that food of his increased so much that hundreds upon hundreds of learned Brahmanas were fed with it.

"'And, O king, it came to pass that having heard of the virtuous Mudgala observant of vows, the *Muni* Durvasa, having space alone for his covering, 47 his accoutrements worn like that of maniac, and his head bare of hair, came there, uttering, O Pandava various insulting words. And having arrived there that best of *Munis* said unto the Brahmana, "Know thou, O foremost of Brahmanas, that I have come hither seeking for food." Thereupon Mudgala said unto the sage, "Thou art welcome!" And then offering to that maniac of an ascetic affected by hunger, water to wash his feet and mouth, that one observant of the vow of feeding guests, respectfully placed before him excellent fare. Affected by hunger, the frantic *Rishi* completely exhausted the food that had been offered unto him. Thereupon, Mudgala furnished him again with food. Then having eaten up all that food, he besmeared his body with the unclean orts and went away as he had come. In this manner, during the next season, he came again and ate up all the food supplied by that wise one leading the *Unchha* mode of life. Thereupon, without partaking any food himself, the sage Mudgala again became engaged in collecting corn, following the *Unchha* mode. Hunger could not disturb his equanimity. Nor could anger, nor guile, nor a sense of degradation, nor agitation, enter into the heart of that best of Brahmanas leading the *Unchha* mode of life along with his son and his wife. In this way, Durvasa having made up his mind, during successive seasons presented himself for six several times before that best of sages living according to the *Unchha* mode; yet that *Muni* could not perceive any agitation in Mudgala's heart; and he found the pure heart of the pure-souled ascetic always pure. Thereupon, well-pleased, the sage addressed Mudgala, saying, "There is not another guileless and charitable being like thee on earth. The pangs of hunger drive away to a distance the sense of righteousness and deprive people of all patience. The tongue, loving delicacies, attracteth men towards them. Life is sustained by food. The mind, moreover, is fickle, and it is hard to keep it in subjection. The concentration of the mind and of the senses surely constitutes ascetic austerities. It must be hard to renounce in a pure spirit a thing earned by pains. Yet, O pious one, all this hath been duly achieved by thee. In thy company we feel obliged and gratified. Self-restraint, fortitude, justice, control of the senses and of faculties, mercy, and virtue, all these are established in thee. Thou hast by thy deeds conquered the different worlds and have thereby obtained admission into paths of beautitude. Ah! even the dwellers of heaven are proclaiming thy mighty deeds of charity. O thou observant of vows, thou shalt go to heaven even in thine own body."

"'Whilst the *Muni* Durvasa was speaking thus, a celestial messenger appeared before Mudgala, upon a car yoked with swans and cranes, hung with a neat work of bells, scented with divine fragrance, painted picturesquely, and possessed of the power of going everywhere at will. And he addressed the Brahmana sage, saying, "O sage, do thou ascend into this chariot earned by thy acts. Thou hast attained the fruit of thy asceticism!"

"'As the messenger of the gods was speaking thus, the sage told him, "O divine messenger, I desire that thou mayst describe unto me the attributes of those that reside there. What are their austerities, and what their purposes? And, O messenger of the gods, what constitutes happiness in heaven, and what are the disadvantages thereof? It is declared by virtuous men of good lineage that friendship with pious people is contracted by only walking with them seven paces. O lord, in the name of that friendship I ask thee, do thou without hesitation tell me the truth, and that which is good for me now. Having heard thee, I shall, according to thy words, ascertain the course I ought to follow."'"

SECTION CCLIX

"'The messenger of the gods said, "O great sage, thou art of simple understanding; since, having secured that celestial bliss which bringeth great honour, thou art still deliberating like an unwise person. O *Muni*, that region which is known as heaven, existeth there above us. Those regions tower high, and are furnished with excellent paths, and are, O sage, always ranged by celestial cars. Atheists, and untruthful persons, those that have not practised ascetic austerities and those that have not performed great sacrifices, cannot repair thither. Only men of virtuous souls, and those of subdued spirits, and those that have their faculties in subjection, and those that have controlled their senses, and those that are free from malice, and persons intent on the practice of charity, and heroes, and men bearing marks of battle, after having, with subdued senses and faculties, performed the most meritorious rites, attain those regions, O Brahmana, capable of being obtained only by virtuous acts, and inhabited by pious men. There, O Mudgala, are established separately myriads of beautiful, shining, and resplendent worlds bestowing every object of desire, owned by those celestial beings, the gods, the *Sadhyas*, and the *Vaiswas*, the great sages, *Yamas*, and the *Dharmas*, and the *Gandharvas* and the *Apsaras*. And there is that monarch of mountains the golden Meru extending over a space of thirty-three thousand *Yojanas*. And there, O Mudgala, are the sacred gardens of the celestials, with Nandana at their head, where sport the persons of meritorious acts. And neither hunger, nor thirst, nor lassitude, nor fear, nor anything that is disgusting or inauspicious is there. And all the odours of that place are delightful, and all the breezes delicious to the touch. And all the sounds there are captivating, O sage, to the ear and the heart. And neither grief, nor decrepitude, nor labour, nor repentance also is there. That world, O *Muni*, obtained as the fruit of one's own acts, is of this nature. Persons repair thither by virtue of their meritorious deeds. And the persons of those that dwell there look resplendent, and this, O Mudgala, solely by virtue of their own acts, and not owing to the merits of father or mothers. And there is neither sweat, nor stench, nor urine there. And there, O *Muni*, dust doth not soils one's garments. And their excellent garlands, redolent of divine fragrance, never fade. And, O Brahmana, they yoke such cars as this (that I have brought). And, O mighty sage, devoid of envy and grief and fatigue and ignorance and malice, men who have attained heaven, dwell in those regions happily. And, O bull among *Munis*, higher and higher over such regions there are others endued with higher celestial virtues. Of these, the beautiful and resplendent regions of Brahma are the foremost. Thither, O Brahmana, repair *Rishis* that have been sanctified by meritorious acts. And there dwell certain beings named *Ribhus*. They are the gods of the gods themselves. Their regions are supremely blessed, and are adored even by the deities. These shine by their own light, and bestow every object of desire. They suffer no pangs that women might cause, do not possess worldly wealth, and are free from guile. The *Ribhus* do not subsist on oblations, nor yet on ambrosia. And they are endued with such celestial forms that they cannot be perceived by the senses. And these eternal gods of the celestials do not desire happiness for happiness' sake, nor do they change at the revolution of a *Kalpa*. Where, indeed, is their decrepitude or dissolution? For them there is neither ecstasy, nor joy, nor happiness. They have neither happiness nor misery. Wherefore should they have anger or aversion then, O *Muni*? O Mudgala, their supreme state is coveted even by the gods. And that crowning emancipation, hard to attain, can never be acquired by people subject to desire. The number of those deities is thirty-three. To their regions repair wise men, after having observed excellent vows, or bestowed gifts according to the ordinance. Thou also hast easily acquired that success by thy charities. Do thou, by effulgence displayed by virtue of thy ascetic austerities, enjoy that condition obtained by thy meritorious acts. Such, O Brahmana, is the bliss of heaven containing various worlds.

"'"Thus have I described unto thee the blessing of the celestial regions. Do thou now hear from me some of the disadvantages thereof. That in the celestial regions a person, while reaping the fruit of the acts he hath already performed, cannot be engaged in any others, and that he must enjoy the consequences of the former until they are completely exhausted, and, further, that he is subject to fall after he hath entirely exhausted his merit, form, in my opinion, the disadvantages of heaven. The fall of a person whose mind hath been steeped in happiness, must, O Mudgala, be pronounced as a fault. And the discontent and regret that must follow one's stay at an inferior seat after one hath enjoyed more auspicious and brighter regions, must be hard to bear. And the consciousness of those about to fall is stupefied, and also agitated by emotions. And as the garlands of those about to fall fade away, fear invadeth their hearts. These mighty drawbacks, O Mudgala, extend even to the regions of Brahma. In the celestial regions, the virtues of men who have performed righteous acts, are countless. And, O *Muni*, this is another of the attributes of the fallen that, by reason of their merits, they take birth among men. And then they attain to high fortune and happiness. If one, however, cannot acquire knowledge here, one cometh by an inferior birth. The fruits of acts done in this world are reaped in the next. This world, O Brahmana, hath been declared to be one of acts; the others, as one of fruit. Thus have I, O Mudgala, asked by thee, described all unto thee. Now, O pious one, with thy favour, we shall easily set out with speed."'

"Vyasa continued, 'Having heard this speech, Mudgala began to reflect in his mind. And having deliberated well, that best of *Munis* spake thus unto the celestial messenger, "O messenger of the gods, I bow unto thee. Do thou, O sire, depart in peace. I have nothing to do with either happiness, or heaven having such prominent defects. Persons who enjoy heaven suffer, after all, huge misery and extreme regret in this world. Therefore, I do not desire heaven. I shall seek for that unfailing region repairing whither people have not to lament, or to be pained, or agitated. Thou hast described unto me these great defects belonging to the celestial regions. Do thou now describe unto me a region free from faults." Thereupon the celestial messenger said, "Above the abode of *Brahma*, there is the supreme seat of Vishnu, pure, and eternal, and luminous known by the name of *Para Brahma*. Thither, O Brahmana, cannot repair persons who are attached to the objects of the senses: nor can those subject to arrogance, covetousness, ignorance, anger, and envy, go to that place. It is only those that are free from affection, and those free from pride, and those free from conflicting emotions, and those that have restrained their senses, and those given to contemplation and *Yoga*, that can repair thither." Having heard these words, the *Muni* bade farewell to the celestial messenger, and that virtuous one leading the *Unchha* mode of life, assumed perfect contentment. And then praise and dispraise became equal unto him; and a brickbat, stone, and gold assumed the same aspect in his eyes. And availing himself of the means of attaining *Brahma*, he became always engaged in meditation. And having obtained power by means of knowledge, and acquired excellent understanding, he attained that supreme state of emancipation which is regarded as Eternal. Therefore, thou also, O Kunti's son, ought not to grieve. Deprived thou hast truly been of a flourishing kingdom, but thou wilt regain it by thy ascetic austerities. Misery after happiness, and happiness after misery, revolve by turns round a man even like the point of a wheel's circumference round the axle. After the thirteenth year hath passed away, thou wilt, O thou of immeasurable might, get back the kingdom possessed before thee by thy father and grandfather. Therefore, let the fever of thy heart depart!"'

Vaisampayana continued, "Having said this to Pandu's son, the worshipful Vyasa went back to his hermitage for the purpose of performing austerities."

SECTION CCLX

Janamejaya said, "While the high-souled Pandavas were living in those woods, delighted with the pleasant conversation they held with the *Munis*, and engaged in distributing the food they obtained from the sun, with various kinds of venison to Brahmanas and others that came to them for edibles till the hour of Krishna's meal, how, O great *Muni*, did Duryodhana and the other wicked and sinful sons of Dhritarashtra, guided by the counsels of Dussasana, Karna and Sakuni, deal with them? I ask thee this. Do thou, worshipful Sir, enlighten me."

Vaisampayana said, "When, O great king, Duryodhana heard that the Pandavas were living as happily in the woods as in a city, he longed, with the artful Karna, Dussasana and others, to do them harm. And while those evil-minded persons were employed in concerting various wicked designs, the virtuous and celebrated ascetic Durvasa, following the bent of his own will, arrived at the city of the Kurus with ten thousand disciples. And seeing the irascible ascetic arrived, Duryodhana and his brothers welcomed him with great humility, self-abasement and gentleness. And himself attending on the *Rishi* as a menial, the prince gave him a right worshipful reception. And the illustrious *Muni* stayed there for a few days, while king Duryodhana, watchful of his imprecations, attended on him diligently by day and night. And sometimes the *Muni* would say, 'I am hungry, O king, give me some food quickly.' And sometimes he would go out for a bath and, returning at a late hour, would say, 'I shall not eat anything today as I have no appetite,' and so saying would disappear from his sight. And sometimes, coming all on a sudden, he would say, 'Feed us quickly.' And at other times, bent on some mischief, he would awake at midnight and having caused his meals to be prepared as before, would carp at them and not partake of them at all. And trying the prince in this way for a while, when the *Muni* found that the king Duryodhana was neither angered, nor annoyed, he became graciously inclined towards him. And then, O Bharata, the intractable Durvasa said unto him, 'I have power to grant thee boons. Thou mayst ask of me whatever lies nearest to thy heart. May good fortune be thine. Pleased as I am with thee, thou mayst obtain from me anything that is not opposed to religion and morals.'"

Vaisampayana continued, "Hearing these words of the great ascetic, Suyodhana felt himself to be inspired with new life. Indeed, it had been agreed upon between himself and Karna and Dussasana as to what the boon should be that he would ask of the *Muni* if the latter were pleased with his reception. And the evil-minded king, bethinking himself of what had previously been decided, joyfully solicited the following favour, saying, 'The great king Yudhishthira is the eldest and the best of our race. That pious man is now living in the forest with his brothers. Do thou, therefore, once become the guest of that illustrious one even as, O Brahmana, thou hast with thy disciples been mine for some time. If thou art minded to do me a favour, do thou go unto him at a time when that delicate and excellent lady, the celebrated princess of Panchala, after having regaled with food the Brahmanas, her husbands and herself, may lie down to rest.' The *Rishi* replied, 'Even so shall I act for thy satisfaction.' And having said this to Suyodhana, that great Brahmana, Durvasa, went away in the very same state in which he had come. And Suyodhana regarded himself to have attained all the objects of his desire. And holding Karna by the hand he expressed great satisfaction. And Karna, too, joyfully addressed the king in the company of his brothers, saying, 'By a piece of singular good luck, thou hast fared well and attained the objects of thy desire. And by good luck it is that thy enemies have been immersed in a sea of dangers that is difficult to cross. The sons of Pandu are now exposed to the fire of Durvasa's wrath. Through their own fault they have fallen into an abyss of darkness.'"

Vaisampayana continued, "O king, expressing their satisfaction in this strain, Duryodhana and others, bent on evil machinations, returned merrily to their respective homes."

SECTION CCLXI

(Draupadi-harana Parva)

Vaisampayana said, "One day, having previously ascertained that the Pandavas were all seated at their ease and that Krishna was reposing herself after her meal, the sage Durvasa, surrounded by ten thousand disciples repaired to that forest. The illustrious and upright king Yudhishthira, seeing that guest arrived, advanced with his brothers to receive him. And joining the palms of his hands and pointing to a proper and excellent seat, he accorded the *Rishis* a fit and respectful welcome. And the king said unto him, 'Return quick, O adorable sir, after performing thy diurnal ablutions and observances.' And that sinless *Muni*, not knowing how the king would be able to provide a feast for him and his disciples, proceeded with the latter to perform his ablutions. And that host of the *Muni*, of subdued passions, went into the stream for performing their ablutions. Meanwhile, O king, the excellent princess Draupadi, devoted to her husbands, was in great anxiety about the food (to be provided for the *Munis*). And when after much anxious thought she came to the conclusion that means there were none for providing a feast, she inwardly prayed to Krishna, the slayer of Kansa. And the princess said, 'Krishna, O Krishna, of mighty arms, O son of Devaki, whose power is inexhaustible, O Vasudeva, O lord of the Universe, who dispellest the difficulties of those that bow down to thee, thou art the soul, the creator and the destroyer of the Universe. Thou, O lord, art inexhaustible and the saviour of the afflicted. Thou art the preserver of the Universe and of all created beings. Thou art the highest of the high, and the spring of the mental perceptions *Akuli* and *Chiti*! 48 O Supreme and Infinite Being, O giver of all good, be thou the refuge of the helpless. O Primordial Being, incapable of being conceived by the soul or the mental faculties or otherwise, thou art the ruler of all and the lord of Brahma. I seek thy protection. O god, thou art ever kindly disposed towards those that take refuge in thee. Do thou cherish me with thy kindness. O thou with a complexion dark as the leaves of the blue lotus, and with eyes red as the corolla of the lily, and attired in yellow robes with, besides, the bright *Kaustubha* gem in thy bosom, thou art the beginning and the end of creation, and the great refuge of all. Thou art the supreme light and essence of the Universe! Thy face is directed towards every point. They call thee Supreme Gem and the depository of all treasures. Under thy protections, O lord of the gods, all evils lose their terror. As thou didst protect me before from Dussasana, do thou extricate me now from this difficulty.'"

Vaisampayana continued, "The great and sovereign God, and Lord of the earth, of mysterious movements, the lord Kesava who is ever kind to the dependents, thus adored by Krishna, and perceiving her difficulty, instantly repaired to that place leaving the bed of Rukmini who was sleeping by his side. Beholding Vasudeva, Draupadi bowed down to him in great joy and informed him of the arrival of the *Munis* and every other thing. And having heard everything Krishna said unto her, 'I am very much afflicted with hunger, do thou give me some food without delay, and then thou mayst go about thy work.' At these words of Kesava, Krishna became confused, and replied unto him, saying, 'The sun-given vessel remains full till I finish my meal. But as I have already taken my meal today, there is no food in it now.' Then that lotus-eyed and adorable being said unto Krishna, 'This is no time for jest, O Krishna.—I am much distressed with hunger, go thou quickly to fetch the vessel and show it to me.' When Kesava, that ornament of the Yadu's race, had the vessel brought unto him,—with such persistence, he looked into it and saw a particle of rice and vegetable sticking at its rim. And swallowing it he said unto her, 'May it please the god Hari, the soul of the Universe, and may that god who partaketh at sacrifices, be satiated with this.' Then the long-armed Krishna, that soother of miseries, said unto Bhimasena, 'Do thou speedily invite the *Munis* to dinner.' Then, O good king, the celebrated Bhimasena quickly went to invite all those *Munis*, Durvasa and others, who had gone to the nearest stream of transparent and cool water to perform their ablutions. Meanwhile, these ascetics, having plunged into the river, were rubbing their bodies and observing that they all felt their stomachs to be full. And coming out of the stream, they began to stare at one another. And turning towards Durvasa, all those ascetics observed, 'Having bade the king make our meals ready, we have come hither for a bath. But how, O regenerate *Rishi*, can we eat anything now, for our stomachs seem to be full to the throat. The repast hath been uselessly prepared for us. What is the best thing to be done now?' Durvasa replied, 'By spoiling the repast, we have done a great wrong to that royal sage, king Yudhishthira. Would not the Pandavas destroy us by looking down upon us with angry eyes? I know the royal sage Yudhishthira to be possessed of great ascetic power. Ye Brahmanas, I am afraid of men that are devoted to Hari. The high-souled Pandavas are all religious men, learned, war-like, diligent in ascetic austerities and religious observances, devoted to Vasudeva, and always observant of rules of good conduct. If provoked, they can consume us with their wrath as fire doth a bale of cotton. Therefore, ye disciples, do ye all run away quickly without seeing them (again)!'"

Vaisampayana continued, "All those Brahmanas, thus advised by their ascetic preceptor, became greatly afraid of the Pandavas and fled away in all directions. Then Bhimasena not beholding those excellent *Munis* in the celestial river, made a search after them here and there at all the landing places. And learning from the ascetics of those places that they had run away, he came back and informed Yudhishthira of what had happened. Then all the Pandavas of subdued senses, expecting them to come, remained awaiting their arrival for some time. And Yudhishthira said, 'Coming dead of night the *Rishis* will deceive us. Oh how, can we escape from this difficulty created by the fates?' Seeing them absorbed in such reflections and breathing long deep sighs at frequent intervals, the illustrious Krishna suddenly appeared to them and addressed them these words: 'Knowing, ye sons of Pritha, your danger from that wrathful *Rishi*, I was implored by Draupadi to come, and (therefore) have I come here speedily. But now ye have not the least fear from the *Rishi* Durvasa. Afraid of your ascetic powers, he hath made himself scarce ere this. Virtuous men never suffer. I now ask your permission to let me return home. May you always be prosperous!'"

Vaisampayana continued, "Hearing Kesava's words, the sons of Pritha, with Draupadi, became easy in mind. And cured of their fever (of anxiety), they said unto him, 'As persons drowning in the wide ocean safely reach the shore by means of a boat, so have we, by thy aid, O lord Govinda, escaped from this inextricable difficulty. Do thou now depart in peace, and may prosperity be thine.' Thus dismissed, he repaired to his capital and the Pandavas too, O blessed lord, wandering from forest to forest passed their days merrily with Draupadi. Thus, O king, have I related to thee the story which thou askedest me to repeat. And it was thus that the machinations of the wicked sons of Dhritarashtra about the Pandavas in the forest, were frustrated."

SECTION CCLXII

Vaisampayana said, "These great warriors of the race of Bharata sojourned like immortals in the great forest of Kamyaka, employed in hunting and pleased with the sight of numerous wild tracts of country and wide reaches of woodland, gorgeous with flowers blossoming in season. And the sons of Pandu, each like unto Indra and the terror of his enemies, dwelt there for some time. And one day those valiant men, the conquerors of their foes, went about in all directions in search of game for feeding the Brahmanas in their company, leaving Draupadi alone at the hermitage, with the permission of the great ascetic Trinavindu, resplendent with ascetic grandeur, and of their spiritual guide Dhaumya. Meanwhile, the famous king of Sindhu, the son of Vriddhakshatra was, with a view to matrimony, proceeding to the kingdom of Salwa, dressed in his best royal apparel and accompanied by numerous princes. And the prince halted in the woods of Kamyaka. And in that secluded place, he found the beautiful Draupadi, the beloved and celebrated wife of the Pandavas, standing at the threshold of the hermitage. And she looked grand in the superb beauty of her form, and seemed to shed a lustre on the woodland around, like lightning illuminating masses of dark clouds. And they who saw her asked themselves, 'Is this an Apsara, or a daughter of the gods, or a celestial phantom?' And with this thought, their hands also joined together, they stood gazing on the perfect and faultless beauty of her form. And Jayadratha, the king of Sindhu, and the son of Vriddhakshatra, struck with amazement at the sight of that lady of faultless beauty, was seized with an evil intention. And inflamed with desire, he said to the prince named Kotika, 'Whose is this lady of faultless form? Is she of the human kind? I have no need to marry if I can secure this exquisitely beautiful creature. Taking her with me, I shall go back to my abode, Oh sir, and enquire who she is and whence she has come and why also that delicate being hath come into this forest beset with thorns. Will this ornament of womankind, this slender-waisted lady of so much beauty, endued with handsome teeth and large eyes, accept me as her lord? I shall certainly regard myself successful, if I obtain the hand of this excellent lady. Go, Kotika, and enquire who her husband may be.' Thus asked, Kotika, wearing a kundala, jumped out of his chariot and came near her, as a jackal approacheth a tigress, and spake unto her these words."

SECTION CCLXIII

"Kotika said, 'Excellent lady, who art thou that standest alone, leaning on a branch of the *Kadamva* tree at this hermitage and looking grand like a flame of fire blazing at night time, and fanned by the wind? Exquisitely beautiful as thou art, how is it that thou feelest not any fear in these forests? Methinks thou art a goddess, or a *Yakshi*, or a *Danavi*, or an excellent *Apsara*, or the wife of a *Daitya*, or a daughter of the *Naga* king, or a *Rakshasi* or the wife of Varuna, or of Yama, or of Soma, or of Kuvera, who, having assumed a human form, wanderest in these forests. Or, hast thou come from the mansions of Dhatri, or of Vidhatri, or of Savitri, or of Vibhu, or of Sakra? Thou dost not ask us who we are, nor do we know who protects thee here! Respectfully do we ask thee, good lady, who is thy powerful father, and, O, do tell us truly the names of thy husband, thy relatives, and thy race, and tell us also what thou dost here. As for us, I am king Suratha's son whom people know by the name of Kotika, and that man with eyes large as the petals of the lotus, sitting on a chariot of gold, like the sacrificial fire on the altar, is the warrior known by the name of Kshemankara, king of Trigarta. And behind him is the famous son of the king of Pulinda, who is even now gazing on thee. Armed with a mighty bow and endued with large eyes, and decorated with floral wreaths, he always liveth on the breasts of mountains. The dark and handsome young man, the scourge of his enemies, standing at the edge of that tank, is the son of Suvala of the race of Ikshwaku. And if, O excellent lady, thou hast ever heard the name of Jayadratha, the king of Sauviras, even he is there at the head of six thousand chariots, with horses and elephants and infantry, and followed by twelve Sauvira princes as his standard-bearers, named Angaraka, Kunjara, Guptaka, Satrunjaya, Srinjaya, Suprabiddha, Prabhankara, Bhramara, Ravi, Sura, Pratapa and Kuhana, all mounted on chariots drawn by chestnut horses and every one of them looking like the fire on the sacrificial altar. The brothers also of the king, viz., the powerful Valahaka, Anika, Vidarana and others, are among his followers. These strong-limbed and noble youths are the flowers of the Sauvira chivalry. The king is journeying in the company of these his friends, like Indra surrounded by the Maruts. O fine-haired lady, do tell us that are unacquainted (with these matters), whose wife and whose daughter thou art.'"

SECTION CCLXIV

Vaisampayana continued, "The princess Draupadi, thus questioned by that ornament of Sivi's race, moved her eyes gently, and letting go her hold of the Kadamva branch and arranging her silken apparel she said, 'I am aware, O prince, that it is not proper for a person like me to address you thus, but as there is not another man or woman here to speak with thee and as I am alone here just now, let me, therefore, speak. Know, worthy sir, that being alone in this forest here, I should not speak unto thee, remembering the usages of my sex. I have learned, O Saivya, that thou art Suratha's son, whom people know by the name of Kotika. Therefore, on my part, I shall now tell thee of my relations and renowned race. I am the daughter of king Drupada, and people know me by the name of Krishna, and I have accepted as my husbands, five persons of whom you may have heard while they were living at Khandavaprastha. Those noble persons, viz., Yudhishthira, Bhimasena, Arjuna, and the two sons of Madri, leaving me here and having assigned unto themselves the four points of the horizon, have gone out on a hunting excursion. The king hath gone to the east, Bhimasena towards the south, Arjuna to the west, and the twin brothers towards the north! Therefore, do ye now alight and dismiss your carriages so that ye may depart after receiving a due welcome from them. The high-souled son of Dharma is fond of guests and will surely be delighted to see you!' Having addressed Saivya's son in this way, the daughter of Drupada, with face beautiful as the moon, remembering well her husband's character for hospitality, entered her spacious cottage."

SECTION CCLXV

Vaisampayana said, "O Bharata, Kotikakhya related to those princes who had been waiting, all that had passed between him and Krishna. And hearing Kotikakhya's words, Jayadratha said to that scion of the race of Sivi, 'Having listened only to her speech, my heart has been lovingly inclined towards that ornament of womankind. Why therefore, hast thou returned (thus unsuccessful)? I tell thee truly, O thou of mighty arms, that having once seen this lady, other women now seem to me like so many monkeys. I having looked at her, she has captivated my heart. Do tell me, O Saivya, if that excellent lady is of the human kind.' Kotika replied, 'This lady is the famous princess Krishna, the daughter of Drupada, and the celebrated wife of the five sons of Pandu. She is the much esteemed and beloved and chaste wife of the sons of Pritha. Taking her with thee, do thou proceed towards Sauvira!'"

Vaisampayana continued, "Thus addressed, the evil-minded Jayadratha, the king of Sindhu, Sauvira and other countries, said, 'I must see Draupadi.' And with six other men he entered that solitary hermitage, like a wolf entering the den of a lion. And he said unto Krishna, 'Hail to thee, excellent lady! Are thy husbands well and those, besides, whose prosperity thou always wishest.' Draupadi replied, 'Kunti's son king Yudhishthira of the race of Kuru, his brothers, myself, and all those of whom thou hast enquired of, are well. Is everything right with thy kingdom, thy government, exchequer, and thy army? Art thou, as sole ruler, governing with justice the rich countries of Saivya, Sivi, Sindhu and others that thou hast brought under thy sway? Do thou, O prince, accept this water for washing thy feet. Do thou also take this seat. I offer thee fifty animals for thy train's breakfast. Besides these, Yudhishthira himself, the son of Kunti, will give thee porcine deer and *Nanku* deer, and does, and antelopes, and *Sarabhas*, and rabbits, and *Ruru* deer, and bears, and *Samvara* deer and gayals and many other animals, besides wild boars and buffaloes and other animals of the quadruped tribe.' Hearing this Jayadratha replied, saying, 'All is well with me. By offering to provide our breakfast, thou hast in a manner actually done it. Come now and ride my chariot and be completely happy. For it becomes not thee to have any regard for the miserable sons of Pritha who are living in the woods, whose energies have been paralysed, whose kingdom hath been snatched and whose fortunes are at the lowest ebb. A woman of sense like thee doth not attach herself to a husband that is poor. She should follow her lord when he is in prosperity but abandon him when in adversity. The sons of Pandu have for ever fallen away from their high state, and have lost their kingdom for all time to come. Thou hast no need, therefore, to partake of their misery from any regard for them. Therefore, O thou of beautiful hips, forsaking the sons of Pandu, be happy by becoming my wife, and share thou with me the kingdoms of Sindhu and Sauvira.'"

Vaisampayana continued, "Hearing these frightful words of the king of Sindhu, Krishna retired from that place, her face furrowed into a frown owing to the contraction of her eye-brows. But disregarding his words from supreme contempt, the slender-waisted Krishna reproving said unto the king of Sindhu, 'Speak not thus again! Art thou not ashamed? Be on thy guard!' And that lady of irreproachable character anxiously expecting the return of her husband, began, with long speeches, to beguile him completely."

SECTION CCLXVI

Vaisampayana said, "The daughter of Drupada, though naturally handsome, was suffused with crimson arising from a fit of anger. And with eyes inflamed and eye-brows bent in wrath, she reproved the ruler of the Suviras, saying, 'Art thou not ashamed, O fool, to use such insulting words in respect of those celebrated and terrible warriors, each like unto Indra himself, and who are all devoted to their duties and who never waver in fight with even hosts of *Yakshas* and *Rakshasas*? O Sauvira, good men never speak ill of learned persons devoted to austerities and endued with learning, no matter whether they live in the wilderness or in houses. It is only wretches that are mean as thou who do so. Methinks there is none in this assemblage of Kshatriya, who is capable of holding thee by the hand to save thee from falling into the pit thou openest under thy feet. In hoping to vanquish king Yudhishthira the just, thou really hopest to separate, stick in hand, from a herd roaming in Himalayan valleys, its leader, huge as a mountain peak and with the temporal juice trickling down its rent temples. Out of childish folly thou art kicking up into wakefulness the powerful lion lying asleep, in order to pluck the hair from off his face! Thou shalt, however, have to run away when thou seest Bhimasena in wrath! Thy courting a combat with the furious Jishnu may be likened to thy kicking up a mighty, terrible, full-grown and furious lion asleep in a mountain cave. The encounter thou speakest of with those two excellent youths—the younger Pandavas—is like unto the act of a fool that wantonly trampleth on the tails of two venomous black cobras with bifurcated tongues. The bamboo, the reed, and the plantain bear fruit only to perish and not to grow in size any further. Like also the crab that conceiveth for her own destruction, thou wilt lay hands upon me who am protected by these mighty heroes!'

"Jayadratha replied, 'I know all this, O Krishna, and I am well aware of the prowess of those princes. But thou canst not frighten us now with these threats. We, too, O Krishna, belong by birth to the seventeen high clans, and are endowed with the six royal qualities. 49 We, therefore, look down upon the Pandavas as inferior men! Therefore, do thou, O daughter of Drupada, ride this elephant or this chariot quickly, for thou canst not baffle us with thy words alone; or, speaking less boastfully, seek thou the mercy of the king of the Sauviras!'

"Draupadi replied, 'Though I am so powerful, why doth the king of Sauvira yet consider me so powerless. Well-known as I am, I cannot, from fear of violence, demean myself before that prince. Even Indra himself cannot abduct her for whose protection Krishna and Arjuna would together follow, riding in the same chariot. What shall I say, therefore, of a weak human being. When Kiriti, that slayer of foes, riding on his car, will, on my account, enter thy ranks, striking terror into every heart, he will consume everything around like fire consuming a stack of dry grass in summer. The warring princes of the Andhaka and the Vrishni races, with Janardana at their head, and the mighty bowmen of the Kaikeya tribe, will all follow in my wake with great ardour. The terrible arrows of Dhananjaya, shot from the string of the *Gandiva* and propelled by his arms fly with great force through the air, roaring like the very clouds. And when thou wilt behold Arjuna shooting from the *Gandiva* a thick mass of mighty arrows like unto a flight of locusts, then wilt thou repent of thine own folly! Bethink thyself of what thou wilt feel when that warrior armed with the *Gandiva*, blowing his conch-shell and with gloves reverberating with the strokes of his bowstring will again and again pierce thy breast with his shafts. And when Bhima will advance towards thee, mace in hand and the two sons of Madri range in all directions, vomiting forth the venom of their wrath, thou wilt then experience pangs of keen regret that will last for ever. As I have never been false to my worthy lords even in thought, so by that merit shall I now have the pleasure of beholding thee vanquished and dragged by the sons of Pritha. Thou canst not, cruel as thou art, frighten me by seizing me with violence, for as soon as those Kuru warriors will espy me they will bring me back to the woods of Kamyaka.'"

Vaisampayana continued, "Then that lady of large eyes, beholding them ready to lay violent hands on her, rebuked them and said, 'Defile me not by your touch!' And in a great alarm she then called upon her spiritual adviser, Dhaumya. Jayadratha, however, seized her by her upper garment, but she pushed him with great vigour. And pushed by the lady, that sinful wretch fell upon the ground like a tree severed from its roots. Seized, however, once more by him with great violence, she began to pant for breath. And dragged by the wretch, Krishna at last ascended his chariot having worshipped Dhaumya's feet. And Dhaumya then addressed Jayadratha and said, 'Do thou, O Jayadratha, observe the ancient custom of the Kshatriyas. Thou canst not carry her off without having vanquished those great warriors. Without doubt, thou shalt reap the painful fruits of this thy despicable act, when thou encounterest the heroic sons of Pandu with Yudhishthira the just at their head!'"

Vaisampayana continued, "Having said these words Dhaumya, entering into the midst of Jayadratha's infantry, began to follow that renowned princess who was thus being carried away by the ravisher."

SECTION CCLXVII

Vaisampayana said, "Meanwhile those foremost of bowmen on the face of the earth, having wandered separately and ranged in all directions, and having slain plenty of deer and buffaloes, at length met together. And observing that great forest, which was crowded with hosts of deer and wild beasts, resounding with the shrill cries of birds, and hearing the shrieks and yells of the denizens of the wilderness, Yudhishthira said unto his brothers, 'These birds and wild beasts, flying towards that direction which is illuminated by the sun, are uttering dissonant cries and displaying an intense excitement. All this only shows that this mighty forest hath been invaded by hostile intruders. Without a moment's delay let us give up the chase. We have no more need of game. My heart aches and seems to burn! The soul in my body, over-powering the intellect, seems ready to fly out. As a lake rid by Garuda of the mighty snake that dwells in it, as a pot drained of its contents by thirsty men, as a kingdom reft of king and prosperity, even so doth the forest of Kamyaka seem to me.' Thus addressed, those heroic warriors drove towards their abode, on great cars of handsome make and drawn by steeds of the *Saindharva* breed exceedingly fleet and possessed of the speed of the hurricane. And on their way back, they beheld a jackal yelling hideously on the wayside towards their left. And king Yudhishthira, regarding it attentively, said unto Bhima and Dhananjaya, 'This jackal that belongs to a very inferior species of animals, speaking to our left, speaketh a language which plainly indicates that the sinful Kurus, disregarding us, have commenced to oppress us by resorting to violence.' After the sons of Pandu had given up the chase and said these words, they entered the grove which contained their hermitage. And there they found their beloved one's maid, the girl Dhatreyika, sobbing and weeping. And Indrasena then quickly alighting from the chariot and advancing with hasty steps towards her, questioned her, O king, in great distress of mind, saying, 'What makes thee weep thus, lying on the ground, and why is thy face so woe-begone and colourless? I hope no cruel wretches have done any harm to the princess Draupadi possessed of incomparable beauty and large eyes and who is the second self of every one of those bulls of the Kuru race? So anxious hath been Dharma's son that if the princess hath entered the bowels of the earth or hath soared to heaven or dived into the bottom of the ocean, he and his brothers will go thither in pursuit of her. Who could that fool be that would carry away that priceless jewel belonging to the mighty and ever-victorious sons of Pandu, those grinders of foes, and which is dear unto them as their own lives? I don't know who the person could be that would think of carrying away that princess who hath such powerful protectors and who is even like a walking embodiment of the hearts of the sons of Pandu? Piercing whose breasts will terrible shafts stick to the ground to-day? Do not weep for her, O timid girl, for know thou that Krishna will come back this very day, and the sons of Pritha, having slain their foes, will again be united with Yagnaseni!' Thus addressed by him, Dhatreyika, wiping her beautiful face, replied unto Indrasena the charioteer, saying, 'Disregarding the five Indra-like sons of Pandu, Jayadratha hath carried away Krishna by force. The track pursued by him hath not yet disappeared, for the broken branches of trees have not yet faded. Therefore, turn your cars and follow her quickly, for the princess cannot have gone far by this time! Ye warriors possessed of the prowess of Indra, putting on your costly bows of handsome make, and taking up your costly bows and quivers, speed ye in pursuit of her, lest overpowered by threats or violence and losing her sense and the colour of her cheeks, she yields herself up to an undeserving wight, even as one poureth forth, from the sacrificial ladle, the sanctified oblation on a heap of ashes. O, see that the clarified butter is not poured into an unigniting fire of paddy chaff; that a garland of flowers is not thrown away in a cemetery. O, take care that the *Soma* juice of a sacrifice is not licked up by a dog through the carelessness of the officiating priests! O, let not the lily be rudely torn by a jackal roaming for its prey in the impenetrable forest. O, let no inferior wight touch with his lips the bright and beautiful face of your wife, fair as the beams of the moon and adorned with the finest nose and the handsomest eyes, like a dog licking clarified butter kept in the sacrificial pot! Do ye speed in this track and let not time steal a march on you.'

"Yudhishthira said, 'Retire, good woman, and control thy tongue. Speak not this way before us. Kings or princes, whoever are infatuated with the possession of power, are sure to come to grief!'"

Vaisampayana continued, "With these words, they departed, following the track pointed out to them, and frequently breathing deep sighs like the hissing of snakes, and twanging the strings of their large bows. And then they observed a cloud of dust raised by the hoofs of the steeds belonging to Jayadratha's army. And they also saw Dhaumya in the midst of the ravisher's infantry, exhorting Bhima to quicken his steps. Then those princes (the sons of Pandu) with hearts undepressed, bade him be of good cheer and said unto him, 'Do thou return cheerfully!' — And then they rushed towards that host with great fury, like hawks swooping down on their prey. And possessed of the prowess of Indra, they had been filled with fury at the insult offered to Draupadi. But at sight of Jayadratha and of their beloved wife seated on his car, their fury knew no bounds. And those mighty bowmen, Bhima and Dhananjaya and the twin brothers and the king, called out Jayadratha to stop, upon which the enemy was so bewildered as to lose their knowledge of directions."

SECTION CCLXVIII

Vaisampayana said, "The hostile Kshatriyas, incensed at sight of Bhimasena and Arjuna, sent up a loud shout in the forest. And the wicked king Jayadratha, when he saw the standards of those bulls of the Kuru race, lost his heart, and addressing the resplendent Yagnaseni seated on his car, said, 'Those five great warriors, O Krishna, that are coming, are I believe, thy husbands. As thou knowest the sons of Pandu well, do thou, O lady of beautiful tresses, describe them one by one to us, pointing out which of them rideth which car!' Thus addressed, Draupadi replied, 'Having done this violent deed calculated to shorten thy life, what will it avail thee now, O fool, to know the names of those great warriors, for, now that my heroic husbands are come, not one of ye will be left alive in battle. However as thou art on the point of death and hast asked me, I will tell thee everything, this being consistent with the ordinance. Beholding king Yudhishthira the just with his younger brothers, I have not the slightest anxiety or fear from thee! That warrior at the top of whose flagstaff two handsome and sonorous tabours called *Nanda* and *Upananda* are constantly played upon,—he, O Sauvira chief, hath a correct knowledge of the morality of his own acts. Men that have attained success always walk in his train. With a complexion like that of pure gold, possessed of a prominent nose and large eyes, and endued with a slender make, that husband of mine is known among people by the name of Yudhishthira, the son of Dharma and the foremost of the Kuru race. That virtuous prince of men granteth life to even a foe that yields. Therefore, O fool, throwing down thy arms and joining thy hands, run to him for thy good, to seek his protection. And that other man whom thou seest with long arms and tall as the full-grown *Sala* tree, seated on his chariot, biting his lips, and contracting his forehead so as to bring the two eye-brows together, is he,—my husband Vrikodara! Steeds of the noblest breed, plump and strong, well-trained and endued with great might, draw the cars of that warrior! His achievements are superhuman. He is known, therefore, by the name of *Bhima* on earth. They that offend him are never suffered to live. He never forgetteth a foe. On some pretext or other he wrecketh his vengeance. Nor is he pacified even after he has wrecked a signal vengeance. And there, that foremost of bowmen, endued with intelligence and renown, with senses under complete control and reverence for the old—that brother and disciple of Yudhishthira—is my husband Dhananjaya! Virtue he never forsaketh, from lust or fear or anger! Nor doth he ever commit a deed that is cruel. Endued with the energy of fire and capable of withstanding every foe, that grinder of enemies is the son of Kunti. And that other youth, versed in every question of morality and profit, who ever dispelleth the fears of the affrighted, who is endued with high wisdom, who is considered as the handsomest person in the whole world and who is protected by all the sons of Pandu, being regarded by them as dearer to them than their own lives for his unflinching devotion to them, is my husband Nakula possessed of great prowess. Endued with high wisdom and having Sahadeva for his second, possessed of exceeding lightness of hand, he fighteth with the sword, making dexterous passes therewith. Thou, foolish man, shall witness today his performances on the field of battle, like unto those of Indra amid the ranks of Daityas! And that hero skilled in weapons and possessed of intelligence and wisdom, and intent on doing what is agreeable to the son of Dharma, that favourite and youngest born of the Pandavas, is my husband Sahadeva! Heroic, intelligent, wise and ever wrathful there is not another man equal unto him in intelligence or in eloquence amid assemblies of the wise. Dearer to Kunti than her own soul, he is always mindful of the duties of Kshatriyas, and would much sooner rush into fire or sacrifice his own life than say anything that is opposed to religion and morals. When the sons of Pandu will have killed thy warriors in battle, then wilt thou behold thy army in the miserable plight of a ship on the sea wrecked with its freight of jewels on the back of a whale. Thus have I described unto thee the prowess of the sons of Pandu, disregarding whom in thy foolishness, thou hast acted so. If thou escapest unscathed from them, then, indeed thou wilt have obtained a new lease of life.'"

Vaisampayana continued, "Then those five sons of Pritha, each like unto Indra, filled with wrath, leaving the panic-stricken infantry alone who were imploring them for mercy, rushed furiously upon the charioteers, attacking them on all sides and darkening the very air with the thick shower of arrows they shot."

SECTION CCLXIX

Vaisampayana said, "Meanwhile, the king of Sindhu was giving orders to those princes, saying, 'Halt, strike, march, quick,' and like. And on seeing Bhima, Arjuna and the twin brothers with Yudhishthira, the soldiers sent up a loud shout on the field of battle. And the warriors of the Sivi, Sauvira and Sindhu tribes, at the sight of those powerful heroes looking like fierce tigers, lost heart. And Bhimasena, armed with a mace entirely of Saikya iron and embossed with gold, rushed towards the Saindhava monarch doomed to death. But Kotikakhya, speedily surrounding Vrikodara with an array of mighty charioteers, interposed between and separated the combatants. And Bhima, though assailed with numberless spears and clubs and iron arrows hurled at him by the strong arms of hostile heroes, did not waver for one moment. On the other hand, he killed, with his mace, an elephant with its driver and fourteen foot-soldiers fighting in the front of Jayadratha's car. And Arjuna also, desirous of capturing the Sauvira king, slew five hundred brave mountaineers fighting in the van of the Sindhu army. And in that encounter, the king himself slew in the twinkling of an eye, a hundred of the best warriors of the Sauviras. And Nakula too, sword in hand, jumping out of his chariot, scattered in a moment, like a tiller sowing seeds, the heads of the combatants fighting in the rear. And Sahadeva from his chariot began to fell with his iron shafts, many warriors fighting on elephants, like birds dropped from the boughs of a tree. Then the king of Trigartas, bow in hand descending from his great chariot, killed the four steeds of the king with his mace. But Kunti's son, king Yudhishthira the just, seeing the foe approach so near, and fighting on foot, pierced his breast with a crescent-shaped arrow. And that hero, thus wounded in the breast began to vomit blood, and fell down upon the ground besides Pritha's son, like an uprooted tree. And king Yudhishthira the just, whose steeds had been slain taking this opportunity, descended with Indrasena from his chariot and mounted that of Sahadeva. And the two warriors, Kshemankara and Mahamuksha, singling out Nakula, began to pour on him from both sides a perfect shower of keen-edged arrows. The son of Madri, however, succeeded in slaying, with a couple of long shafts, both those warriors who had been pouring on him an arrowy shower—like clouds in the rainy season. Suratha, the king of Trigartas, well-versed in elephant-charges, approaching the front of Nakula's chariot, caused it to be dragged by the elephant he rode. But Nakula, little daunted at this, leaped out of his chariot, and securing a point of vantage, stood shield and sword in hand, immovable as a hill. Thereupon Suratha, wishing to slay Nakula at once, urged towards him his huge and infuriate elephant with trunk upraised. But when the beast came near, Nakula with his sword severed from his head both trunk and tusks. And that mail-clad elephant, uttering a frightful roar, fell headlong upon the ground, crushing its riders by the fall. And having achieved this daring feat, the heroic son of Madri, getting up on Bhimasena's car, obtained a little rest. And Bhima too, seeing prince Kotikakhya rush to the encounter, cut off the head of his charioteer with a horse-shoe arrow. That prince did not even perceive that his driver was killed by his strong-armed adversary, and his horses, no longer restrained by a driver, ran about on the battle-field in all directions. And seeing that prince without a driver turn his back, that foremost of smiters, Bhima the son of Pandu, went up to him and slew him with a bearded dart. And Dhananjaya also cut off with his sharp crescent-shaped arrows, the heads, as well as the bows of all the twelve Sauvira heroes. And the great warrior killed in battle, with the arrow, the leaders of the Ikshwakus and the hosts of Sivis and Trigartas and Saindhavas. And a great many elephants with their colours, and chariots with standards, were seen to fall by the hand of Arjuna. And heads without trunks, and trunks without heads, lay covering the entire field of battle. And dogs, and herons and ravens, and crows, and falcons, and jackals, and vultures, feasted on the flesh and blood of warriors slain on that field. And when Jayadratha, the king of Sindhu, saw that his warriors were slain, he became terrified and anxious to run away leaving Krishna behind. And in that general confusion, the wretch, setting down Draupadi there, fled for his life, pursuing the same forest path by which he had come. And king Yudhishthira the just, seeing Draupadi with Dhaumya walking before, caused her to be taken up on a chariot by the heroic Sahadeva, the son of Madri. And when Jayadratha had fled away Bhima began to mow down with his iron-arrows such of his followers as were running away striking each trooper down after naming him. But Arjuna perceiving that Jayadratha had run away exhorted his brother to refrain from slaughtering the remnant of the Saindhava host. And Arjuna said, 'I do not find on the field of battle Jayadratha through whose fault alone we have experienced this bitter misfortune! Seek him out first and may success crown thy effort! What is the good of thy slaughtering these troopers? Why art thou bent upon this unprofitable business?'"

Vaisampayana continued, "Bhimasena, thus exhorted by Arjuna of great wisdom, turning to Yudhishthira, replied, saying, 'As a great many of the enemy's warriors have been slain and as they are flying in all directions, do thou, O king, now return home, taking with thee Draupadi and the twin brothers and high-souled Dhaumya, and console the princess after getting back to our asylum! That foolish king of Sindhu I shall not let alone as long as he lives, even if he find a shelter in the infernal regions or is backed by Indra himself!' And Yudhishthira replied, saying, 'O thou of mighty arms remembering (our sister) Dussala and the celebrated Gandhari, thou shouldst not slay the king of Sindhu even though he is so wicked!'"

Vaisampayana continued, "Hearing these words, Draupadi was greatly excited. And that highly intelligent lady in her excitement said to her two husbands, Bhima and Arjuna with indignation mixed with modesty, 'If you care to do what is agreeable to me, you must slay that mean and despicable wretch, that sinful, foolish, infamous and contemptible chief of the Saindhava clan! That foe who forcibly carries away a wife, and he that wrests a kingdom, should never be forgiven on the battle-field, even though he should supplicate for mercy!' Thus admonished, those two valiant warriors went in search of the Saindhava chief. And the king taking Krishna with him returned home, accompanied by his spiritual adviser. And on entering the hermitage, he found it was laid over with seats for the ascetics and crowded with their disciples and graced with the presence of Markandeya and other Brahmanas. And while those Brahmanas were gravely bewailing the lot of Draupadi, Yudhishthira endued with great wisdom joined their company, with his brothers. And beholding the king thus come back after having defeated the Saindhava and the Sauvira host and recovered Draupadi, they were all elated with joy! And the king took his seat in their midst. And the excellent princess Krishna entered the hermitage with the two brothers.

"Meanwhile Bhima and Arjuna, learning the enemy was full two miles ahead of them urged their horses to greater speed in pursuit of him. And the mighty Arjuna performed a wonderful deed, killing the horse of Jayadratha although they were full two miles ahead of them. Armed with celestial weapons undaunted by difficulties he achieved this difficult feat with arrows inspired with *Mantras*. And then the two warriors, Bhima and Arjuna, rushed towards the terrified king of Sindhu whose horses had been slain and who was alone and perplexed in mind. And the latter was greatly grieved on seeing his steeds slain. And beholding Dhananjaya do such a daring deed, and intent on running away, he followed the same forest track by which he had come. And Phalguna, seeing the Saindhava chief so active in his fright, overtook him and addressed him saying, 'Possessed of so little manliness, how couldst thou dare to take away a lady by force? Turn round, O prince; it is not meet that thou shouldst run away! How canst thou act so, leaving thy followers in the midst of thy foes?' Although addressed by the sons of Pritha thus, the monarch of Sindhu did not even once turn round. And then bidding him to what he chose the mighty Bhima overtook him in an instant, but the kind Arjuna entreated him not to kill that wretch."

SECTION CCLXX

Vaisampayana said, "Jayadratha flying for his life upon beholding those two brothers with upraised arms, was sorely grieved and bolted off with speed and coolness. But the mighty and indignant Bhimasena, descending from his chariot, ran after him thus fleeing, and seized him by the hair of his head. And holding him high up in the air, Bhima thrust him on the ground with violence. And seizing the prince by the head, he knocked him about. And when the wretch recovered consciousness, he groaned aloud and wanted to get up on his legs. But that hero endued with mighty arms kicked him on the head. And Bhima pressed him on the breast with his knees as well as with his fists. And the prince thus belaboured, soon became insensible. Then Phalguna dissuaded the wrathful Bhimasena from inflicting further chastisement on the prince, by reminding him of what Yudhishthira had said regarding (their sister) Dussala. But Bhima replied, saying, 'This sinful wretch hath done a cruel injury to Krishna, who never can bear such treatment. He, therefore, deserveth to die at my hands! But what can I do? The king is always overflowing with mercy, and thou, too, art constantly putting obstacles in my way from a childish sense of virtue!' Having said these words, Vrikodara, with his crescent-shaped arrow, shaved the hair of the prince's head, heaving five tufts in as many places. Jayadratha uttered not a word at this. Then Vrikodara, addressing the foe said, 'If thou wishest to live, listen to me. O fool! I shall tell thee the means to attain that wish! In public assemblies and in open courts thou must say,—I am the slave of the Pandavas.—on this condition alone, I will pardon thee thy life! This is the customary rule of conquest on the field of battle.' Thus addressed and treated, king Jayadratha said to the mighty and fierce warrior who always looked awful, 'Be it so!' And he was trembling and senseless and begrimed with dust. Then Arjuna and Vrikodara, securing him with chains, thrust him into a chariot. And Bhima, himself mounting that chariot, and accompanied by Arjuna, drove towards the hermitage. And approaching Yudhishthira seated there, he placed Jayadratha in that condition before the king. And the king, smiling, told him to set the Sindhu prince at liberty. Then Bhima said unto the king, 'Do thou tell Draupadi that this wretch hath become the slave of the Pandavas.' Then his eldest brother said unto him affectionately, 'If thou hast any regard for us, do thou set this wretch at liberty!' And Draupadi too, reading the king's mind, said, 'Let him off! He hath become a slave of the king's and thou, too, hast disfigured him by leaving five tufts of hair on his head.' Then that crest-fallen prince, having obtained his liberty, approached king Yudhishthira and bowed down unto him. And seeing those *Munis* there, he saluted them also. Then the kind-hearted king Yudhishthira, the son of Dharma, beholding Jayadratha in that condition, almost supported by Arjuna, said unto him, 'Thou art a free man now; I emancipate thee! Now go away and be careful not to do such thing again; shame to thee! Thou hadst intended to take away a lady by violence, even though thou art so mean and powerless! What other wretch save thee would think of acting thus?' Then that foremost king of Bharata's race eyed with pity that perpetrator of wicked deeds, and believing that he had lost his senses, said, 'Mayst thy heart grow in virtue! Never set thy heart again on immoral deeds! Thou mayst depart in peace now with thy charioteers, cavalry and infantry.' Thus addressed by Yudhishthira, the prince, O Bharata, was overpowered with shame, and bending down his head, he silently and sorrowfully wended his way to the place where the Ganga debouches on the plains. And imploring the protection of the god of three eyes, the consort of Uma, he did severe penance at that place. And the three-eyed god, pleased with his austerities deigned to accept his offerings in person. And he also granted him a boon! Do thou listen, O monarch, how the prince received that boon! Jayadratha, addressing that god, asked the boon, 'May I be able to defeat in battle all the five sons of Pandu on their chariots!' The god, however, told him 'This cannot be.' And Maheswara said, 'None can slay or conquer them in battle. Save Arjuna, however, thou shall be able to only check them (once) on the field of battle! The heroic Arjuna, with mighty arms, is the god incarnate styled *Nara*. He practised austerities of old in the Vadari forest. The God *Narayana* is his friend. Therefore, he is unconquerable of the very gods. I myself have given him the celestial weapon called *Pasupata*. From the regents also of all the ten cardinal points, he has acquired the thunder-bolt and other mighty weapons. And the great god Vishnu who is the Infinite Spirit, the Lord Preceptor of all the gods, is the Supreme Being without attributes, and the Soul of the Universe, and existeth pervading the whole creation. At the termination of a cycle of ages, assuming the shape of the all-consuming fire, he consumed the whole Universe with mountains and seas and islands and hills and woods and forests. And after the destruction of the *Naga* world also in the subterranean regions in the same way, vast masses of many-coloured and loud-pealing clouds, with streaks of lightning, spreading along the entire welkin, had appeared on high. Then pouring down water in torrents thick as axles of cars, and filling the space everywhere, these extinguishing that all-consuming fire! When at the close of four thousand *Yugas* the Earth thus became flooded with water, like one vast sea, and all mobile creatures were hushed in death, and the sun and the moon and the winds were all destroyed, and the Universe was devoid of planets and stars, the Supreme Being called Narayana, unknowable by the senses, adorned with a thousand heads and as many eyes and legs, became desirous of rest. And the serpent Sesha, looking terrible with his thousand hoods, and shining with the splendour of ten thousand suns, and white as the *Kunda* flower or the moon or a string of pearls, or the white lotus, or milk, or the fibres of a lotus stalk, served for his conch. And that adorable and omnipotent God thus slept on the bosom of the deep, enveloping all space with nocturnal gloom. And when his creative faculty was excited, he awoke and found the Universe denuded of everything. In this connection, the following *sloka* is recited respecting the meaning of *Narayana*. "Water was created by (the *Rishi*) *Nara,* and it formed his corpus; therefore do we hear it styled as *Nara.* And because it formed his *Ayana* (resting-place) therefore is he known as *Narayana*." As soon as that everlasting Being was engaged in meditation for the re-creation of the Universe, a lotus flower instantaneously came into existence from his navel, and the four-faced *Brahma* came out of that navel-lotus. And then the Grandsire of all creatures, seating himself on that flower and finding that the whole Universe was a blank, created in his own likeness, and from his will, the (nine) great *Rishis, Marichi* and others. And these in their turn observing the same thing, completed the creation, by creating *Yakshas, Rakshas, Pisachas,* reptiles, men, and all mobile and immobile creatures. The Supreme Spirit hath three conditions. In the form of Brahma, he is the Creator, and in the form of Vishnu he is the Preserver, and in his form as Rudra, he is the Destroyer of the Universe! O king of Sindhu, hast thou not heard of the wonderful achievements of Vishnu, described to thee by the *Munis* and the Brahmanas learned in the *Vedas*? When the world was thus reduced to one vast sea of water, with only the heavens above, the Lord, like a fire-fly at night-time during the rainy season, moved about hither and thither in search of stable ground, with the view of rehabilitating his creation, and became desirous of raising the Earth submerged in water. *What shape shall I take to rescue the Earth from this flood!*—So thinking and contemplating with divine insight, he bethought himself of the shape of a wild boar fond of sporting in water. And assuming the shape of a sacrificial boar shining with effulgence and instinct with the *Vedas* and ten *Yojanas* in length, with pointed tusks and a complexion like dark clouds, and with a body huge as a mountain, and roaring like a conglomeration of clouds, the Lord plunged into the waters, and lifted up the Earth with one of his tusks, and replaced it in its proper sphere. At another time, the mighty Lord, assuming a wonderful form with a body half lion, half man, and squeezing his hands, repaired to the court of the ruler of the *Daityas*. That progenitor of the *Daityas*, the son of *Diti*, who was the enemy of the (gods), beholding the Lord's peculiar form, burst out into passion and his eyes became inflamed with rage. And Hiranya-Kasipu, the war-like son of Diti and the enemy of the gods, adorned with garlands and looking like a mass of dark clouds, taking up his trident in hand and roaring like the clouds, rushed on that being half lion, half man. Then that powerful king of wild beasts, half man, half lion, taking a leap in the air, instantly rent the *Daitya* in twain by means of his sharp claws. And the adorable lotus-eyed Lord of great effulgence, having thus slain the *Daitya* king for the well-being of all creatures, again took his birth in the womb of *Aditi* as son of Kasyapa. And at the expiration of a thousand years she was delivered of that superhuman conception. And then was born that Being, of the hue of rain-charged clouds with bright eyes and of dwarfish stature. He had the ascetic's staff and water-pot in hand, and was marked with the emblem of a curl of hair on the breast. And that adorable Being wore matted locks and the sacrificial thread, and he was stout and handsome and resplendent with lustre. And that Being, arriving at the sacrificial enclosure of Vali, king of the *Danavas*, entered the sacrificial assembly with the aid of Vrihaspati. And beholding that dwarf-bodied Being, Vali was well-pleased and said unto him, "I am glad to see thee, O Brahmana! Say what is it that thou wantest from me!" Thus addressed by Vali, the dwarf-god replied with a smile, saying, "So be it! Do thou, lord of the *Danavas*, give me three paces of ground!" And Vali contented to give what that Brahmana of infinite power had asked. And while measuring with his paces the space he sought, Hari assumed a wonderful and extraordinary form. And with only three paces he instantly covered this illimitable world. And then that everlasting God, Vishnu, gave it away unto Indra. This history which has just been related to thee, is celebrated as the "*Incarnation of the Dwarf.*" And from him, all the gods had their being, and after him the world is said to be *Vaishnava*, or pervaded by Vishnu. And for the destruction of the wicked and the preservation of religion, even He hath taken his birth among men in the race of the Yadus. And the adorable Vishnu is styled Krishna. These, O king of Sindhu, are the achievements of the Lord whom all the worlds worship and whom the learned describe as without beginning and without end, unborn and Divine! They call Him, the unconquerable Krishna with conchshell, discus and mace, and adorned with the emblem of a curl of hair, Divine, clad in silken robes of yellow hue, and the best of those versed in the art of war. Arjuna is protected by Krishna the possessor of these attributes. That glorious and lotus-eyed Being of infinite power, that slayer of hostile heroes, riding in the same chariot with Pritha's son, protecteth him! He is, therefore, invincible; the very gods cannot resist his power, still less can one with human attributes vanquish the son of Pritha in battle! Therefore, O king, thou must let him alone! Thou shalt, however, be able to vanquish for a single day only, the rest of Yudhishthira's forces along with thine enemies—the four sons of Pandu!'"

Vaisampayana continued, "Having said these words unto that prince, the adorable Hara of three eyes, the destroyer of all sins, the consort of Uma, and lord of wild beasts, the destroyer of (Daksha's) sacrifice, the slayer of Tripura and He that had plucked out the eyes of Bhaga, surrounded by his dwarfish and hunch-backed and terrible followers having frightful eyes and ears and uplifted arms, vanished, O tiger among kings, from that place with his consort Uma! And the wicked Jayadratha also returned home, and the sons of Pandu continued to dwell in the forest of Kamyaka."

SECTION CCLXXI

Janamejaya said, "What did those tigers among men, the Pandavas, do, after they had suffered such misery in consequence of the ravishment of Draupadi?"

Vaisampayana said, "Having defeated Jayadratha and rescued Krishna, the virtuous king Yudhishthira took his seat by the side of that best of *Munis*. And among those foremost of ascetics who were expressing their grief upon hearing Draupadi's misfortune, Yudhishthira, the son of Pandu, addressed Markandeya, saying, 'O adorable Sire, amongst the gods and the ascetics, thou art known to have the fullest knowledge of both the past as well as the future. A doubt existeth in my mind, which I would ask thee to solve! This lady is the daughter of Drupada; she hath issued from the sacrificial altar and hath not been begotten of the flesh; and she is highly blessed and is also the daughter-in-law of the illustrious Pandu. I incline to think that Time, and human Destiny that dependeth on our acts, and the Inevitable, are irresistible in respect of creatures. (If it were not so), how could such a misfortune afflict this wife of ours so faithful and virtuous, like a false accusation of theft against an honest man? The daughter of Drupada hath never committed any sinful act, nor hath she done anything that is not commendable: on the contrary, she hath assiduously practised the highest virtues towards Brahmanas. And yet the foolish king Jayadratha had carried her away by force. In consequence of this act of violence on her, that sinful wretch hath his hair shaved off his head and sustained also, with all his allies, defeat in battle. It is true we have rescued her after slaughtering the troops of Sindhu. But the disgrace of this ravishment of our wife during our hours of carelessness, hath stained us, to be sure. This life in the wilderness is full of miseries. We subsist by chase; and though dwelling in the woods, we are obliged to slay the denizens thereof that live with us! This exile also that we suffer is due to the act of deceitful kinsmen! Is there any one who is more unfortunate than I am? Hath thou ever seen or heard of such a one before?'"

SECTION CCLXXII

"Markandeya said, 'O bull of the Bharata race, even Rama suffered unparalleled misery, for the evil-minded Ravana, king of the Rakshasas, having recourse to deceit and overpowering the vulture Jatayu, forcibly carried away his wife Sita from his asylum in the woods. Indeed, Rama, with the help of Sugriva, brought her back, constructing a bridge across the sea, and consuming Lanka with his keen-edged arrows.'

"Yudhishthira said, 'In what race was Rama born and what was the measure of his might and prowess? Whose son also was Ravana and for what was it that he had any misunderstanding with Rama? It behoveth thee, O illustrious one, to tell me all this in detail; for I long to hear the story of Rama of great achievements!'

"Markandeya said, 'Listen, O prince of Bharata's race, to this old history exactly as it happened! I will tell thee all about the distress suffered by Rama together with his wife. There was a great king named Aja sprung from the race of Ikshwaku. He had a son named Dasaratha who was devoted to the study of the Vedas and was ever pure. And Dasaratha had four sons conversant with morality and profit known by the names, respectively, of Rama, Lakshmana, Satrughna, and the mighty Bharata. And Rama had for his mother Kausalya, and Bharata had for his mother Kaikeyi, while those scourges of their enemies Lakshmana and Satrughna were the sons of Sumitra. And Janaka was the king of Videha, and Sita was his daughter. And Tashtri himself created her, desiring to make her the beloved wife of Rama. I have now told thee the history of both Rama's and Sita's birth. And now, O king, I will relate unto thee the birth of Ravana. That Lord of all creatures and the Creator of the Universe viz., the Self-create Prajapati himself—that god possessed of great ascetic merit—is the grandfather of Ravana. And Pulastya hath a mighty son called Vaisravana begotten of a cow. But his son, leaving his father, went to his grandfather. And, O king, angered at this, his father then created a second self of himself. And with half of his own self that regenerate one became born of Visrava for wrecking a vengeance on Vaisravana. But the Grandsire, pleased with Vaisravana, gave him immortality, and sovereignty of all the wealth of the Universe, the guardianship of one of the cardinal points, the friendship of Isana, and a son named Nalakuvera. And he also gave him for his capital Lanka, which was guarded by hosts of Rakshasas, and also a chariot called Pushpaka capable of going everywhere according to the will of the rider. And the kingship of the Yakshas and the sovereignty over sovereigns were also his.'"

SECTION CCLXXIII

"Markandeya said, 'The Muni named Visrava, who was begotten of half the soul of Pulastya, in a fit of passion, began to look upon Vaisravana with great anger. But, O monarch, Kuvera, the king of the Rakshasas, knowing that his father was angry with him, always sought to please him. And, O best of Bharata's race, that king of kings living in Lanka, and borne upon the shoulders of men, sent three Rakshasa women to wait upon his father. Their names, O king, were Pushpotkata, Raka and Malini. And they were skilled in singing and dancing and were always assiduous in their attentions on that high-souled Rishi. And those slender-waisted ladies vied with one another, O king, in gratifying the Rishi. And that high-souled and adorable being was pleased with them and granted them boons. And to every one of them he gave princely sons according to their desire. Two sons—those foremost of Rakshasas named Kumvakarna and the Ten-headed Ravana,—both unequaled on earth in prowess, were born to Pushpotkata. And Malini had a son named Vibhishana, and Raka had twin children named Khara and Surpanakha. And Vibhishana surpassed them all in beauty. And that excellent person was very pious and assiduously performed all religious rites. But that foremost of Rakshasas, with ten heads, was the eldest to them all. And he was religious, and energetic and possessed of great strength and prowess. And the Rakshasa Kumvakarna was the most powerful in battle, for he was fierce and terrible and a thorough master of the arts of illusion. And Khara was proficient in archery, and hostile to the Brahmanas, subsisting as he did on flesh. And the fierce Surpanakha was constant source of trouble to the ascetics. And the warriors, learned in the Vedas and diligent in ceremonial rites, all lived with their father in the Gandhamadana. And there they beheld Vaisravana seated with their father, possessed of riches and borne on the shoulders of men. And seized with jealousy, they resolved upon performing penances. And with ascetic penances of the most severe kind, they gratified Brahma. And the Ten-headed Ravana, supporting life by means of air alone and surrounded by the five sacred fires and absorbed in meditation, remained standing on one leg for a thousand years. And Kumvakarna with head downwards, and with restricted diet, was constant in austerities. And the wise and magnanimous Vibhishana, observing fasts and subsisting only on dry leaves and engaged in meditation, practised severe austerities for a long period. And Khara and Surpanakha, with cheerful hearts, protected and attended on them while they were performing those austerities. And at the close of a thousand years, the invincible Ten-headed One, cutting off his own heads, offered them as offering to the sacred fire. And at this act of his, the Lord of the Universe was pleased with him. And then Brahma, personally appearing to them, bade them desist from those austerities and promised to grant boons unto every one of them. And the adorable Brahma said, "I am pleased with you, my sons! Cease now from these austerities and ask boons of me! Whatever your desires may be, they, with the single exception of that of immortality, will be fulfilled! As thou hast offered thy heads to the fire from great ambition, they will again adorn thy body as before, according to thy desire. And thy body will not be disfigured and thou shall be able to assume any form according to thy desire and become the conqueror of thy foes in battle. There is no doubt of this!" thereupon Ravana said, "May I never experience defeat at the hands of Gandharvas, Celestials, Kinnaras, Asuras, Yakshas, Rakshasas, Serpents and all other creatures!" Brahma said, "From those that hast named, thou shalt never have cause of fear; except from men (thou shalt have no occasion for fear). Good betide thee! So hath it been ordained by me!"'

"Markandeya said, 'Thus addressed, the Ten-headed (Ravana) was highly gratified, for on account of his perverted understanding, the man-eating one slighted human beings. Then the great Grandsire addressed Kumbhakarna as before. His reason being clouded by darkness, he asked for long-lasting sleep. Saying, "It shall be so!" Brahma then addressed Vibhishana, "O my son, I am much pleased with thee! Ask any boon thou pleasest!" Thereupon, Vibhishana replied, "Even in great danger, may I never swerve from the path of righteousness, and though ignorant, may I, O adorable Sire, be illumined with the light of divine knowledge!" And Brahma replied, "O scourge of thy enemies, as thy soul inclines not to unrighteousness although born in the *Rakshasa race*, I grant thee immortality!"'

"Markandeya continued, 'Having obtained this boon, the Ten-headed Rakshasa defeated Kuvera in battle and obtained from him the sovereignty of Lanka. That adorable Being, leaving Lanka and followed by Gandharvas, Yakshas, Rakshas, and Kinnaras, went to live on mount Gandhamadana. And Ravana forcibly took from him the celestial chariot *Pushpaka*. And upon this Vaisravana cursed him, saying, "This chariot shall never carry thee; it shall bear him who will slay thee in battle! And as thou hast insulted me, thy elder brother, thou shalt soon die!"

"'The pious Vibhishana, O King, treading in the path followed by the virtuous and possessed of great glory, followed Kuvera. That adorable Lord of wealth, highly pleased with his younger brothers, invested him with the command of the Yaksha and Raksha hosts. On the other hand, the powerful and man-eating *Rakshasas* and *Pisachas,* having assembled together, invested the Ten-headed Ravana with their sovereignty. And Ravana, capable of assuming any form at will and terrible in prowess, and capable also of passing through the air, attacked the gods and the *Daityas* and wrested from them all their valuable possessions. And as he had terrified all creatures, he was called *Ravana.* And Ravana, capable of mustering any measure of might inspired the very gods with terror.'"

SECTION CCLXXIV

"Markandeya said, 'Then the *Brahmarshis*, the *Siddhas* and the *Devarshis*, with *Havyavaha* as their spokesman, sought the protection of Brahma. And Agni said, "That powerful son of Visrava, the Ten-headed cannot be slain on account of thy boon! Endued with great might he oppresseth in every possible way the creatures of the earth. Protect us, therefore, O adorable one! There is none else save thee to protect us!"

"'Brahma said, "O Agni, he cannot be conquered in battle by either the gods or the *Asuras*! I have already ordained that which is needful for that purpose. Indeed his death is near! Urged by me, the four-headed God hath already been incarnate for that object. Even Vishnu, that foremost of smiters will achieve that object!"'

"Markandeya continued, 'Then the Grandsire also asked Sakra, in their presence, "Be thou, with all the celestials, born on earth! And beget ye on monkeys and bears, heroic sons possessed of great strength and capable of assuming any form at will as allies of Vishnu!" And at this, the gods, the *Gandharvas* and the *Danavas* quickly assembled to take counsel as to how they should be born on earth according to their respective parts. And in their presence the boon-giving god commanded a *Gandharvi*, by name Dundubhi saying, "Go there for accomplishing this object!" And Dundubhi hearing these words of the Grandsire was born in the world of men as the hunchbacked *Manthara*. And all the principal celestials, with Sakra and others begot offspring upon the wives of the foremost of monkeys and bears. And those sons equaled their sires in strength and fame. And they were capable of splitting mountain peaks and their weapons were stones and trees of the *Sala* and the *Tala* species. And their bodies were hard as adamant, and they were possessed of very great strength. And they were all skilled in war and capable of mustering any measure of energy at will. And they were equal to a thousand elephants in might, and they resembled the wind in speed. And some of them lived wherever they liked, while others lived in forests. And the adorable Creator of the Universe, having ordained all this, instructed *Manthara* as to what she would have to do. And Manthara quick as thought, understood all his words, and went hither and thither ever engaged in fomenting quarrels.'"

SECTION CCLXXV

"Yudhishthira said, 'O adorable one, thou hast described to me in detail the history of the birth of Rama and others. I wish to learn the cause of their exile. Do thou, O Brahmana, relate why the sons of Dasaratha—the brothers Rama and Lakshmana—went to the forest with famous princess of Mithila.'

"Markandeya said, 'The pious king Dasaratha, ever mindful of the old and assiduous in religious ceremonies, was greatly pleased when these sons were born. And his sons gradually grew up in might and they became conversant with the Vedas together with all their mysteries, and with the science of arms. And when after having gone through the Brahmacharya vows the princes were married, king Dasaratha became happy and highly pleased. And the intelligent Rama, the eldest of them all, became the favourite of his father, and greatly pleased the people with his charming ways. And then, O Bharata, the wise king, considering himself old in years took counsel with his virtuous ministers and spiritual adviser for installing Rama as regent of the kingdom. And all those great ministers were agreed that it was time to do so. And, O scion of Kuru's race, king Dasaratha was greatly pleased to behold his son,—that enhancer of Kausalya's delight— possessed of eyes that were red, and arms that were sinewy. And his steps were like those of a wild elephant. And he had long arms and high shoulders and black and curly hair. And he was valiant, and glowing with splendour, and not inferior to Indra himself in battle. And he was well-versed in holy writ and was equal to Vrihaspati in wisdom. An object of love with all the people, he was skilled in every science. And with senses under complete control, his very enemies were pleased to behold him. And he was terror of the wicked and the protector of the virtuous. And possessed of intelligence and incapable of being baffled, he was victorious over all and never vanquished by any. And, O descendant of Kurus, beholding his son— that enhancer of Kausalya's joy—king Dasaratha became highly pleased. And reflecting on Rama's virtues, the powerful and mighty king cheerfully addressed the family priest, saying, "Blessed be thou, O Brahmana! This night of the Pushya constellation will bring in a very auspicious conjunction. Let, therefore, materials be collected and let Rama also be invited. This

Pushya constellation will last till tomorrow. And Rama, therefore, should be invested by me and my ministers as prince-regent of all my subjects!"

"'Meanwhile Manthara (the maid of Kaikeyi), hearing these words of the king, went to her mistress, and spoke unto her as was suited to the occasion. And she said, "Thy great ill-luck, O Kaikeyi, hath this day been proclaimed by the king! O unlucky one, mayst thou be bitten by a fierce and enraged snake of virulent poison! Kausalya, indeed, is fortunate, as it is her son that is going to be installed on the throne. Where, indeed, is thy prosperity, when thy son obtaineth not the kingdom?"

"'Hearing these words of her maid, the slender-waisted and beautiful Kaikeyi put on all her ornaments, and sought her husband in a secluded place. And with a joyous heart, and smiling pleasantly, she addressed these words to him with all the blandishments of love, "O king, thou art always true to thy promises. Thou didst promise before to grant me an object of my desire. Do thou fulfil that promise now and save thyself from the sin of unredeemed pledge!" The king replied, saying, "I will grant thee a boon. Ask thou whatever thou wishest! What man undeserving of death shall be slain today and who that deserves death is to be set at liberty? Upon whom shall I bestow wealth to-day, or whose wealth shall be confiscated? Whatever wealth there is in this world, save what belongeth to Brahmanas, is mine! I am the king of kings in this world, and the protector of all the four classes! Tell me quickly, O blessed lady, what that object is upon which thou hast set thy heart!" Hearing these words of the king, and tying him fast to his pledge, and conscious also of her power over him, she addressed him in these words, "I desire that Bharata be the recipient of that investiture which thou hast designed for Rama, and let Rama go into exile living in the forest of Dandaka for fourteen years as an ascetic with matted locks on head and robed in rags and deer-skins!" Hearing these disagreeable words of cruel import, the king, O chief of the Bharata race, was sorely afflicted and became utterly speechless! But the mighty and virtuous Rama, learning that his father had been thus solicited, went into the forest so that the king's truth might remain inviolate. And, blessed be thou, he was followed by the auspicious Lakshmana—that foremost of bowmen and his wife Sita, the princess of Videha and daughter of Janaka. And after Rama had gone into the forest, king Dasaratha took leave of his body, agreeably to the eternal law of time. And knowing that Rama not near and that the king was dead, queen Kaikeyi, causing Bharata to be brought before her, addressed him in these words, "Dasaratha hath gone to heaven and both Rama and Lakshmana are in the forest! Take thou this kingdom which is so extensive and whose peace there is no rival to disturb." Thereupon the virtuous Bharata replied unto her saying, "Thou hast done a wicked deed, having slain thy husband and exterminated this family from lust of wealth alone! Heaping infamy on my head, O accursed woman of our race, thou hast, O mother, attained this, thy object!" And having said these words, the prince wept aloud. And having proved his innocence before all the subjects of that realm he set out in the wake of Rama, desiring to bring him back. And placing Kausalya and Sumitra and Kaikeyi in the vehicles at the van of his train, he proceeded with a heavy heart, in company with Satrughna. And he was accompanied by Vasishtha and Vamadeva, and other Brahmanas by thousands and by the people of the cities and the provinces, desiring to bring back Rama. And he saw Rama with Lakshmana, living on the mountains of Chitrakuta with bow in hand and decked with the ornaments of ascetics. Bharata, however, was dismissed by Rama, who was determined to act according to the words of his father. And returning, Bharata ruled at Nandigrama, keeping before him, his brother's wooden sandals. And Rama fearing a repetition of intrusion by the people of Ayodhya, entered into the great forest towards the asylum of Sarabhanga. And having paid his respects to Sarabhanga, he entered the forest of Dandaka and took up his abode on the banks of beautiful river Godavari. And while living there, Rama was inveigled into hostilities with Khara, then dwelling in Janasthana, on account of Surpanakha. And for the protection of the ascetics the virtuous scion of Raghu's race slew fourteen thousand Rakshasas on earth, and having slain those mighty Rakshasas, Khara and Dushana, the wise descendant of Raghu once more made that sacred forest free from danger.

"'And after these Rakshasas had been slain, Surpanakha with mutilated nose and lips, repaired to Lanka—the abode of her brother (Ravana). And when that Rakshasa woman, senseless with grief and with dry blood-stains on her face, appeared before Ravana, she fell down at his feet. And beholding her so horribly mutilated, Ravana became senseless with wrath and grinding his teeth sprung up from his seat. And dismissing his ministers, he enquired of her in private, saying, "Blessed sister, who hath made thee so, forgetting and disregarding me? Who is he that having got a sharp-pointed spear hath rubbed his body with it? Who is he that sleepeth in happiness and security, after placing a fire close to his head? Who is he that hath trodden upon a revengeful snake of virulent poison? Who indeed, is that person who standeth with his hand thrust into the mouth of the maned lion!" Then flames of wrath burst forth from his body, like those that are emitted at night from the hollows of a tree on fire. His sister then related unto him the prowess of Rama and the defeat of the Rakshasas with Khara and Dushana at their head. Informed of the slaughter of his relatives, Ravana, impelled by Fate, remembered Maricha for slaying Rama. And resolving upon the course he was to follow and having made arrangements for the government of his capital, he consoled his sister, and set out on an aerial voyage. And crossing the Trikuta and the Kala mountains, he beheld the vast receptacle of deep waters—the abode of the Makaras. Then crossing the Ocean, the Ten headed Ravana reached Gokarna—the favourite resort of the illustrious god armed with the trident. And there Ravana met with his old friend Maricha who, from fear of Rama himself, had adopted an ascetic mode of life.'"

SECTION CCLXXVI

"Markandeya said, 'Beholding Ravana come, Maricha received him with a respectful welcome, and offered him fruits and roots. And after Ravana had taken his seat, and rested himself a while, Maricha skilled in speech, sat beside Ravana and addressed him who was himself as eloquent in speech, saying, "Thy complexion hath assumed an unnatural hue; is it all right with thy kingdom, O king of the Rakshasas? What hath brought thee here? Do thy subjects continue to pay thee the same allegiance that they used to pay thee before? What business hath brought thee here? Know that it is already fulfilled, even if it be very difficult of fulfilment!" Ravana, whose heart was agitated with wrath and humiliation informed him briefly of the acts of Rama and the measures that were to be taken. And on hearing his story, Maricha briefly replied to him, saying, "Thou must not provoke Rama, for I know his strength! Is there a person who is capable of withstanding the impetus of his arrows? That great man hath been the cause of my assuming my present ascetic life. What evil-minded creature hath put thee up to this course calculated to bring ruin and destruction on thee?" To this Ravana indignantly replied, reproaching him thus, "If thou dost not obey my orders, thou shall surely die at my hands." Maricha then thought within himself, "When death is inevitable, I shall do his biddings; for it is better to die at the hands of one that is superior." Then he replied to the lord of the Rakshasas saying, "I shall surely render thee whatever help I can!" Then the Ten-headed Ravana said unto him, "Go and tempt Sita, assuming the shape of a deer with golden horns and a golden skin! When Sita will observe thee thus, she will surely send away Rama to hunt thee. And then Sita will surely come within my power, and I shall forcibly carry her away. And then that wicked Rama will surely die of grief at the loss of his wife. Do thou help me in this way!"

"'Thus addressed, Maricha performed his obsequies (in anticipation) and with a sorrowful heart, followed Ravana who was in advance of him. And having reached the hermitage of Rama of difficult achievements, they both did as arranged beforehand. And Ravana appeared in the guise of an ascetic with head shaven, and adorned with a *Kamandala*, and a treble staff. And Maricha appeared in the shape of a deer. And Maricha appeared before the princess of Videha in that guise. And impelled by Fate, she sent away Rama after that deer. And Rama, with the object of pleasing her, quickly took up his bow, and leaving Lakshmana behind to protect her, went in pursuit of that deer. And armed with his bow and quiver and scimitar, and his fingers encased in gloves of *Guana* skin, Rama went in pursuit of that deer, after the manner of Rudra following the stellar deer 50 in days of yore. And that Rakshasa enticed away Rama to a great distance by appearing before him at one time and disappearing from his view at another. And when Rama at last knew who and what that deer was, viz., that he was a *Rakshasa*, that illustrious descendant of Raghu's race took out an infallible arrow and slew that Rakshasa, in the disguise of a deer. And struck with Rama's arrow, the Rakshasa, imitating Rama's voice, cried out in great distress, calling upon Sita and Lakshmana. And when the princess of Videha heard that cry of distress, she urged Lakshmana to run towards the quarter from whence the cry came. Then Lakshmana said to her, "Timid lady, thou hast no cause of fear! Who is so powerful as to be able to smite Rama? O thou of sweet smiles, in a moment thou wilt behold thy husband Rama!" Thus addressed, the chaste Sita, from that timidity which is natural to women, became suspicious of even the pure Lakshmana, and began to weep aloud. And that chaste lady, devoted to her husband, harshly reproved Lakshmana, saying, "The object which thou, O fool, cherishest in thy heart, shall never be fulfilled! I would rather kill myself with a weapon or throw myself from the top of a hill or enter into a blazing fire than live with a sorry wretch like thee, forsaking my husband Rama, like a tigress under the protection of a jackal!"

"'When the good natured Lakshmana, who was very fond of his brother, heard these words, he shut his ears (with his hands) and set out on the track that Rama had taken. And Lakshmana set out without casting a single glance on that lady with lips soft and red like the *Bimba* fruit. Meanwhile, the Rakshasa Ravana, wearing a genteel guise though wicked at heart, and like unto fire enveloped in a heap of ashes, showed himself there. And he appeared there in the disguise of a hermit, for forcibly carrying away that lady of blameless character. The virtuous daughter of Janaka, seeing him come, welcomed him with fruits and root and a seat. Disregarding these and assuming his own proper shape, that bull among Rakshasas began to re-assure the princess of Videha in these words, "I am, O Sita, the king of the Rakshasas, known by the name of Ravana! My delightful city, known by the name of Lanka is on the other side of the great ocean! There among beautiful women, thou wilt shine with me! O lady of beautiful lips, forsaking the ascetic Rama do thou become my wife!" Janaka's daughter of beautiful lips, hearing these and other words in the same strain, shut her ears and replied unto him, saying, "Do not say so! The vault of heaven with all its stars may fall down, the Earth itself may be broken into fragments, fire itself may change its nature by becoming cool, yet I cannot forsake the descendant of Raghu! How can a she-elephant, who hath lived with the mighty leader of a herd with rent temples forsake him and live with a hog? Having once tasted the sweet wine prepared from honey or flowers, how can a woman, I fancy, relish the wretched arrak from rice?" Having uttered those words, she entered the cottage, her lips trembling in wrath and her arms moving to and fro in emotion. Ravana, however, followed her thither and intercepted her further progress. And rudely scolded by the Rakshasa, she swooned away. But Ravana seized her by the hair of her head, and rose up into the air. Then a huge vulture of the name of Jatayu living on a mountain peak, beheld that helpless lady thus weeping and calling upon Rama in great distress while being carried away by Ravana.'"

SECTION CCLXXVII

"Markandeya said, 'That heroic king of the vultures, Jatayu, having Sampati for his uterine brother and Arjuna himself for his father, was a friend of Dasaratha. And beholding his daughter-in-law Sita on the lap of Ravana, that ranger of the skies rushed in wrath against the king of the Rakshasas. And the vulture addressed Ravana, saying, "Leave the princess of Mithila, leave her I say! How canst thou, O Rakshasa, ravish her when I am alive? If thou dost not release my daughter-in-law, thou shalt not escape from me with life!" And having said these words Jatayu began to tear the king of the Rakshasas with his talons. And he mangled him in a hundred different parts of his body by striking him with his wings and beaks. And blood began to flow as copiously from Ravana's body as water from a mountain spring. And attacked thus by that vulture desirous of Rama's good, Ravana, taking up a sword, cut off the two wings of that bird. And having slain that king of the vultures, huge as a mountain-peak shooting forth above the clouds, the Rakshasa rose high in the air with Sita on his lap. And the princess of Videha, wherever she saw an asylum of ascetics, a lake, a river, or a tank, threw down an ornament of hers. And beholding on the top of a mountain five foremost of monkeys, that intelligent lady threw down amongst them a broad piece of her costly attire. And that beautiful and yellow piece of cloth fell, fluttering through the air, amongst those five foremost of monkeys like lightning from the clouds. And that Rakshasa soon passed a great way through the firmament like a bird through the air. And soon the Rakshasa beheld his delightful and charming city of many gates, surrounded on all sides by high walls and built by Viswakrit himself. And the king of the Rakshasa then entered his own city known by the name of Lanka, accompanied by Sita.

"'And while Sita was being carried away, the intelligent Rama, having slain the great deer, retraced his steps and saw his brother Lakshmana (on the way). And beholding his brother, Rama reproved him, saying, "How couldst thou come hither, leaving the princess of Videha in a forest that is haunted by the Rakshasa?" And reflecting on his own enticement to a great distance by that Rakshasa in the guise of a deer and on the arrival of his brother (leaving Sita alone in the asylum), Rama was filled with agony. And quickly advancing towards Lakshmana while reproving him still, Rama asked him, "O Lakshmana, is the princess of Videha still alive? I fear she is no more!" Then Lakshmana told him everything about what Sita had said, especially that unbecoming language of hers subsequently. With a burning heart Rama then ran towards the asylum. And on the way he beheld a vulture huge as a mountain, lying in agonies of death. And suspecting him to be a Rakshasa, the descendant of the Kakutstha race, along with Lakshmana rushed towards him, drawing with great force his bow to a circle. The mighty vulture, however, addressing them both, said, "Blessed be ye, I am the king of the vultures, and friend of Dasaratha!" Hearing these words of his, both Rama and his brother put aside their excellent bow and said, "Who is this one that speaketh the name of our father in these woods?" And then they saw that creature to be a bird destitute of two wings, and that bird then told them of his own overthrow at the hands of Ravana for the sake of Sita. Then Rama enquired of the vulture as to the way Ravana had taken. The vulture answered him by a nod of his head and then breathed his last. And having understood from the sign the vulture had made that Ravana had gone towards the south, Rama reverencing his father's friend, caused his funeral obsequies to be duly performed. Then those chastisers of foes, Rama and Lakshmana, filled with grief at the abduction of the princess of Videha, took a southern path through the Dandaka woods beholding along their way many uninhabited asylums of ascetics, scattered over with seats of Kusa grass and umbrellas of leaves and broken water-pots, and abounding with hundreds of jackals. And in that great forest, Rama along with Sumatra's son beheld many herds of deer running in all directions. And they heard a loud uproar of various creatures like what is heard during a fast spreading forest conflagration. And soon they beheld a headless Rakshasa of terrible mien. And that Rakshasa was dark as the clouds and huge as a mountain, with shoulders broad as those of a Sola tree, and with arms that were gigantic. And he had a pair of large eyes on his breast, and the opening of his mouth was placed on his capacious belly. And that Rakshasa seized Lakshmana by the hand, without any difficulty. And seized by the Rakshasa the son of Sumitra, O Bharata, became utterly confounded and helpless. And casting his glances on Rama, that headless Rakshasa began to draw Lakshmana towards that part of his body where his mouth was. And Lakshmana in grief addressed Rama, saying, "Behold my plight! The loss of thy kingdom, and then the death of our father, and then the abduction of Sita, and finally this disaster that hath overwhelmed me! Alas, I shall not behold thee return with the princess of Videha to Kosala and seated on thy ancestral throne as the ruler of the entire Earth! They only that are fortunate will behold thy face, like unto the moon emerged from the clouds, after thy coronation bath in water sanctified with Kusa grass and fried paddy and black peas!" And the intelligent Lakshmana uttered those and other lamentations in the same strain. The illustrious descendant, however, of Kakutstha's race undaunted amid danger, replied unto Lakshmana, saying, "Do not, O tiger among men, give way to grief! What is this thing when I am here? Cut thou off his right arm and I shall cut off his left." And while Rama was still speaking so, the left arm of the monster was severed by him, cut off with a sharp scimitar, as if indeed, that arm were a stalk of the *Tila corn*. The mighty son of Sumitra then beholding his brother standing before him struck off with his sword the right arm also of that Rakshasa. And Lakshmana also began to repeatedly strike the Rakshasa under the ribs, and then that huge headless monster fell upon the ground and expired quickly. And then there came out from the Rakshasa's body a person of celestial make. And he showed himself to the brothers, staying for a moment in the skies, like the Sun in his effulgence in the firmament. And Rama skilled in speech, asked him, saying, "Who art thou? Answer *me* who enquire of thee? Whence could such a thing happen? All this seems to me to be exceedingly wonderful!" Thus addressed by Rama, that being replied unto him, saying, "I am, O prince, a Gandharva of the name of Viswavasu! It was through the curse of a Brahmana that I had to assume the form and nature of a Rakshasa. As to thyself, O Rama, Sita hath been carried away with violence by king Ravana who dwelleth in Lanka. Repair thou unto Sugriva who will give thee his friendship. There, near enough to the peak of *Rishyamuka* is the lake known by the name of *Pampa* of sacred water and cranes. There dwelleth, with four of his counsellors, Sugriva, the brother of the monkey-king Vali decked with a garland of gold. Repairing unto him, inform of thy cause of sorrow. In plight very much like thy own, he will render thee assistance. This is all that we can say. Thou wilt, without doubt, see the daughter of Janaka! Without doubt Ravana and others are known to the king of the monkeys!" Having said these words, that celestial being of great effulgence made himself invisible, and those heroes, both Rama and Lakshmana, wondered much.'"

SECTION CCLXXVIII

"Markandeya said, 'Afflicted with grief at the abduction of Sita, Rama had not to go much further before he came upon *Pampa*—that lake which abounded with lotuses of various kinds. And fanned by the cool, delicious and fragrant breezes in those woods, Rama suddenly remembered his dear spouse. And, O mighty monarch, thinking of that dear wife of his, and afflicted at the thought of his separation from her, Rama gave way to lamentations. The son of Sumitra then addressed him saying, "O thou that givest proper respect to those that deserve it, despondency such as this should not be suffered to approach thee, like illness that can never touch an old man leading a regular life! Thou hast obtained information of Ravana and of the princess of Videha! Liberate her now with exertion and intelligence! Let us now approach Sugriva, that foremost of monkeys, who is even now on the mountain top! Console thyself, when I, thy disciple and slave and ally, am near!" And addressed by Lakshmana in these and other words of the same import, Rama regained his own nature and attended to the business before him. And bathing in the waters of *Pampa* and offering oblations therewith unto their ancestors, both those heroic brothers, Rama and Lakshmana, set out (for *Rishyamuka*). And arriving at *Rishyamuka* which abounded with fruits and roots and trees, those heroes beheld five monkeys on the top of the mountain-peak. And seeing them approach, Sugriva sent his counsellor the intelligent Hanuman, huge as the Himavat-mountains, to receive them. And the brothers, having first exchanged words with Hanuman, approached Sugriva. And then, O king, Rama made friends with Sugriva. And when Rama informed Sugriva of the object he had in view, Sugriva showed him the piece of cloth that Sita had dropped among the monkeys, while being carried away by Ravana. And having obtained from him those credentials, Rama himself installed Sugriva—that foremost of monkeys—in sovereignty of all the monkeys of Earth. And Rama also pledged himself to slay Vali in battle. And having come to that understanding and placing the fullest confidence in each other, they all repaired to *Kiskindhya*, desirous of battle (with Vali). And arriving at *Kiskindhya*, Sugriva sent forth a loud roar deep as that of a cataract. Unable to bear that challenge, Vali was for coming out (but his wife) Tara stood in way, saying, "Himself endued with great strength, the way in which Sugriva is roaring, showeth, I ween, that he hath found assistance! It behoveth thee not, therefore, to go out!" Thus addressed by her, that king of the monkeys, the eloquent Vali, decked in a golden garland replied unto Tara of face beautiful as the moon, saying, "Thou understandest the voice of every creature. Tell me after reflection whose help it is that this brother in name only of mine hath obtained!" Thus addressed by him Tara endued with wisdom and possessed of the effulgence of the moon, answered her lord after a moment's reflection, saying, "Listen, O monarch of the monkeys! That foremost of bowmen, endued with great might, Rama the son of Dasaratha, whose spouse hath been ravished, hath made an alliance offensive and defensive with Sugriva! And his brother the intelligent Lakshmana also of mighty arms, the unvanquished son of Sumitra, standeth beside him for the success of Sugriva's object. And Mainda and Dwivida, and Hanuman the son of *Pavana*, and Jamvuman, the king of the bears, are beside Sugriva as his counsellors. All these illustrious ones are endued with great strength and intelligence. And these all, depending upon the might and energy of Rama, are prepared for thy destruction!" Hearing these words of hers that were for his benefit, the king of the monkeys disregarded them altogether. And filled with jealousy, he also suspected her to have set her heart on Sugriva! And addressing Tara in harsh words, he went out of his cave and coming before Sugriva who was staying by the side of the mountains of Malyavat, he spoke unto him thus, "Frequently vanquished before by me, fond as thou art of life, thou art allowed by me to escape with life owing to thy relationship with me! What hath made thee wish for death so soon?" Thus addressed by Vali, Sugriva, that slayer of foes, as if addressing Rama himself for informing him of what had happened, replied unto his brother in these words of grave import, "O king, robbed by thee of my wife and my kingdom also, what need have I of life? Know that it is for this that I have come!" Then addressing each other in these and other words of the same import, Vali and Sugriva rushed to the encounter, fighting with *Sala* and *Tala* trees and stones. And they struck each other down on the earth. And leaping high into the air, they struck each other with their fists. And mangled by each other's nail and teeth, both of them were covered with blood. And the two heroes shone on that account like a pair of blossoming *Kinshukas*. And as they fought with each other, no difference (in aspect) could be observed so as to distinguish them. Then Hanuman placed on Sugriva's neck a garland of flowers. And that hero thereupon shone with that garland on his neck, like the beautiful and huge peak of *Malya* with its cloudy belt. And Rama, recognising Sugriva by that sign, then drew his foremost of huge bows, aiming at Vali as his mark. And the twang of Rama's bow resembled the roar of an engine. And Vali, pierced in the heart by that arrow, trembled in fear. And Vali, his heart having been pierced through, began to vomit forth blood. And he then beheld standing before him Rama with Sumatra's son by his side. And reproving that descendant of Kakutstha's race, Vali fell down on the ground and became senseless. And Tara then beheld that lord of hers possessed of the effulgence of the Moon, lying prostrate on the bare earth. And after Vali had been thus slain, Sugriva regained possession of Kishkindhya, and along with it, of the widowed Tara also of face beautiful as the moon. And the intelligent Rama also dwelt on the beautiful breast of the Malyavat hill for four months, duly worshipped by Sugriva all the while.

"'Meanwhile Ravana excited by lust, having reached his city of Lanka, placed Sita in an abode, resembling *Nandana* itself, within a forest of *Asokas*, that looked like an asylum of ascetics. And the large-eyed Sita passed her days there in distress, living on fruits and roots, practising ascetic austerities with fasts, attired in ascetic garb, and waning thin day by day, thinking of her absent lord. And the king of the *Rakshasas* appointed many *Rakshasa* women armed with bearded darts and swords and lances and battle-axes and maces and flaming brands, for guarding her. And some of these had two eyes, and some three, and some had eyes on their foreheads. And some had long tongues and some had none. And some had three breasts and some had only one leg. And some had three matted braids on their heads, and some had only one eye. And these, and others of blazing eyes and hair stiff as the camel's, stood beside Sita surrounding her day and night most watchfully. And those *Pisacha* women of frightful voice and terrible aspect always addressed that large-eyed lady in the harshest tones. And they said, "Let us eat her up, let us mangle her, let us tear her into pieces, her, that is, that dwelleth here disregarding our lord!" And filled with grief at the separation from her lord, Sita drew a deep sigh and answered those *Rakshasa* women, saying, "Reverend ladies, eat me up without delay! I have no desire to live without that husband of mine, of eyes like lotus-leaves and locks wavy, and blue in hue! Truly I will, without food and without the least love of life, emaciate my limbs, like a she-snake (hybernating) within a *Tala* tree. Know this for certain that I will never seek the protection of any other person than the descendant of Raghu. And knowing this, do what ye think fit!" And hearing these words of hers, those *Rakshasas* with dissonant voice went to the king of the *Rakshasas*, for representing unto him all she had said. And when those *Rakshasas* had gone away, one of their number known by the name of *Trijata*, who was virtuous and agreeable in speech, began to console the princess of Videha. And she said, "Listen, O Sita! I will tell thee something! O friend, believe in what I say! O thou of fair hips, cast off thy fears, and listen to what I say. There is an intelligent and old chief of the *Rakshasas* known by the name of Avindhya. He always seeketh Rama's good and hath told me these words for thy sake! 'Reassuring and cheering her, tell Sita in my name, saying: "Thy husband the mighty Rama is well and is waited upon by Lakshmana. And the blessed descendant of Raghu hath already made friends with Sugriva, the king of the monkeys, and is ready to act for thee!"' And, O timid lady, entertain thou no fear on account of Ravana, who is censured by the whole world, for, O daughter, thou art safe from him on account of Nalakuvera's curse. Indeed, this wretch had been cursed before for his having violated his daughter-in-law, Rambha. This lustful wretch is not able to violate any woman by force. Thy husband will soon come, protected by Sugriva and with the intelligent son of Sumitra in his train, and will soon take thee away hence! O lady, I have had a most terrible dream of evil omen, indicating the destruction of this wicked-minded wretch of Pulastya's race! This night wanderer of mean deeds is, indeed, most wicked and cruel. He inspireth terror in all by the defects of his nature and the wickedness of his conduct. And deprived of his senses by Fate, he challengeth the very gods. In my vision I have seen every indication of his downfall. I have seen the Ten-headed, with his crown shaven and body besmeared with oil, sunk in mire, and the next moment dancing on a chariot drawn by mules. I have seen Kumbhakarna and others, perfectly naked and with crowns shaven, decked with red wreaths and unguents, and running towards the southern direction. Vibhishana alone, with umbrella over his head, and graced with a turban, and with body decked with white wreaths and unguents, I beheld ascending the summit of the White hill. And I saw four of his counsellors also, decked with white wreaths and unguents, ascending the summit of that hill along with him. All this bodeth that these alone will be saved from the impending terror. The whole earth with its oceans and seas will be enveloped with Rama's arrows. O lady, thy husband will fill the whole earth with his fame. I also saw Lakshmana, consuming all directions (with his arrows) and ascending on a heap of bones and drinking thereon honey and rice boiled in milk. And thou, O lady, hast been beheld by me running towards a northernly direction, weeping and covered with blood and protected by a tiger! And, O princess of Videha, soon wilt thou find happiness, being united, O Sita, with thy lord, that descendant of Raghu accompanied by his brother!' Hearing these words of *Trijata*, that girl with eyes like those of a young gazelle, once more began to entertain hopes of a union with her lord. And when at last those fierce and cruel *Pisacha* guards came back, they saw her sitting with *Trijata* as before.'"

SECTION CCLXXIX

"Markandeya said, 'And while the chaste Sita was dwelling there afflicted with melancholy and grief on account of her lord, attired in mean garb, with but a single jewel (on the marital thread on her wrist), and incessantly weeping, seated on a stone, and waited upon by *Rakshasa* women, Ravana, afflicted by the shafts of the god of desire, came to her and approached her presence. And inflamed by desire, that conqueror in battle of the gods, the *Danavas*, the *Gandharvas*, the *Yakshas*, and the *Kimpurushas*, attired in celestial robes and possessing handsome features, decked with jewelled earrings and wearing a beautiful garland and crown, entered the *Asoka* woods, like an embodiment of the vernal season. And dressed with care, Ravana looked like the *Kalpa* tree in Indra's garden. But though adorned with every embellishment, that inspired her only with awe, like a beautified banian in the midst of a cemetery. And that night wanderer, having approached the presence of that slender-waisted lady, looked like the planet Saturn in the presence of *Rohini*. And smitten with the shafts of the god of the flowery emblem he accosted that fair-hipped lady then affrighted like a helpless doe, and told her these words, "Thou hast, O Sita, shown thy regard for thy lord too much! O thou of delicate limbs, be merciful unto me. Let thy person be embellished now (by these maids in waiting). O excellent lady, accept me as thy lord! And, O thou of the most beautiful complexion, attired in costly robes and ornaments, take thou the first place among all the women of my household. Many are the daughters of the celestials and also the *Gandharvas* that I possess! I am lord also of many *Danava* and *Daitya* ladies! One hundred and forty millions of *Pisachas*, twice as many man-eating Rakshasa of terrible deed, and thrice as many Yaksha do my bidding! Some of these are under the sway of my brother who is the lord of all treasures. In my drinking hall, O excellent lady of beautiful thighs, Gandharvas and Apsaras wait on me as they do on my brother! I am, again, the son of that regenerate *Rishi* Visravas himself of high ascetic merit. I am renowned, again, as the fifth Regent of the Universe! And, O beautiful lady, of food and edibles and drinks of the very best kind, I have as much as the Lord himself of the celestials! Let all thy troubles consequent on a life in the woods cease! O thou of fair hips, be my Queen, as Mandodari herself!" Thus addressed by him, the beautiful princess of Videha, turning away and regarding him as something less than a straw, replied unto that wanderer of the night. And at that time the princess of Videha, that girl of beautiful hips, had her deep and compact bosom copiously drenched by her inauspicious tears shed ceaselessly. And she who regarded her husband as her god, answered that mean wretch, saying, "By sheer ill-luck it is, O king of the Rakshasas, that I am obliged to hear such words of grievous import spoken by thee! Blessed be thou, O Rakshasa fond of sensual pleasures, let thy heart be withdrawn from me! I am the wife of another, ever devoted to my husband, and, therefore, incapable of being possessed by thee! A helpless human being that I am, I cannot be a fit wife for thee! What joy can be thine by using violence towards an unwilling woman? Thy father is a wise Brahmana, born of Brahma and equal unto that Lord himself of the creation! Why dost thou not, therefore, thyself being equal to a Regent of the Universe, observe virtue? Disgracing thy brother, that king of the Yakshas, that adorable one who is the friend of Maheswara himself, that lord of treasures, how is it that thou feelest no shame?" Having said these words, Sita began to weep, her bosom shivering in agitation, and covering her neck and face with her garments. And the long and well-knit braid, black and glossy, falling from the head of the weeping lady, looked like a black snake. And hearing these cruel words uttered by Sita, the foolish Ravana, although thus rejected, addressed Sita once more, saying, "O lady, let the god having the *Makara* for his emblem burn me sorely. I will, however, on no account, O thou of sweet smiles and beautiful hips, approach thee, as thou art unwilling! What can I do to thee that still feelest a regard for Rama who is only a human being and, therefore, our food?" Having said those words unto that lady of faultless features, the king of the *Rakshasa* made himself invisible then and there and went away to the place he liked. And Sita, surrounded by those *Rakshasa* women, and treated with tenderness by *Trijata*, continued to dwell there in grief.'"

SECTION CCLXXX

"Markandeya said, 'Meanwhile the illustrious descendant of Raghu, along with his brother, hospitably treated by Sugriva, continued to dwell on the breast of the *Malyavat* hill, beholding every day the clear blue sky. And one night, while gazing from the mountain-top on the bright moon in the cloudless sky surrounded by planets and stars and stellar bodies, that slayer of foes was suddenly awakened (to a remembrance of Sita) by the cold breezes fragrant with the perfumes of the lily, lotus and other flowers of the same species. And virtuous Rama, dejected in spirits at the thought of Sita's captivity in the abode of the Rakshasa, addressed the heroic Lakshmana in the morning saying, "Go, Lakshmana and seek in Kishkindhya that ungrateful king of the monkeys, who understands well his own interest and is even now indulging in dissipations, that foolish wretch of his race whom I have installed on a throne and to whom all apes and monkeys and bears owe allegiance, that fellow for whose sake, O mighty-armed perpetuator of Raghu's race, Vali was slain by me with thy help in the wood of Kishkindhya! I regard that worst of monkeys on earth to be highly ungrateful, for, O Lakshmana, that wretch hath now forgotten me who am sunk in such distress! I think he is unwilling to fulfil his pledge, disregarding, from dullness of understanding, one who hath done him such services! If thou findest him luke-warm and rolling in sensual joys, thou must then send him, by the path Vali hath been made to follow, to the common goal of all creatures! If, on the other hand, thou seest that foremost of monkeys delight in our cause, then, O descendant of Kakutstha, shouldst thou bring him hither with thee! Be quick, and delay not!" Thus addressed by his brother, Lakshmana ever attentive to the behests and welfare of his superiors, set out taking with him his handsome bow with string and arrows. And reaching the gates of Kishkindhya he entered the city unchallenged. And knowing him to be angry, the monkey-king advanced to receive him. And with his wife, Sugriva, the king of the monkeys, with a humble heart, joyfully received him with due honours. And the dauntless son of Sumitra then told him what Rama had said. And having heard everything in detail, O mighty monarch, Sugriva, the king of the monkeys with his wife and servants, joined his hands, and cheerfully said unto Lakshmana, that elephant among men, these words: "I am, O Lakshmana, neither wicked, nor ungrateful, nor destitute of virtue! Hear what efforts I have made for finding out Sita's place of captivity! I have despatched diligent monkeys in all directions. All of them have stipulated to return within a month. They will, O hero, search the whole earth with her forests and hills and seas, her villages and towns and cities and mines. Only five nights are wanting to complete that month, and then thou wilt, with Rama, hear tidings of great joy!"

"'Thus addressed by that intelligent king of the monkeys, the high-souled Lakshmana became appeased, and he in his turn worshipped Sugriva. And accompanied by Sugriva, he returned to Rama on the breast of the Malyavat hill. And approaching him, Lakshmana informed him of the beginning already made in respect of his undertaking. And soon thousands of monkey-chiefs began to return, after having carefully searched the three quarters of the earth, viz., the North, the East and the West. But they that had gone towards the South did not make their appearance. And they that came back represented to Rama, saying that although they had searched the whole earth with her belt of seas, yet they could not find either the princess of Videha or Ravana. But that descendant of Kakutstha's race, afflicted at heart, managed to live yet, resting his hopes (of hearing Sita's tidings) on the great monkeys that had gone towards the South.

"'After the lapse of two months, several monkeys seeking with haste the presence of Sugriva, addressed him, saying, "O king, that foremost of monkeys, the son of *Pavana*, as also Angada, the son of Vali, and the other great monkeys whom thou hadst despatched to search the southern region, have come back and are pillaging that great and excellent orchard called *Madhuvana*, which was always guarded by Vali and which hath been well-guarded by thee also after him!" Hearing of this act of liberty on their part, Sugriva inferred the success of their mission, for it is only servants that have been crowned with success that can act in this way. And that intelligent and foremost of monkeys communicated his suspicions to Rama. And Rama also, from this, guessed that the princess of Mithila had been seen. Then Hanuman and the other monkeys, having refreshed themselves thus, came towards their king, who was then staying with Rama and Lakshmana. And, O Bharata, observing the gait of Hanuman and the colour of his face, Rama was confirmed in the belief that Hanuman had really seen Sita. Then those successful monkeys with Hanuman at their head, duly bowed unto Rama and Lakshmana and Sugriva. And Rama then taking up his bow and quiver, addressed those monkeys, saying, "Have you been successful? Will ye impart life unto me? Will ye once more enable me to reign in Ayodhya after having slain my enemy in battle and rescued the daughter of Janaka? With the princess of Videha unrescued, and the foe unslain in battle, I dare not live, robbed of wife and honour!" Thus addressed by Rama, the son of *Pavana*, replied unto him, saying, "I bring thee good news, O Rama; for Janaka's daughter hath been seen by me. Having searched the southern region with all its hills, forests, and mines for some time, we became very weary. At length we beheld a great cavern. And having beheld it, we entered that cavern which extended over many *Yojanas*. It was dark and deep and overgrown with trees and infested by worms. And having gone a great way through it, we came upon sun-shine and beheld a beautiful palace. It was, O Raghava, the abode of the *Daitya Maya*. And there we beheld a female ascetic named *Prabhavati* engaged in ascetic austerities. And she gave us food and drink of various kinds. And having refreshed ourselves therewith and regained our strength, we proceeded along the way shown by her. At last we came out of the cavern and beheld the brimy sea, and on its shores, the *Sahya*, the *Malaya* and the great *Dardura* mountains. And ascending the mountains of *Malaya*, we beheld before us the vast ocean. 51 And beholding it we felt sorely grieved in mind. And dejected in spirits and afflicted with pain and famishing with hunger, we despaired of returning with our lives. Casting our eyes on the great ocean extending over many hundreds of *Yojanas* and abounding in whales and alligators and other aquatic animals, we became anxious and filled with grief. We then sat together, resolved to die there of starvation. And in course of conversation we happened to talk of the vulture *Jatayu*. Just then we saw a bird huge as a mountain, of frightful form, and inspiring terror into every heart, like a second son of Vinata. 52 And coming upon us unawares for devouring us, he said, 'Who are ye that are speaking thus of my brother *Jatayu*? I am his elder brother, by name *Sampati*, and am the king of birds. Once upon a time, we two, with the desire of outstripping each other, flew towards the sun. My wings got burnt, but those of *Jatayu* were not. That was the last time I saw my beloved brother *Jatayu*, the king of vultures! My wings burnt, I fell down upon the top of this great mountain where I still am!' When he finished speaking, we informed him of the death of his brother in a few words and also of this calamity that hath befallen thee! And, O king, the powerful Sampati hearing this unpleasant news from us, was greatly afflicted and again enquired of us, saying, 'Who is this Rama and why was Sita carried off and how was Jatayu slain? Ye foremost of monkeys I wish to hear everything in detail!' We then informed him of everything about this calamity of thine and of the reason also of our vow of starvation. That king of birds then urged us (to give up our vow) by these words of his: 'Ravana is, indeed, known to me. Lanka is his capital. I beheld it on the other side of the sea in a valley of the *Trikuta* hills! Sita must be there. I have little doubt of this!' Hearing these words of his, we rose up quickly and began, O chastiser of foes, to take counsel of one another for crossing the ocean! And when none dared to cross it, I, having recourse to my father, crossed the great ocean which is a hundred *Yojanas* in width. And having slain the *Rakshasis* on the waters, I saw the chaste Sita within Ravana's harem, observing ascetic austerities, eager to behold her lord, with matted locks on head, and body besmeared with filth, and lean, and melancholy and helpless. Recognising her as Sita by those unusual signs, and approaching that worshipful lady while alone, I said, 'I am, O Sita, an emissary of Rama and monkey begotten by *Pavana*! 53 Desirous of having a sight of thee, hither have I come travelling through the skies! Protected by Sugriva, that monarch of all the monkeys, the royal brothers Rama and Lakshmana are in peace! And Rama, O lady, with Sumitra's son, hath enquired of thy welfare! And Sugriva also, on account of his friendship (with Rama and Lakshmana) enquireth of thy welfare. Followed by all the monkeys, thy husband will soon be here. Confide in me, O adorable lady, I am a monkey and not a *Rakshasa*!' Thus addressed by me, Sita seemed to meditate for a moment and then replied to me, saying, 'From the words of *Avindhya* I know that thou art Hanuman! O mighty-armed one, Avindhya is an old and respected *Rakshasa*! He told me that Sugriva is surrounded by counsellors like thee. Thou mayst depart now!' And with these words she gave me this jewel as a credential. And, indeed, it was by means of this jewel that the faultless Sita had been able to support her existence. And the daughter of Janaka further told me as a token from her, that by thee, O tiger among men, a blade of grass (inspired with *Mantras* and thus converted into a fatal weapon) had once been shot at a crow while ye were on the breast of the mighty hill known by the name of *Chitrakuta*! And this she said as evidence of my having met her and hers being really the princess of Videha. I then caused myself to be seized by Ravana's soldiers, and then set fire to the city of Lanka!'"

SECTION CCLXXXI

"Markandeya said, 'It was on the breast of that very hill where Rama was seated with those foremost of monkeys that great monkey chiefs at the command of Sugriva, began to flock together. The father-in-law of Vali, the illustrious Sushena, accompanied by a thousand crores of active apes, came to Rama. And those two foremost of monkeys endued with mighty energy, viz., Gaya and Gavakshya, each accompanied by a hundred crores of monkeys, showed themselves there. And, O king, Gavakshya also of terrible mien and endued with a bovine tail, showed himself there, having collected sixty thousand crores of monkeys. And the renowned Gandhamadana, dwelling on the mountains of the same name, collected a hundred thousand crores of monkeys. And the intelligent and mighty monkey known by the name of Panasa mustered together fifty-two crores of monkeys. 54 And that foremost and illustrious of monkeys named Dadhimukha of mighty energy mustered a large army of monkeys possessed of terrible prowess. And Jamvuvan showed himself there with a hundred thousand crores of black bears of terrible deeds and faces having the *Tilaka* mark. 55 And these and many other chiefs of monkey-chiefs, countless in number, O king, came there for aiding Rama's cause. And endued with bodies huge as mountain-peaks and roaring like lions, loud was the uproar that was heard there made by those monkeys running restlessly from place to place. And some of them looked like mountain-peaks, and some looked like buffaloes. And some were of the hue of autumnal clouds and the faces of some were red as vermillion. And some rose high, and some fell down, and some cut capers, and some scattered the dust, as they mustered together from various directions. And that monkey army, vast as the sea at full tide, encamped there at Sugriva's bidding. And after those foremost of monkeys had mustered from every direction, the illustrious descendant of Raghu, with Sugriva by his side, set out in an auspicious moment of a very fair day under a lucky constellation, accompanied by that host arrayed in order of battle, as if for the purpose of destroying all the worlds. And Hanuman, the son of the Wind-god, was in the van of that host, while the rear was protected by the fearless son of Sumitra. And surrounded by the monkey-chiefs, those princes of Raghu's house with fingers cased in *guana* skin, shone, as they went, like the Sun and the Moon in the midst of the planets. And that monkey host armed with stones and *Sola* and *Tola* trees, looked very much like a far-extending field of corn under the morning sun. And that mighty army, protected by Nala and Nila and Angada and Kratha and Mainda and Dwivida, marched forth for achieving the purpose of Raghava. And encamping successively, without interruption of any kind, on wide and healthy tracts and valleys abounding with fruits and roots and water and honey and meat, the monkey host at last reached the shores of the brimy sea. And like unto a second ocean, that mighty army with its countless colours, having reached the shores of sea, took up its abode there. Then the illustrious son of Dasaratha, addressing Sugriva amongst all those foremost monkeys, spoke unto him these words that were suited to the occasion, "This army is large. The ocean also is difficult to cross. What contrivance, therefore, commends itself to thee for crossing the ocean?" At these words, many vain-glorious monkeys answered, "We are fully able to cross the sea." This answer, however, was not of much use, as all could not avail of that means. Some of the monkeys proposed to cross the sea in boats, and some in rafts of various kinds. Rama, however, conciliating them all, said, "This cannot be. The sea here is a full hundred *Yojanas* in width. All the monkeys, ye heroes, will not be able to cross it. This proposal, therefore, that ye have made, is not consonant to reason. Besides we have not the number of boats necessary for carrying all our troops. How, again, can one like us raise such obstacles in the way of the merchants? Our army is very large. The foe wilt make a great havoc if a hole is detected. Therefore, to cross the sea in boats and rafts doth not recommend itself to me. I will, however, pray to the Ocean for the necessary means. Foregoing food, I will lie down on the shore. He will certainly show himself to me. If, however, he doth not show himself, I will chastise him then by means of my great weapons that are more blazing than fire itself and are incapable of being baffled!" Having said these words, both Rama and Lakshmana touched water 56 and duly laid themselves down on a bed of *kusa* grass on the seashore. The divine and illustrious Ocean then, that lord of male and female rivers, surrounded by aquatic animals, appeared unto Rama in a vision. And addressing Rama in sweet accents, the genius of the Ocean, surrounded by countless mines of gems, said, "O son of Kausalya, tell me what aid, O bull among men, I am to render thee! I also have sprung from the race of Ikshwaku and am, therefore, a relative of thine!" Rama replied unto him, saying, "O lord of rivers, male and female, I desire thee to grant me a way for my troops, passing along which I may slay the Ten-headed (Ravana), that wretch of Pulastya's race! If thou dost not grant the way I beg of thee, I will then dry thee up by means of my celestial arrows inspired with *mantras*!" And hearing these words of Rama, the genius of Varuna's abode, joining his hands, answered in great affliction, "I do not desire to put any obstacle in thy way. I am no foe of thine! Listen, O Rama, to these words, and having listened, do what is proper! If, at thy command, I get a way for the passage of thy army, others then, from strength of their bows, will command me to do the same! In thy army there is a monkey of the name of Nala, who is a skilful mechanic. And endued with great strength, Nala is the son of *Tashtri*, the divine artificer of the Universe. And whether it is wood, or grass or stone, that he will throw into my waters, I will support the same on my surface, and thus wilt thou have a bridge (over which to pass)!" And having said these words, the genius of the Ocean disappeared. And Rama awaking, called Nala unto him and said, "Build thou a bridge over the sea! Thou alone, I am sure, art able to do it!" And it was by this means that the descendant of Kakutstha's race caused a bridge to be built that was ten *Yojanas* in width and a hundred *Yojanas* in length. And to this day that bridge is celebrated over all the world by the name of *Nala's bridge*. And having completed that bridge, Nala, of body huge as a hill, came away at the command of Rama.

"'And while Rama was on this side of the ocean, the virtuous Vibhishana, the brother of the king of the Rakshasas accompanied by four of his counsellors, came unto Rama. And the high-souled Rama received him with due welcome. Sugriva, however, feared, thinking he might be a spy. The son of Raghu, meanwhile perfectly satisfied (with Vibhishana) in consequence of the sincerity of his exertions and the many indications of his good conduct, worshipped him with respect. And he also installed Vibhishana in the sovereignty of all the Rakshasas and made him his own junior counsellor, and a friend of Lakshmana's. And it was under Vibhishana's guidance, O king, that Rama with all his troops crossed the great ocean by means of that bridge in course of a month. And having crossed the ocean and arrived at Lanka, Rama caused its extensive and numerous gardens to be devastated by his monkeys. And while Rama's troops were there, two of Ravana's counsellors and officers, named Suka and Sarana, who had come as spies, having assumed the shape of monkeys, were seized by Vibhishana. And when those wanderers of the night assumed their real Rakshasa forms, Rama showed them his troop and dismissed them quietly. And having quartered his troops in those woods that skirted the city, Rama then sent the monkey Angada with great wisdom as his envoy to Ravana.'"

SECTION CCLXXXII

"Markandeya said, 'Having quartered his army in those groves abounding with food and water and with fruits and roots, the descendant of Kakutstha began to watch over them with care. Ravana, on the other hand, planted in his city many appliances constructed according to the rules of military science. And his city, naturally impregnable on account of its strong ramparts and gate-ways, had seven trenches, that were deep and full of water to the brim and that abounded with fishes and sharks and alligators, made more impregnable still by means of pointed stakes of *Khadira* wood. And the ramparts, heaped with stones, were made impregnable by means of catapults. And the warriors (who guarded the walls) were armed with earthen pots filled with venomous snakes, and with resinous powders of many kinds. And they were also armed with clubs, and fire-brands and arrows and lances and swords and battle-axes. And they had also *Sataghnis* 57 and stout maces steeped in wax. 58 And at all the gates of the city were planted movable and immovable encampments manned by large numbers of infantry supported by countless elephants and horses. And Angada, having reached one of the gates of the city, was made known to the Rakshasas. And he entered the town without suspicion or fear. And surrounded by countless Rakshasas, that hero in his beauty looked like the Sun himself in the midst of masses of clouds. And having approached the hero of Pulastya's race in the midst of his counsellors, the eloquent Angada saluted the king and began to deliver Rama's message in these words, "That descendant of Raghu, O king, who ruleth at Kosala and whose renown hath spread over the whole world, sayeth unto thee these words suited to the occasion. Accept thou that message and act according to it! Provinces and towns, in consequence of their connection with sinful kings incapable of controlling their souls, are themselves polluted and destroyed. By the violent abduction of Sita, thou alone hast injured me! Thou, however, wilt become the cause of death to many unoffending persons. Possessed of power and filled with pride, thou hast, before this, slain many *Rishis* living in the woods, and insulted the very gods. Thou hast slain also many great kings and many weeping women. For those transgressions of thine, retribution is about to overtake thee! I will slay thee with thy counsellors. Fight and show thy courage! 59 O wanderer of the night, behold the power of my bow, although I am but a man! Release Sita, the daughter of Janaka!

If thou dost not release her, I shall make the Earth divested of all Rakshasas with my keen-edged arrows!" Hearing these defiant words of the enemy, king Ravana bore them ill, becoming senseless with wrath. And thereupon four Rakshasas skilled in reading every sign of their master, seized Angada like four hawks seizing a tiger. With those Rakshasas, however, holding him fast by his limbs, Angada leaped upwards and alighted on the palace terrace. And as he leaped up with a great force, those wanderers of the night fell down the earth, and bruised by the violence of the fall, had their ribs broken. And from the golden terrace on which he had alighted, he took a downward leap. And overleaping the walls of Lanka, he alighted to where his comrades were. And approaching the presence of the lord of Kosala and informing him of everything, the monkey Angada endued with great energy retired to refresh himself, dismissed with due respect by Rama.

"'The descendant of Raghu then caused the ramparts of Lanka to be broken down by a united attack of all those monkeys endued with the speed of the wind. Then Lakshmana, with Vibhishana and the king of the bears marching in the van, blew up the southern gate of the city that was almost impregnable. Rama then attacked Lanka with a hundred thousand crores of monkeys, all possessed of great skill in battle, and endued with reddish complexions like those of young camels. And those crores of greyish bears with long arms, and legs and huge paws, and generally supporting themselves on their broad haunches, were also urged on to support the attack. And in consequence of those monkeys leaping up and leaping down and leaping in transverse directions, the Sun himself, his bright disc completely shaded, became invisible for the dust they raised. And the citizens of Lanka beheld the wall of their town assume all over a tawny hue, covered by monkeys of complexions yellow as the ears of paddy, and grey as *Shirisha* flowers, and red as the rising Sun, and white as flax or hemp. And the Rakshasas, O king, with their wives and elders, were struck with wonders at that sight. And the monkey warriors began to pull down pillars made of precious stones and the terraces and tops of palatial mansions. And breaking into fragments the propellers of catapults and other engines, they began to cast them about in all directions. And taking up the *Sataghnis* along with the discs, the clubs, and stones, they threw them down into the city with great force and loud noise. And attacked thus by the monkeys, those Rakshasas that had been placed on the walls to guard them, fled precipitately by hundreds and thousands.

"'Then hundreds of thousands of Rakshasas, of terrible mien, and capable of assuming any form at will, came out at the command of the king. And pouring a perfect shower of arrows and driving the denizens of the forest, those warriors, displaying great prowess, adorned the ramparts.

And soon those wanderers of the night, looking like masses of flesh, and of terrible mien, forced the monkeys to leave the walls. And mangled by the enemies' lances, numerous monkey-chiefs fell down from the ramparts, and crushed by the falling columns and gate-ways, numerous Rakshasas also fell down to rise no more. And the monkeys and the brave Rakshasas that commenced to eat up the foe, struggled, seizing one another by the hair, and mangling and tearing one another with their nails and teeth. And the monkeys and the Rakshasas roared and yelled frightfully, and while many of both parties were slain and fell down to rise no more, neither side gave up the contest. And Rama continued all the while to shower a thick downpour of arrows like the very clouds. And the arrows he shot, enveloping Lanka, killed large numbers of Rakshasas. And the son of Sumitra, too, that mighty bowman incapable of being fatigued in battle, naming particular Rakshasas stationed on the ramparts, slew them with his clothyard shafts. And then the monkey host, having achieved success was withdrawn at the command of Rama, after it had thus pulled down the fortifications of Lanka and made all objects within the city capable of being aimed at by the besieging force.'"

SECTION CCLXXXIII

"Markandeya said, 'And while those troops (thus withdrawn) were reposing themselves in their quarters, many little Rakshasas and *Pisachas* owning Ravana as their leader, penetrated amongst them. And among these were *Parvana, Patana, Jambha, Khara, Krodha-vasa, Hari, Praruja, Aruja* and *Praghasa*, and others. And as these wicked ones were penetrating (the monkey host) in their invisible forms, Vibhishana, who had the knowledge thereof, broke the spell of their invisibility. And once seen, O king, by the powerful and long-leaping monkeys, they were all slain and prostrated on the earth, deprived of life. And unable to endure this, Ravana marched out at the head of his troops. And surrounded by his terrible army of Rakshasas and *Pisachas*, Ravana who was conversant with the rules of warfare like a second *Usanas* invested the monkey host, having disposed his troops in that array which is named after *Usanas* himself. And beholding Ravana advancing with his army disposed in that array, Rama, following the mode recommended by Vrihaspati, disposed his troops in counter array for opposing that wanderer of the night. And coming up quickly, Ravana began to fight with Rama. And Lakshmana singled out Indrajit, and Sugriva singled out Virupakshya, and Nikharvata fought with Tara, and Nala with Tunda, and Patusa with Panasa. And each warrior, advancing up to him whom he regarded as his match, began to fight with him on that field of battle, relying on the strength of his own arms, and that encounter, so frightful to timid persons, soon became terrible and fierce like that between the gods and the *Asuras* in the days of old. And Ravana covered Rama with a shower of darts and lances and swords, and Rama also afflicted Ravana with his whetted arrows of iron furnished with the sharpest points, and in the same way Lakshmana smote the contending Indrajit with arrows capable of penetrating into the most vital parts and Indrajit also smote Sumitra's son with an arrowy shower. And Vibhishana showered upon Prahasta and Prahasta showered upon Vibhishana, without any regard for each other a thick downpour of winged arrows furnished with the sharpest points. And thus between those mighty warriors there came about an encounter of celestial weapons of great force, at which the three worlds with their mobile and immobile creatures were sorely distressed.'"

SECTION CCLXXXIV

"Markandeya said, 'Then Prahasta, suddenly advancing up to Vibhishana and uttering a loud yell, struck him with his mace. But though struck with that mace of terrible force, the mighty-armed Vibhishana of great wisdom, without wavering in the least, stood still as the mountains of Himavat. Then Vibhishana, taking up a huge and mighty javelin furnished with a hundred bells, inspired it with *mantras* and hurled it at the head of his adversary. And by the impetuosity of that weapon rushing with the force of the thunderbolt, Prahasta's head was severed off, and he thereupon looked like a mighty tree broken by the wind. And beholding that wanderer of the night, Prahasta, thus slain in battle, Dhumraksha rushed with great impetuosity against the monkey-host. And beholding the soldiers of Dhumraksha, looking like the clouds and endued with terrible mien, advancing up towards them, the monkey-chief suddenly broke and fled. And seeing those foremost of monkeys suddenly give way, that tiger among monkeys, Hanuman, the son of Pavana, began to advance. And beholding the son of Pavana staying still on the field of battle, the retreating monkeys, O king, one and all quickly rallied. Then mighty and great and fearful was the uproar that arose there in consequence of the warriors of Rama and Ravana rushing against each other. And in that battle which raged terribly the field soon became miry with blood. And Dhumraksha afflicted the monkey-host with volleys of winged shafts. Then that vanquisher of foes, Hanuman, the son of Pavana, quickly seized that advancing leader of the Rakshasa. And the encounter that took place between that monkey and the Rakshasa hero, each desirous of defeating the other, was fierce and terrible, like that of Indra and Prahlada (in days of yore). And the Rakshasa struck the monkey with his maces and spiked clubs while the monkey struck the Rakshasa with trunks of trees unshorn of their branches. Then Hanuman, the son of Pavana, slew in great wrath that Rakshasa along with his charioteer and horses and broke his chariot also into pieces. And beholding Dhumraksha, that foremost of Rakshasa, thus slain, the monkeys, abandoning all fear, rushed against the Rakshasa army with great valour. And slaughtered in large numbers by the victorious and powerful monkeys, the Rakshasas became dispirited and fled in fear to Lanka. And the surviving wreck of the Rakshasa army, having reached the city, informed king Ravana of everything that had happened. And hearing from them that Prahasta and that mighty archer Dhumraksha, had both, with their armies, been slain by the powerful monkeys, Ravana drew a deep sigh and springing up from his excellent seat, said,—the time is come for Kumbhakarna to act.—And having said this, he awoke, by means of various loud-sounding instruments, his brother Kumbhakarna from his deep and prolonged slumbers. And having awaked him with great efforts, the Rakshasa king, still afflicted with anxiety, addressed the mighty Kumbhakarna and said unto him when seated at his ease on his bed, having perfectly recovered consciousness and self-possession, these words, "Thou, indeed, art happy, O Kumbhakarna, that canst enjoy profound and undisturbed repose, unconscious of the terrible calamity that hath overtaken us! Rama with his monkey host hath crossed the Ocean by a bridge and disregarding us all is waging a terrible war (against us). I have stealthily brought away his wife Sita, the daughter of Janaka, and it is to recover her that he hath come hither, after having made a bridge over the great Ocean. Our great kinsmen also, Prahasta and others, have already been slain by him. And, O scourge of thy enemies, there is not another person, save thee, that can slay Rama! Therefore, O warrior, putting on thy armour, do thou set out this day for the purpose of vanquishing Rama and his followers! The two younger brothers of Dushana, viz., Vajravega and Promathin, will join thee with their forces!" And having said this unto the mighty Kumbhakarna, the Rakshasa king gave instructions to Vajravega and Promathin as to what they should do. And accepting his advice, those two warlike brothers of Dushana quickly marched out of the city, preceded by Kumbhakarna.'"

SECTION CCLXXXV

"Markandeya said, 'Then Kumbhakarna set out from the city, accompanied by his followers. And soon he beheld the victorious monkey troops encamped before him. And passing them by with the object of seeking out Rama, he beheld the son of Sumitra standing at his post, bow in hand. Then the monkey warriors, speedily advancing towards him, surrounded him on all sides. And then they commenced to strike him with numberless large trees. And many amongst them fearlessly began to tear his body with their nails. And those monkeys began to fight with him in various ways approved by the laws of warfare. And they soon overwhelmed that chief of the Rakshasas with a shower of terrible weapons of various kinds. And attacked by them thus, Kumbhakarna only laughed at them and began to eat them up. And he devoured those foremost of monkeys known by the name of Chala, and Chandachala, and Vajravahu. And beholding that fearful act of the *Rakshasa*, other monkeys were frightened and set forth a loud wail of fear. And hearing the screams of those monkey-leaders, Sugriva boldly advanced towards Kumbhakarna. And that high-souled king of the monkeys swiftly approaching the *Rakshasa*, violently struck him on the head with the trunk of a *Sala* tree. And though the high-souled Sugriva always prompt in action broke that *Sala* tree on the head of Kumbhakarna, he failed to make any impression on that *Rakshasa*. And then, as if roused from his torpor by that blow, Kumbhakarna stretching forth his arms seized Sugriva by main force. And beholding Sugriva dragged away by the *Rakshasa*, the heroic son of Sumitra, that delighter of his friends, rushed towards Kumbhakarna. And that slayer of hostile heroes, Lakshmana, advancing towards Kumbhakarna, discharged at him an impetuous and mighty arrow furnished with golden wings. And that arrow, cutting through his coat of mail and penetrating into his body, passed through it outright and struck into the earth, stained with the *Rakshasa's* blood. Kumbhakarna then, having his breast thus bored through, released the king of monkeys. And taking up a huge mass of stone as his weapon, the mighty warrior Kumbhakarna then rushed towards the son of Sumitra, aiming it at him. And as the *Rakshasa* rushed towards him, Lakshmana cut off his upraised arms by means of a couple of keen-edged shafts furnished with heads resembling razors. But as soon as the two arms of the Rakshasa were thus cut off, double that number of arms soon appeared on his person. Sumitra's son, however, displaying his skill in weapons, soon by means of similar arrows cut off those arms also, each of which had seized a mass of stone. At this, that *Rakshasa* assumed a form enormously huge and furnished with numerous heads and legs and arms. Then the son of Sumitra rived, with a *Brahma* weapon, that warrior looking like an assemblage of hill. And rent by means of that celestial weapon, that *Rakshasa* fell on the field of battle like a huge tree with spreading branches suddenly consumed by heaven's thunderbolt. And beholding Kumbhakarna endued with great activity and resembling the *Asura* Vritra himself, deprived of life and prostrated on the field of battle, the *Rakshasa* warriors fled in fear. And beholding the *Rakshasa* warriors running away from the field of battle, the younger brother of Dushana, rallying them, rushed in great wrath upon the son of Sumitra. Sumitra's son, however, with a loud roar, received with his winged shafts both those wrathful warriors, Vajravega and Promathin, rushing towards him. The battle then, O son of Pritha, that took place between those two younger brothers of Dushana on the one hand and the intelligent Lakshmana on the other, was exceedingly furious and made the bristles of the spectators stand on end. And Lakshmana overwhelmed the two *Rakshasas* with a perfect shower of arrows. And those two *Rakshasa* heroes, on the other hand, both of them excited with fury, covered Lakshmana with an arrowy hail. And that terrible encounter between Vajravega and Promathin and the mighty-armed Lakshmana lasted for a short while. And Hanuman, the son of Pavana, taking up a mountain peak, rushed towards one of the brothers, and with that weapon took the life of the Rakshasa Vajravega. And that mighty monkey, Nala, also, with a large mass of rock, crushed Promathin, that other younger brother of Dushana. The deadly struggle, however, between the soldiers of Rama and Ravana, rushing against one another, instead of coming to an end even after this, raged on as before. And hundreds of *Rakshasas* were slain by the denizens of the forest, while many of the latter were slain by the former. The loss, however, in killed, of the *Rakshasas* was far greater than that of the monkeys.

SECTION CCLXXXVI

"Markandeya said, 'Learning that Kumbhakarna had with his followers, fallen in battle as also that great warrior Prahasta, and Dhumraksha too of mighty energy, Ravana then addressed his heroic son Indrajit saying, "O slayer of foes, slay thou in battle Rama and Sugriva and Lakshmana. My good son, it was by thee that this blazing fame of mine had been acquired by vanquishing in battle that wielder of the thunderbolt, the thousand-eyed Lord of Sachi! Having the power of appearing and vanishing at thy will, slay thou, O smiter of foes, my enemies by means, O thou foremost of all wielders of weapons, of thy celestial arrows received as boons (from the gods)! Rama and Lakshmana and Sugriva are incapable of enduring the bare touch of thy weapons. What shall I say, therefore, of their followers? That cessation of hostilities which could not be brought about by either Prahasta or Kumbhakarna in battle, be it thine, O mighty-armed one, to bring about! Slaying my enemies with all their army by means of thy keen-edged shafts, enhance my joy to-day, O son, as thou didst once before by vanquishing Vasava!" Thus addressed by him, Indrajit said—So be it,—and encased in mail he quickly ascended his chariot, and proceeded, O king, towards the field of battle. And then that bull amongst *Rakshasas* loudly announcing his own name, challenged Lakshmana endued with auspicious marks, to a single combat. And Lakshmana, thus challenged, rushed towards that *Rakshasa*, with his bow and arrows, and striking terror into his adversary's heart by means of the flapping of his bow-string on the leathern case of his left hand. And the encounter that took place between those warriors that defied each other's prowess and each of whom was desirous of vanquishing the other, and both of whom were conversant with celestial weapons, was terrible in the extreme. But when the son of Ravana found that he could not by his arrows gain any advantage over his adversary, that foremost of mighty warriors mustered all his energy. And Indrajit then began to hurl at Lakshmana with great force numberless javelins. The son of Sumitra, however, cut them into fragments by means of his own keen-edged arrows. And those javelins, thus cut into pieces by the keen-edged arrows of Lakshmana, dropped down upon the ground. Then the handsome Angada, the son of Vali, taking up a large tree, rushed impetuously at Indrajit and struck him with it on the head. Undaunted at this, Indrajit of mighty energy sought to smite Angada with a lance. Just at that juncture, however, Lakshmana cut into pieces the lance taken up by Ravana's son. The son of Ravana then took up a mace and struck on the left flank that foremost of monkeys, the heroic Angada who was then staying close beside him. Angada, the powerful son of Vali, little recking that stroke, hurled at Indrajit a mighty Sala stem. And hurled in wrath by Angada for the destruction of Indrajit, that tree, O son of Pritha, destroyed Indrajit's chariot along with his horses and charioteer. And thereupon jumping from his horseless and driverless car, the son of Ravana disappeared from sight, O king, by aid of his powers of illusion. And beholding that *Rakshasa*, abundantly endued with powers of illusion, disappear so suddenly, Rama proceeded towards that spot and began to protect his troops with care. Indrajit, however, with arrows, obtained as boons from the gods, began to pierce both Rama and mighty Lakshmana in every part of their bodies. Then the heroic Rama and Lakshmana both continued to contend with their arrows against Ravana's son who had made himself invisible by his powers of illusion. But Indrajit continued to shower in wrath all over those lions among men his keen-edged shafts by hundreds and thousands. And seeking that invisible warrior who was ceaselessly showering his arrows, the monkeys penetrated into every part of the firmament, armed with huge masses of stone. Them as well as the two brothers, however, the invisible *Rakshasa* began to afflict with his shafts. Indeed, the son of Ravana, concealing himself by his powers of illusion, furiously attacked the monkey host. And the heroic brothers Rama and Lakshmana, pierced all over with arrows, dropped down on the ground like the Sun and the Moon fallen down from the firmament.'"

SECTION CCLXXXVII

"Markandeya said, 'Beholding both the brothers Rama and Lakshmana prostrate on the ground, the son of Ravana tied them in a net-work of those arrows of his which he had obtained as boons. And tied by Indrajit on the field of battle by means of that arrowy net, those heroic tigers among men resembled a couple of hawks immured in a cage. And beholding those heroes prostrate on the ground pierced with hundreds of arrows, Sugriva with all the monkeys stood surrounding them on all sides. And the king of the monkeys stood there, accompanied by Sushena and Mainda and Dwivida, and Kumuda and Angada and Hanuman and Nila and Tara and Nala. And Vibhishana, having achieved success in another part of the field, soon arrived at that spot, and roused those heroes from insensibility, awakening them by means of the weapon called *Prajna*. 60 Then Sugriva soon extracted the arrows from their bodies. And by means of that most efficacious medicine called the *Visalya*, 61 applied with celestial *mantras*, those human heroes regained their consciousness. And the arrow having been extracted from their bodies, those mighty warriors in a moment rose from their recumbent posture, their pains and fatigue thoroughly alleviated. And beholding Rama the descendant of Ikshwaku's race, quite at his ease, Vibhishana, O son of Pritha, joining his hands, told him these words, "O chastiser of foes, at the command of the king of the Guhyakas, a Guhyaka hath come from the White mountains, bringing with him his water! 62 O great king, this water is a present to thee from Kuvera, so that all creatures that are invisible may, O chastiser of foes, become visible to thee! This water laved over the eyes will make every invisible creature visible to thee, as also to any other person to whom thou mayst give it!" —Saying— *So be it*, —Rama took that sacred water, and sanctified his own eyes therewith. And the high-minded Lakshmana also did the same. And Sugriva and Jambuvan, and Hanuman and Angada, and Mainda and Dwivida, and Nila and many other foremost of the monkeys, laved their eyes with that water. And thereupon it exactly happened as Vibhishana had said, for, O Yudhishthira, soon did the eyes of all these became capable of beholding things that could not be seen by the unassisted eye!

"'Meanwhile, Indrajit, after the success he had won, went to his father. And having informed him of the feats he had achieved, he speedily returned to the field of battle and placed himself at the van of his army. The son of

Sumitra then, under Vibhishana's guidance, rushed towards that wrathful son of Ravana coming back, from desire of battle, to lead the attack. And Lakshmana, excited to fury and receiving a hint from Vibhishana, and desiring to slay Indrajit who had not completed his daily sacrifice, smote with his arrows that warrior burning to achieve success. And desirous of vanquishing each other, the encounter that took place between them was exceedingly wonderful like that (in days of yore) between the Lord of celestials and Prahrada. And Indrajit pierced the son of Sumitra with arrows penetrating into his very vitals. And the son of Sumitra also pierced Ravana's son with arrows of fiery energy. And pierced with Lakshmana's arrows, the son of Ravana became senseless with wrath. And he shot at Lakshmana eight shafts fierce as venomous snakes. Listen now, O Yudhishthira, as I tell thee how the heroic son of Sumitra then took his adversary's life by means of three winged arrows possessed of the energy and effulgence of fire! With one of these, he severed from Indrajit's body that arm of his enemy which had grasped the bow. With the second he caused that other arm which had held the arrows, to drop down on the ground. With the third that was bright and possessed of the keenest edge, he cut off his head decked with a beautiful nose and bright with earrings. And shorn of arms and head, the trunk became fearful to behold. And having slain the foe thus, that foremost of mighty men then slew with his arrows the charioteer of his adversary. And the horses then dragged away the empty chariot into the city. And Ravana then beheld that car without his son on it. And hearing that his son had been slain, Ravana suffered his heart to be overpowered with grief. And under the influence of extreme grief and affliction, the king of the Rakshasas suddenly cherished the desire of killing the princess of Mithila. And seizing a sword, the wicked Rakshasa hastily ran towards that lady staying within the *Asoka* wood longing to behold her lord. Then Avindhya beholding that sinful purpose of the wicked wretch, appeased his fury. Listen, O Yudhishthira, to the reasons urged by Avindhya! That wise Rakshasa said, "Placed as thou art on the blazing throne of an empire, it behoveth thee not to slay a woman! Besides, this woman is already slain, considering that she is a captive in thy power! I think, she would not be slain if only her body were destroyed. Slay thou her husband! He being slain, she will be slain too! Indeed, not even he of an hundred sacrifices (Indra) is thy equal in prowess! The gods with Indra at their head, had repeatedly been affrighted by thee in battle!" With these and many other words of the same import, Avindhya succeeded in appeasing Ravana. And the latter did, indeed, listen to his counsellor's speech. And that wanderer of the night, then, resolved to give battle himself, sheathed his sword, and issued orders for preparing his chariot.'"

SECTION CCLXXXVIII

"Markandeya said, 'The Ten-necked (Ravana), excited to fury at the death of his beloved son, ascended his car decked with gold and gems. And surrounded by terrible *Rakshasas* with various kinds of weapons in their hands, Ravana rushed towards Rama, fighting with numerous monkey-chiefs. And beholding him rushing in wrath towards the monkey army, Mainda and Nila and Nala and Angada, and Hanuman and Jambuvan, surrounded him with all their troops. And those foremost of monkeys and bears began to exterminate with trunks of trees, the soldiers of the Ten-necked (Ravana), in his very sight. And beholding the enemy slaughtering his troops, the *Rakshasa* king, Ravana, possessed of great powers of illusion, began to put them forth. And forth from his body began to spring hundreds and thousands of *Rakshasas* armed with arrows and lances and double-edged swords in hand. Rama, however, with a celestial weapon slew all those *Rakshasas*. The king of the *Rakshasas* then once more put forth his prowess of illusion. The Ten-faced, producing from his body numerous warriors resembling, O Bharata, both Rama and Lakshmana, rushed towards the two brothers. And then those *Rakshasas*, hostile to Rama and Lakshmana and armed with bows and arrows, rushed towards Rama, and beholding that power of illusion put forth by the king of *Rakshasas*, that descendant of Ikshwaku's race, the son of Sumitra, addressed Rama in these heroic words, "Slay those *Rakshasas*, those wretches with forms like thy own!" And Rama, thereupon slew those and other *Rakshasas* of forms resembling his own. And that time Matali, the charioteer of Indra, approached Rama on the field of battle, with a car effulgent as the Sun and unto which were yoked horses of a tawny hue. And Matali said, "O son of Kakutstha's race, this excellent and victorious car, unto which have been yoked this pair of tawny horses, belongs to the Lord of celestials! It is on this excellent car, O tiger among men, that Indra hath slain in battle hundreds of *Daityas* and *Danavas*! Therefore, O tiger among men, do thou, riding on the car driven by me, quickly slay Ravana in battle! Do not delay in achieving this!" Thus addressed by him, the descendant of Raghu's race, however, doubted the truthful words of Matali, thinking this is another illusion produced by the *Rakshasas*—Vibhishana then addressed him saying, "This, O tiger among men, is no illusion of the wicked Ravana! Ascend thou this chariot quickly, for this, O thou of great effulgence, belongeth to Indra!" The descendant of Kakutstha then cheerfully said unto Vibhishana, "So be it", and riding on that car, rushed wrathfully upon Ravana. And when Ravana, too, rushed against his antagonist, a loud wail of woe was set up by the creatures of the Earth, while the celestials in heaven sent forth a leonine roar accompanied by beating of large drums. The encounter then that took place between the Ten-necked *Rakshasa* and that prince of Raghu's race, was fierce in the extreme. Indeed, that combat between them hath no parallel elsewhere. And the *Rakshasa* hurled at Rama a terrible javelin looking like Indra's thunderbolt and resembling a Brahmana's curse on the point of utterance. 63 Rama, however, quickly cut into fragments that javelin by means of his sharp arrows. And beholding that most difficult feat, Ravana was struck with fear. But soon his wrath was excited and the Ten-necked hero began to shower on Rama whetted arrows by thousands and tens of thousands and countless weapons of various kinds, such as rockets and javelins and maces and battle-axes and darts of various kinds and Shataghnis and *whetted shafts*. And beholding that terrible form of illusion displayed by the Ten-necked *Rakshasa*, the monkeys fled in fear in all directions. Then the descendant of Kakutstha, taking out of his quiver an excellent arrow furnished with handsome wings and golden feathers and a bright and beautiful head, fixed it on the bow with *Brahmasira* mantra. And beholding that excellent arrow transformed by Rama, with proper *mantras* into a Brahma weapon, the celestials and the Gandharvas with Indra at their head, began to rejoice. And the gods and the *Danavas* and the *Kinnaras* were led by the display of that *Brahma* weapon to regard the life of their Rakshasa foe almost closed. Then Rama shot that terrible weapon of unrivalled energy, destined to compass Ravana's death, and resembling the curse of a Brahmana on the point of utterance. And as soon, O Bharata, as that arrow was shot by Rama from his bow drawn to a circle, the *Rakshasa* king with his chariot and charioteer and horses blazed up, surrounded on all sides by a terrific fire. And beholding Ravana slain by Rama of famous achievements, the celestials, with the *Gandharvas* and the *Charanas*, rejoiced exceedingly. And deprived of universal dominion by the energy of the Brahma weapon, the five elements forsook the illustrious Ravana, and were consumed by the *Brahma* weapon, the physical ingredients of Ravana's body. His flesh and blood were all reduced to nothingness,—so that the ashes even could not be seen.'"

SECTION CCLXXXIX

"Markandeya said, 'Having slain Ravana, that wretched king of the *Rakshasas* and foe of the celestials, Rama with his friends and Sumitra's son rejoiced exceedingly. And after the Ten-necked (*Rakshasa*) hath been slain, the celestials with the *Rishis* at their head, worshipped Rama of mighty arms, blessing and uttering the word *Jaya* repeatedly. And all the celestials and the *Gandharvas* and the denizens of the celestial regions gratified Rama of eyes like lotus leaves, with hymns and flowery showers. And having duly worshipped Rama, they all went away to those regions whence they had come. And, O thou of unfading glory, the firmament at that time looked as if a great festival was being celebrated.

"'And having slain the Ten-necked *Rakshasa*, the lord Rama of worldwide fame, that conqueror of hostile cities, bestowed Lanka on Vibhishana. Then that old and wise counsellor (of Ravana) known by the name of Avindhya, with Sita walking before him but behind Vibhishana who was at the front, came out of the city. And with great humility Avindhya said unto the illustrious descendant of Kakutstha, "O illustrious one, accept thou this goddess, Janaka's daughter of excellent conduct!" Hearing these words, the descendant of Ikshwaku's race alighted from his excellent chariot and beheld Sita bathed in tears. And beholding that beautiful lady seated within her vehicle, afflicted with grief, besmeared with filth, with matted locks on head, and attired in dirty robes, Rama, afraid of the loss of his honour, said unto her, "Daughter of Videha, go withersover thou likest! Thou art now free! What should have been done by me, hath been done! O blessed lady, owning me for thy husband, it is not meet that thou shouldst grow old in the abode of the *Rakshasa*! It is for this I have slain that wanderer of the night! But how can one like us, acquainted with every truth of morality, embrace even for a moment a woman that had fallen into other's hands? O princess of Mithila whether thou art chaste or unchaste, I dare not enjoy thee, now that thou art like sacrificial butter lapped by a dog!" Hearing these cruel words, that adorable girl suddenly fell down in great affliction of heart, like a plantain tree severed from its roots. And the colour that was suffusing her face in consequence of the joy she had felt, quickly disappeared, like watery particles on a mirror blown thereon by the breath of the mouth. And hearing these words of Rama, all the monkeys also with Lakshmana became still as dead. Then the divine and pure-souled Brahma of four faces, that Creator of the Universe himself sprung from a lotus, showed himself on his car to Raghu's son. And Sakra and Agni and Vayu, and Yama and Varuna and the illustrious Lord of the *Yakshas*, and the holy *Rishis*, and king Dasaratha also in a celestial and effulgent form and on car drawn by swans, showed themselves. And then the firmament crowded with celestials and *Gandharvas* became as beautiful as the autumnal welkin spangled with stars. And rising up from the ground, the blessed and famous princess of Videha, in the midst of those present spoke unto Rama of wide chest, these words, "O prince, I impute no fault to thee, for thou art well acquainted with the behaviour that one should adopt towards both men and women. But hear thou these words of mine! The ever-moving Air is always present within every creature. If I have sinned, let him forsake my vital forces! If I have sinned, Oh, then let Fire, and Water, and Space, and Earth, like Air (whom I have already invoked), also forsake my vital forces! And as, O hero, I have never, even in my dreams, cherished the image of any other person, so be thou my lord as appointed by the gods." After Sita had spoken, a sacred voice, resounding through the whole of that region, was heard in the skies, gladdening the hearts of the high-souled monkeys. And the Wind-god was heard to say, "O son of Raghu, what Sita hath said is true! I am the god of Wind. The princess of Mithila is sinless! Therefore, O king, be united with thy wife!" And the god of Fire said, "O son of Raghu, I dwell within the bodies of all creatures! O descendant of Kakutstha, the princess of Mithila is not guilty of even the minutest fault!" And Varuna then said, "O son of Raghu, the humours in every creature's body derive their existence from me! I tell thee, let the princess of Mithila be accepted by thee!" And Brahma himself then said, "O descendant of Kakutstha, O son, in thee that art honest and pure and conversant with the duties of royal sages, this conduct is not strange. Listen, however, to these words of mine! Thou hast, O hero, slain this enemy of the gods, the *Gandharvas*, the *Nagas*, the *Yakshas*, the *Danavas*, and the great *Rishis*! It was through my grace that he had hitherto been unslayable of all creatures. And indeed, it was for some reason that I had tolerated him for some time! The wretch, however, abducted Sita for his own destruction. And as regards Sita, I protected her through Nalakuvera's curse. For that person had cursed Ravana of old, saying, that if he ever approached an unwilling woman, his head should certainly be split into a hundred fragments. Let no suspicion, therefore, be thine! O thou of great glory, accept thy wife! Thou hast indeed, achieved a mighty feat for the benefit of the gods, O thou that art of divine effulgence!" And last of all Dasaratha said, "I have been gratified with thee, O child! Blessed be thou,

I am thy father Dasaratha! I command thee to take back thy wife, and rule thy kingdom, O thou foremost of men!" Rama then replied, "If thou art my father, I salute thee with reverence, O king of kings! I shall indeed, return, at thy command, to the delightful city of Ayodhya!"'

"Markandeya continued, 'Thus addressed, his father, O bull of the Bharata race, gladly answered Rama, the corners of whose eyes were of a reddish hue, saying, "Return to Ayodhya and rule thou that kingdom! O thou of great glory, thy fourteen years (of exile) have been completed." Thus addressed by Dasaratha, Rama bowed to the gods, and saluted by his friends he was united with his wife, like the Lord of the celestials with the daughter of Puloman. And that chastiser of foes then gave a boon to Avindhya. And he also bestowed both riches and honours on the *Rakshasa* woman named *Trijata*. And when Brahma with all the celestials having Indra at their head, said unto Rama, "O thou that ownest Kausalya for thy mother, what boons after thy heart shall we grant thee?" Rama, thereupon, prayed them to grant him firm adherence to virtues and invincibility in respect of all foes. And he also asked for the restoration to life of all those monkeys that had been slain by the *Rakshasas*, and after Brahma had said—So be it, those monkeys, O king, restored to life, rose up from the field of battle, and Sita too, of great good fortune, granted unto Hanuman a boon, saying, "Let thy life, O son, last as long as (the fame of) Rama's achievements! And, O Hanuman of yellow eyes, let celestial viands and drinks be ever available to thee through my grace!"'

"'Then the celestials with Indra at their head all disappeared in the very sight of those warriors of spotless achievements. And beholding Rama united with the daughter of Janaka, the charioteer of Sakra, highly pleased, addressed him in the midst of friends, and said these words, "O thou of prowess that can never be baffled thou hast dispelled the sorrow of the celestials, the *Gandharvas*, the *Yakshas*, the *Asuras*, the *Nagas*, and human beings! As long, therefore, as the Earth will hold together, so long will all creatures with the celestials, the *Asuras*, the *Gandharvas*, the *Yakshas*, the *Rakshasas*, and the *Pannagas*, speak of thee." And having said these words unto Rama, Matali worshipped that son of Raghu, and having obtained the leave of that foremost of wielders of weapons, he went away, on that same chariot of solar effulgence. And Rama also, with Sumatra's son and Vibhishana, and accompanied by all the monkeys with Sugriva at their head, placing Sita in the van and having made arrangements for the protection of Lanka, recrossed the ocean by the same bridge. And he rode on that beautiful and sky-ranging chariot called the *Pushpaka* that was capable of going everywhere at the will of the rider. And that subduer of passions was surrounded by his principal counsellors in order of precedence. And arriving at that part of the sea-shore where he had formerly laid himself down, the virtuous king, with all the monkeys, pitched his temporary abode. And the son of Raghu then, bringing the monkeys before him in due time, worshipped them all, and gratifying them with presents of jewels and gems, dismissed them one after another. And after all the monkey-chiefs, and the apes with bovine tails, and the bears, had gone away, Rama re-entered Kishkindhya with Sugriva. And accompanied by both Vibhishana and Sugriva, Rama re-entered Kishkindhya riding on the *Pushpaka* car and showing the princess of Videha the woods along the way. And having arrived at Kishkindhya, Rama, that foremost of all smiters, installed the successful Angada as prince-regent of the kingdom. And accompanied by the same friends as also by Sumitra's son, Rama proceeded towards his city along the same path by which he had come. And having reached the city of Ayodhya, the king despatched Hanuman thence as envoy to Bharata. And Hanuman, having ascertained Bharata's intentions from external indications, gave him the good news (of Rama's arrival). And after the son of Pavana had come back, Rama entered *Nandigrama*. And having entered that town, Rama beheld Bharata besmeared with filth and attired in rags and seated with his elder brother's sandals placed before him. And being united, O bull of Bharata race, with both Bharata and Shatrughna, the mighty son of Raghu, along with Sumitra's son, began to rejoice exceedingly. And Bharata and Shatrughna also, united with their eldest brother, and beholding Sita, both derived great pleasure. And Bharata then, after having worshipped his returned brother, made over to him with great pleasure, the kingdom that had been in his hands as a sacred trust. And Vasishtha and Vamadeva then together installed that hero in the sovereignty (of Ayodhya) at the eighth Muhurta 64 of the day under the asterism called *Sravana*. And after his installation was over, Rama gave leave to well-pleased Sugriva the king of the monkeys, along with all his followers, as also to rejoicing Vibhishana of Pulastya's race, to return to their respective abodes. And having worshipped them with various articles of enjoyment, and done everything that was suitable to the occasion, Rama dismissed those friends of his with a sorrowful heart. And the son of Raghu then, having worshiped that *Pushpaka* chariot, joyfully gave it back unto Vaisravana. And then assisted by the celestial *Rishi* (Vasishtha), Rama performed on the banks of the *Gomati* ten horse-sacrifices without obstruction of any kind and with treble presents unto Brahmanas.'"

SECTION CCLXL

"Markandeya said, 'It was thus, O mighty-armed one, that Rama of immeasurable energy had suffered of old such excessive calamity in consequence of his exile in the woods! O tiger among men, do not grieve, for, O chastiser of foes, thou art *Kshatriya*! Thou too treadest in the path in which strength of arms is to be put forth,—the path that leadeth to tangible rewards. Thou hast not even a particle of sin. Even the celestials with Indra at their head, and the *Asuras* have to tread in the path that is trod by thee! It was after such afflictions that the wielder of the thunderbolt, aided by the *Maruts*, slew *Vritra*, and the invincible *Namuchi* and the Rakshasi of long tongue! He that hath assistance, always secureth the accomplishment of all his purposes! What is that which cannot be vanquished in battle by him that hath Dhananjaya for his brother? This Bhima, also, of terrible prowess, is the foremost of mighty persons. The heroic and youthful sons of Madravati again are mighty bowmen. With allies such as these, why dost thou despair, O chastiser of foes? These are capable of vanquishing the army of the wielder himself of the thunderbolt with the *Maruts* in the midst. Having these mighty bowmen of celestial forms for thy allies, thou, O bull of Bharata race, art sure to conquer in battle all thy foes! Behold, this Krishna, the daughter of Drupada, forcibly abducted by the wicked-minded Saindhava from pride of strength and energy, hath been brought back by these mighty warriors after achieving terrible feats! Behold, king Jayadratha was vanquished and lay powerless before thee! The princess of Videha was rescued with almost no allies by Rama after the slaughter in battle of the Ten-necked *Rakshasa* of terrible prowess! Indeed, the allies of Rama (in that contest) were monkeys and black-faced bears, creatures that were not even human! Think of all this, O king, in thy mind! Therefore, O foremost of Kurus, grieve not for all (that hath occurred), O bull of the Bharata race! Illustrious persons like thee never indulge in sorrow, O smiter of foes!'"

Vaisampayana continued, "It was thus that the king was comforted by Markandeya. And then that high-souled one, casting off his sorrows, once more spoke unto Markandeya."

SECTION CCLXLI

(Pativrata-mahatmya Parva)

"Yudhishthira said, 'O mighty sage, I do not so much grieve for myself or these my brothers or the loss of my kingdom as I do for this daughter of Drupada. When we were afflicted at the game of the dice by those wicked-souled ones, it was Krishna that delivered us. And she was forcibly carried off from the forest by Jayadratha. Hast thou even seen or heard of any chaste and exalted lady that resembleth this daughter of Drupada?'

"Markandeya said, 'Listen, O king, how the exalted merit of chaste ladies, O Yudhishthira, was completely obtained by a princess named Savitri. There was a king among the Madras, who was virtuous and highly pious. And he always ministered unto the Brahmanas, and was high-souled and firm in promise. And he was of subdued senses and given to sacrifices. And he was the foremost of givers, and was able, and beloved by both the citizens and the rural population. And the name of that lord of Earth was Aswapati. And he was intent on the welfare of all beings. And that forgiving (monarch) of truthful speech and subdued senses was without issue. And when he got old, he was stricken with grief at this. And with the object of raising offspring, he observed rigid vows and began to live upon frugal fare, having recourse to the Brahmacharya mode of life, and restraining his senses. And that best of kings, (daily) offering ten thousand oblations to the fire, recited Mantras in honour of *Savitri* 65 and ate temperately at the sixth hour. And he passed eighteen years, practising such vows. Then when the eighteen years were full, *Savitri* was pleased (with him). And O king, issuing with great delight, in embodied form, from the *Agnihotra* fire, the goddess showed herself to that king. And intent on conferring boons, she spoke these words unto the monarch, "I have been gratified, O king, with thy *Brahmacharya* practices, thy purity and self-restraint and observance of vows, and all thy endeavours and veneration! Do thou, O mighty king, O Aswapati, ask for the boon that thou desirest! Thou ought, however, by no means show any disregard for virtue." Thereat Aswapati said, "It is with the desire of attaining virtue that I have been engaged in this task. O goddess, may many sons be born unto me worthy of my race! If thou art pleased with me, O goddess, I ask for this boon. The twice-born ones have assured me that great merit lieth in having offspring!" *Savitri* replied, "O king, having already learnt this thy intention, I had spoken unto that lord, the Grandsire, about thy sons. Through the favour granted by the Self-create, there shall speedily be born unto thee on earth a daughter of great energy. It behoveth thee not to make any reply. Well-pleased, I tell thee this at the command of the Grandsire."'

"Markandeya said, 'Having accepted *Savitri's* words and saying, "*So be it!*" the king again gratified her and said, "May this happen soon!" On *Savitri* vanishing away, the monarch entered his own city. And that hero began to live in his kingdom, ruling his subjects righteously. And when some time had elapsed, that king, observant of vows, begat offspring on his eldest queen engaged in the practice of virtue. And then, O bull of the Bharata race, the embryo in the womb of the princess of Malava increased like the lord of stars in the heavens during the lighted fortnight. And when the time came, she brought forth a daughter furnished with lotus-like eyes. And that best of monarchs, joyfully performed the usual ceremonies on her behalf. And as she had been bestowed with delight by the goddess *Savitri* by virtue of the oblations offered in honour of that goddess, both her father, and the Brahmanas named her *Savitri*. And the king's daughter grew like unto *Sree* herself in an embodied form. And in due time, that damsel attained her puberty. And beholding that graceful maiden of slender waist and ample hips, and resembling a golden image, people thought, "We have received a goddess." And overpowered by her energy, none could wed that girl of eyes like lotus-leaves, and possessed of a burning splendour.

"'And it came to pass that once on the occasion of a *parva*, having fasted and bathed her head, she presented herself before the (family) deity and caused the Brahmanas to offer oblations with due rites to the sacrificial fire. And taking the flowers that had been offered to the god, that lady, beautiful as *Sree* herself, went to her high-souled sire. And having reverenced the feet of her father and offering him the flowers she had brought, that maiden of exceeding grace, with joined hands, stood at the side of the king. And seeing his own daughter resembling a celestial damsel arrived at puberty, and unsought by people, the king became sad. And the king said, "Daughter, the time for bestowing thee is come! Yet none asketh thee. Do thou (therefore) thyself seek for a husband equal to thee in qualities! That person who may be desired by thee should be notified to me. Do thou choose for thy husband as thou listest. I shall bestow thee with deliberation. Do thou, O auspicious one, listen to me as I tell thee the words which I heard recited by the twice-born ones. The father that doth not bestow his daughter cometh by disgrace. And the husband that knoweth not his wife in her season meeteth with disgrace. And the son that doth not protect his mother when her husband is dead, also suffereth disgrace. Hearing these words of mine, do thou engage thyself in search of a husband. Do thou act in such a way that we may not be censured by the gods!"'

"Markandeya said, 'Having said these words to his daughter and his old counsellors, he instructed the attendants to follow her, saying, — Go! Thereat, bashfully bowing down unto her father's feet, the meek maid went out without hesitation, in compliance with the words of her sire. And ascending a golden car, she went to the delightful asylum of the royal sages, accompanied by her father's aged counsellors. There, O son, worshipping the feet of the aged ones, she gradually began to roam over all the woods. Thus the king's daughter distributing wealth in all sacred regions, ranged the various places belonging to the foremost of the twice-born ones.'"

SECTION CCLXLII

"Markandeya continued, 'On one occasion, O Bharata, when that king, the lord of the Madras, was seated with Narada in the midst of his court, engaged in conversation, Savitri, accompanied by the king's counsellors, came to her father's abode after having visited various sacred regions and asylums. And beholding her father seated with Narada, she worshipped the feet of both by bending down her head. And Narada then said, "Whither had this thy daughter gone? And, O king, whence also doth she come? Why also dost thou not bestow her on a husband, now that she hath arrived at the age of puberty?" Aswapati answered, saying, "Surely it was on this very business that she had been sent, and she returneth now (from her search). Do thou, O celestial sage, listen, even from her as to the husband she hath chosen herself!"'

"Markandeya continued, 'Then the blessed maid, commanded by her father with the words,—*Relate everything in detail*,—regarded those words of her sire as if they were those of a god, and spoke unto him thus, "There was, amongst the Salwas, a virtuous Kshatriya king known by the name of Dyumatsena. And it came to pass that in course of time he became blind. And that blind king possessed of wisdom had an only son. And it so happened that an old enemy dwelling in the vicinity, taking advantage of the king's mishap, deprived him of his kingdom. And thereupon the monarch, accompanied by his wife bearing a child on her breast, went into the woods. And having retired into the forests, he adopted great vows and began to practise ascetic austerities. And his son, born in the city, began to grow in the hermitage. That youth, fit to be my husband, I have accepted in my heart for my lord!". At these words of hers, Narada said, "Alas, O king, Savitri hath committed a great wrong, since, not knowing, she hath accepted for her lord this Satyavan of excellent qualities! His father speaketh the truth and his mother also is truthful in her speech. And it is for this that the Brahmanas have named the son *Satyavan*. In his childhood he took great delight in horses, and used to make horses of clay. And he used also to draw pictures of horses. And for this that youth is sometimes called by the name of *Chitraswa*." The king then asked, "And is prince Satyavan, who is devoted to his father, endued with energy and intelligence and forgiveness and courage?" Narada replied, saying, "In energy Satyavan is like unto the sun, and in wisdom like unto Vrihaspati! And he is brave like unto the lord of the celestials and forgiving like unto the Earth herself!" Aswapati then said, "And is the prince Satyavan liberal in gifts and devoted to the Brahmanas? Is he handsome and magnanimous and lovely to behold?" Narada said, "In bestowal of gifts according to his power, the mighty son of Dyumatsena is like unto Sankriti's son Rantideva. In truthfulness of speech and devotion unto Brahmanas, he is like Sivi, the son of Usinara. And he is magnanimous like Yayati, and beautiful like the Moon. And in beauty of person he is like either of the twin Aswins. And with senses under control, he is meek, and brave, and truthful! And with passion in subjection he is devoted to his friends, and free from malice and modest and patient. Indeed, briefly speaking, they that are possessed of great ascetic merit and are of exalted character say that he is always correct in his conduct and that honour is firmly seated on his brow." Hearing this, Aswapati said, "O reverend sage, thou tellest me that he is possessed of every virtue! Do thou now tell me his defects if, indeed, he hath any!" Narada then said, "He hath one only defect that hath overwhelmed all his virtues. That defect is incapable of being conquered by even the greatest efforts. He hath only one defect, and no other. Within a year from this day, Satyavan, endued with a short life will cast off his body!" Hearing these words of the sage, the king said, "Come, O Savitri, go thou and choose another for thy lord, O beautiful damsel! That one great defect (in this youth) existeth, covering all his merits. The illustrious Narada honoured by even the gods, sayeth, that Satyavan will have to cast off his body within a year, his days being numbered!" At these words of her father, Savitri said, "The death can fall but once; a daughter can be given away but once; and once only can a person say, *I give away*! These three things can take place only once. Indeed, with a life short or long, possessed of virtues or bereft of them, I have, for once, selected my husband. Twice I shall not select. Having first settled a thing mentally, it is expressed in words, and then it is carried out into practice. Of this my mind is an example!" Narada then said, "O best of men, the heart of thy daughter Savitri wavereth not! It is not possible by any means to make her swerve from this path of virtue! In no other person are those virtues that dwell in Satyavan. The bestowal of thy daughter, therefore, is approved by me!" The king said, "What thou hast said, O illustrious one, should never be disobeyed, for thy words are true! And I shall act as thou hast said, since thou art my preceptor!" Narada said, "May the bestowal of thy daughter Savitri be attended with peace! I shall now depart. Blessed be all of ye!"'

"Markandeya continued, 'Having said this, Narada rose up into the sky and went to heaven. On the other hand, the king began to make preparations for his daughter's wedding!'"

SECTION CCLXLIII

"Markandeya said, 'Having pondered over these words (of Narada) about his daughter's marriage, the king began to make arrangements about the nuptials. And summoning all the old Brahmanas, and *Ritwijas* together with the priests, he set out with his daughter on an auspicious day. And arriving at the asylum of Dyumatsena in the sacred forest, the king approached the royal sage on foot, accompanied by the twice-born ones. And there he beheld the blind monarch of great wisdom seated on a cushion of *Kusa* grass spread under *Sala* tree. And after duly reverencing the royal sage, the king in an humble speech introduced himself. Thereupon, offering him the *Arghya*, a seat, and a cow, the monarch asked his royal guest, — *Wherefore is this visit?* — Thus addressed the king disclosed everything about his intentions and purpose with reference to Satyavan. And Aswapati said, "O royal sage, this beautiful girl is my daughter named Savitri. O thou versed in morality, do thou, agreeably to the customs of our order, take her from me as thy daughter-in-law!" Hearing these words, Dyumatsena said, "Deprived of kingdom, and taking up our abode in the woods, we are engaged in the practice of virtue as ascetics with regulated lives. Unworthy of a forest life, how will thy daughter, living in the sylvan asylum, bear this hardship?" Aswapati said, "When my daughter knoweth, as well as myself, that happiness and misery come and go (without either being stationary), such words as these are not fit to be used towards one like me! O king, I have come hither, having made up my mind! I have bowed to thee from friendship; it behoveth thee not, therefore, to destroy my hope! It behoveth thee not, also, to disregard me who, moved by love, have come to thee! Thou art my equal and fit for an alliance with me, as indeed, I am thy equal and fit for alliance with thee! Do thou, therefore, accept my daughter for thy daughter-in-law and the wife of the good Satyavan!" Hearing these words Dyumatsena said, "Formerly I had desired an alliance with thee. But I hesitated, being subsequently deprived of my kingdom. Let this wish, therefore, that I had formerly entertained, be accomplished this very day. Thou art, indeed, a welcome guest to me!"

"'Then summoning all the twice-born ones residing in the hermitages of that forest, the two kings caused the union to take place with due rites. And having bestowed his daughter with suitable robes and ornaments, Aswapati went back to his abode in great joy. And Satyavan, having obtained a wife possessed of every accomplishment, became highly glad, while she also rejoiced exceedingly upon having gained the husband after her own heart. And when her father had departed, she put off all her ornaments, and clad herself in barks and cloths dyed in red. And by her services and virtues, her tenderness and self-denial, and by her agreeable offices unto all, she pleased everybody. And she gratified her mother-in-law by attending to her person and by covering her with robes and ornaments. And she gratified her father-in-law by worshipping him as a god and controlling her speech. And she pleased her husband by her honeyed speeches, her skill in every kind of work, the evenness of her temper, and by the indications of her love in private. And thus, O Bharata, living in the asylum of those pious dwellers of the forest, they continued for some time to practise ascetic austerities. But the words spoken by Narada were present night and day in the mind of the sorrowful Savitri.'"

SECTION CCLXLIV

"Markandeya said, 'At length, O king, after a long time had passed away, the hour that had been appointed for the death of Satyavan arrived. And as the words that had been spoken by Narada were ever present in the mind of Savitri, she had counted the days as they passed. And having ascertained that her husband would die on the fourth day following, the damsel fasted day and night, observing the *Triratra* vow. And hearing of her vow, the king became exceedingly sorrowful and rising up soothed Savitri and said these words, "This vow that thou hast begun to observe, O daughter of a king, is exceedingly hard; for it is extremely difficult to fast for three nights together!" And hearing these words, Savitri said, "Thou needst not be sorry, O father! This vow I shall be able to observe! I have for certain undertaken this task with perseverance; and perseverance is the cause of the successful observance of vows." And having listened to her, Dyumatsena said, "I can by no means say unto thee, *Do thou break thy vow.* One like me should, on the contrary, say, — *Do thou complete thy vow!*" And having said this to her, the high-minded Dyumatsena stopped. And Savitri continuing to fast began to look (lean) like a wooden doll. And, O bull of the Bharata race, thinking that her husband would die on the morrow, the woe-stricken Savitri, observing a fast, spent that night in extreme anguish. And when the Sun had risen about a couple of hand Savitri thinking within herself — *To-day is that day*, finished her morning rites, and offered oblations to the flaming fire. And bowing down unto the aged Brahmanas, and her father-in-law, and mother-in-law, she stood before them with joined hands, concentrating her senses. And for the welfare of Savitri, all the ascetics dwelling in that hermitage, uttered the auspicious benediction that she should never suffer widowhood. And Savitri immersed in contemplation accepted those words of the ascetics, mentally saying, — *So be it!* — And the king's daughter, reflecting on those words of Narada, remained, expecting the hour and the moment.

"'Then, O best of the Bharatas, well-pleased, her father-in-law and mother-in-law said these words unto the princess seated in a corner, "Thou hast completed the vow as prescribed. The time for thy meal hath now arrived; therefore, do thou what is proper!" Thereat Savitri said, "Now that

I have completed the purposed vow, I will eat when the Sun goes down. Even this is my heart's resolve and this my vow!"

"Markandeya continued, 'And when Savitri had spoken thus about her meal, Satyavan, taking his axe upon his shoulders, set out for the woods. And at this, Savitri said unto her husband, "It behoveth thee not to go alone! I will accompany thee. I cannot bear to be separated from thee!" Hearing these words of hers, Satyavan said, "Thou hast never before repaired to the forest. And, O lady, the forest-paths are hard to pass! Besides thou hast been reduced by fast on account of thy vow. How wouldst thou, therefore, be able to walk on foot?" Thus addressed, Savitri said, "I do not feel langour because of the fast, nor do I feel exhaustion. And I have made up my mind to go. It behoveth thee not, therefore, to prevent me!" At this, Satyavan said, "If thou desirest to go, I will gratify that desire of thine. Do thou, however, take the permission of my parents, so that I may be guilty of no fault!"'

"Markandeya continued, 'Thus addressed by her lord, Savitri of high vows saluted her father-in-law and mother-in-law and addressed them, saying, "This my husband goeth to the forest for procuring fruits. Permitted by my revered lady-mother and father-in-law, I will accompany him. For to-day I cannot bear to be separated from him. Thy son goeth out for the sake of the sacrificial fire and for his reverend superiors. He ought not, therefore, to be dissuaded. Indeed, he could be dissuaded if he went into the forest on any other errand. Do ye not prevent me! I will go into the forest with him. It is a little less than a year that I have not gone out of the asylum. Indeed, I am extremely desirous of beholding the blossoming woods!" Hearing these words Dyumatsena said, "Since Savitri hath been bestowed by her father as my daughter-in-law, I do not remember that she hath ever spoken any words couching a request. Let my daughter-in-law, therefore, have her will in this matter. Do thou, however, O daughter, act in such a way that Satyavan's work may not be neglected!"'

"Markandeya continued, 'Having received the permission of both, the illustrious Savitri, departed with her lord, in seeming smiles although her heart was racked with grief. And that lady of large eyes went on, beholding picturesque and delightful woods inhabited by swarms of peacocks. And Satyavan sweetly said unto Savitri, "Behold these rivers of sacred currents and these excellent trees decked with flowers!" But the faultless Savitri continued to watch her lord in all his moods, and recollecting the words of the celestial sage, she considered her husband as already dead. And with heart cleft in twain, that damsel, replying to her lord, softly followed him expecting that hour.'"

SECTION CCLXLV

"Markandeya said, 'The powerful Satyavan then, accompanied by his wife, plucked fruits and filled his wallet with them. And he then began to fell branches of trees. And as he was hewing them, he began to perspire. And in consequence of that exercise his head began to ache. And afflicted with toil, he approached his beloved wife, and addressed her, saying, "O Savitri, owing to this hard exercise my head acheth, and all my limbs and my heart also are afflicted sorely! O thou of restrained speech, I think myself unwell, I feel as if my head is being pierced with numerous darts. Therefore, O auspicious lady, I wish to sleep, for I have not the power to stand." Hearing these words, Savitri quickly advancing, approached her husband, and sat down upon the ground, placing his head upon her lap. And that helpless lady, thinking of Narada's words, began to calculate the (appointed) division of the day, the hour, and the moment. The next moment she saw a person clad in red attire with his head decked with a diadem. And his body was of large proportions and effulgent as the Sun. And he was of a darkish hue, had red eyes, carried a noose in his hand, and was dreadful to behold. And he was standing beside Satyavan and was steadfastly gazing at him. And seeing him, Savitri gently placed her husband's head on the ground, and rising suddenly, with a trembling heart, spake these words in distressful accents, "Seeing this thy superhuman form, I take thee to be a deity. If thou will tell me, O chief of the gods, who thou art and what also thou intendst to do!" Thereat, Yama replied, "O Savitri, thou art ever devoted to thy husband, and thou art also endued with ascetic merit. It is for this reason that I hold converse with thee. Do thou, O auspicious one, know me for Yama. This thy lord Satyavan, the son of a king, hath his days run out. I shall, therefore, take him away binding him in this noose. Know this to be my errand!" At these words Savitri said, "I had heard that thy emissaries come to take away mortals, O worshipful one! Why then, O lord, hast thou come in person?"'

"Markandeya continued, 'Thus addressed by her, the illustrious lord of *Pitris*, with a view to oblige her, began to unfold to her truly all about his intentions. And Yama said, "This prince is endued with virtues and beauty of person, and is a sea of accomplishments. He deserveth not to be borne away by my emissaries. Therefore is it that I have come personally." Saying this, Yama by main force pulled out of the body of Satyavan, a person of the measure of the thumb, bound in noose and completely under subjection. And when Satyavan's life had thus been taken out, the body, deprived of breath, and shorn of lustre, and destitute of motion, became unsightly to behold. And binding Satyavan's vital essence, Yama proceeded in a southerly direction. Thereupon, with heart overwhelmed in grief, the exalted Savitri, ever devoted to her lord and crowned with success in respect of her vows, began to follow Yama. And at this, Yama said, "Desist, O Savitri! Go back, and perform the funeral obsequies of thy lord! Thou art freed from all thy obligations to thy lord. Thou hast come as far as it is possible to come." Savitri replied, "Whither my husband is being carried, or whither he goeth of his own accord, I will follow him thither. This is the eternal custom. By virtue of my asceticism, of my regard for my superiors, of my affection for my lord, of my observance of vows, as well as of thy favour, my course is unimpeded. It hath been declared by wise men endued with true knowledge that by walking only seven paces with another, one contracteth a friendship with one's companion. Keeping that friendship (which I have contracted with thee) in view, I shall speak to thee something. Do thou listen to it. They that have not their souls under control, acquire not merit by leading the four successive modes of life, viz.,—celibacy with study, domesticity, retirement into the woods, and renunciation of the world. That which is called religious merit is said to consist of true knowledge. The wise, therefore, have declared religious merit to be the foremost of all things and not the passage through the four successive modes. By practising the duties of even one of these four modes agreeable to the directions of the wise, we have attained to true merit, and, therefore, we do not desire the second or the third mode, viz., celibacy with study or renunciation. It is for this again that the wise have declared religious merit to be the foremost of all things!" Hearing these words of hers, Yama said, "Do thou desist! I have been pleased with these words of thine couched in proper letters and accents, and based on reason. Do thou ask for a boon! Except the life of thy husband, O thou of faultless features, I will bestow on thee any boon that thou mayst solicit!" Hearing these words, Savitri said, "Deprived of his kingdom and bereft also of sight, my father-in-law leadeth a life of retirement in our sylvan asylum. Let that king through thy favour attain his eye-sight, and become strong like either fire or the Sun!" Yama said, "O thou of faultless features, I grant thee this boon! It will even be as thou hast said! It seems that thou art fatigued with thy journey. Do thou desist, therefore, and return! Suffer not thyself to be weary any longer!" Savitri said, "What weariness can I feel in the presence of my husband? The lot that is my husband's is certainly mine also. Whither thou carriest my husband, thither will I also repair! O chief of the celestials, do thou again listen to me! Even a single interview with the pious is highly desirable; friendship with them is still more so. And intercourse with the virtuous can never be fruitless. Therefore, one should live in the company of the righteous!" Yama said, "These words that thou hast spoken, so fraught with useful instruction, delight the heart and enhance the wisdom of even the learned. Therefore, O lady, solicit thou a second boon, except the life of Satyavan!" Savitri said, "Sometime before, my wise and intelligent father-in-law was deprived of his kingdom. May that monarch regain his kingdom. And may that superior of mine never renounce his duties! Even this is the second boon that I solicit!" Then Yama said,—"The king shall soon regain his kingdom. Nor shall he ever fall off from his duties. Thus, O daughter of a king have I fulfilled thy desire. Do thou now desist! Return! Do not take any future trouble!" Savitri said, "Thou hast restrained all creatures by thy decrees, and it is by thy decrees that thou takest them away, not according to thy will. Therefore it is, O god, O divine one, that people call thee *Yama*! Do thou listen to the words that I say! The eternal duty of the good towards all creatures is never to injure them in thought, word, and deed, but to bear them love and give them their due. As regards this world, everything here is like this (husband of mine). Men are destitute of both devotion and skill. The good, however, show mercy to even their foes when these seek their protection." Yama said, "As water to the thirsty soul, so are these words uttered by thee to me! Therefore, do thou, O fair lady, if thou will, once again ask for any boon except Satyavana's life!" At these words Savitri replied, "That lord of earth, my father, is without sons. That he may have a hundred sons begotten of his loins, so that his line may be perpetuated, is the third boon I would ask of thee!" Yama said, "Thy sire, O auspicious lady, shall obtain a hundred illustrious sons, who will perpetuate and increase their father's race! Now, O daughter of a king, thou hast obtained thy wish. Do thou desist! Thou hast come far enough." Savitri said, "Staying by the side of my husband, I am not conscious of the length of the way I have walked. Indeed, my mind rusheth to yet a longer way off. Do thou again, as thou goest on, listen to the words that I will presently utter! Thou art the powerful son of Vivaswat. It is for this that thou art called *Vatvaswata* by the wise. And, O lord, since thou dealest out equal law unto all created things, thou hast been designated the *lord of justice*! One reposeth not, even in one's own self, the confidence that one doth in the righteous. Therefore, every one wisheth particularly for intimacy with the righteous. It is goodness of heart alone that inspireth the confidence of all creatures. And it is for this that people rely particularly on the righteous." And hearing these words, Yama said, "The words that thou utterest, O fair lady, I have not heard from any one save thee; I am highly pleased with this speech of thine. Except the life of Satyavan, solicit thou, therefore, a fourth boon, and then go thy way!"

Savitri then said, "Both of me and Satyavan's loins, begotten by both of us, let there be a century of sons possessed of strength and prowess and capable of perpetuating our race! Even this is the fourth boon that I would beg of thee!" Hearing these words of hers, Yama replied, "Thou shalt, O lady, obtain a century of sons, possessed of strength and prowess, and causing thee great delight. O daughter of a king, let no more weariness be thine! Do thou desist! Thou hast already come too far!" Thus addressed, Savitri said, "They that are righteous always practise eternal morality! And the communion of the pious with the pious is never fruitless! Nor is there any danger to the pious from those that are pious. And verily it is the righteous who by their truth make the Sun move in the heaven. And it is the righteous that support the earth by their austerities! And, O king, it is the righteous upon whom both the past and the future depend! Therefore, they that are righteous, are never cheerless in the company of the righteous. Knowing this to be the eternal practice of the good and righteous, they that are righteous continue to do good to others without expecting any benefit in return. A good office is never thrown away on the good and virtuous. Neither interest nor dignity suffereth any injury by such an act. And since such conduct ever adheres to the righteous, the righteous often become the protectors of all." Hearing these words of hers, Yama replied, "The more thou utterest such speeches that are pregnant with great import, full of honeyed phrases, instinct with morality, and agreeable to mind, the more is the respect that I feel for thee! O thou that art so devoted to thy lord, ask for some incomparable boon!" Thus addressed, Savitri said, "O bestower of honours, the boon thou hast already given me is incapable of accomplishment without union with my husband. Therefore, among other boons, I ask for this, may this Satyavan be restored to life! Deprived of my husband, I am as one dead! Without my husband, I do not wish for happiness. Without my husband, I do not wish for heaven itself. Without my husband, I do not wish for prosperity. Without my husband, I cannot make up my mind to live! Thou thyself hast bestowed on me the boon, namely, of a century of sons; yet thou takest away my husband! I ask for this boon, 'May Satyavan be restored to life,' for by that thy words will be made true.'"

"Markandeya continued, 'Thereupon saying,—*So be it*,—Vivaswat's son, Yama, the dispenser of justice, untied his noose, and with cheerful heart said these words to Savitri, "Thus, O auspicious and chaste lady, is thy husband freed by me! Thou wilt be able to take him back free from disease. And he will attain to success! And along with thee, he will attain a life of four hundred years. And celebrating sacrifices with due rites, he will achieve great fame in this world. And upon thee Satyavan will also beget a century of sons. And these Kshatriyas with their sons and grandsons will all be kings, and will always be famous in connection with thy name. And thy father also will beget a hundred sons on thy mother Malavi. And under the name of the *Malavas*, thy Kshatriya brothers, resembling the celestials, will be widely known along with their sons and daughters!" And having bestowed these boons on Savitri and having thus made her desist, Yama departed for his abode. Savitri, after Yama had gone away, went back to the spot where her husband's ash-coloured corpse lay, and seeing her lord on the ground, she approached him, and taking hold of him, she placed his head on her lap and herself sat down on the ground. Then Satyavan regained his consciousness, and affectionately eyeing Savitri again and again, like one come home after a sojourn in a strange land, he addressed her thus, "Alas, I have slept long! Wherefore didst thou not awake me? And where is that same sable person that was dragging me away?" At these words of his, Savitri said, "Thou hast, O bull among men, slept long on my lap! That restrainer of creatures, the worshipful Yama, had gone away. Thou art refreshed, O blessed one, and sleep hath forsaken thee, O son of a king! If thou art able, rise thou up! Behold, the night is deep!"'

"Markandeya continued, 'Having regained consciousness, Satyavan rose up like one who had enjoyed a sweet sleep, and seeing every side covered with woods, said, "O girl of slender waist, I came with thee for procuring fruits. Then while I was cutting wood I felt a pain in my head. And on account of that intense pain about my head I was unable to stand for any length of time, and, therefore, I lay on thy lap and slept. All this, O auspicious lady, I remember. Then, as thou didst embrace me, sleep stole away my senses. I then saw that it was dark all around. In the midst of it I saw a person of exceeding effulgence. If thou knowest everything, do thou then, O girl of slender waist, tell me whether what I saw was only a dream or a reality!" Thereupon, Savitri addressed him, saying, "The night deepens. I shall, O prince, relate everything unto thee on the morrow. Arise, arise, may good betide thee! And, O thou of excellent vows, come and behold thy parents! The sun hath set a long while ago and the night deepens. Those rangers of the night, having frightful voices, are walking about in glee. And sounds are heard, proceeding from the denizens of the forest treading through the woods. These terrible shrieks of jackals that are issuing from the south and the east make my heart tremble (in fear)!" Satyavan then said, "Covered with deep darkness, the wilderness hath worn a dreadful aspect. Thou wilt, therefore, not be able to discern the tract, and consequently wilt not be able to go!" Then Savitri replied, "In consequence of a conflagration having taken place in the forest today a withered tree standeth aflame, and the flames being stirred by the wind are discerned now and then. I shall fetch some fire and light these faggots around. Do thou dispel all anxiety.

I will do all (this) if thou darest not go, for I find thee unwell. Nor wilt thou be able to discover the way through this forest enveloped in darkness. Tomorrow when the woods become visible, we will go hence, if thou please! If, O sinless one, it is thy wish, we shall pass this night even here!" At these words of hers, Satyavan replied, "The pain in my head is off; and I feel well in my limbs. With thy favour I wish to behold my father and mother. Never before did I return to the hermitage after the proper time had passed away. Even before it is twilight my mother confineth me within the asylum. Even when I come out during the day, my parents become anxious on my account, and my father searcheth for me, together with all the inhabitants of the sylvan asylums. Before this, moved by deep grief, my father and mother had rebuked me many times and often, saying, — *Thou comest having tarried long*! I am thinking of the pass they have today come to on my account, for, surely, great grief will be theirs when they miss me. One night before this, the old couple, who love me dearly, wept from deep sorrow and said into me, 'Deprived of thee, O son, we cannot live for even a moment. As long as thou livest, so long, surely, we also will live. Thou art the crutch of these blind ones; on thee doth perpetuity of our race depend. On thee also depend our funeral cake, our fame and our descendants!' My mother is old, and my father also is so. I am surely their crutch. If they see me not in the night, what, oh, will be their plight! I hate that slumber of mine for the sake of which my unoffending mother and my father have both been in trouble, and I myself also, am placed in such rending distress! Without my father and mother, I cannot bear to live. It is certain that by this time my blind father, his mind disconsolate with grief, is asking everyone of the inhabitants of the hermitage about me! I do not, O fair girl, grieve so much for myself as I do for my sire, and for my weak mother ever obedient to her lord! Surely, they will be afflicted with extreme anguish on account of me. I hold my life so long as they live. And I know that they should be maintained by me and that I should do only what is agreeable to them!"'

"Markandeya continued, 'Having said this, that virtuous youth who loved and revered his parents, afflicted with grief held up his arms and began to lament in accents of woe. And seeing her lord overwhelmed with sorrow the virtuous Savitri wiped away the tears from his eyes and said, "If I have observed austerities, and have given away in charity, and have performed sacrifice, may this night be for the good of my father-in-law, mother-in-law and husband! I do not remember having told a single falsehood, even in jest. Let my father-in-law and mother-in-law hold their lives by virtue of the truth!" Satyavan said, "I long for the sight of my father and mother! Therefore, O Savitri, proceed without delay. O beautiful damsel, I swear by my own self that if I find any evil to have befallen my father and mother, I will not live. If thou hast any regard for virtue, if thou wishest me to live, if it is thy duty to do what is agreeable to me, proceed thou to the hermitage!" The beautiful Savitri then rose and tying up her hair, raised her husband in her arms. And Satyavan having risen, rubbed his limbs with his hands. And as he surveyed all around, his eyes fell upon his wallet. Then Savitri said unto him, "Tomorrow thou mayst gather fruits. And I shall carry thy axe for thy ease." Then hanging up the wallet upon the bough of a tree, and taking up the axe, she re-approached her husband. And that lady of beautiful thighs, placing her husband's left arm upon her left shoulder, and embracing him with her right arms, proceeded with elephantic gait. Then Satyavan said, "O timid one, by virtue of habit, the (forest) paths are known to me. And further, by the light of the moon between the trees, I can see them. We have now reached the same path that we took in the morning for gathering fruits. Do thou, O auspicious one, proceed by the way that we had come: thou needst not any longer feel dubious about our path. Near that tract overgrown with *Palasa* tree, the way diverges into two. Do thou proceed along the path that lies to the north of it. I am now well and have got back my strength. I long to see my father and mother!" Saying this Satyavan hastily proceeded towards the hermitage.'"

SECTION CCLXLVI

"Markandeya said, 'Meanwhile the mighty Dyumatsena, having regained his sight, could see everything. And when his vision grew clear he saw everything around him. And, O bull of the Bharata race, proceeding with his wife Saivya to all the (neighbouring) asylums in search of his son, he became extremely distressed on his account. And that night the old couple went about searching in asylums, and rivers, and woods, and floods. And whenever they heard any sound, they stood rising their heads, anxiously thinking that their son was coming, and said, "O yonder cometh Satyavan with Savitri!" And they rushed hither and thither like maniacs, their feet torn, cracked, wounded, and bleeding, pierced with thorns and *Kusa* blades. Then all the Brahmanas dwelling in that hermitage came unto them, and surrounding them on all sides, comforted them, and brought them back to their own asylum. And there Dyumatsena with his wife surrounded by aged ascetics, was entertained with stories of monarchs of former times. And although that old couple desirous of seeing their son, was comforted, yet recollecting the youthful days of their son, they became exceedingly sorry. And afflicted with grief, they began to lament in piteous accerts, saying, "Alas, O son, alas, O chaste daughter-in-law, where are you?" Then a truthful Brahmana of the name of Suvarchas spake unto them, saying, "Considering the austerities, self-restraint, and behaviour of his wife Savitri, there can be no doubt that Satyavan liveth!" And Gautama said, "I have studied all the *Vedas* with their branches, and I have acquired great ascetic merit. And I have led a celibate existence, practising also the *Brahmacharya* mode of life. I have gratified Agni and my superiors. With rapt soul I have also observed all the vows: and I have according to the ordinance, frequently lived upon air alone. By virtue of this ascetic merit, I am cognisant of all the doings of others. Therefore, do thou take it for certain that Satyavan liveth." Thereupon his disciple said, "The words that have fallen from the lips of my preceptor can never be false. Therefore, Satyavan surely liveth." And the *Rishi* said, "Considering the auspicious marks that his wife Savitri beareth and all of which indicate immunity from widowhood, there can be no doubt that Satyavan liveth!" And Varadwaja said, "Having regard to the ascetic merit, self-restraint, and conduct of his wife Savitri, there can be no doubt that Satyavan liveth." And Dalbhya said, "Since thou hast regained thy sight, and since Savitri hath gone away after completion of the vow, without taking any food, there can be no doubt that Satyavan liveth." And Apastamba said, "From the manner in which the voices of birds and wild animals are being heard through the stillness of the atmosphere on all sides, and from the fact also of thy having regained the use of thy eyes, indicating thy usefulness for earthly purposes once more, there can be no doubt that Satyavan liveth." And Dhaumya said, "As thy son is graced with every virtue, and as he is the beloved of all, and as he is possessed of marks betokening a long life, there can be no doubt that Satyavan liveth."'

"Markandeya continued, 'Thus cheered by those ascetics of truthful speech, Dyumatsena pondering over those points, attained a little ease. A little while after, Savitri with her husband Satyavan reached the hermitage during the night and entered it with a glad heart. The Brahmanas then said, "Beholding this meeting with thy son, and thy restoration to eye-sight, we all wish thee well, O lord of earth. Thy meeting with thy son, the sight of thy daughter-in-law, and thy restoration to sight—constitute a threefold prosperity which thou hast gained. What we all have said must come to pass: there can be no doubt of this. Henceforth thou shalt rapidly grow in prosperity." Then, O Pritha's son, the twice-born ones lighted a fire and sat themselves down before king Dyumatsena. And Saivya, and Satyavan, and Savitri who stood apart, their hearts free from grief, sat down with the permission of them all. Then, O Partha, seated with the monarch those dwellers of the woods, actuated by curiosity, asked the king's son, saying, "Why didst thou not, O illustrious one, come back earlier with thy wife? Why hast thou come so late in the night? What obstacle prevented thee! We do not know, O son of a king, why thou hast caused such alarm to us, and to thy father and mother. It behoveth thee to tell us all about this." Thereupon, Satyavan said, "With the permission of my father, I went to the woods with Savitri. There, as I was hewing wood in the forest, I felt a pain in my head. And in consequence of the pain, I fell into a deep sleep.—This is all that I remember. I had never slept so long before I have come so late at night, in order that ye might not grieve (on my account). There is no other reason for this." Gautama then said, "Thou knowest not then the cause of thy father's sudden restoration to sight. It, therefore, behoveth Savitri to relate it. I wish to hear it (from thee), for surely thou art conversant with the mysteries of good and evil. And, O Savitri, I know thee to be like the goddess *Savitri* herself in splendour. Thou must know the cause of this. Therefore, do thou relate it truly! If it should not be kept a secret, do thou unfold it unto us!" At these words of Gautama Savitri said, "It is as ye surmise. Your desire shall surely not be unfulfilled. I have no secret to keep. Listen to the truth then! The high-souled Narada had predicted the death of my husband. To-day was the appointed time. I could not, therefore, bear to be separated from my husband's company. And after he had fallen asleep, Yama, accompanied by his messengers, presented himself before him, and tying him, began to take him away towards the region inhabited by the *Pitris*. Thereupon I began to praise that august god, with truthful words. And he granted me five boons, of which do ye hear from me! For my father-in-law I have obtained these two boons, viz., his restoration to sight as also to his kingdom. My father also hath obtained a hundred sons. And I myself have obtained a hundred sons. And my husband Satyavan hath obtained a life of four hundred years. It was for the sake of my husband's life that I had observed that vow. Thus have I narrated unto you in detail the cause by which this mighty misfortune of mine was afterwards turned into happiness." The *Rishis* said, "O chaste lady of excellent disposition, observant of vows and endued with virtue, and sprung from an illustrious line, by thee hath the race of this foremost of kings, which was overwhelmed with calamities, and was sinking in an ocean of darkness, been rescued."'

"Markandeya continued, 'Then having applauded and reverenced that best of women, those *Rishis* there assembled bade farewell to that foremost of kings as well as to his son. And having saluted them thus, they speedily went, in peace with cheerful hearts, to their respective abodes.'"

SECTION CCLXLVII

"Markandeya continued, 'When the night had passed away, and the solar orb had risen, those ascetics, having performed their morning rites, assembled together. And although those mighty sages again and again spake unto Dyumatsena of the high fortune of Savitri, yet they were never satisfied. And it so happened, O king, that there came to that hermitage a large body of people from Salwa. And they brought tidings of the enemy of Dyumatsena having been slain by his own minister. And they related unto him all that had happened, viz., how having heard that the usurper had been slain with all his friends and allies by his minister, his troops had all fled, and how all the subjects had become unanimous (on behalf of their legitimate king), saying, "Whether possessed of sight or not, even he shall be our king!" And they said, "We have been sent to thee in consequence of that resolve. This car of thine, and this army also consisting of four kinds of forces, have arrived for thee! Good betide thee, O King! Do thou come! Thou hast been proclaimed in the city. Do thou for ever occupy the station belonging to thy father and grand-father!" And beholding the king possessed of sight and able-bodied, they bowed down their heads, their eyes expanded with wonder. Then having worshipped those old and Brahmanas dwelling in the hermitage and honoured by them in return, the king set out for his city. And surrounded by the soldiers, Saivya also accompanied by Savitri, went in a vehicle furnished with shining sheets and borne on the shoulders of men. Then the priests with joyful hearts installed Dyumatsena on the throne with his high-souled son as prince-regent. And after the lapse of a long time, Savitri gave birth to a century of sons, all warlike and unretreating from battle, and enhancing the fame of Salwa's race. And she also had a century of highly powerful uterine brothers born unto Aswapati, the lord of the Madras, by Malavi. Thus, O son of Pritha, did Savitri raise from pitiable plight to high fortune, herself, and her father and mother, her father-in-law and mother-in-law, as also the race of her husband. And like that gentle lady Savitri, the auspicious daughter of Drupada, endued with excellent character, will rescue you all.'"

Vaisampayana said, "Thus exhorted by that high-souled sage, the son of Pandu, O king, with his mind free from anxiety, continued to live in the forest of Kamyaka. The man that listeneth with reverence to the excellent story of Savitri, attaineth to happiness, and success in everything, and never meeteth with misery!"

SECTION CCLXLVIII

Janamejaya said,—"What, O Brahmana, was that great fear entertained by Yudhishthira in respect of Karna, for which Lomasa had conveyed to the son of Pandu a message of deep import from Indra in these words, *That intense fear of thine which thou dost never express to any one, I will remove after Dhananjaya goeth from hence?* And, O best of ascetics, why was it that the virtuous Yudhishthira never expressed it to any one?"

Vaisampayana said, "As thou askest me, O tiger among kings, I will relate that history unto thee! Do thou listen to my words, O best of the Bharatas! After twelve years (of their exile) had passed away and the thirteenth year had set in, Sakra, ever friendly to the sons of Pandu, resolved to beg of Karna (his ear-rings). And, O mighty monarch, ascertaining this intention of the great chief of the celestials about (Karna's) ear-rings, Surya, having effulgence for his wealth, went unto Karna. And, O foremost of kings, while that hero devoted to the Brahmanas and truthful in speech was lying down at night at his ease on a rich bed overlaid with a costly sheet, the effulgent deity, filled with kindness and affection for his son, showed himself, O Bharata, unto him in his dreams. And assuming from ascetic power the form of a handsome Brahmana versed in the *Vedas*, Surya sweetly said unto Karna these words for his benefit, 'O son, do thou O Karna, listen to these words of mine, O thou foremost of truthful persons! O mighty-armed one, I tell thee to-day from affection, what is for thy great good! With the object, O Karna, of obtaining thy ear-rings, Sakra, moved by the desire of benefiting the sons of Pandu, will come unto thee, disguised as a Brahmana! He, as well as all the world, knoweth thy character, viz., that when solicited by pious people, thou givest away but never takest in gift! Thou, O son, givest unto Brahmanas wealth or any other thing that is asked of thee and never refusest anything to anybody. Knowing thee to be such, the subduer himself of Paka will come to beg of thee thy ear-rings and coat of mail. When he beggeth the ear-rings of thee, it behoveth thee not to give them away, but to gratify him with sweet speeches to the best of thy power. Even this, is for thy supreme good! While asking thee for the ear-rings, thou shalt, with various reasons, repeatedly refuse Purandara who is desirous of obtaining them, offering him, instead, various other kinds of wealth, such as gems and women and kine, and citing various precedents. If thou, O Karna, givest away thy beautiful ear-rings born with thee, thy life being shortened, thou wilt meet with death! Arrayed in thy mail and ear-rings, thou wilt, O bestower of honours, be incapable of being slain by foes in battle! Do thou lay to heart these words of mine! Both these jewelled ornaments have sprung from *Amrita*. Therefore, they should be preserved by thee, if thy life is at all dear to thee.'

"Hearing these words, Karna said, 'Who art thou that tellest me so, showing me such kindness? If it pleaseth thee, tell me, O illustrious one, who thou art in the guise of a Brahmana!'—The Brahmana thereupon said, 'O son, I am he of a thousand rays! Out of affection, I point out to thee the path! Act thou according to my words, as it is for thy great good to do so!' Karna replied, 'Surely, this itself is highly fortunate for me that the god himself of splendour addresses me today, seeking my welfare. Listen, however, to these words of mine! May it please thee, O bestower of boons, it is only from affection that I tell thee this! If I am dear to thee, I should not be dissuaded from the observance of my vow! O thou that are possessed of the wealth of effulgence, the whole world knoweth this to be my vow that, of a verity, I am prepared to give away life itself unto superior Brahmanas! If, O best of all rangers of the sky, Sakra cometh to me, disguised as a Brahmana, to beg for the benefit of the sons of Pandu, I will, O chief of the celestials, give him the ear-rings and the excellent mail, so that my fame which hath spread over the three worlds may not suffer any diminution! For persons like us, it is not fit to save life by a blame-worthy act. On the contrary, it is even proper for us to meet death with the approbation of the world and under circumstances bringing fame. Therefore, will I bestow upon Indra the ear-rings with my coat of mail! If the slayer himself of Vala and Vritra cometh to ask for the ear-rings for the benefit of the sons of Pandu, that will conduce to my fame, leading at the same time to *his* infamy! O thou possessed of splendour, I wish for fame in this world, even if it is to be purchased with life itself, for they that have fame enjoy the celestial regions, while they that are destitute of it are lost. Fame keepeth people alive in this world even like a mother, while infamy killeth men even though they may move about with bodies undestroyed. O lord of the worlds, O thou possessed of the wealth of effulgence, that fame is the life of men is evidenced by an ancient *sloka* sung by the Creator himself,—*In the next world it is fame that is the chief support of a person, while in this world pure fame lengthens life*. Therefore, by giving away my ear-rings and mail with both of which I was born I will win eternal fame! And by duly giving away the same to Brahmanas according to the ordinance, by offering up my body (as a gift to the gods) in the sacrifice of war, by achieving feats difficult of performance, and by conquering my foes in fight, I will acquire nothing but renown. And by dispelling on the field of battle the fears of the affrighted that may beg for their lives, and relieving old men and boys and Brahmanas from terror and anxiety, I will win excellent fame and the highest heaven. My fame is to be protected with the sacrifice of even my life. Even this, know thou, is my vow! By giving away such a valuable gift to Maghavan disguised as a Brahmana, I will, O god, acquire in this world the most exalted state.'"

SECTION CCLXLIX

"Surya said, 'Never do, O Karna, anything that is harmful to thy self and thy friends; thy sons, thy wives, thy father, and thy mother; O thou best of those that bear life, people desire renown (in this world) and lasting fame in heaven, without wishing to sacrifice their bodies. But as thou desirest undying fame at the expense of thy life, she will, without doubt, snatch away thy life! O bull among men, in this world, the father, the mother, the son, and other relatives are of use only to him that is alive. O tiger among men, as regard kings, it is only when they are alive that prowess can be of any use to them. Do thou understand this? O thou of exceeding splendour, fame is for the good of these only that are alive! Of what use is fame to the dead whose bodies have been reduced to ashes? One that is dead cannot enjoy renown. It is only when one is alive that one can enjoy it. The fame of one that is dead is like a garland of flowers around the neck of a corpse. As thou reverest me, I tell thee this for thy benefit, because thou art a worshipper of mine! They that worship me are always protected by me. That also is another reason for my addressing thee thus! Thinking again, O mighty-armed one, that *this one revereth me with great reverence*, I have been inspired with love for thee! Do thou, therefore, act according to my words! There is, besides some profound mystery in all this, ordained by fate. It is for this, that I tell thee so. Do thou act without mistrust of any kind! O bull among men, it is not fit for thee to know this which is a secret to the very gods. Therefore, I do not reveal that secret unto thee. Thou wilt, however, understand it in time. I repeat what I have already said. Do thou, O Radha's son, lay my words to heart! When the wielder of the thunder-bolt asketh thee for them, do thou never give him thy ear-rings! O thou of exceeding splendour, with thy handsome ear-rings, thou lookest beautiful, even like the Moon himself in the clear firmament, between the *Visakha* constellation! Dost thou know that fame availeth only the person that is living. Therefore, when the lord of the celestials will ask the ear-rings, thou shouldst, O son, refuse him! Repeating again and again answers fraught with various reasons, thou wilt, O sinless one, be able to remove the eagerness of the lord of the celestial for the possession of the ear-rings. Do thou, O Karna, alter Purandara's purpose by urging answers fraught with reason and grave import and adorned with sweetness and suavity. Thou dost always, O tiger among men, challenge him that can draw the bow with his left hand, and heroic Arjuna also will surely encounter thee in fight. But when furnished with thy ear-rings, Arjuna will never be able to vanquish thee in fight even if Indra himself comes to his assistance. Therefore, O Karna, if thou wishest to vanquish Arjuna in battle, these handsome ear-rings of thine should never be parted with to Sakra.'"

SECTION CCC

"Karna said, 'As thou, O lord of splendour, knowest me for thy worshipper, so also thou knowest that there is nothing which I cannot give away in charity, O thou of fiery rays! Neither my wives, nor my sons, nor my own self, nor my friends, are so dear to me as thou, on account of the veneration I feel for thee, O lord of splendour! Thou knowest, O maker of light, that high-souled persons bear a loving regard for their dear worshippers. *Karna revereth me and is dear to me. He knoweth no other deity in heaven,*—thinking this thou hast, O lord, said unto me what is for my benefit. Yet, O thou of bright rays, again do I beseech thee with bended head, again do I place myself in thy hands. I will repeat the answer I have already given. It behoveth thee to forgive me! Death itself is not fraught with such terrors for me as untruth! As regards especially the Brahmanas, again, I do not hesitate to yield up my life even for them! And, O divine one, respecting what thou hast said unto me of Phalguna, the son of Pandu, let thy grief born of thy anxiety of heart, O lord of splendour, be dispelled touching him and myself; for I shall surely conquer Arjuna in battle! Thou knowest, O deity, that I have great strength of weapons obtained from Jamadagnya and the high-souled Drona. Permit me now, O foremost of celestials, to observe my vow, so that unto him of the thunderbolt coming to beg of me, I may give away even my life!'

"Surya said, 'If O son, thou givest away thy ear-rings to the wielder of the thunder-bolt, O thou of mighty strength, thou shouldst also, for the purpose of securing victory, speak unto him, saying,—*O thou of a hundred sacrifices, I shall give thee ear-rings under a condition.*—Furnished with the ear-rings, thou art certainly incapable of being slain by any being. Therefore, it is, O son, that desirous of beholding thee slain in battle by Arjuna, the destroyer of the Danavas desireth to deprive thee of thy ear-rings. Repeatedly adoring with truthful words that lord of the celestials, viz., Purandara armed with weapons incapable of being frustrated, do thou also beseech him, saying, "Give me an infallible dart capable of slaying all foes, and I will, O thousand-eyed deity, give the ear-rings with the excellent coat of mail!" On this condition shouldst thou give the ear-rings unto Sakra.

With that dart, O Karna, thou wilt slay foes in battle: for, O mighty-armed one, that dart of the chief of the celestials doth not return to the hand that hurleth it, without slaying enemies by hundreds and by thousands!'"

Vaisampayana continued, "Having said this, the thousand-rayed deity suddenly vanished away. The next day, after having told his prayers, Karna related his dream unto the Sun. And Vrisha related unto him the vision he had seen, and all that had passed between them in the night. Thereupon, having heard everything, that enemy of Swarbhanu, that lord, the resplendent and divine Surya, said unto him with a smile, 'It is even so!' Then Radha's son, that slayer of hostile heroes, knowing all about the matter, and desirous of obtaining the dart, remained in expectation of Vasava."

SECTION CCCI

Janamejaya said, "What was that secret which was not revealed to Karna by the deity of warm rays? Of what kind also were those ear-rings and of what sort was that coat of mail? Whence, too, was that mail and those ear-rings? All this, O best of men. I wish to hear! O thou possessed of the wealth of asceticism, do tell me all this!"

Vaisampayana said, "I will, O monarch, tell thee that secret which was not revealed by the deity possessed of the wealth of effulgence. I will also describe unto thee those ear-rings and that coat of mail. Once on a time, O king, there appeared before Kuntibhoja a Brahmana of fierce energy and tall stature, bearing a beard and matted locks, and carrying a staff in his hand. And, he was agreeable to the eye and of faultless limbs, and seemed to blaze forth in splendour. And he was possessed of a yellow-blue complexion like that of honey. And his speech was mellifluous, and he was adorned with ascetic merit and a knowledge of the *Vedas*. And that person of great ascetic merit, addressing king Kuntibhoja, said, 'O thou that are free from pride, I wish to live as a guest in thy house feeding on the food obtained as alms from thee! Neither thy followers, nor thou thyself, shall ever act in such a way as to produce my displeasure! If, O sinless one, it liketh thee, I would then live in thy house thus! I shall leave thy abode when I wish, and come back when I please. And, O king, no one shall offend me in respect of my food or bed.' — Then Kuntibhoja spake unto him these words cheerfully, 'Be it so, and more.' And he again said unto him, 'O thou of great wisdom, I have an illustrious daughter named Pritha. And she beareth an excellent character, is observant of vow, chaste, and of subdued senses. And she shall attend on thee and minister unto thee with reverence. And thou wilt be pleased with her disposition!' And having said this to that Brahmana and duly paid him homage, the king went to his daughter Pritha of large eyes, and spake thus unto her, 'O child, this eminently pious Brahmana is desirous of dwelling in my house! I have accepted his proposal, saying, —So be it, relying, O child, on thy aptitude and skill in ministering unto Brahmanas. It, therefore, behoveth thee to act in such a manner that my words may not be untrue. Do thou give him with alacrity whatever this reverend Brahmana possessed of ascetic merit and engaged in the study of the Vedas, may want. Let everything that this Brahmana asketh for be given to him cheerfully. A Brahmana is the embodiment of pre-eminent energy: he is also the embodiment of the highest ascetic merit. It is in consequence of the virtuous practices of Brahmanas that the sun shineth in the heavens. It was for their disregard of Brahmanas that were deserving of honour that the mighty *Asura* Vatapi, as also Talajangha, was destroyed by the curse of the Brahmanas. For the present, O child, it is a highly virtuous one of that order that is entrusted to thy keep. Thou shouldst always tend this Brahmana with concentrated mind. O daughter, I know that, from childhood upwards, thou hast ever been attentive to Brahmanas, and superiors, and relatives, and servants, and friends, to thy mothers and myself. I know thou bearest thyself well, bestowing proper regard upon everyone. And, O thou of faultless limbs, in the city of the interior of my palace, on account of thy gentle behaviour, there is not one, even among the servants, that is dissatisfied with thee. I have, therefore, thought thee fit to wait upon all Brahmanas of wrathful temper. Thou art, O Pritha, a girl and has been adopted as my daughter. Thou art born in the race of the Vrishnis, and art the favourite daughter of Sura. Thou wert, O girl, given to me gladly by thy father himself. The sister of Vasudeva by birth, thou art (by adoption) the foremost of my children. Having promised me in these words,—*I will give my first born*,—thy father gladly gave thee to me while thou wert yet in thy infancy. It is for this reason that thou art my daughter. Born in such a race and reared in such a race, thou hast come from one happy state to another like a lotus transferred from one lake to another. O auspicious girl, women, specially they that are of mean extraction, although they may with difficulty be kept under restraint, become in consequence of their unripe age, generally deformed in character. But thou, O Pritha, art born in a royal race, and thy beauty also is extraordinary. And then, O girl, thou art endued with every accomplishment. Do thou, therefore, O damsel, renouncing pride and haughtiness and a sense of self-importance, wait upon and worship the boon-giving Brahmana, and thereby attain, O Pritha, to an auspicious state! By acting thus, O auspicious and sinless girl, thou wilt surely attain to auspiciousness! But if on the contrary, thou stirrest up the anger of this best of the twice-born ones, my entire race will be consumed by him!'"

SECTION CCCII

"Kunti said, 'According to thy promise, I will, O king, with concentrated mind, serve that Brahmana. O foremost of kings, I do not say this falsely. It is my nature to worship Brahmanas. And, as in the present case, my doing so would be agreeable to thee, even this would be highly conducive to my welfare. Whether that worshipful one cometh in the evening, or in morning, or at night or even at midnight, he will have no reason to be angry with me! O foremost of kings, to do good by serving the twice-born ones, observing all thy commands, is what I consider to be highly profitable to me, O best of men! Do thou, therefore, O foremost of monarchs rely on me! That best of Brahmanas, while residing in thy house, shall never have cause for dissatisfaction, I tell thee truly. I shall, O king, be always attentive to that which is agreeable to this Brahmana, and what is fraught also with good to thee. O sinless one! I know full well that Brahmanas that are eminently virtuous, when propitiated bestow salvation, and when displeased, are capable of bringing about destruction upon the offender. Therefore, I shall please this foremost of Brahmanas. Thou wilt not, O monarch, come to any grief from that best of regenerate persons, owing to any act of mine. In consequence of the transgressions of monarchs, Brahmanas, O foremost of kings, became the cause of evil to them, as Chyavana had become, in consequence of the act of Sukanya. I will, therefore, O king, with great regularity, wait upon that best of Brahmanas according to thy instructions in that respect!' And when she had thus spoken at length, the king embraced and cheered her, and instructed her in detail as to what should be done by her. And the king said, 'Thou shall, O gentle maid, act even thus, without fear, for my good as also thy own, and for the good of thy race also, O thou of faultless limbs!' And having said this the illustrious Kuntibhoja, who was devoted to the Brahmanas, made over the girl Pritha to that Brahmana, saying, 'This my daughter, O Brahmana, is of tender age and brought up in luxury. If, therefore, she transgresses at any time, do thou not take that to heart! Illustrious Brahmanas are never angry with old men, children, and ascetics, even if these transgress frequently. In respect of even a great wrong forgiveness is due from the regenerate. The worship, therefore, O best of Brahmanas, that is offered to the best of one's power and exertion, should be acceptable!' Hearing these words of the monarch, the Brahmana said, 'So be it!' Thereupon, the king became highly pleased and assigned unto him apartments that were white as swans or the beams of the moon. And in the room intended for the sacrificial fire, the king placed a brilliant seat especially constructed for him. And the food and other things that were offered unto the Brahmana were of the same excellent kind. And casting aside idleness and all sense of self-importance, the princess addressed herself with right good will to wait upon the Brahmana. And the chaste Kunti, endued with purity of conduct, went thither for serving the Brahmana. And duly waiting upon that Brahmana as if he were a very god, she gratified him highly."

SECTION CCCIII

Vaisampayana said, "And that maiden of rigid vows, O mighty monarch, by serving with a pure heart, that Brahmana of rigid vows, succeeded in gratifying him. And, O foremost of kings, saying, 'I will come back in the morning,' that best of Brahmanas sometimes came in the evening or in night. Him, however, the maiden worshipped at all hours with sumptuous food and drink and bed. And as day after day passed away, her attentions to him, in respect of food and seat and bed, increased instead of undergoing any diminution. And, O king, even when the Brahmana reproved her, finding fault with any of her arrangements, or addressed her in harsh words, Pritha did not do anything that was disagreeable to him. And on many occasions the Brahmana came back after the appointed hour had long passed away. And on many occasions (such as the depth of night) when food was hard to procure, he said, 'Give me food!' But on all those occasions saying, 'All is ready,'—Pritha held before him the fare. And even like a disciple, daughter, or a sister, that blameless gem of a girl with a devoted heart, O king, gratified that foremost of Brahmanas. And that best of Brahmanas became well-pleased with her conduct and ministrations. And he received those attentions of hers, valuing them rightly. And, O Bharata, her father asked her every morning and evening saying, 'O daughter, is the Brahmana satisfied with thy ministrations?' And that illustrious maiden used to reply, 'Exceedingly well!' And thereupon, the high-souled Kuntibhoja experienced the greatest delight. And when after a full year that best of ascetics was unable to find any fault whatever in Pritha, who was engaged in ministering unto him, well-pleased he said unto her, 'O gentle maid, I have been well-pleased with thy attentions, O beautiful girl! Do thou, O blessed girl, ask even for such boons as are difficult of being obtained by men in this world, and obtaining which, thou mayst surpass in fame all the women in this world.' At these words of his, Kunti said, 'Everything hath already been done in my behalf since thou, O chief of those that are versed in the *Vedas*, and my father also, have been pleased with me! As regards the boons, I consider them as already obtained by me, O Brahmana!' The Brahmana thereupon said, 'If, O gentle maid, thou dost not, O thou of sweet smiles, wish to obtain boons from me, do thou then take this *mantra* from me for invoking the celestials! Any one amongst the celestials whom thou mayst invoke by uttering this *mantra*, will appear before thee and be under thy power. Willing or not, by virtue of this *mantra*, that deity in gentle guise, and assuming the obedient attitude of slave, will become subject to thy power!'"

Vaisampayana continued, "Thus addressed, that faultless maiden could not, O king, from fear of a curse, refuse for the second time compliance with the wishes of that best of the twice-born ones. Then, O king, that Brahmana imparted unto that girl of faultless limbs those *mantras* which are recited in the beginning of the *Atharvan Veda*. And, O king, having imparted unto her those *mantras*, he said unto Kuntibhoja. 'I have, O monarch, dwelt happily in thy house, always worshipped with due regard and gratified by thy daughter. I shall now depart.' And saying this, he vanished there and then. And beholding that Brahmana vanish there and then, the king was struck with amazement. And the monarch then treated his daughter Pritha with proper regard."

SECTION CCCIV

Vaisampayana said, "When that foremost of Brahmanas had gone away on some other errand, the maiden began to ponder over the virtue of those *mantras*. And she said to herself, 'Of what nature are those *mantras* that have been bestowed on me by that high-souled one? I shall without delay test their power.' And as she was thinking in this way, she suddenly perceived indications of the approach of her season. And her season having arrived, while she was yet unmarried, she blushed in shame. And it came to pass that as she was seated in her chamber on a rich bed, she beheld the solar orb rising in the east. And both the mind and the eyes of that maiden of excellent waist became rivetted fast upon the solar orb. And she gazed and gazed on that orb without being satiated with the beauty of the morning Sun. And she suddenly became gifted with celestial sight. And then she beheld that god of divine form accoutred in mail and adorned with ear-rings. And at sight of the god, O lord of men, she became curious as to the (potency of the) *mantras*. And thereupon that maiden resolved to invoke him. And having recourse to *Pranayama*, she invoked the Maker of day. And thus invoked by her, O king, the Maker of day speedily presented himself. And he was of a yellowish hue like honey, and was possessed of mighty arms, and his neck was marked with lines like those of a conchshell. And furnished with armlets, and decked with a diadem, he came smiling, and illumining all the directions. And it was by *Yoga* power that he divided himself in twain, one of which continued to give heat, and the other appeared before Kunti. And he addressed Kunti in words that were exceedingly sweet, saying, 'O gentle maiden, over-powered by the *mantras*, I come hither obedient to thee. Subject as I am to thy power, what shall I do, O queen? Tell me, for I shall do whatever thou mayst command.' Hearing these words of the deity, Kunti said, 'O worshipful one, go thou back to the place thou hast come from! I invoked thee from curiosity alone. Pardon me, O worshipful one!' Surya then said, 'O damsel of slender waist, I will, even as thou hast said, return to the place I have come from! Having called a celestial, it is not, however, proper to send him away in vain. Thy intention, O blessed one, it is to have from Surya a son furnished with a coat of mail and ear-rings, and who in point of prowess would be beyond compare in this world! Do thou, therefore, O damsel of elephantine gait, surrender thy person to me!

Thou shall then have, O lady, a son after thy wish! O gentle girl, O thou of sweet smiles, I will go back after having known thee! If thou do not gratify me to-day by obeying my word, I shall in anger curse thee, thy father and that Brahmana also. For thy fault, I will surely consume them all, and I shall inflict condign punishment on that foolish father of thine that knoweth not this transgression of thine and on that Brahmana who hath bestowed the *mantras* on thee without knowing thy disposition and character! Yonder are all the celestials in heaven, with Purandara at their head, who are looking at me with derisive smiles at my being deceived by thee, O lady! Look at those celestials, for thou art now possessed of celestial sight! Before this I have endued thee with celestial vision, in consequence of which thou couldst see me!'"

Vaisampayana continued, "Thereupon the princess beheld the celestials standing in the firmament, each in his proper sphere, even as she saw before her that highly resplendent deity furnished with rays, viz., Surya himself. And beholding them all, the girl became frightened and her face was suffused with blushes of shame. And then she addressed Surya, saying, 'O lord of rays, go thou back to thy own region. On account of my maidenhood, this outrage of thine is fraught with woe to me! It is only one's father, mother, and other superiors, that are capable of giving away their daughter's body. Virtue I shall never sacrifice, seeing that in this world the keeping of their persons inviolate is deemed as the highest duty of Women, and is held in high regard! O thou possessed of wealth of splendour, it is only to test the power of my *mantras* that I have, from mere childishness, summoned thee. Considering that this hath been done by a girl of tender years, it behoveth thee, O lord, to forgive her!' Then Surya said, 'It is because I consider thee a girl that, O Kunti, I am speaking to thee so mildly. To one that is not so I would not concede this. Do thou, O Kunti, surrender thyself! Thou shalt surely attain happiness thereby. Since, O timid maiden, thou hast invoked me with *mantras*, it is not proper for me to go away without any purpose being attained, for, if I do so I shall then, O thou of faultless limbs, be the object of laughter in the world, and, O beauteous damsel, a bye-word with all the celestials. Do thou, therefore, yield to me! By that thou shalt obtain a son even like myself, and thou shalt also be much praised in all the world.'"

SECTION CCCV

Vaisampayana said, "Although that noble girl addressed him in various sweet words, yet she was unable to dissuade that deity of a thousand rays. And when she failed to dissuade the dispeller of darkness, at last from fear of a curse, she reflected, O king, for a long time!—'How may my innocent father, and that Brahmana also, escape the angry Surya's curse for my sake? Although energy and asceticism are capable of destroying sins, yet even honest persons, if they be of unripe age, should not foolishly court them. By foolishly acting in that way I have today been placed in a frightful situation. Indeed, I have been placed entirely within the grasp of this deity. Ye how can I do what is sinful by taking it on myself to surrender my person to him?'"

Vaisampayana continued, "afflicted with fear of a curse, and thinking much within herself, an utter stupefaction of the senses came upon her. And she was so confounded that she could not settle what to do. Afraid, on the one hand, O king, of the reproach of friends if she obeyed the deity, and, on the other, of his curse if she disobeyed him, the damsel at last, O foremost of kings, said these words unto that god, in accents tremulous with bashfulness, 'O god, as my father and mother and friends are still living, this violation of duty on my part should not take place. If, O god, I commit this unlawful act with thee, the reputation of this race shall be sacrificed in this world on my account. If thou, however, O thou foremost of those that impart heat, deem this to be a meritorious act, I shall then fulfil thy desire even though my relatives may not have bestowed me on thee! May I remain chaste after having surrendered my person to thee! Surely, the virtue, the reputation, the fame, and the life of every creature are established in thee!' Hearing these words of hers, Surya replied, 'O thou of sweet smiles, neither thy father, nor thy mother, nor any other superior of thine, is competent to give thee away! May good betide thee, O beauteous damsel! Do thou listen to my words! It is because a virgin desireth the company of every one, that she hath received the appellation of *Kanya*, from the root *kama* meaning to desire. Therefore, O thou of excellent hips and the fairest complexion, a virgin is, by nature, free in this world. Thou shalt not, O lady, by any means, be guilty of any sin by complying with my request. And how can I, who am desirous of the welfare of all creatures, commit an unrighteous act? That all men and women should be bound by no restraints, is the law of nature. The opposite condition is the perversion of the natural state. Thou shalt remain a virgin after having gratified me. And thy son shall also be mighty-armed and illustrious.' Thereupon Kunti said, 'If, O dispeller of darkness, I obtain a son from thee, may he be furnished with a coat of mail and ear-rings, and may he be mighty-armed and endued with great strength!' Hearing these words of hers, Surya answered, 'O gentle maiden, thy son shall be mighty-armed and decked with ear-rings and a celestial coat of mail. And both his ear-rings and coat of mail will be made of *Amrita*, and his coat will also be invulnerable.' Kunti then said, 'If the excellent mail and ear-rings of the son thou wilt beget on me, be, indeed, made of *Amrita*, then, O god, O worshipful deity, let thy purpose be fulfilled! May he be powerful, strong, energetic, and handsome, even like thee, and may he also be endued with virtue!' Surya then said, 'O princess, O excellent damsel, these ear-rings had been given to me by Aditi. O timid lady, I will bestow them, as also this excellent mail, on thy son!' Kunti then said, 'Very well, O worshipful one! If my son, O lord of light, become so, I will, as thou sayest, gratify thee!'"

Vaisampayana continued, "Hearing these words of hers Surya said, 'So be it!' And that ranger of the skies, that enemy of Swarbhanu, with soul absorbed in *Yoga*, entered into Kunti, and touched her on the navel. At this, that damsel, on account of Surya's energy, became stupefied. And that reverend lady then fell down on her bed, deprived of her senses. Surya then addressed her, saying, 'I will now depart, O thou of graceful hips! Thou shalt bring forth a son who will become the foremost of all wielders of weapons. At the same time thou shalt remain a virgin.'"

Vaisampayana continued, "Then, O foremost of kings, as the highly effulgent Surya was about to depart, that girl bashfully said unto him, 'So be it!' And it was thus that the daughter of king Kuntibhoja, importuned by Surya, had after soliciting a son from him, fallen down stupefied on that excellent bed, like a broken creeper. And it was thus that deity of fierce rays, stupefying her, entered into her by virtue of *Yoga* power, and placed his own self within her womb. The deity, however, did not sully her by deflowering her in the flesh. And after Surya had gone away, that girl regained her consciousness."

SECTION CCCVI

Vaisampayana said, "It was, O lord of earth, on the first day of the lighted fortnight during the tenth month of the year that Pritha conceived a son like the lord himself of the stars in the firmament. And that damsel of excellent hips from fear of her friends, concealed her conception, so that no one knew her condition. And as the damsel lived entirely in the apartments assigned to the maidens and carefully concealed her condition, no one except her nurse knew the truth. And in due time that beauteous maiden, by the grace of deity, brought forth a son resembling a very god. And even like his father, the child was equipped in a coat of mail, and decked with brilliant ear-rings. And he was possessed of leonine eyes and shoulders like those of a bull. And no sooner was the beauteous girl delivered of a child, then she consulted with her nurse and placed the infant in a commodious and smooth box made of wicker work and spread over with soft sheets and furnished with a costly pillow. And its surface was laid over with wax, and it was encased in a rich cover. And with tears in her eyes, she carried the infant to the river Aswa, and consigned the basket to its waters. And although she knew it to be improper for an unmarried girl to bear offspring, yet from parental affection, O foremost of kings, she wept piteously. Do thou listen to the words Kunti weepingly uttered, while consigning the box to the waters of the river Aswa, 'O child, may good betide thee at the hands of all that inhabit the land, the water, the sky, and the celestial regions. May all thy paths be auspicious! May no one obstruct thy way! And, O son, may all that come across thee have their hearts divested of hostility towards thee: And may that lord of waters, Varuna, protect thee in water! And may the deity that rangeth the skies completely protect thee in the sky. And may, O son, that best of those that impart heat, viz., Surya, thy father, and from whom I have obtained thee as ordained by Destiny, protect thee everywhere! And may the *Adityas* and the *Vasus*, the *Rudras* and the *Sadhyas*, the *Viswadevas* and the *Maruts*, and the cardinal points with the great Indra and the regents presiding over them, and, indeed, all the celestials, protect thee in every place! Even in foreign lands I shall be able to recognise thee by this mail of thine! Surely, thy sire, O son, the divine Surya possessed of the wealth of splendour, is blessed, for he will with his celestial sight behold thee going down the current! Blessed also is that lady who will, O thou that are begotten by a god, take thee for her son, and who will give thee suck when thou art thirsty! And what a lucky dream hath been dreamt by her that will adopt thee for her son, thee that is endued with solar splendour, and furnished with celestial mail, and adorned with celestial ear-rings, thee that hast expansive eyes resembling lotuses, a complexion bright as burnished copper or lotus leaves, a fair forehead, and hair ending in beautiful curls! O son, she that will behold thee crawl on the ground, begrimed with dust, and sweetly uttering inarticulate words, is surely blessed! And she also, O son, that will behold thee arrive at thy youthful prime like maned lion born in Himalayan forests, is surely blessed!'"

"O king, having thus bewailed long and piteously, Pritha laid the basket on the waters of the river Aswa. And the lotus-eyed damsel, afflicted with grief on account of her son and weeping bitterly, with her nurse cast the basket at dead of night, and though desirous of beholding her son often and again, returned, O monarch, to the palace, fearing lest her father should come to know of what had happened. Meanwhile, the basket floated from the river Aswa to the river Charmanwati, and from the Charmanwati it passed to the Yamuna, and so on to the Ganga. And carried by the waves of the Ganga, the child contained in the basket came to the city of Champa ruled by a person of the *Suta* tribe. Indeed, the excellent coat of mail and those ear-rings made of *Amrita* that were born with his body, as also the ordinance of Destiny, kept the child alive."

SECTION CCCVII

Vaisampayana said, "And it came to pass that at this time a *Suta* named Adhiratha, who was a friend of Dhritarashtra, came to the river Ganga, accompanied by his wife. And, O king, his wife named Radha was unparalleled on earth for beauty. And although that highly blessed dame had made great endeavours to obtain a son, yet she had failed, O represser of foes, to obtain one. And on coming to the river Ganga, she beheld a box drifting along the current. And containing articles capable of protecting from dangers and decked with unguents, that box was brought before her by the waves of the Janhavi. And attracted by curiosity, the lady caused it to be seized. And she then related all unto Adhiratha of the charioteer caste. And hearing this Adhiratha took away the box from the water-side, and opened it by means of instruments. And then he beheld a boy resembling the morning Sun. And the infant was furnished with golden mail, and looked exceedingly beautiful with a face decked in ear-rings. And thereupon the charioteer, together with his wife, was struck with such astonishment that their eyes expanded in wonder. And taking the infant on his lap, Adhiratha said unto his wife, 'Ever since I was born, O timid lady, I had never seen such a wonder. This child that hath come to us must be of celestial birth. Surely, sonless as I am, it is the gods that have sent him unto me!' Saying this, O lord of earth, he gave the infant to Radha. And thereat, Radha adopted, according to the ordinance, that child of celestial form and divine origin, and possessed of the splendour of the filaments of the lotus and furnished with excellent grace. And duly reared by her, that child endued with great prowess began to grow up. And after Karna's adoption, Adhiratha had other sons begotten by himself. And seeing the child furnished with bright mail and golden ear-rings, the twice-born ones named him Vasusena. And thus did that child endued with great splendour and immeasurable prowess became the son of the charioteer, and came to be known as Vasusena and Vrisha. And Pritha learnt through spies that her own son clad in celestial mail was growing up amongst the Angas as the eldest son of a charioteer (Adhiratha). And seeing that in process of time his son had grown up, Adhiratha sent him to the city named after the elephant. And there Karna put up with Drona, for the purpose of learning arms. And that powerful youth contracted a friendship with Duryodhana. And having acquired all the four kinds of weapons from Drona, Kripa, and Rama, he became famous in the world as a mighty bowman. And after having contracted a friendship with Dhritarashtra's son, he became intent on injuring the sons of Pritha. And he was always desirous of fighting with the high-souled Phalguna. And, O king, ever since they first saw each other, Karna always used to challenge Arjuna, and Arjuna, on his part, used to challenge him. This, O foremost of kings, was without doubt, the secret known to the Sun, viz., begot by himself on Kunti, Karna was being reared in the race of the *Sutas*. And beholding him decked with his earrings and mail, Yudhishthira thought him to be unslayable in fight, and was exceedingly pained at it. And when, O foremost of monarchs, Karna after rising from the water, used at mid-day to worship the effulgent Surya with joined hands, the Brahmanas used to solicit him for wealth. And at that time there was nothing that he would not give away to the twice-born ones. And Indra, assuming the guise of a Brahmana, appeared before him (at such a time) and said, 'Give me!' And thereupon Radha's son replied unto him, 'Thou art welcome!'"

SECTION CCCVIII

Vaisampayana said, "And when the king of the celestials presented himself in the guise of a Brahmana, beholding him, Karna said, 'Welcome!' And not knowing his intention, Adhiratha's son addressed the Brahmana, saying, 'Of a necklace of gold, and beauteous damsels, and villages with plenty of kine, which shall I give thee?' Thereupon the Brahmana replied, 'I ask thee not to give me either a necklace of gold, or fair damsels, or any other agreeable object. To those do thou give them that ask for them. If, O sinless one, thou art sincere in thy vow, then wilt thou, cutting off (from thy person) this coat of mail born with thy body, and these ear-rings also, bestow them on me! I desire, O chastiser of foes, that thou mayst speedily give me these; for, this one gain of mine will be considered as superior to every other gain!' Hearing these words, Karna said, 'O Brahmana, I will give thee homestead land, and fair damsels, and kine, and fields; but my mail and ear-rings I am unable to give thee!'"

Vaisampayana continued, "Although thus urged with various words by Karna, still, O chief of the Bharata race, that Brahmana did not ask for any other boon. And although Karna sought to pacify him to the best of his power, and worshipped him duly, yet that best of Brahmanas did not ask for any other boon. And when that foremost of Brahmanas did not ask for any other boon, Radha's son again spake unto him with a smile, 'My mail, O regenerate one, hath been born with my body, and this pair of ear-rings hath arisen from *Amrita*. It is for these that I am unslayable in the worlds. Therefore, I cannot part with them. Do thou, O bull among Brahmanas, accept from me the entire kingdom of the earth, rid of enemies and full of prosperity! O foremost of regenerate ones, if I am deprived of my ear-rings, and the mail born with my body, I shall be liable to be vanquished by the foes!'"

Vaisampayana continued, "When the illustrious slayer of Paka refused to ask for any other boon, Karna with a smile again addressed him, saying, 'O god of gods, even before this, I had recognised thee, O Lord! O Sakra, it is not proper for me to confer on thee any unprofitable boon, for thou art the very lord of the celestials! On the contrary, being as thou art the Creator and lord of all beings, it is thou that shouldst confer boons on me!

If, O god, I give thee this coat of mail and ear-rings, then I am sure to meet with destruction, and thou shalt also undergo ridicule! Therefore, O Sakra, take my earrings and excellent mail in exchange for something conferred by thee on me! Otherwise, I will not bestow them on thee!' Thereupon Sakra replied, 'Even before I had come to thee, Surya had known of my purpose and without doubt, it is he that hath unfolded everything unto thee! O Karna, be it as thou wishest! O son, except the thunder-bolt alone, tell me what it is that thou desirest to have!'"

Vaisampayana continued, "Hearing these words of Indra, Karna was filled with delight and seeing that his purpose was about to be accomplished he approached Vasava, and intent upon obtaining a dart incapable of being baffled, he addressed Indra, saying, 'Do thou, O Vasava, in exchange for my coat of mail and ear-rings, give me a dart incapable of being baffled, and competent to destroy hosts of enemies when arrayed in order of battle!' Thereupon, O ruler of earth, fixing his mind for a moment on the dart (for bringing it there), Vasava thus spake unto Karna, 'Do thou give me thy ear-rings, and the coat of mail born with thy body, and in return take this dart on these terms! When I encounter the *Daitya* in battle, this dart that is incapable of being baffled, hurled by my hand, destroyeth enemies by hundreds, and cometh back to my hand after achieving its purpose. In thy hand, however, this dart, O son of *Suta*, will slay only one powerful enemy of thine. And having achieved that feat, it will, roaring and blazing, return to me!' Thereat Karna said, 'I desire to slay in fierce fight even one enemy of mine, who roareth fiercely and is hot as fire, and of whom I am in fear!' At this, Indra said, 'Thou shall slay such a roaring and powerful foe in battle. But that one whom thou seekest to slay, is protected by an illustrious personage. Even He whom persons versed in the Vedas call *'the invincible Boar,'* and *'the incomprehensible Narayana,'* even that Krishna himself, is protecting him!' Thereupon Karna replied, 'Even if this be so, do thou, O illustrious one give me the weapon that will destroy only one powerful foe! I shall, on my part, bestow on thee my mail and ear-rings, cutting them off my person. Do thou, however, grant that my body, thus wounded, may not be unsightly!' Hearing this, Indra said, 'As thou, O Karna, art bent upon observing the truth, thy person shall not be unsightly, or shall any scar remain on it. And, O thou best of those that are graced with speech, O Karna, thou shall be possessed of complexion and energy of thy father himself. And if, maddened by wrath, thou hurlest this dart, while there are still other weapons with thee, and when thy life also is not in imminent peril, it will fall even on thyself.' Karna answered, 'As thou directest me, O Sakra, I shall hurl this *Vasavi* dart only when I am in imminent peril! Truly I tell thee this!'"

Vaisampayana continued, "Thereupon, O king, taking the blazing dart, Karna began to peel off his natural mail. And beholding Karna cutting his own body, the entire host of celestials and men and *Danavas* set up a leonine roar. And Karna betrayed no contortions of face while peeling his mail. And beholding that hero among men thus cutting his body with an weapon, smiling ever and anon, celestial kettle-drums began to be played upon and celestial flowers began to be showered on him. And Karna cutting off the excellent mail from his person, gave it to Vasava, still dripping. And cutting off his ear-rings also from off his ears, he made them over to Indra. And it is for this fact that he came to be called Karna. And Sakra, having thus beguiled Karna that made him famous in the world, thought with a smile that the business of the sons of Pandu had already been completed. And having done all this, he ascended to heaven. And hearing that Karna had been beguiled, all the sons of Dhritarashtra became distressed and shorn of pride. And the sons of Pritha, on the other hand, learning that such plight had befallen the son of the charioteer, were filled with joy."

Janamejaya said, "Where were those heroes, the sons of Pandu, at that time? And from whom did they hear this welcome news? And what also did they do, when the twelfth year of their exile passed away? Do thou, O illustrious one, tell me all this!"

Vaisampayana said, "Having defeated the chief of the Saindhavas, and rescued Krishna, and having outlived the entire term of their painful exile in the woods, and having listened to the ancient stories about gods and *Rishis* recited by Markandeya, those heroes among men returned from their asylum in Kamyaka to the sacred Dwaitavana, with all their cars, and followers, and accompanied by their charioteers, their kine, and the citizens who had followed them."

SECTION CCCIX

(Aranya Parva)

Janamejaya said, "Having felt great affliction on account of the abduction of their wife and having rescued Krishna thereafter, what did the Pandavas next do?"

Vaisampayana said, "Having felt great affliction on account of the abduction of Krishna, king Yudhishthira of unfading glory, with his brothers, left the woods of Kamyaka and returned to the delightful and picturesque Dwaitavana abounding in trees and containing delicious fruits and roots. And the sons of Pandu with their wife Krishna began to reside there, living frugally on fruits and practising rigid vows. And while those repressers of foes, the virtuous king Yudhishthira, the son of Kunti, and Bhimasena, and Arjuna, and those other sons of Pandu born of Madri, were dwelling in Dwaitavana, practising rigid vows, they underwent, for the sake of a Brahmana, great trouble, which, however, was destined to bring about their future happiness. I will tell thee all about the trouble which those foremost of Kurus underwent while living in those woods, and which in the end brought about their happiness. Do thou listen to it! Once on a time, as a deer was butting about, it chanced that the two sticks for making fire and a churning staff belonging to a Brahmana devoted to ascetic austerities, struck fast into its antlers. And, thereupon, O king, that powerful deer of exceeding fleetness with long bounds, speedily went out of the hermitage, taking those articles away. And, O foremost of Kurus, seeing those articles of his thus carried away, the Brahmana, anxious on account of his *Agnihotra*, quickly came before the Pandavas. And approaching without loss of time Ajatasatru seated in that forest with his brothers, the Brahmana, in great distress, spake these words, 'As a deer was butting about, it happened, O king, that my fire-sticks and churning staff which had been placed against a large tree stuck fast to its antlers. O king, that powerful deer of exceeding fleetness hath speedily gone out of the hermitage with long bounds, taking those articles away. Tracking that powerful deer, O king, by its foot-prints, do ye, ye sons of Pandu, bring back those articles of mine, so that my *Agnihotra* may not be stopped!' Hearing these words of the Brahmana, Yudhishthira became exceedingly concerned. And the son of Kunti taking up his bow sallied out with his brothers. And putting on their corselets and equipped with their bows, those bulls among men, intent upon serving the Brahmana, swiftly sallied out in the wake of the deer. And descrying the deer at no great distance, those mighty warriors discharged at it barbed arrows and javelins and darts, but the sons of Pandu could not pierce it by any means. And as they struggled to pursue and slay it, that powerful deer became suddenly invisible. And losing sight of the deer, the noble-minded sons of Pandu, fatigued and disappointed and afflicted with hunger and thirst, approached a banian tree in that deep forest, and sat down in its cool shade. And when they had sat down, Nakula stricken with sorrow and urged by impatience, addressed his eldest brother of the Kuru race, saying, 'In our race, O king, virtue hath never been sacrificed, nor hath there been loss of wealth from insolence. And being asked, we have never said to any creature, Nay! Why then in the present case have we met with this disaster?'"

SECTION CCCX

"Yudhishthira said, 'There is no limit to calamities. Nor is it possible to ascertain either their final or efficient cause. It is the Lord of justice alone who distributeth the fruits of both virtue and vice.' Thereupon Bhima said, 'Surely, this calamity hath befallen us, because I did not slay the *Pratikamin* on the very spot, when he dragged Krishna as a slave into the assembly.' And Arjuna said, 'Surely, this calamity hath befallen us because I resented not those biting words piercing the very bones, uttered by the *Suta's* son!' And Sahadeva said, 'Surely, O Bharata, this calamity hath befallen us because I did not slay Sakuni when he defeated thee at dice!'"

Vaisampayana continued, "Then king Yudhishthira addressed Nakula saying, 'Do thou, O son of Madri, climb this tree and look around the ten points of the horizon. Do thou see whether there is water near us or such trees as grow on watery grounds! O child, these thy brothers are all fatigued and thirsty.' Thereupon saying, 'So be it,' Nakula speedily climbed up a tree, and having looked around, said unto his eldest brother, 'O king, I see many a tree that groweth by the water-side, and I hear also the cries of cranes. Therefore, without doubt, water must be somewhere here.' Hearing these words, Kunti's son Yudhishthira, firm in truth, said, 'O amiable one, go thou and fetch water in these quivers!' Saying, 'So be it,' at the command of his eldest brother Nakula quickly proceeded towards the place where there was water and soon came upon it. And beholding a crystal lake inhabited by cranes he desired to drink of it, when he heard these words from the sky, 'O child, do not commit this rash act! This lake hath already been in my possession. Do thou, O son of Madri, first answer my questions and then drink of this water and take away (as much as thou requirest).' Nakula, however, who was exceedingly thirsty, disregarding these words, drank of the cool water, and having drunk of it, dropped down dead. And, O represser of foes, seeing Nakula's delay, Yudhishthira the son of Kunti said unto Sahadeva, the heroic brother of Nakula, 'O Sahadeva, it is long since our brother, he who was born immediately before thee, hath gone from hence! Do thou, therefore, go and bring back thy uterine brother, together with water.' At this, Sahadeva, saying, 'So be it,' set out in that direction; and coming to the spot, beheld his brother lying dead on the ground. And afflicted at the death of his brother, and suffering severely from thirst, he advanced towards the water, when these words were heard by him, 'O child, do not commit this rash act! This lake hath already been in my possession. First answer my question, and then drink of the water and take away as much as thou mayst require.' Sahadeva, however, who was extremely thirsty, disregarding these words, drank of the water, and having drunk of it, dropped down dead. Then Yudhishthira, the son of Kunti, said unto Vijaya, 'It is long since, O Vibhatsu, that thy two brothers have gone, O represser of foes! Blessed be thou! Do thou bring them back, together with water. Thou art, O child, the refuge of us all when plunged in distress!' Thus addressed, the intelligent Gudakesa, taking his bow and arrows and also his naked sword, set out for that lake of waters. And reaching that spot, he whose car was drawn by white steeds beheld those tigers among men, his two younger brothers who had come to fetch water, lying dead there. And seeing them as if asleep, that lion among men, exceedingly aggrieved, raised his bow and began to look around that wood. But he found none in that mighty forest. And, being fatigued, he who was capable of drawing the bow by his left hand as well, rushed in the direction of the water. And as he was rushing (towards the water), he heard these words from the sky, 'Why dost thou approach this water? Thou shalt not be able to drink of it by force. If thou, O Kaunteya, can answer the question I will put to thee, then only shalt thou drink of the water and take away as much as thou requirest, O Bharata!' Thus forbidden, the son of Pritha said, 'Do thou forbid me by appearing before me! And when thou shalt be sorely pierced with my arrows, thou wilt not then again speak in this way!' Having said this, Partha covered all sides with arrows inspired by *mantras*. And he also displayed his skill in shooting at an invisible mark by sound alone. And, O bull of the Bharata race, sorely afflicted with thirst, he discharged barbed darts and javelins and iron arrows, and showered on the sky innumerable shafts incapable of being baffled. Thereupon, the invisible Yaksha said, 'What need of all this trouble, O son of Pritha? Do thou drink only after answering my questions! If thou drink, however, without answering my questions, thou shalt die immediately after.' Thus addressed, Pritha's son Dhananjaya capable of drawing the bow with his left hand as well, disregarding those words, drank of the water, and immediately after dropped down dead. And (seeing Dhananjaya's delay) Kunti's son Yudhishthira addressed Bhimasena, saying, 'O represser of foes, it is a long while that Nakula and Sahadeva and Vibhatsu have gone to fetch water, and they have not come yet, O Bharata! Good betide thee! Do thou bring them back, together with water!' Thereupon saying, 'So be it,' Bhimasena set out for that place where those tigers among men, his brothers, lay dead. And beholding them, Bhima afflicted though he was with thirst, was exceedingly distressed. And that mighty armed hero thought all that to have been the act of some Yaksha or Rakshasa. And Pritha's son Vrikodara thought, 'I shall surely have to fight today. Let me, therefore, first appease my thirst.' Then that bull of the Bharata race rushed forward with the intention of drinking. Thereupon the Yaksha said, 'O child, do not commit this rash act! This lake hath already been in my possession. Do thou first answer my questions, and then drink and take away as much water as thou requirest!'"

Vaisampayana continued, "Thus addressed by that Yaksha of immeasurable energy, Bhima, without answering his questions, drank of the water. And as soon as he drank, he fell down dead on the spot. Then thinking that his brothers had left him long since, Yudhishthira waited for some time. And the king said unto himself again and again, 'Why is it that the two sons of Madri are delaying? And why doth the wielder also of the *Gandiva* delay? And why doth Bhima too, endued with great strength, delay? I shall go to search for them!' And resolved to do this, the mighty-armed Yudhishthira then rose up, his heart burning in grief. And that bull among men, the royal son of Kunti thought within himself. 'Is this forest under some malign influence? Or, is it infested by some wicked beasts? Or, have they all fallen, in consequence of having disregarded some mighty being? Or, not finding water in the spot whither those heroes had first repaired, they have spent all this time in search through the forest? What is that reason for which those bulls among men do not come back?' And speaking in this strain, that foremost of monarchs, the illustrious Yudhishthira, entered into that mighty forest where no human sound was heard and which was inhabited by deer and bears and birds, and which was adorned with trees that were bright and green, and which echoed with the hum of the black-bee and the notes of winged warblers. As he was proceeding along, he beheld that beautiful lake which looked as if it had been made by the celestial artificer himself. And it was adorned with flowers of a golden hue and with lotuses and *Sindhuvars*. And it abounded with canes and *Ketakas* and *Karaviras* and *Pippalas*, and fatigued with toil, Yudhishthira saw that tank and was struck with wonder."

SECTION CCCXI

Vaisampayana said, "Yudhishthira saw his brothers, each possessed of the glory of Indra himself, lying dead like the Regents of the world dropped from their spheres at the end of the *Yuga*. And beholding Arjuna lying dead, with his bow and arrows dropped on the ground, and also Bhimasena and the twins motionless and deprived of life, the king breathed a hot and long sigh, and was bathed in tears of grief. And beholding his brothers lying dead, the mighty armed son of Dharma with heart racked in anxiety, began to lament profusely, saying, 'Thou hadst, O mighty-armed Vrikodara, vowed, saying,—*I shall with mace smash the thighs of Duryodhana in battle!* O enhancer of the glory of the Kurus, in thy death, O mighty-armed and high-souled one, all that hath become fruitless now! The promises of men may be ineffectual; but why have the words of the gods uttered in respect of thee been thus fruitless? O Dhananjaya, while thou wert in thy mother's lying-in-room, the gods had said,—*O Kunti, this thy son shall not be inferior to him of a thousand eyes!* And in the northern Paripatra mountains, all beings had sung, saying,—*The prosperity (of this race), robbed by foes will be recovered by this one without delay. No one will be able to vanquish him in battle, while there will be none whom he will not be able to vanquish.* Why then hath that Jishnu endued with great strength been subject to death? Oh, why doth that Dhananjaya, relying on whom we had hitherto endured all this misery, lie on the ground blighting 66 all my hopes! Why have those heroes, those mighty sons of Kunti, Bhimasena and Dhananjaya, came under the power of the enemy,—those who themselves always slew their foes, and whom no weapons could resist! Surely, this vile heart of mine must be made of adamant, since, beholding these twins lying today on the ground it doth not split! Ye bulls among men, versed in holy writ and acquainted with the properties of time and place, and endued with ascetic merit, ye who duly performed all sacred rites, why lie ye down, without performing acts deserving of you? Alas, why lie ye insensible on the earth, with your bodies unwounded, ye unvanquished ones, and with your vows untouched?' And beholding his brothers sweetly sleeping there as (they usually did) on mountain slopes, the high souled king, overwhelmed with grief and bathed in sweat, came to a distressful condition. And saying,—It is even so—that virtuous lord of men, immersed in an ocean of grief anxiously proceeded to ascertain the cause (of that catastrophe). And that mighty-armed and high-souled one, acquainted with the divisions of time and place, could not settle his course of action. Having thus bewailed much in this strain, the virtuous Yudhishthira, the son of *Dharma* or *Tapu*, restrained his soul and began to reflect in his mind as to who had slain those heroes. 'There are no strokes of weapons upon these, nor is any one's foot-print here. The being must be mighty I ween, by whom my brothers have been slain. Earnestly shall I ponder over this, or, let me first drink of the water, and then know all. It may be that the habitually crooked-minded Duryodhana hath caused this water to be secretly placed here by the king of the *Gandharvas*. What man of sense can trust wicked wight of evil passions with whom good and evil are alike? Or, perhaps, this may be an act of that wicked-souled one through secret messengers of his.' And it was thus that that highly intelligent one gave way to diverse reflections. He did not believe that water to have been tainted with poison, for though dead no corpse-like pallor was on them. 'The colour on the faces of these my brothers hath not faded!' And it was thus that Yudhishthira thought. And the king continued, 'Each of these foremost of men was like unto a mighty cataract. Who, therefore, save Yama himself who in due time bringeth about the end of all things, could have baffled them thus.' And having concluded this for certain, he began to perform his ablutions in that lake. And while he descended into it, he heard these words from the sky, uttered by the Yaksha,—'I am a crane, living on tiny fish. It is by me that thy younger brothers have been brought under the sway of the lord of departed spirits. If thou, O prince, answer not the questions put by me, even thou shalt number the fifth corpse. Do not, O child, act rashly! This lake hath already been in my possession. Having answered my questions first, do thou, O Kunti's son, drink and carry away (as much as thou requirest)!' Hearing these words, Yudhishthira said, 'Art thou the foremost of the Rudras, or of the Vasus, or of the Marutas? I ask, what god art thou? This could not have been done by a bird! Who is it that hath overthrown the four mighty mountains, viz., the Himavat, the Paripatra, the Vindhya, and the Malaya? Great is the feat done by thee, thou foremost of strong persons! Those whom neither gods, nor *Gandharvas* nor *Asuras*, nor *Rakshasas* could endure in mighty conflict, have been slain by thee! Therefore, exceedingly wonderful is the deed done by thee! I do not know what thy business may be, nor do I know thy purpose. Therefore, great is the curiosity and fear also that have taken possession of me. My mind is greatly agitated, and as my head also is aching, I ask thee, therefore, O worshipful one, who art thou that stayest here?' Hearing these words the Yaksha said, 'I am, good betide thee, a Yaksha, and not an amphibious bird. It is by me that all these brothers of thine, endued with mighty prowess, have been slain!'"

Vaisampayana continued, "Hearing these accursed words couched in harsh syllabus, 67 Yudhishthira, O king, approaching the Yaksha who had spoken then, stood there. And that bull among the Bharatas then beheld that Yaksha of unusual eyes and huge body tall like a palmyra-palm and looking like fire or the Sun, and irresistible and gigantic like a mountain, staying on a tree, and uttering a loud roar deep as that of the clouds. And the Yaksha said, 'These thy brothers, O king, repeatedly forbidden by me, would forcibly take away water. It is for this that they have been slain by me! He that wisheth to live, should not, O king, drink this water! O son of Pritha, act not rashly! This lake hath already been in my possession. Do thou, O son of Kunti, first answer my questions, and then take away as much as thou likest!' Yudhishthira said, 'I do not, O Yaksha, covet, what is already in thy possession! O bull among male beings, virtuous persons never approve that one should applaud his own self (without boasting, I shall, therefore, answer thy questions, according to my intelligence). Do thou ask me!' The Yaksha then said, 'What is it that maketh the Sun rise? Who keeps him company? Who causeth him to set? And in whom is he established?' Yudhishthira answered, '*Brahma* maketh the Sun rise; the gods keep him company; *Dharma* causeth him to set; and he is established in truth.' 68 The Yaksha asked, 'By what doth one become learned? By what doth he attain what is very great? How can one have a second? And, O king, how can one acquire intelligence?' Yudhishthira answered, 'It is by the (study of the) *Srutis* that a person becometh learned; it is by ascetic austerities that one acquireth what is very great; it is by intelligence that a person acquireth a second and it is by serving the old that one becometh wise.' 69 The Yaksha asked, 'What constituteth the divinity of the Brahmanas? What even is their practice that is like that of the pious? What also is the human attribute of the Brahmanas? And what practice of theirs is like that of the impious?' Yudhishthira answered, 'The study of the *Vedas* constitutes their divinity; their asceticism constitutes behaviour that is like that of the pious; their liability to death is their human attribute and slander is their impiety.' The Yaksha asked, 'What institutes the divinity of the Kshatriyas? What even is their practice that is like that of the pious? What is their human attribute? And what practice of theirs is like that of the impious?' Yudhishthira answered, 'Arrows and weapons are their divinity; celebration of sacrifices is that act which is like that of the pious; liability to fear is their human attribute; and refusal of protection is that act of theirs which is like that of the impious.' The Yaksha asked, 'What is that which constitutes the *Sama* of the sacrifice? What the *Yajus* of the sacrifice? What is that which is the refuge of a sacrifice? And what is that which sacrifice cannot do without?' Yudhishthira answered, 'Life is the *Sama* of the sacrifice; the mind is the *Yajus* of the sacrifice; the *Rik* is that which is the refuge of the sacrifice; and it is *Rik* alone which sacrifice cannot do without.' 70 The Yaksha asked, 'What is of the foremost value to those that cultivate? What is of the foremost value to those that sow? What is of the foremost value to those that wish for prosperity in this world? And what is of the foremost value to those that bring forth?' Yudhishthira answered, 'That which is of the foremost value to those that cultivate is rain; that of the foremost value to those that sow is seed; that of the foremost value to those that bring forth is offspring.' 71 The Yaksha asked, 'What person, enjoying all the objects of the senses, endued with intelligence, regarded by the world and liked by all beings, though breathing, doth not offer anything to these five, viz., gods, guests, servants, *Pitris*, and himself, though endued with breath, is not yet alive.' The Yaksha asked, 'What is weightier than the earth itself? What is higher than the heavens? What is fleeter than the wind? And what is more numerous than grass?' Yudhishthira answered, 'The mother is weightier than the earth; the father is higher than the heaven; the mind is fleeter than the wind; and our thoughts are more numerous than grass.' The Yaksha asked, 'What is that which doth not close its eyes while asleep? What is that which doth not move after birth? What is that which is without heart? And what is that which swells with its own impetus?' Yudhishthira answered, 'A fish doth not close its eyes while asleep; an egg doth not move after birth; a stone is without heart; and a river swelleth with its own impetus.' The Yaksha asked, 'Who is the friend of the exile? Who is the friend of the householder? Who is the friend of him that ails? And who is the friend of one about to die?' Yudhishthira answered, 'The friend of the exile in a distant land is his companion; the friend of the householder is the wife; the friend of him that ails is the physician; and the friend of him about to die is charity.' The Yaksha asked,— 'Who is the guest of all creatures? What is the eternal duty? What, O foremost of kings, is *Amrita*? And what is this entire Universe?' Yudhishthira answered,—'*Agni* is the guest of all creatures; the milk of kine is *amrita*; *Homa* (therewith) is the eternal duty; and this Universe consists of air alone.' 72 The Yaksha asked,—'What is that which sojourneth alone? What is that which is re-born after its birth? What is the remedy against cold? And what is the largest field?' Yudhishthira answered,—'The sun sojourneth alone; the moon takes birth anew; fire is the remedy against cold; and the Earth is the largest field.' The Yaksha asked,—'What is the highest refuge of virtue? What of fame? What of heaven? And what, of happiness?' Yudhishthira answered,—'Liberality is the highest refuge of virtue; gift, of fame; truth, of heaven; and good behaviour, of happiness.' The Yaksha asked,—'What is the soul of man? Who is that friend bestowed on man by the gods? What is man's chief support? And what also is his chief refuge?' Yudhishthira answered,—'The son is a man's soul; the wife is the friend bestowed on man by the gods; the clouds are his chief support; and gift is his chief refuge.' The

Yaksha asked,—'What is the best of all laudable things? What is the most valuable of all his possessions? What is the best of all gains? And what is the best of all kinds of happiness?' Yudhishthira answered,—"The best of all laudable things is skill; the best of all possessions is knowledge; the best of all gains is health; and contentment is the best of all kinds of happiness.' The Yaksha asked,—'What is the highest duty in the world? What is that virtue which always beareth fruit? What is that which if controlled, leadeth not to regret? And who are they with whom an alliance cannot break?' Yudhishthira answered,—'The highest of duties is to refrain from injury; the rites ordained in the *Three (Vedas)* always bear fruit; the mind, if controlled, leadeth to no regret; and an alliance with the good never breaketh.' The Yaksha asked,— 'What is that which, if renounced, maketh one agreeable? What is that which, if renounced, leadeth to no regret? What is that which, if renounced, maketh one wealthy? And what is that which if renounced, maketh one happy?' Yudhishthira answered,—'Pride, if renounced, maketh one agreeable; wrath, if renounced leadeth to no regret; desire, if renounced, maketh one wealthy; and avarice, if renounced, maketh one happy.' The Yaksha asked,—'For what doth one give away to Brahmanas? For what to mimes and dancers? For what to servants? And for what to the king?' Yudhishthira answered,—'It is for religious merit that one giveth away to Brahmanas; it is for fame that one giveth away to mimes and dancers; it is for supporting them that one giveth away to servants; and it is for obtaining relief from fear that one giveth to kings.' The Yaksha asked,—'With what is the world enveloped? What is that owing to which a thing cannot discover itself? For what are friends forsaken? And for what doth one fail to go to heaven?' Yudhishthira answered,—'The world is enveloped with darkness. Darkness doth not permit a thing to show itself. It is from avarice that friends are forsaken. And it is connection with the world for which one faileth to go to heaven.' The Yaksha asked,—'For what may one be considered as dead? For what may a kingdom be considered as dead? For what may a *Sraddha* be considered as dead? And for what, a sacrifice?' Yudhishthira answered,—'For want of wealth may a man be regarded as dead. A kingdom for want of a king may be regarded as dead. A *Sraddha* that is performed with the aid of a priest that hath no learning may be regarded as dead. And a sacrifice in which there are no gifts to Brahmanas is dead.' The Yaksha asked,—'What constitutes the way? What hath been spoken of as water? What, as food? And what, as poison? Tell us also what is the proper time of a *Sraddha*, and then drink and take away as much as thou likest!' Yudhishthira answered,—'They that are good constitute the way. 73 Space hath been spoken of as water. 74 The cow is food. 75 A request is poison. And a Brahmana is regarded as the proper time of a *Sraddha*. 76 I do not know what thou mayst think of all this, O Yaksha?' The

Yaksha asked,—'What hath been said to be the sign of asceticism? And what is true restraint? What constitutes forgiveness. And what is shame?' Yudhishthira answered,—'Staying in one's own religion is asceticism; the restraint of the mind is of all restraints the true one; forgiveness consists in enduring enmity; and shame, in withdrawing from all unworthy acts.' The Yaksha asked,—'What, O king is said to be knowledge? What, tranquillity? What constitutes mercy? And what hath been called simplicity?' Yudhishthira answered,—'True knowledge is that of Divinity. True tranquillity is that of the heart. Mercy consists in wishing happiness to all. And simplicity is equanimity of heart.' The Yaksha asked,—'What enemy is invincible? What constitutes an incurable disease for man? What sort of a man is called honest and what dishonest?' Yudhishthira answered,—'Anger is an invincible enemy. Covetousness constitutes an incurable disease. He is honest that desires the weal of all creatures, and he is dishonest who is unmerciful.' The Yaksha asked,—'What, O king, is ignorance? And what is pride? What also is to be understood by idleness? And what hath been spoken of as grief?' Yudhishthira answered,—'True ignorance consists in not knowing one's duties. Pride is a consciousness of one's being himself an actor or sufferer in life. Idleness consists in not discharging one's duties, and ignorance in grief.' The Yaksha asked,—'What hath steadiness been said by the *Rishis* to be? And what, patience? What also is a real ablution? And what is charity?' Yudhishthira answered,—'Steadiness consists in one's staying in one's own religion, and true patience consists in the subjugation of the senses. A true bath consists in washing the mind clean of all impurities, and charity consists in protecting all creatures.' The Yaksha asked,—'What man should be regarded as learned, and who should be called an atheist? Who also is to be called ignorant? What is called desire and what are the sources of desire? And what is envy?' Yudhishthira answered,—'He is to be called learned who knoweth his duties. An atheist is he who is ignorant and so also he is ignorant who is an atheist. Desire is due to objects of possession, and envy is nothing else than grief of heart.' The Yaksha asked,—'What is pride, and what is hypocrisy? What is the grace of the gods, and what is wickedness?' Yudhishthira answered,—'Stolid ignorance is pride. The setting up of a religious standard is hypocrisy. The grace of the gods is the fruit of our gifts, and wickedness consists in speaking ill of others.' The Yaksha asked,—'Virtue, profit, and desire are opposed to one another. How could things thus antagonistic to one another exist together?' Yudhishthira answered,—'When a wife and virtue agree with each other, then all the three thou hast mentioned may exist together.' The Yaksha asked,—'O bull of the Bharata race, who is he that is condemned to everlasting hell? It behoveth thee to soon answer the question that I ask!' Yudhishthira answered,—'He that summoneth a poor Brahmana promising to make him a gift and then tells him that he hath nothing to give, goeth to everlasting hell. He also must go to everlasting hell, who imputes falsehood to the *Vedas*, the scriptures, the Brahmanas, the gods, and the ceremonies in honour of the *Pitris*. He also goeth to everlasting hell who though in possession of wealth, never giveth away nor enjoyeth himself from avarice, saying, he hath none.' The Yaksha asked, —'By what, O king, birth, behaviour, study, or learning doth a person become a Brahmana? Tell us with certitude!' Yudhishthira answered, —'Listen, O Yaksha! It is neither birth, nor study, nor learning, that is the cause of *Brahmanahood*, without doubt, it is behaviour that constitutes it. One's behaviour should always be well-guarded, especially by a Brahmana. He who maintaineth his conduct unimpaired, is never impaired himself. Professors and pupils, in fact, all who study the scriptures, if addicted to wicked habits, are to be regarded as illiterate wretches. He only is learned who performeth his religious duties. He even that hath studied the four Vedas is to be regarded as a wicked wretch scarcely distinguishable from a Sudra (if his conduct be not correct). He only who performeth the *Agnihotra* and hath his senses under control, is called a Brahmana!' The Yaksha asked, —'What doth one gain that speaketh agreeable words? What doth he gain that always acteth with judgment? What doth he gain that hath many friends? And what he, that is devoted to virtue?' Yudhishthira answered, —'He that speaketh agreeable words becometh agreeable to all. He that acteth with judgment obtaineth whatever he seeketh. He that hath many friends liveth happily. And he that is devoted to virtue obtaineth a happy state (in the next world).' The Yaksha asked, — 'Who is truly happy? What is most wonderful? What is *the* path? And what is *the* news? Answer these four questions of mine and let thy dead brothers revive.' Yudhishthira answered, —'O amphibious creature, a man who cooketh in his own house, on the fifth or the sixth part of the day, with scanty vegetables, but who is not in debt and who stirreth not from home, is truly happy. Day after day countless creatures are going to the abode of Yama, yet those that remain behind believe themselves to be immortal. What can be more wonderful than this? Argument leads to no certain conclusion, the *Srutis* are different from one another; there is not even one *Rishi* whose opinion can be accepted by all; the truth about religion and duty is hid in caves: therefore, that alone is the path along which the great have trod. This world full of ignorance is like a pan. The sun is fire, the days and nights are fuel. The months and the seasons constitute the wooden ladle. Time is the cook that is cooking all creatures in that pan (with such aids); this is *the news*.' The Yaksha asked, —'Thou hast, O represser of foes, truly answered all my questions! Tell us now who is truly a man, and what man truly possesseth every kind of wealth.' Yudhishthira answered, —'The report of one's good action reacheth heaven and spreadeth over the earth.

As long as that report lasteth, so long is a person to whom the agreeable and the disagreeable, weal and woe, the past and the future, are the same, is said to possess every kind of wealth.' The Yaksha said,—'Thou hast, O king truly answered who is a man, and what man possesseth every kind of wealth. Therefore, let one only amongst thy brothers, whom thou mayst wish, get up with life!' Yudhishthira answered,—'Let this one that is of darkish hue, whose eyes are red, who is tall like a large *Sala* tree, whose chest is broad and arms long, let this Nakula, O Yaksha, get up with life!' The Yaksha rejoined,—'This Bhimasena is dear unto thee, and this Arjuna also is one upon whom all of you depend! Why, then, O king, dost thou wish a step-brother to get up with his life! How canst thou, forsaking Bhima whose strength is equal to that of ten thousand elephants, wish Nakula to live? People said that this Bhima was dear to thee. From what motive then dost thou wish a step-brother to revive? Forsaking Arjuna the might of whose arm is worshipped by all the sons of Pandu, why dost thou wish Nakula to revive?' Yudhishthira said,—'If virtue is sacrificed, he that sacrificeth it, is himself lost. So virtue also cherisheth the cherisher. Therefore taking care that virtue by being sacrificed may not sacrifice us, I never forsake virtue. Abstention from injury is the highest virtue, and is, I ween, even higher than the highest object of attainment. I endeavour to practise that virtue. Therefore, let Nakula, O Yaksha, revive! Let men know that the king is always virtuous! I will never depart from my duty. Let Nakula, therefore, revive! My father had two wives, Kunti and Madri. Let both of them have children. This is what I wish. As Kunti is to me, so also is Madri. There is no difference between them in my eye. I desire to act equally towards my mothers. Therefore, let Nakula live.' The Yaksha said,—'Since abstention from injury is regarded by thee as higher than both profit and pleasure, therefore, let all thy brothers live, O bull of Bharata race!'"

SECTION CCCXII

Vaisampayana continued,—"Then agreeable to the words of the Yaksha the Pandavas rose up; and in a moment their hunger and thirst left them. Thereupon Yudhishthira said, 'I ask thee that art incapable of being vanquished and that standest on one leg in the tank, what god art thou, for I cannot take thee for a Yaksha! Art thou the foremost of the Vasus, or of the Rudras, or of the chief of the Maruts? Or art thou the lord himself of the celestials, wielder of the thunder-bolt! Each of these my brothers is capable of fighting as hundred thousand warriors, and I see not the warrior that can slay them all! I see also that their senses have refreshed, as if they have sweetly awaked from slumber. Art thou a friend of ours, or even our father himself?' At this the Yaksha replied,—'O child, I am even thy father, the Lord of justice, possessed of great prowess! Know, bull of the Bharata race, that I came hither desirous of beholding thee! Fame, truth, self-restraint, purity, candour, modesty, steadiness, charity, austerities and *Brahmacharya*, these are my body! And abstention from injury, impartiality, peace, penances, sanctity, and freedom from malice are the doors (through which I am accessible). Thou art always dear to me! By good luck thou art devoted to the five; 77 and by good luck also thou hast conquered the six. 78 Of the six, two appear in the first part of life; two in the middle part thereof; and the remaining two at the end, in order to make men repair to the next world. I am, good betide thee, the lord of justice! I came hither to test thy merit. I am well-pleased to witness thy harmlessness; and, O sinless one, I will confer boons on thee. Do thou, O foremost of kings, ask of me boons. I shall surely confer them, O sinless one! Those that revere me, never come by distress!' Yudhishthira said,—'A deer was carrying away the Brahmana's fire-sticks. Therefore, the first boon that I shall ask, is, may that Brahmana's adorations to *Agni* be not interrupted!' The Yaksha said,—'O Kunti's son endued with splendour, it was I who for examining thee, was carrying away, in the guise of a deer, that Brahmana's fire-sticks!'"

Vaisampayana continued,—"Thereupon that worshipful one said,—'I give thee this boon! Good betide thee! O thou that are like unto an immortal, ask thou a fresh boon!' Yudhishthira said,—'We have spent these twelve years in the forest; and the thirteenth year is come. May no one recognise us, as we spend this year somewhere.'"

Vaisampayana continued,—"Thereat that worshipful one replied,—'I give this boon unto thee!' And then reassuring Kunti's son having truth for prowess, he also said, 'Even if, O Bharata, ye range this (entire) earth in your proper forms none in the three worlds shall recognise you. Ye perpetuators of the Kuru race, through my grace, ye will spend this thirteenth year, secretly and unrecognised, in Virata's kingdom! And every one of you will be able at will to assume any form he likes! Do ye now present the Brahmana with his fire-sticks. It was only to test you that I carried them away in the form of a deer! O amiable Yudhishthira, do thou ask for another boon that thou mayst like! I will confer it on thee. O foremost of men, I have not yet been satisfied by granting boons to thee! Do thou my son, accept a third boon that is great and incomparable! Thou, O king, art born of me, and Vidura of portion or mine!' Thereat Yudhishthira said,—'It is enough that I have beheld thee with my senses, eternal God of gods as thou art! O father, whatever boon thou wilt confer on me I shall surely accept gladly! May I, O lord, always conquer covetousness and folly and anger, and may my mind be ever devoted to charity, truth, and ascetic austerities!' The Lord of justice said,—'Even by nature, O Pandava, hast thou been endued with these qualities, for thou art the Lord of justice himself! Do thou again attain what thou asked for!'"

Vaisampayana continued,—"Having said these words, the worshipful Lord of justice, who is the object of contemplation of all the worlds, vanished therefrom; and the high-souled Pandavas after they had slept sweetly were united with one another. And their fatigue dispelled, those heroes returned to the hermitage, and gave back that Brahmana his firesticks. That man who pursueth this illustrious and fame-enhancing story of the revival (of the Pandavas) and the meeting of father and son (Dharma and Yudhishthira), obtaineth perfect tranquillity of mind, and sons and grandsons, and also a life extending over a hundred years! And the mind of that man that layeth this story to heart, never delighteth in unrighteousness, or in disunion among friends, or misappropriation of other person's property, or staining other people's wives, or in foul thoughts!"

SECTION CCCXIII

Vaisampayana continued,—"Commanded by the Lord of justice to thus spend in disguise the thirteenth year of non-discovery, the high-souled Pandavas, observant of vows and having truth for prowess, sat before those learned and vow-observing ascetics that from regard were dwelling with them in their exile in the forest. And with joined hands they said these words, with the intention of obtaining permission to spend the thirteenth year in the manner indicated. And they said, 'Ye know well that the sons of Dhritarashtra have by deceit deprived us of our kingdom, and have also done us many other wrongs! We have passed twelve years in the forest in great affliction. The thirteenth year only, which we are to spend unrecognised, yet remaineth. It behoveth you to permit us now to spend this year in concealment! Those rancorous enemies of ours, Suyodhana, the wicked-minded Karna, and Suvala's son should they discover us, would do mighty wrong to the citizens and our friends! Shall we all with the Brahmanas, be again established in our own kingdom?' Having said this, that pure-spirited son of Dharma king Yudhishthira, overwhelmed with grief and with accents choked in tears, swooned away. Thereupon the Brahmanas, together with his brothers began to cheer him up. Then Dhaumya spake unto the king these words fraught with mighty meaning,— 'O king, thou art learned and capable of bearing privations, art firm in promise, and of subdued sense! Men of such stamp are not overwhelmed by any calamity whatever. Even the high-souled gods themselves have wandered over various places in disguise, for the purpose of overcoming foes. Indra for the purpose of overcoming his foes, dwelt in disguise in the asylum of Giriprastha, in Nishadha and thus attained his end. Before taking his birth in the womb of Aditi, Vishnu for the purpose of destroying the *Daityas* passed a long time unrecognised, assuming the form of the *Haya-griba* (Horse-necked). Then how disguising himself in the form of a dwarf, he by his prowess deprived Vali of his kingdom, hath been heard by thee! And thou hast also heard how Hutasana entering into water and remaining in concealment, achieved the purpose of the gods. And O thou versed in duty, thou hast heard how Hari with the view of overcoming his foes, entered into Sakra's thunder-bolt, and lay concealed there. And, O sinless one, thou hast heard of the office the regenerate *Rishi* Aurva at one time performed for the gods, remaining concealed in his mother's womb. And O child, living in concealment in every part of the earth, Vivaswat, endued with excellent energy, at last entirely burnt up all his foes. And living disguised in the abode of Dasaratha, Vishnu of dreadful deeds slew the Ten-necked one in battle. Thus remaining in disguise in various places, high-souled persons have before this conquered their enemies in battle.' Thus cheered by these words of Dhaumya, the virtuous Yudhishthira, relying on his own wisdom and also that acquired from the scriptures regained his composure. Then that foremost of strong persons, the mighty-armed Bhimasena endued with great strength encouraging the king greatly, spake these words, 'Looking up to thy face (for permission), the wielder of the *Gandiva*, acting according to his sense of duty hath not yet, O king, shown any rashness! And although fully able to destroy the foe, Nakula and Sahadeva of dreadful prowess have been ever prevented by me! Never shall we swerve from that in which thou wilt engage us! Do thou tell us what is to be done! We shall speedily conquer our enemies!' When Bhimasena had said this, the Brahmanas uttered benedictions on the Bharatas, and then obtaining their permission, went to their respective quarters. And all those foremost of *Yatis* and *Munis* versed in the Vedas, exceedingly desirous of again beholding the Pandavas, went back to their homes. And accompanied by Dhaumya, these heroes, the five learned Pandavas equipped in vows set out with Krishna. And each versed in a separate science, and all proficient in *mantras* and cognisant of when peace was to be concluded and when war was to be waged those tigers among men, about to enter upon a life of non-recognition, the next day proceeded for a Krose and then sat themselves down with the view of taking counsel of each other."

Footnote 1: It means these six things, unfavourable to crops—excessive rain, drought, rats, locusts, birds, and a neighbouring hostile king.

Footnote 2: In as much as the rites performed by the Sudras have their origin in the Vedas.

Footnote 3: More literally, the state of the gods. It may appropriately be remarked here that the ordinary Hindu gods, of the post-Vedic period, like the gods of Ancient Greece and Italy, were simply a class of superhuman beings, distinctly contra-distinguished from the Supreme Spirit, the *Paramatman* or *Parabrahma*. After death, a virtuous man was supposed to be transformed into one of these so-called gods.

Footnote 4: This is the well-known and popular doctrine of transmigration of souls.

Footnote 5: The word in the text is *Kora-dushakas*, supposed by Wilson to be the *Paspalum frumentacea* (*vide* Dict.).

Footnote 6: The word in the text is *mlecchibhutam*. The Sanskrit grammar affords a great facility for the formation of verbs from substantives. *Mlecchify* may be hybrid, but it correctly and shortly signifies the Sanskrit word.

Footnote 7: *Pushya* is the eighth lunar asterism consisting of three stars, of which one is, the Cancer. (Vide Wilson's Diet.).

Footnote 8: An Indian creeper of the order of *Goertnera racemosa*. It bears large white flowers of much fragrance.

Footnote 9: They, therefore, that lead deathless lives can enjoy this bliss from day to day for ever.

Footnote 10: It is difficult to understand how all that Vaka says can be an answer to Indra's question. The chief of the gods enquires: What are the joys of those that lead deathless lives? Vaka breaks away unto a confused rigmarole about the merits of independence and the religious merit of entertaining guests and servants. All the printed editions have the passage as rendered here.

Footnote 11: The ceremony of *Swastivachana* is described to be "a religious rite, preparatory to any important observance, in which the Brahmanas strew boiled rice on the ground, and invoke the blessings of the gods on the ceremony about to commence" (*Vide* Wilson's Diet). A flowery car was, probably, one of celestial make that the kings procured from heaven by performing costly rites and ceremonies. These were sometimes exhibited to the people, and prior to these exhibitions, the ceremony of *Swastivachana* was performed.

Footnote 12: A man is said to sell the Vedas who lectures on the Vedas taking fees from the hearers.

Footnote 13: *Japa* is the silent recitation of particular *Mantras*.

Footnote 14: *Mantras* are particular formulae of worship. They are for the most part rhythmic compositions, believed to be of great efficacy.

Footnote 15: The *Homa* is that sacrificial rite which consists of pouring libations of clarified butter into fire.

Footnote 16: *Vedamayi nou*. Lit, a boat made of the Vedas.

Footnote 17: *Vishada* is the original. It means discontent, but here it means more a mixture of discontent, perplexity and confusion than mere discontent.

Footnote 18: A form of Hindu etiquette at parting.

Footnote 19: It is so very difficult to translate the word *Karma*,—religion and morals were invariably associated with each other in ancient Hindu mind.

Footnote 20: Agni or fire was supposed to convey the oblations offered by men to the gods.

Footnote 21: *Kumara* means a boy, hence a prince. Here Kartika the war-god is meant.

Footnote 22: By carrying their oblations to the gods.

Footnote 23: Portions of the Vedas.

Footnote 24: *Raga* means love.

Footnote 25: Kama is the name of the god of love, Indian Cupid.

Footnote 26: The body, the exciting Cause of our actions is an *uktha*, the soul of the vivifier of the body is the second *uktha*, and the Supreme Spirit, the inciter of the soul is the third.

Footnote 27: The word of God.

Footnote 28: In Hindu Mythology there are no gods who destroy sacrifices. It is only the Asuras who do so. The Burdwan translator renders this passage,—"fifteen other gods belonging to western nations or *Asuras*." It is noticeable that the beings that were denounced as *Asuras* by the Hindus were worshipped as Gods (*Asuras*) by the followers of Zarathustra.

Footnote 29: In connection with the names of these Mitra-gods, it is to be remembered that Mitra was the name of the principal god of the ancient Persians.

Footnote 30: *Avala* is a common name of women. It means one who has no vala or strength or power. The word is also used as an adjective.

Footnote 31: According to the Hindus, the sun rises from and sets behind two hills respectively. He rises from the *Udaya* or Sun-rise hill and sets behind the *Asta* or sun-set hill.

Footnote 32: *Raudra*—belonging to Rudra, the god of fury, violence, war, &c.

Footnote 33: *Devasena* literally means the celestial army. This fable seems to be an allegorical representation of the attempts made by Indra to procure a leader for the celestial host.

Footnote 34: Anger personified is a deity.

Footnote 35: Another name of gods, so named from their having only three stages of life—viz., infancy, childhood, and youth—and being exempt from the fourth—old age.

Footnote 36: i.e., good and evil spirits.

Footnote 37: One of the ensigns of royalty in Hindustan.

Footnote 38: Brahma.

Footnote 39: Devasenapati is the original. It may mean either the *pati* (leader) of the *sena* (forces) of *devas* or the *pati* (husband) of Devasena.

Footnote 40: A kind of missile.

Footnote 41: Another kind of weapon.

Footnote 42: The word in the text is "Agrahara," which, as Nilakantha explains, means here, "That which is first taken from a heap after the dedication of a portion to the Viswadevas." What Draupadi means to say is, that she always took care to feed those Brahmanas with food "first" taken from the stores, without, in fact, having taken anything there from the use of anybody else.

Footnote 43: Lit, Soldiers that have sworn to conquer or die. A full Akshauhini of these soldiers was owned by Krishna, who gave them to Duryodhana to fight for him. The story of Krishna's offering to Duryodhana the choice between these soldiers on the one side, and himself sworn not to fight but only to aid with his counsels on the other, is given in full in the Udyoga Parva. Duryodhana, from folly, accepted the former, who were all slain by Arjuna.

Footnote 44: The vow of the Asuras was (according to the Burdwan Pundits) never to drink wine. It is more rational to suppose that Karna swears to give up the refined manners and practices of the Arvas and adopt those of the Asuras till the consummation of the cherished desire.

Footnote 45: A very small measure.

Footnote 46: Picking up for support (1) ears of corn and (2) individual grains, left on the field by husbandmen after they have gathered and carried away the sheaves, are called the Sila and the Unchha modes of life.

Footnote 47: Naked.

Footnote 48: Both these words are of doubtful meaning. It seems they are employed in the Vedas to denote the faculties of knowledge and the moral sense respectively.

Footnote 49: The six acts of a king are peace, war, marching, halting, sowing dissention, and seeking protection.

Footnote 50: Tard-mrigam. Formerly Prajapati, assuming the Form of a deer, followed his daughter from lust, and Rudra, armed with a trident, pursued Prajapati and struck off his head. That deer-head of Prajapati severed from the trunk, became the star, or rather constellation, called Mrigasiras.

Footnote 51: Abode of Varuna in the original.

Footnote 52: Garuda.

Footnote 53: Pavana, the God of the wind.

Footnote 54: There is a difference of reading here. Some texts read fifty seven.

Footnote 55: A difference of reading is observable here.

Footnote 56: As a purificatory ceremony, called the Achamana. To this day, no Hindu can perform any ceremony without going through the Achamana in the first instance.

Footnote 57: Lit. an engine killing a hundred. Perhaps, some kind of rude cannon.

Footnote 58: Perhaps, brands or torches steeped in wax, intended to be thrown in a burning state, amongst the foe. Readers of Indian history know how Lord Lake was repulsed from Bharatpore by means of huge bales of cotton, steeped in oil, rolled from the ramparts of that town, in a burning state, towards the advancing English.

Footnote 59: Lit. be a Purusha (male)! Manhood would not be appropriate in connection with a Rakshasa.

Footnote 60: This weapon could restore an insensible warrior to consciousness, as the Sam-mohana weapon could deprive one of consciousness.

Footnote 61: Visalya a medicinal plant of great efficacy in healing cuts and wounds. It is still cultivated in several parts of Bengal. A medical friend of the writer tested the efficacy of the plant known by that name and found it to be much superior to either gallic acid or tannic acid in stopping blood.

Footnote 62: The Guhyakas occupy, in Hindu mythology, a position next only to that of the gods, and superior to that of the Gandharvas who are the celestial choristers. The White mountain is another name of Kailasa, the peak where Siva hath his abode.

Footnote 63: According to both Vyasa and Valmiki, there is nothing so fierce as a Brahmana's curse. The very thunderbolt of Indra is weak compared to a Brahmana's curse. The reason is obvious. The thunder smites the individual at whom it may be aimed. The curse of Brahmana smites the whole race, whole generation, whole country.

Footnote 64: Abhijit is lit. the eighth muhurta of the day, a muhurta being equal to an hour of 48 minutes, i.e. the thirtieth part of a whole day and night. The Vaishnava asterism is as explained by Nilakantha, the Sravava.

Footnote 65: Also called Gayatri, the wife of Brahma.

Footnote 66: Samhritya—killing.

Footnote 67: Lit. Letters.

Footnote 68: Behind the plain and obvious meanings of the words employed both in the question and the answer, there is a deeper signification of a spiritual kind. I think Nilakantha has rightly understood the passage. By Aditya, which of course commonly means the Sun, is indicated the unpurified soul (from adatte sabdadin indriadivis &c.). The first question then, becomes, 'Who is it that exalteth the unpurified soul?' The act of exaltation implies a raising of the soul from its earthly connections. The answer to this is, 'Brahma, i.e., Veda or self-knowledge.' The second question—'What are those that keep company with the soul during its progress of purification?' The answer is, 'Self-restraint and other qualities, which are all of a god-like or divine nature.' The third question is.—Who lead the soul to its place (state) of rest? The answer is, 'Dharma, *i.e.*, rectitude, morality, and religious observances.' It is often asserted that one must pass through the observances (Karma) before attaining to a state of Rest or Truth or Pure Knowledge. The last question is,—'On what is the soul established!' The answer, according to all that has been previously said, is 'Truth or Pure Knowledge.' For the soul that is emancipated from and raised above all carnal connections, is no longer in need of observances and acts (Karma) but stays unmoved in True Knowledge (Janana).

Footnote 69: Nilakantha explains both Dhriti and Dwitiya in a spiritual sense. There is no need, however, of a spiritual explanation here. By Dhriti is meant steadiness of intelligence; by Dwitiya lit, a second. What Yudhishthira says is that a steady intelligence serves the purposes of a helpful companion.

Footnote 70: Nilakantha explains this correctly, as I imagine, by supposing that by 'sacrifice' is meant the spiritual sacrifice for the acquisition of pure knowledge. In the objective sacrifice which one celebrates, the Sama, the Yajus, and the Rik mantras are all necessary. In the subjective sacrifice the acquisition of true knowledge, life and mind are as necessary as the mantras from the Sama and the Yajur Vedas in an objective one. And as no objective sacrifice can do without the Riks, being principally dependent on them, so the subjective sacrifices for acquiring true knowledge can never do without prayerfulness, which, I imagine, is represented as the Riks. To understand this passage thoroughly would require an intimate acquaintance with the ritual of a sacrifice like the Agnishtoma or any other of that kind.

Footnote 71: Some texts read apatatam for uvapatam. If the former be the correct reading, the meaning would be—'What is the best of things that fall?' Nilakantha explains both avapatam nivapatam in a spiritual sense. By the first he understands—'They that offer oblation to the gods,' and by the second, 'They that offer oblations to the Pitris.' The necessity of a spiritual interpretation, however, is not very apparent.

Footnote 72: Yudhishthira has the authority of the Srutis for saying that the one pervading element of the universe is air.

Footnote 73: The word used in the question is *dik*, literally, direction. Obviously, of course, it means in this connection way. Yudhishthira answers that the way which one is to tread along is that of the good.

Footnote 74: The *Srutis* actually speak of space as water. These are questions to test Yudhishthira's knowledge of the Vedic cosmogony.

Footnote 75: The *Srutis* speak of the cow as the only food, in the following sense. The cow gives milk. The milk gives butter. The butter is used in Homa. The Homa is the cause of the clouds. The clouds give rain. The rain makes the seed to sprout forth and produce food. Nilakantha endeavours to explain this in a spiritual sense. There is however, no need of such explanation here.

Footnote 76: What Yudhishthira means to say is that there is no special time for a Sraddha. It is to be performed whenever a good and able priest may be secured.

Footnote 77: That is, tranquillity of mind, self-restraint, abstention from sensual pleasures, resignation, and Yoga meditation.

Footnote 78: That is, hunger, thirst, sorrow, bluntness of mortal feeling, decrepitude, and death.